Patricia L. Wolleat

PSYCHOTHERAPY AND THE LAW

PSYCHOTHERAPY
AND LAW
THE

Edited by

LOUIS EVERSTINE
**Research Fellow
Mental Research Institute;
Director of Research and Evaluation
Emergency Treatment Center
Palo Alto, California**

DIANA SULLIVAN EVERSTINE
**Research Fellow
Mental Research Institute;
Director, Emergency Treatment Center
Palo Alto, California**

Grune & Stratton, Inc.
Harcourt Brace Jovanovich, Publishers
Orlando   New York   San Diego   Boston   London
San Francisco   Tokyo   Sydney   Toronto

Library of Congress Cataloging-in-Publication Data

Psychotherapy and the law.

Includes bibliographies and index.
1. Psychology, Forensic. 2. Insanity—Jurisprudence—United
States. 3. Evidence, Expert—United States. 4. Psychotherapy
ethics. I. Everstine, Louis, 1933–   . II. Everstine, Diana Sullivan,
1944–   . [DNLM: 1, Ethics, Medical. 2. Ethics, Professional. 3.
Psychotherapy—United States—legislation. WM 33 AA1 P9]
KF8922.P79 1986   347'.066   86–11938
ISBN 0–8089–1780–3   342.766

Grune & Stratton, Inc.
Orlando, Florida 32887

Distributed in the United Kingdom by
Grune & Stratton, Ltd.
24/28 Oval Road, London NW 1

Library of Congress Catalog Number 86–11938
International Standard Book Number 0–8089–1780–3
Printed in the United States of America
86 87 88 89   10 9 8 7 6 5 4 3 2 1

Contents

Foreword

The all too frequent conflicts between the law and psychotherapy are due to two factors: A misunderstanding by each of the role of the other, and extravagant expectations of the law as to what psychotherapy can routinely accomplish. Papers such as those contained in this volume may help to bring those conflicts into perspective.

As the preface to the book points out, the law seeks the truth, while psychotherapy seeks to promote health. But the law needs more than truth in the sense of merely determining what happened at a given place and time. It must also ascertain culpability and that generally depends on intent. Since intent, or the ability to form intent, is entirely subjective, the law often expectantly turns to behavioral science for assistance.

If the law stopped at that point, perhaps our discord would be minimal. But some judges, in both the criminal and civil fields, have looked to psychotherapists for predictions of an individual's future behavior, dangerousness in particular. It has taken all of us considerable soul-searching to come to the realization that such predictability is beyond reasonable expectations.

In the 1975 case of People v. Burnick (14 Cal. 3d 306), I made this observation for a majority of the California Supreme Court: "In the light of recent studies, it is no longer heresy to question the reliability of psychiatric predictions. Psychiatrists themselves would be the first to admit that however desirable an infallible crystal ball might be, it is not among the tools of their profession. It must be conceded that psychiatrists still experience considerable difficulty in confidently and accurately diagnosing mental illness. Yet those difficulties are multiplied manyfold when psychiatrists venture from diagnosis to prognosis and undertake to predict the consequences of such illness . . . ."

Justice William O. Douglas elaborated on this subject in a 1972 opinion for the United States Supreme Court (Murel v. Baltimore City Criminal Court, 407 U.S. 355, 364): "A diagnosis of mental illness tells us nothing about whether the person so diagnosed is or is not dangerous. Some mental patients are dangerous, some are not. Perhaps the psychiatrist is an expert at deciding whether a person is mentally ill, but is he an expert at predicting which of the persons so diagnosed are dangerous? Sane people, too, are dangerous, and it may legitimately be inquired whether there is anything in the education, training or experience of psychiatrists which renders them particularly adept at predicting dangerous behavior. Predictions of dangerous behavior, no matter who makes them, are incredibly inaccurate, and there is a growing consensus that psychiatrists are not uniquely qualified to predict dangerous behavior and are, in fact, less accurate in their predictions than other professionals."

The Douglas views may be somewhat hyperbolic, but there is at least a germ of truth in them. As Mark Twain once observed, "Wagner's music is better than it sounds." Yet I must concede that a majority of the California Supreme Court erred in what the preface describes as "the notorious case of Tarasoff v. the Regents of the University of California." I make that concession not merely from 20/20 hindsight; I differed with the major premise at the time the opinion was originally rendered.

The *Tarasoff* case imposed a duty on psychotherapists not only to have warned a potential victim if they "in fact determined" a serious danger was imminent, but if they "should have so determined." It was the latter requirement that suggested departure from the world of reality into the wonderland of clairvoyance.

On the other hand, many psychotherapists will not concede any duty whatever to warn a potential victim of imminent danger. That, I suggest, is unrealistic insulation from the modest responsibility that every citizen in modern society must assume.

Let me give an example: if Sara Jane Moore had seen a psychotherapist as a patient, told the doctor that as soon as she left the office she intended to shoot President Ford as he left the St. Francis Hotel in San Francisco— where he was known to be staying—and showed the doctor the gun she intended to use, can the therapy profession possibly justify a failure to notify law enforcement officers of an impending tragedy? That was the point of my separate opinion in *Tarasoff:* if the psychotherapist does *in fact* have the information on which to anticipate specific violence on a named individual, he or she has a duty to warn. That, I believe, can be distinguished from a nebulous requirement of *should have* known.

I commend the ambitious effort of this volume to build a bridge between two of society's significant professions. Perhaps this effort will contribute, as Walt Whitman hoped, to ending "life's stormy conflicts, nor victory, nor defeat—no more time's dark events, charging like ceaseless clouds across the sky."

Stanley Mosk
Justice of the California Supreme Court

Preface

A meeting of the minds between lawyers and mental health professionals occurs too rarely. This lack is partly one of communication, because the two disciplines do speak different languages. Moreover, they inhabit different cultures and thus have differing aims. The legal enterprise, for example, seeks to discover truth, while psychotherapy and the other helping professions seek to promote health. There is no necessary incompatibility here, but profound ideological differences exist. Like Pyramus and Thisbe, whose legend was parodied by Shakespeare in "A Midsummer Night's Dream," two lovers must profess their love through a make-believe.

The premise of this book is that a dialogue between legal and clinical practitioners can be fostered. In the beginning, it requires that the same topics be addressed by representatives of both disciplines, and its future will be assured when conferences and seminars are organized jointly to span the two fields. The former aim is achieved in the present collection of papers by attorneys, law professors, and psychotherapists, in which each subject is treated in dual versions. These paired essays are not so much complementary (e.g., "Fishback's reply to Rotweiler") as they are prismatic—the same objects seen from varied perspectives.

Since agreement between and among the authors of these chapters was not sought, it is their *differences* that represent the book's distinctive point of view. Suffice it to say that they are vast. For instance, the paper by Leonard Rubenstein argues that clinical testimony on criminal responsibility is inherently counterproductive, while the one by David Shapiro presents concepts that, if applied, could improve its accuracy. In another sharp contrast, Robert Weisberg and Michael Wald propose criteria for strengthening the law on reporting suspected child abuse, while Gary Heymann argues that even the current law can be stultifying to psychotherapy.

The chasm that separates psychotherapy and the law is starkly seen in the notorious case of *Tarasoff v. the Regents of the University of California* that is referred to so often in the pages that follow. Few cases of this century have more richly stirred the controversy between courtroom and consulting room than this tragic sequel to a brutal murder. In their understandable revulsion to the crime, the California Supreme Court justices chose to deliver a stinging rebuke to the mental health establishment. By ruling as they did, the justices changed the nature of therapeutic training and practice in myriad ways. With time, new "case law" has somewhat softened the blow on the one hand (and toughened it on the other), but the fact remains that the court implied that an entire profession had adopted unethical practices.

In ruling against a therapist at the University of California, the *Tarasoff* court decided that this clinician had neglected his common-law obligation to protect human life. By reasoning thus, the court demonstrated its lack of sympathetic awareness of the therapy experience. The point that was missed is that a therapeutic relationship can be an intensely intimate form of interaction between two persons. Even though he did not warn the likely victim of his client, the therapist meant to *protect the client*. The nonaction for which he was judged negligent was a well-intentioned impulse to preserve a semblance of the rapport with this person that he had arduously won. By any accepted standard of therapy, the clinician failed miserably to divert the client from his murderous purpose. Obviously, this standard was not the one that the court applied. Therein lies the gulf.

We can expect that there will be many similar misadventures in which the justice system and the health care system are working at cross-purposes. Someday, by means of exchanges such as the one represented by this book, it will be an easier matter to resolve the kind of mutual confusion of motives that characterized the *Tarasoff* imbroglio. Until then, a major arena for confrontation will be the courtroom, where individual cases, with all their perplexities and ambiguities, will be debated.

It has been observed that hard cases make bad law. But it is through cases that the law comes alive; and, life being what it is, there are no easy cases.

Acknowledgments

Some years ago, when our friend and colleague Arthur M. Bodin was elected to the presidency of the California State Psychological Association, he asked us to form a new statewide committee. Thus was born the first Committee on Privacy and Confidentiality of the state association, of which there have been several successors. We admire Bodin's range of vision in inaugurating this valuable resource to the psychologists of California, and note that his concern has been echoed by other state (as well as national) professional organizations.

The work of the Committee had two major phases, the first ending with publication of our collaborative article in the *American Psychologist,* "Privacy and Confidentiality in Psychotherapy," in 1980. The second phase began when Gary M. Heymann, an original committee member, assumed the chairmanship in 1981. The Committee became an activist group that answered the specific questions of therapists by telephone and by mail, contributed articles to the CSPA newsletter, and advocated for legislative changes. We are pleased to include a chapter by Heymann in this volume.

As we grew in knowledge of the subjects of this book, we encountered an extremely important paper by Attorney Richard J. Kohlman, "Malpractice Liability for Failing to Report Child Abuse." This eloquent account of the discovery of a tragic abuse, its investigation, and culmination in a civil trial, moved us to feel the urgency of these issues more deeply. Of the sources of inspiration that have sustained our work on the book, our friendship with Kohlman has been bountiful.

We are grateful not least to Attorney Richard Alexander for his careful reading of text and thoughtful suggestions. The typing, copying, and mailing of drafts was ably done by Karl Stager, Sharon Lucas, Theresa Coombs and Harriet Vanderaa. We thank the editorial and production staff at Grune & Stratton for their perseverance and support.

Finally, each of the contributors to these chapters will know how much we admire their efforts. With them, we marvel how patience finds its reward.

Contributors

Ronald Jay Cohen, Ph.D.
    Adjunct Professor of Psychology, Department of Psychology, St. John's University, Jamaica, New York
Diana Sullivan Everstine, Ph.D.
    Research Fellow, Mental Research Institute; Director, Emergency Treatment Center, Palo Alto, California
Louis Everstine, Ph.D., M.P.H.
    Research Fellow, Mental Research Institute; Director of Research and Evaluation, Emergency Treatment Center, Palo Alto, California
Gary M. Heymann, Ph.D.
    Palo Alto, California
Paul D. Lipsitt, LL.B., Ph.D.
    Lecturer on Psychology, Department of Psychiatry, Harvard Medical School; Director, Mental Health-Law Program, Erich Lindemann Mental Health Center, Government Center Boston, Massachusetts
William E. Mariano
    Attorney at Law, Mariano & Mariano, New York, New York
C. J. Meyers, Ph.D., M.L.S.
    Chief, Criminal Justice Mental Health Program, Highland General Hospital, Oakland, California
David G. Miller
    Attorney at Law, Gair, Gair & Conason, New York, New York
Leonard S. Rubenstein
    Attorney at Law, Mental Health Law Project, Washington, D.C.
David L. Shapiro, Ph.D.
    Diplomate, American Board of Forensic Psychology, Baltimore, Maryland
Ralph Slovenko
    Professor of Law and Psychiatry, Wayne State University, Detroit, Michigan

Michael Wald
        Professor, Stanford Law School, Stanford University, Stanford,
        California
Robert Weisberg
        Associate Professor, Stanford Law School, Stanford University,
        Stanford, California
William J. Winslade, Ph.D., J.D.
        Associate Professor of Medical Humanities, Institute for the Medical
        Humanities, University of Texas Medical Branch, Galveston, Texas
Derek Wolman
        Attorney at Law, Mariano & Mariano, New York, New York

Introduction

Louis Everstine

1

Law and Psychotherapy:
The State of the Relationship

Psychotherapy is the second oldest profession, because it consists in talking with a person for a fee. Among the health disciplines, psychotherapy strives to do the most with the fewest resources, for the following reasons. Like surgery, it seeks to alleviate pain, but the pain of emotional distress is the most acute that human beings know. Like engineering and architecture, it has a scientific base, but that base has no comparable history and its contribution until now can only be described as naive.[1] Properly conceived, psychotherapy is an art. Because of the poignant sensitivity of its subject, it can be placed foremost among the healing arts.

Even though it is an applied discipline with limited scientific foundation, psychotherapy is not without an evolutionary past. Refinement in the forms and methods of this art began with Freud, and yet developments in recent years have brought such changes that Freud would scarcely recognize current therapeutic techniques. Even so, change for the sake of change has produced its share of improvement—as Freud would graciously acknowledge. The current American awareness of the hazards of psychological stress, for example, is surely a positive trend, accompanied as it currently is by a passionate resolve, on the part of many people, to better their physical health. Nor would it be possible to imagine Western culture without its programs to promote mental health, its attempts to "cure" addiction in

---

[1] The scientific study of human behavior began with the establishment of the first psychological laboratory by Wilhelm Wundt at Leipzig in 1879. Few applied disciplines rest upon such a recent foundation of empirical research than does psychotherapy.

PSYCHOTHERAPY AND THE LAW
ISBN 0-8089-1780-3

every form, and its efforts to gain control of the emotional forces that can exacerbate disease.

Clearly, psychotherapy is here to stay. It has taken a prideful place among the health professions, and its usefulness is a proven fact. Hence the question "Does psychotherapy work?" has a certain irrelevance, while "How does therapy work?" is the more compelling issue today. And although that question goes far beyond the scope of this book, the subject will not be ignored in the pages that follow.

Some of the current questions surrounding the field of psychotherapy lend themselves to a distinctly philosophical frame of reference. There has arisen within the field itself a certain amount of soul-searching, and from outside sources have come a series of probing investigations into the aims and procedures of the art. Recently, the National Commission on the Insanity Defense sought to define the term "insanity" for the purpose of informing legislators and the courts; the products of its labors (1983) are yet to be judged. Within the discipline itself, debate ensues on a wide range of topics, perhaps originating with and stimulated by the work of Thomas Szasz. For at least 20 years, in a series of books and public pronouncements, Szasz has cast and polished his unwavering case. Asking the rhetorical question "Is therapy ethical?" Szasz has concluded that it is not—categorically not (1963, 1970). More recently, he has wielded his ideological chain saw against the subdiscipline of forensic psychiatry (1976). And for all his strident iconoclasm, he remains a member of the psychiatric profession and continues to teach the subject in a school of medicine. Even though these concerns imply that Szasz is nominally an expert on human motivation, it is difficult to understand whether he wishes to improve psychiatry or to destroy it.

Other internal debate has arisen within psychotherapy over issues such as the following:

- Who is the true client of the psychotherapist (e.g., the person who has sought help, members of his or her family, his or her employer, a government agency, society-at-large)? Monahan (1980) has contributed a penetrating analysis of this subject.
- What is the liability (i.e., professional responsibility) of the therapist to his or her client; this topic has been the subject of many scholarly writings, among which Slovenko's *Psychiatry and Law* (1973) is recognized as a classic.
- What is private and what is public about the therapeutic relationship (i.e., what are the limits of confidentiality, and how much of what happens in therapy can properly be revealed in a court of law)?

These issues were defined and discussed by the editors of this book in earlier writings (Everstine, et al., 1980, Everstine and Everstine, 1983, chap. 13).

The foregoing are among many dilemmas therapists themselves are endeavoring to resolve. To some extent, this forum has taken on an institutional character, as evidenced by the formation of the Law and Society Association, the American Academy of Forensic Psychologists, and the American Psychology-Law Society (with its numerous local chapters in large communities), to cite a few. For the most part, these efforts parallel those of the newly constituted field of biomedical ethics, but a major difference is that the latter inquiry can be traced only to the time of Hippocrates. The ethical dilemmas posed by psychotherapy have an even earlier origin, for therapy is no more or less than a species of relationship between people. The ethical concerns that arise in this context are based upon the primitive requirements of concern that one human being owes another.

Although this book can encompass only a small portion of this complex field of inquiry, each of the subjects discussed here represents a piece of the larger puzzle. The following topics, addressed in this chapter, exemplify key issues in the complex interplay between psychotherapy and the law:

- the question of insanity;
- the question of dangerousness; and
- the question of mental process or functioning.

Each question has importance for the eventual improvement of the tenuous liaison that has been entered into by the justice system and the therapeutic establishment.

THE QUESTION OF INSANITY

The insanity question rests upon a legal principle of the first magnitude—namely the *intent* to commit a crime or to commit a civil wrong. For guilt to be established in either case, intention must be either proven or assumed.[2] Actions resulting wholly from accidental sources are excused from blame regardless of how illegal or hurtful those actions may be.[3] In Western culture, the concept of accidental cause is extended to acts done when a person is not in full possession of his or her faculties. This is the concept of "diminished capacity," which, in its various interpretations, has served as a Rosetta Stone for the legal conceptualization of insanity.

Because the purpose of a court of law is to determine guilt or innocence, and this judgment depends upon intent, an initial branch of the decision tree

---

[2] The legal attribution of intention to a person who is believed to have committed a crime takes this form: A person who is "of sound mind" is believed to be capable of intending "the rational and probable consequences of his [or her] acts" (from standard jury instructions). Hence lack of intent in committing an act may imply a related lack of soundness of mind.

[3] The gray area of "preventable accident" is avoided here for the purpose of showing the key issues in a focused light.

concerns sanity versus insanity.[4] That is, an inference of intention presupposes a prior inference that the person was sane at the moment when the action was done. If sanity can readily be inferred, the problem becomes trivial. But when sanity is called into question, for one reason or another, an extremely delicate instrument of standards and criteria is set in motion. Some of its component parts will be described and examined here.

For a psychotherapist, insanity is not the first question but the ultimate question. None would admit to being unable to recognize it on sight, and few would admit to having diagnosed it where it did not exist. In short, any therapist feels qualified to decide whether or not a person is sane. The most basic lessons of his or her training program will have emphasized this distinction, and the more fundamental case examples of his or her internship will have stressed the importance of accuracy in this the grossest of diagnostic choices.

That there are a number of specific categories within the general class "insanity" (and of course an infinitely large variety of types within the class "normality") has no bearing on the matter. That some therapists prefer to use the term "schizophrenia" and others "psychosis" is a semantic quibble and irrelevant.[5] A person is sane or not. One cannot be sane and insane at the same time. And although few lay persons can, with ease, decide whether a particular person fits within one category or the other, surely a therapist can. If not, who needs therapists?

These observations may cast light upon a recent development within organized psychiatry. Shortly after the infamous verdict in the case of *U.S. v. Hinckley* was handed down, the American Psychiatric Association convened a task force to study the beleaguered insanity defense. The findings of this group were startling, to say the least: They concluded that psychiatrists should *not* be consulted by the courts about whether or not a person was responsible for the commission of a crime. Further, they argued that there is no reason to seek a psychiatric opinion concerning whether or not an accused person is sane or insane, because "sanity is, of course, a legal issue, not a medical one" (quoted by American Bar Association, 1983, p. 143). By that assertion, the professional organization seems to be requesting that its own members be excused on grounds of diminished capacity.

This development is the more surprising because, several years ago, the same American Psychiatric Association announced with pride the publication of a major text on diagnosis that had required intensive deliberation by

---

[4] At an even more basic level, the sanity versus insanity issue must be decided before a trial even begins. The subject of competence to stand trial will be addressed in Chapters 6 and 7 of this book.

[5] For this discussion, "insanity" is defined as an illness of such type or severity that it requires the person to be hospitalized. The terms "psychosis" and "schizophrenia" will be used interchangeably with "insanity," as will "psychotic" and "schizophrenic" with "insane."

many therapists over a long period of time. The *Diagnostic and Statistical Manual of Mental Disorders: III* (1980) replaced an earlier version and was soon adopted by hospitals and other mental institutions, health insurers, and private psychotherapists throughout the nation. The purpose of the revised manual was to improve the accuracy and relevance of the complex process of differential diagnosis. In principle, this manual has enhanced the skills of therapists to choose among the many kinds and degrees of schizophrenia (psychosis) on the one hand and the many kinds and degrees of neurosis (now called "adjustment disorder") on the other. To the extent that the principle applies in practice, a well-trained therapist will be the more astute diagnostician. And this trend may make it more likely, in the future, that psychotherapy will once again accept the challenge of making such coarse diagnostic decisions as sane versus insane.

Also, in the wake of *U.S. v. Hinckley,* have come revisions of legislation in several states that change the traditional verdict of "not guilty by reason of insanity" to "guilty but mentally ill" (see, for example, Hall, 1983). To a large extent, this new verdict was intended to appease those who believed that in some trials such as that of John Hinckley, or that of Dan White for murdering the mayor and a supervisor of San Francisco, justice was not served. Whether or not the scale has thus been tipped in favor of the needs of the community against the rights of the individual will be settled in actual cases that will test these laws, as Hall and others (e.g., Dorsey, 1982; Rubenstein, 1983) have pointed out. The new verdict was expressly rejected, however, in the report of the National Commission on the Insanity Defense, which stated, "The [Commission] recommends that an alternative verdict of 'guilty but mentally ill' not be adopted in any jurisdiction" (1983, p. 3). This advice was received too late to influence the thinking of some state legislatures, but it may lead to more mature insight by others.

In California, an even more salient step has been taken toward enabling the prosecution to prove a defendant's guilt. Effective on the first day of January 1983, a new law abolished the concept of diminished capacity as a mitigating factor in a criminal case. In effect, one's guilt or innocence in respect to a criminal charge can no longer be based upon one's "state of mind" at the time the act in question occurred. Nevertheless, in the *sentencing* phase of a trial (when punishment is assigned after guilt has been established), a form of insanity plea *can* be entered. In the latter instance, the defense must show that the person did not know what he or she was doing *and* did not know the difference between right and wrong in respect to what was being done. This development in California is thought to be the strictest interpretation of the requirement for proving insanity in the nation.

Issues that are raised by newly minted versions of the insanity defense are discussed in detail in Chapters 4 and 5, on criminal responsibility, in this volume. For now, it should be noted that it is becoming more and more difficult for a person to be excused of doing something criminal because of the "accident" of mental defect. Put another way, the likelihood has increased that mentally ill persons will be forced to suffer criminal punishment in some form or degree. This emerging state of affairs is less a legal development than a social trend. It means that public outrage has accomplished a certain change in the way society responds to deviant behavior. The cry of "law and order" has elicited at least a temporary response in the form of suppression of a measure of civil liberty. For some, this change may seem long overdue, but others may see it as unnecessarily severe. With time and reflection, there may be a reversal of the trend.

From both a legal and a diagnostic viewpoint, the determination of clinical responsibility has an inherent flaw because it requires that judgments be made about a past state of mind. Because the accused person may have done the alleged deed some considerable time before he or she was arrested, and the diagnostic examination must be conducted still later, the examiner must attempt to form a clear picture of the accused as he or she was before the alleged crime took place. The clinician must filter out of this assessment the effects of events that have occurred since the crime (e.g., the arrest, possible incarceration, accusation in a courtroom, advice and warning by an attorney). Quite apart from the question of sanity or insanity, the clinician must weigh his or her own notions about the possible guilt of the person being examined—who might have been no more than an innocent bystander at the scene of the crime. These issues are important, to be sure, but they can be placed in the following perspective.

A description of a person's intention prior to the commission of a crime is one among many postdictive kinds of reasoning that are nonetheless valid. Although the assessment is not as objective as one made today on the basis of facts concerning today, it still follows the proper inductive sequence of culling an array of data to make a generalization. This inquiry into a state of mind at time A minus 1 consists of asking for reports of behavior occurring at that time and explanations of that behavior. In most cases when mental illness is detected by such a procedure, the critical variable is the *discrepancy* between behavior described and behavior explained—for example, "I hit him because he was staring at me," or "I followed her because the voices told me to do it." This type of evidence is not weakened by virtue of being stated in the past tense (i.e., as a retrospective report). To these findings can be added knowledge of even earlier events concerning the person, such as a prior episode of illness or a chronic history of hospital treatment for similar symptoms.

In short, postdictive diagnosis of sanity or insanity is logically possible. Although not certain or simple, it by no means deserves to be dismissed as a form of "hearsay" evidence. Its accuracy is a function of the skill and integrity of the clinician, but its evidentiary relevance is sound. And although some therapists may refuse to indulge in such historical diagnostic work, others can claim to do it artfully. It is significant that one psychiatrist was permitted to examine Dan White on the same day that the murders were committed; in testimony, the psychiatrist said that White was not mentally ill on that day.[6]

The affair of poor Hinckley invokes other demons. More than any other, this case gave a bad "rap" to the insanity defense. And more than others the case enables us to see, as through a microscope, a view of human frailty and the nature of insanity that may have evaded us before. In this case, the fault lies not with the judge, the jury, "those lawyers," the discipline of psychotherapy, the justice system, the penal code, Congress, the Constitution, or "the times we live in." The fault lies in ourselves. As a species, we are such overevolved creatures that we can oscillate between the opposites of sane and insane with astounding ease. Although a person cannot inhabit both conditions at once, the Hinckley case has brought to awareness the quantum changes that can occur from day to day to day in a person's mental ecology.

It is useful to reflect that insanity is transient—it comes and it goes, and it does not necessarily last forever; and it is not a progressive disease, in that it does not necessarily worsen with the passing of time. Proof of the temporary nature of insanity is the fact that in most mental hospitals an average stay for an *acutely* ill patient is 1 week; in hospitals where *chronic* mental illness is treated, the average stay is less than 1 month (Keisling, 1983, p. 343). Evidence of the changeable nature of the illness is that chronic schizophrenia can recur on 20 or 30 or more occasions during a lifetime, with periods of relative recovery interspersed.

These considerations suggest that the best analogy between mental illness and a physical disorder is with cardiovascular accident or stroke, which can afflict a person repeatedly and without warning. And before the widespread application of antibiotic drugs for the treatment of tuberculosis, that disease resembled insanity because it would "flare up" again and again with relentless force, and new episodes could seldom be predicted or prevented. A key distinction between these major disorders of psyche and soma is that the body can become increasingly more debilitated as the effects of a physical malfunction deepen and spread; by contrast, the mental apparatus is

---

[6] Because this case is not nationally known, a few details are worth noting here. White killed Mayor George Moscone and Supervisor Harvey Milk in San Francisco in 1978. The following year, he was convicted of manslaughter and sentenced to 8 years in prison. At the trial, a succession of psychiatrists and psychologists testified in his behalf, presumably establishing that White was so mentally unstable at the time of the assassinations that he did not harbor malice toward his victims. One therapist said that he was clinically depressed as shown by, for example, his obsession with a certain snack food (hence the "Twinkies defense"); one referred to White's gun as his "teddy bear." The testimony of these expert witnesses was so compelling to the jury that White escaped the gas chamber, and after 5 years of incarceration, he was granted parole. On October 21, 1985, he took his own life. In addition to the three wholly unnatural deaths, other casualties may have been the principle of diminished capacity and justice.

extremely resilient and capable of renewal without loss.[7] Rejuvenation from emotional disease can be complete and permanent, whereas only limited recovery can reasonably be expected from bodily trauma.

The best description of insanity that I know is: living in a fantasy world. It is obvious that insanity thus construed is a relative proposition, but there are more subtle implications. For example, "living" in a fantasy implies just that—as opposed to thinking in fantasy terms or "having" a fantasy. The insane person quite literally dwells in a realm of unreality in which his or her *overt* behavior is motivated by, and controlled by, the fantasy itself. Hence the flights of fancy of the creative person (a composer of music, a teller of tales, a scientific discoverer) are sane because they are contained within the context of words and numbers and symbols. There is no boundary between fantasy life and real life for the insane person. As an example, there came a time in the horrendous career of Adolf Hitler when he was living within and for his fantasies in the most demented way. Surely no one will deny that Hitler was mad in the end.

There is no need to retry *U.S. v. Hinckley,* but for the purpose of this analysis some observations are worth noting. It may be that the prosecution unwisely ignored the question of sane versus insane *motivation* when it attempted to show that Hinckley was fully responsible for his crime. A fraction of the argument in favor of judging the man sane was that Hinckley was striving to achieve a certain notoriety by becoming a presidential assassin. This point, if it had been pressed more strenuously, would have supported the contention that he should have been held responsible for his deeds.

When Hinckley pulled the trigger he was sane because he was firing a gun at people for a realistic reason. That is, he set in motion a sequence of events that eventually satisfied his motive, because by doing so he earned a version of the label he sought. (The title "would-be presidential assassin" is not, after all, synonymous with "crazy person.") In a sense, Hinckley's assassination attempt may have been his most lucid act in recent years. The defense attorneys won their case for Hinckley by introducing irrelevant testimony about his history of mental illness. In showing that he had a long record of bizarre behavior and psychiatric treatment, the defense was able to evoke the stereotype of "once crazy, always crazy." The success of this strategy is all the more amazing when one realizes that it diverted attention from the ugly event itself, in which one man was maimed and others were seriously injured.

When Hinckley roamed about the country in pursuit of Jodie Foster, he indeed was living in a fantasy world. The belief that one can force another person to love him or her is a quintessential example of what is meant by

---

[7] Of necessity, the organic psychoses and the dementias associated with senility are excluded from this discussion.

primitive thinking. To have acted on this belief, as Hinckley did repeatedly over a long period of time, means that he was insane during that interval.[8] Nothing worked that this pathetic man tried, and none of his thoughts about his beloved were confirmed by another human being. The psychological state in which he dwelt is exactly what the concept of diminished capacity was meant to describe.

By contrast, when Hinckley embarked on his quest to kill the president, the behavior that he displayed was chillingly efficient. He planned the assault carefully and infiltrated the perimeter of security with apparent ease. When the moment came, this inept nonperson, this Caliban, knew what he was about. He was aware that he was holding a loaded gun and that within a certain range it could wound or kill. When a person walks voluntarily into a life-or-death situation, there are some thoughts one cannot not think.

Posterity will ignore the disposition of Hinckley's case. Whether he is confined in St. Elizabeth's Hospital or Leavenworth Prison is of no historical significance. The lesson to be learned from this affair is of another quality, on a different plane, and is revealed by turning the coin both ways. First, most people would agree that a person such as Hinckley does not deserve to receive psychiatric treatment at an expense of public funds. Conversely, *many inmates of our prisons are insane*. This fact may not seem remarkable, except that it raises a compelling question: Is it just for a mentally ill person to be confined to a prison cell? More than a hundred years ago, the use of chains to control the behavior of insane persons was abolished. Have we found a 20th-century means to achieve the same result?[9]

The verdict "guilty but insane" is a cop-out, and like most cop-outs, it does not work. The same person cannot simultaneously be crazy and responsible, because one is a fish and the other a bird. In each case that is brought forward to be judged, it will be necessary to choose one category or the other. That choice must be carefully weighed because upon it rests a moral guide to action.

Insane persons deserve to be offered some form of care for their illness—whether or not they are guilty of committing a crime. Until they are well again, the imposing of punishment will be a travesty. Because they are insane, they cannot be expected to understand either the punishment or its purpose. But the issue is not the effectiveness of one form of retaliation or another. It is priorities, in which the interests of social justice must yield to

---

[8] In sharp contrast, the preponderance of evidence suggests that Dan White was not mentally ill for a single day of his life.

[9] A recent article by Teplin (1984) describes this development in detail: "The criminal justice system may have become the institution that cannot say no. Persons rejected as inappropriate for the mental health system are readily accepted by the criminal justice system. As a result, the jails and prisons may have become the long-term repository for mentally ill individuals who, in a previous era, would have been institutionalized within a psychiatric facility. . . . the way we treat our mentally ill is criminal" (pp. 795, 799).

the needs of personal health and well-being. Each of us has the obligation to cast aside other considerations when we are given an opportunity to save the life of a mind.

THE QUESTION OF DANGEROUSNESS

Many have deplored the practice of admitting testimony by psychotherapists in the prediction of dangerousness, but few have advanced a remedy. Among several detailed analyses of this subject, the work of Dix (1980) is the most comprehensive, that of Stone (1975) the most pessimistic, and that of Megargee (1976) the most perceptive. The verdict until now on the ability of clinicians to perform this task is, at best, an embarrassment to the profession. Estimates of the efficacy of clinical prediction range, for example, from (1) unproven until now (Dix, 1980, pp. 573–581); (2) negligible in some cases (Kozol, Boucher, & Garofalo, 1972, p. 383); and (3) negligible in most cases (Ennis & Litwack, 1974, *passim;* Cocozza & Steadman, 1976, *passim*). In fact, so few kind words have been written about this function of the therapist that one might wonder why some still undertake it. It may be because attorneys and judges will seek this kind of information and no one else has the temerity to supply it, or perhaps it is a pure product of vanity on the part of clinicians. This section will present a new approach to the detection of dangerousness that may resolve the current dilemma.

In general, prediction is a thankless task. Very few people endeavor to make a living at it, with the exception of investment counselors and those lugubrious soothsayers who forecast the weather on television. Unless one is prepared to be proven wrong about 50 percent of the time and can justify the risk, prophesy is not an occupation for those who seek security. This point was made by Ennis and Litwack (1974) when they likened the prediction of dangerousness by psychotherapists to flipping a coin. In essence, if anyone can do it, why ask a therapist? On reflection, the therapist could ask himself or herself, "Why bother?"

The reason many therapists continue to indulge themselves in the conceit that they can predict behavior is that they have been doing it for as long as they can remember. That is, they have been carrying out the task of *prognosis* for so long that the habit is scarcely conscious. By "prognosis" is simply meant a procedure of forecasting the length and severity of a course of illness—in this case, a mental illness. The prognosis is usually attached to a diagnosis and plan of treatment and consists of a statement as terse as "guarded" or "poor" or as ponderous as "freedom from major symptoms likely within 6 months, with possible chronic recurrence of mild depressive episodes." After long experience with this form of expression, the process of composing prognostic statements approaches that of automatic writing.

Small wonder then that the history of prognosis in psychotherapy is a tale of lost causes. Most prognoses, no matter how well thought through or carefully crafted, have a half-life of about 3 weeks. That is in no way astounding when one considers how fraught with contradictions people are and how often they conspire to fox those who try to judge them. The fact is that people are not very predictable, especially with respect to specific actions or even to specific classes of actions. Violent acts in particular and violent behavior in general fit well within this observation.[10]

To summarize, psychotherapists have the delusion that they can make predictions because they are accustomed to writing prognostic statements in case records. Prognosis is an enfeebled form of prophesy that has few pretentions to accuracy. Not much can be expected of it because people are, by nature, resistant to being forced into a mold or to having their futures preordained. Thus the wish to predict, in respect to human actions, may be a vain hope indeed. It would surely be an easier task to foretell the extent to which a recommended diet will reduce high blood pressure, or the likelihood of a patient recovering from infectious pneumonia, or even the length of time that a terminal cancer patient will live. It may be easier still to prophesy the behavior of a quark or the dynamic properties of a micromolecular structure than to say what a certain person will or will not do on one fine day in May.

What *can* psychotherapists do? As advertised, they can make diagnoses, and they can provide treatment for people. Hence it would be in the best interests of the profession to confine itself to these functions in which its expertise is beyond question. It may be that its reputation vis-a-vis the justice system will improve in the bargain.

Diagnosing a person's current mental or emotional state or level of adjustment is a skill for which many clinicians are justly proud. Because a diagnosis is meant to refer to the client's present condition, the examiner can steer a middle course between the shoals of postdiction and prediction alike. He or she is of course expected to specify that the resulting diagnosis applies only to the client's condition *today*. This time-limited view can be used to foresee a future state or condition, if desired, but the risk of making that kind of generalization must be borne by whoever makes the generality.

At first glance, this approach may seem to be a cop-out of the highest rank. For if a diagnosis applies to the person only on the day it was pronounced, how can it be used in any but the narrowest context (i.e., for anything other than record-keeping purposes)? If a judge is struggling with a decision about the kind and length of sentence to impose, of what value is a label that was attached to the person last week or last month? Even if the diagnosis was supplied by a well-qualified clinician, aided by the *Diagnostic*

---

[10] As a matter of official policy, the American Psychiatric Association seems to have reached the same conclusion several years ago: "In an *amicus* civil brief filed before the U.S. Supreme Court in October 1979, [the association] stated that psychiatrists have no expertise to make accurate predictions of future violent behavior" (Roche Report, 1981, p. 4).

and Statistical Manual: III to ensure that he or she chose the descriptive terms with a high level of precision, how would the best available clinical statement help this jurist carry out his or her task? Answers to these questions lie in a deeper examination of the clinician's other (therapeutic) role.

A diagnosis, in practical terms, is no more or less than a codified version of the plan for treatment. Assuming that the person being diagnosed has some form or degree of mental illness or defect (i.e., is not "perfectly normal"), the diagnosis crystalizes the therapist's view of those aspects of a client's current condition that should be changed. In effect, in labeling a person as suffering from one or another psychosis or neurosis, the therapist is producing a statement of intention to provide treatment of some type or to refer the person to another specific source of treatment. In that sense, a diagnosis is the first clause in a plan for therapeutic action.

It is difficult to conceive of a diagnosis that is not accompanied by an obligation, on the part of the clinician, to see to it that care is provided for the disorder. For example, a complete diagnostic statement will resemble this one in form: "Because the client suffers from acute agoraphobia, a course of treatment by behavior modification methods is recommended." Or, "The client is severely depressed and may be self-destructive; he [or she] should be hospitalized (if necessary, involuntarily) for at least a 3-day period of observation and evaluation for possible chemotherapy." Through this combination of assessment and recommended treatment plan, the therapist can fulfill a duty to the client while performing the amazing feat of avoiding use of the future tense.

How do these comments pertain to the prediction of dangerousness? Precisely by addressing correctly both the needs of the court and the capability of clinicians. By not asking too much, the justice system can be served; and by not promising too much, the standards of psychotherapy can be maintained. The following is a proposed blueprint for this long-sought reconciliation.

When diagnosis and treatment plan replace prognostication, the court will be offered two main categories of information: (1) what is wrong with the person (on the day of the examination); and (2) what should be done about it. If, of course, the person is found to be free of pathology, he or she will stand before the court as accused, and at least no psychological mitigating circumstances need be considered by the judge or jury. Conversely, when a mental disorder *is* present, the court will be given whatever facts are needed to substantiate the diagnosis. Most important, the kind and extent of treatment needed to alleviate this pathological condition will be described. The court can then decide whether the recommended treatment is to be provided by a prison-based mental health care system or in the community should release be granted.

With respect to dangerousness, diagnosis is a far superior art to progno-

Table 1-1

Decision Matrix for Acting on Diagnostic Evidence

		Psychological State	
		Psychotic	Nonpsychotic
Potential For Violence	Dangerous	Hospitalization	Treatment plus warning to potential victim(s)
	Not dangerous	Hospitalization	—

sis. The clinician is asked to locate the person on a continuum of dangerousness, ranging from mild to severe, on the day of the examination. The severity of dangerousness is dealt with by means of intervention that begins soon and continues for as many days as are required to reduce the danger to an acceptable level. Hence the concept of treatment can fill the "black hole" left by unreliable prediction.

With this approach, the team of psychotherapist and judge (or jury or parole board or probation department or other decision-making entity of the system) faces relatively few contingencies. These can be ordered on two dimensions, namely those of psychological state and potential for violence, as shown in Table 1-1. In the decision matrix of Table 1-1, two cells imply that hospitalization should be implemented, one cell indicates that no action need be taken, and the fourth recommends that treatment be accompanied by a warning to potential victim(s). The latter provision will be discussed in more detail below.

When a person is found to be *psychotic,* it is axiomatic that he or she be given hospital care for an indefinite period of time. This is a cardinal principle of the mental health profession. It is considered to be a vital part of each clinician's *duty of care* to his or her client (Everstine and Everstine, 1983, pp. 230, 231), and any evasion of that mandate to provide care would be unconscionable. Hence the procedure to be followed in caring for a psychotic person has no element of ambiguity. If the person will agree to voluntary hospitalization, so much the better. If not, some form of coercion must be applied. In most jurisdictions a psychotherapist can make the decision to hospitalize a person against his or her will, and with this authority goes a responsibility to do so when the safety of the psychotic person or other people is at issue.

If the psychotic person is diagnosed as being *dangerous* as well, a request for his or her admission to a hospital ward (whether or not the ward is located in a prison) should include this appraisal of potential for violence. Of course this information will affect the security precautions taken by hospital staff and, to some extent, the nature of the treatment provided, at least at the beginning of the hospital stay. With time, the hospital staff will reassess and confirm or revise these combined diagnoses of psychosis and dangerousness. In that way the status of the person with respect to the decision matrix can be revised and perhaps transferred from one cell of the matrix to another. In this context, diagnosis is an evolutionary process that renews itself on a daily basis. Prediction has no such powers of rejuvenation.

Foremost among the cells of the matrix is the one where "dangerous" and "nonpsychotic" converge. Within this category fit some of the most difficult cases requiring cooperation between the mental health and justice systems. Persons who merit this nonpsychotic/dangerous description are those who are not hospitalizable by any just criterion but who nevertheless represent a menace to the community.[11] Most exhibit poor impulse control, and many already have criminal records. This category includes the psychopaths, whose potential threat to society has been well described by Dix (1980, pp. 550–571), that rarer breed the sociopaths, and the vast majority of common criminals. Although they are by definition not insane, their penchant for dangerousness implies that they could benefit from some form of mental health care.

When a need for treatment is demonstrated, it should be offered. Although the offer may not be accepted, or the acceptance may be lacking in motivation for change, a *duty of care* requires that the offer be made. Unfortunately, a potentially violent client is the least likely client to come forward for assistance at a public clinic or to the therapist's private practice. Often such a person applies for therapy only because he or she has been ordered to do so by a parole board, probation officer, or sentencing judge. Yet because nonpsychotic/dangerous persons may need treatment most of all, the fact that they are more resistive to therapy and less capable of benefiting has little relevance. Unless these people can readily be referred by the justice system to the mental health system, and unless the latter responds appropriately, the liaison between these two institutions will wither and die. Nonpsychotic dangerousness is a pivotal cell in the decision matrix, and the tough choices concerning release or incarceration depend upon what is promised for the disposition of people in that category. If they are to be set free, some social force must be activated to control their dangerous tendencies and to induce eventual change. Psychotherapy is thought to be the best available medium for the application of this force.

The role of the therapist as society's agent does not end with the attempt to deter violence by treatment. As will be explored in further detail in

---

[11] This distinction between psychotic and nonpsychotic dangerousness is by no means a new conception. For instance, it has been referred to instructively by both Dix (1980, pp. 545, 546) and Hall (1983, p. 2).

Chapters 10 and 11, the duty of care that must be discharged by a clinician toward a client is counterbalanced by an equally stringent duty to warn. That is, a therapist who concludes (today) that a client is potentially violent toward a certain person must issue some sort of warning to that intended victim (as soon as possible). The timing and adequacy of this warning may well become an issue in a subsequent civil action against the therapist should the warning fall short of preventing a threatened act. In deciding on the merits of a lawsuit against a therapist for negligence in failing properly to warn, a court will be guided by the legal precedents of the *Tarasoff* decision[12] and its many offspring.

Warning potential victims is a relatively new legal requirement of clinicians, even though many have done it without being required and the principle has existed for centuries in common law. No one doubts that most therapists are well-meaning people who abhor violence, but some have been reluctant to issue warnings to nonclients because of their loyalty to the threat-making clients themselves. It was on the grounds of protecting the confidentiality of a clinic patient that the negligent therapists in *Tarasoff* justified their failure to issue a direct warning to the ultimate victim. The confidentiality privilege has its own foundation in common law, and in defense of the therapists it can be said that they were wrong for the right reasons.

This principle of warning the intended victim about a potentially violent, nonpsychotic person is the capstone of the diagnostic approach to dangerousness that is presented here. In effect, diagnosis of dangerousness is inadequate unless it is followed by treatment, and treatment is insufficient unless anchored by the resolve to warn those who may be menaced by the client's dangerous tendencies. In this way, a person who is released to the community by the justice system can, in theory, be helped toward rehabilitation, and, in practical terms, the community will be afforded a measure of protection. The therapist can be seen, in metaphor, as an officer of the court in such cases. His or her attendant responsibility to reduce the incidence of violence may be considered oppressive to many therapists, but some will see fit to accept it.

From one point of view, the relationship between law and psychotherapy will seethe with conflict unless there is accord on the problem of violence. The court is at pains to prevent it, and therapy is hard-pressed to cure it. By the terms of the present theory, detente will depend upon new definitions of the roles of those who participate on both sides of the liaison. Each side seeks the same ends, and each should offer the other a measure of tolerance concerning the means.

---

[12] *Tarasoff v. Regents of the University of California.* 17 Cal. 3d 425, 131 Cal. Rptr. 14, 551P. 2d 334 (1976).

In summary, these observations on dangerousness were put forward:

- Dangerousness can be diagnosed.
- Dangerousness can be treated, whether by hospitalization or by psychotherapy outside a hospital setting.[13]
- Psychotic dangerousness is a sufficient condition for hospitalization.
- Nonpsychotic dangerousness is not a sufficient condition for hospitalization.
- In whatever setting treatment is provided, the clinician has an obligation to deter the dangerous person from doing harm.
- At the very least, deterrence can consist in warning those who may be in danger.
- A person who is dangerous at one moment may be more or less dangerous at another moment. Hence the diagnosis of dangerousness is not an event but a process.

Finally, this psychotherapist can affirm that, even though no guarantees are intended, dangerousness is a clinical issue, not a legal one.

LEGAL PROCESS AND MENTAL PROCESS

An observer of court procedure once remarked that the law has two faces, namely the law as written and the law as interpreted by instructions to a jury. This point is especially well taken when one considers how often cases are reversed on appeal because a jury was not properly instructed. The following commentary is not meant to be critical of the law or of the guidelines by which jury trials are conducted, but to show that psychotherapy can inform the court process with an awareness of how people think.

As an aspect of court procedure, jury instruction has a rich common-law tradition. That is, both its form and content have evolved largely by custom as opposed to legislation. Its logic and syntax were made, not born. Through a continual process of test and revision, appeal and revocation, addendum and condensation, these authoritarian phrases were molded into the rules of the game. In the trial ritual, they can be likened to the lines of scripture that are read by a minister into a sermon at various points, serving as signposts to the lesson being taught. As literature, they can be read as examples of high English rhetoric.

The reader will find the jury instruction liturgy compressed into a single volume in most states, and for a psychotherapist who would serve the court it makes a valuable text. For the purpose of the present discussion, examples

---

[13] The reader who wishes to explore the subject of treatment methods for dangerous and potentially violent persons may consult Stone, 1975; Everstine et al., 1977; Everstine et al., 1981; Everstine and Everstine, 1983. Excellent compendia of articles on this issue were provided by Martin (1978) and Hays, et al. (1981).

are taken from *California Jury Instructions, Criminal (CALJIC)* (1970).[14] What is noteworthy about jury instructions is that they are predicated on certain assumptions about what jury members can and cannot do. That qualifies as a subject germane to the study of human behavior, capability, and motivation. Hence it lies within the province of psychotherapy.

Much of what occurs in a courtroom, whether the case is a civil or a criminal matter, involves the presentation of information concerning mental processes. Intent, premeditation, and bias are psychological states, for example, and knowledge of right and wrong implies a rudimentary form of mental functioning. These processes are officially defined for the purposes of conducting a trial, and those who take part in the drama are expected to ask questions or to testify about them in accordance with preestablished guidelines. That these guidelines were established long ago does not necessarily give them a rational basis. Perhaps some of these rules were based upon a view of people that is no longer valid; or perhaps they arose from a wish-fulfillment fantasy about the way people *should* function. In either case, a fresh inquiry into what a jury is told about itself and what is expected of it may be useful.

The following quotations list some typical clauses, excerpted at random from the jury instruction manual:

"You will disregard it and form your own opinion" (*CALJIC,* 1970, 17.30, p. 561).

"You should disregard any or all of the comments if they do not agree with your views" (*CALJIC,* 1970, 17.32, p. 563).

"The subject of penalty or punishment is not to be discussed or considered by you" (*CALJIC,* 1970, 17.43, p. 568).

"You must not consider. . . . You will regard that fact as being conclusively proved. . . . You must not speculate. . . . You must never speculate. . . . Such matter is to be treated as though you had never heard of it" (*CALJIC,* 1970, 1.02, p. 5).

One after the other, these imperatives reverberate across the consciousness of a psychotherapist, arousing perplexity if not consternation. The first question is, Can jury members do what is required? The second is, Will they?

Practical instances of the use of these and other more specific instructions to a jury often find their way into press reports of trial deliberations. This account, for example, appeared in the San Francisco *Chronicle*'s story on the California case of Gerald Gallego, who was later convicted of murdering a young couple:

> Judge Spellberg warned the prospective jurors that occasionally they might glimpse Gallego . . . being escorted through the courthouse halls in handcuffs.

---

[14] The designation "criminal" refers specifically to the criminal, as opposed to the civil case.

"You are not to draw inferences of guilt [from this]" Spellberg said. ["Trial Opens," 1982, p. 46]

In a more celebrated case, the civil suit of Al Davis against the National Football League (for the right to move his team from Oakland to Los Angeles), the judge instructed the jury to disregard a quotation from a magazine interview. The quotation, which had been shown to the courtroom on a large screen, included this statement by Davis to the interviewer: "I didn't hate Hitler. He captivated me." The following day, Judge Harry Pregerson said to the jury:

I noted one passage that referred to German military tactics and Hitler. . . . I am certain that passage does not reflect the true feelings of Mr. Davis. The passage had to do with Mr. Davis' perception of the war when he was 10 years old. . . .

    If I had seen that excerpt before it was used, I would not have permitted it. The excerpt was inflammatory and should not have been used. ["Raiders' Judge," 1981, p. 6]

Pregerson then asked the jury members whether any of them was unable to "completely and entirely disregard that excerpt." After each one of the jurors had confirmed his or her ability to "disregard" as instructed, Pregerson told them to write a note to the court clerk if they later felt that the quotation had affected them so deeply that they were unable to disregard it. As far as is known, no such note was received.

    In these two unlike case examples, the two judges were using accepted procedure by issuing their cautionary orders to the juries. Each communicated his concerns straightforwardly, and each made an unambiguous plea for fairness on the part of the jury in forming its opinion. Even so, as a practical matter, it is doubtful that these judges were successful in their mutual aim. The reason is that they were employing a psychological principle that does not exist.

    The concept of "blotting it out" of one's mind may be the legacy of an antiquated view of human reasoning. The notion of free will, which was popular in the philosophy of mind of the 18th and 19th centuries, meant that a person can think or not think what he or she wishes. Thought that is regulated by the force of will can be released or suppressed or altered, as desired, by the person who does the thinking. Suffice it to say that this is not a current view of the way the mind works. At present, we are much more inclined to look upon thought and the storage of mental contents as an *interactional* process. In that conceptualization, the mind is not a self-contained system that operates autonomously from the world it perceives. People interact first with their environment and with each other, and thought follows by consequence—as a means to represent the information derived from those encounters. This interactional view sees thinking as an open system, constantly benefiting from (and influenced by) ideas and interpretations that are supplied by other people. The medium of change and growth is human communication.[15]

With even the best of intentions, a person is not likely to be capable of disregarding clearly perceived objects and events whose meaning and significance to a trial are obvious. When the event is one so dramatic as seeing a defendant in handcuffs, or the object so riveting as the sight of a plaintiff's words projected upon a screen, it is likely that the experience itself will make an indelible impression. In effect, to disregard after the fact what was so forcefully registered by the senses is no mean accomplishment. Whether or not the jurors did so in the cases cited is unknown but, if they did, all credit is due their iron-clad consciences.

People often do as they are told—especially when ordered by a judge; but they are seldom so facile that they can erase from their memories a vivid experience. When weighing evidence at the end of a trial, in the snug harbor of a jury room, jurors can dedicate themselves to carrying out the judge's instructions, but some will succeed and some will fail. Of those who fail, some will have been unable to purge their minds of the information labeled as taboo, and others will recall it all the more vividly *because* attention was called to it by the judge. In short, the jury instructions may achieve their purpose with certain jurors, accomplish nothing with others, and have the opposite effect upon still others. With these as possible outcomes, the judge would have done well to save his or her breath.

To review, the activity of disregarding is not one that people do easily or by the mere exercise of will. Evolution has put a premium upon careful regard of our environment as a survival skill (i.e., it is useful to "pay attention," and with lack of attention may come an element of risk). Trying not to think of something can also lead to the kind of closed-loop process which in the obsessive-compulsive variety of neurosis may be hazardous to one's health.

The concepts introduced above apply equally to jury instructions such

---

[15] The theory of repression does not pertain to this issue. Freud made repression a central concept, upon which he based the notion of unconscious thought processes that dominate the everyday expression of one's personality. In fact, the discovery of repression *led to* the identification of a subconscious mind. Repression, however, is a restricted concept with a limited application, as indicated by the following definition: "The active process of keeping out and ejecting, banishing from consciousness, ideas or impulses that are unacceptable to it" (Hinsie and Campbell, 1970, p. 660). Hence the repressed idea is one that cannot be kept within the conscious mind because it evokes emotional pain. It becomes forgotten for a specific reason and serves a unique purpose, namely to protect the ego from harm. This function is very different from the kind of forgetting that is required of jurors in a court of law. There is ample motivation for the forgetting of a thought that may threaten the self, but none whatever for forgetting the details of testimony or of some event that has occurred in a courtroom. The difference is as compelling as that between the experience of having a toothache and sympathizing with another person's toothache pain.

as "You must not consider" and "You must never speculate," because
these admonitions in the negative are as easily disobeyed as obeyed. Each
time a person is told not to do this or that, the implied counterargument is
that what is being prohibited may be worth doing.[16] Further, the judge may
compromise his or her own impartiality by interjecting comments of this
kind for reasons that could appear prejudiced.

When admonished not to consider some event or situation, the person
might ask reflectively, "Why not?" Later reflection may lead to asking,
"What would be the harm in considering _____?" or, "Where would it
lead me in my thinking if I did consider _____?" The more inquisitive may
proceed to questions such as, "Why did the judge say that?" and "What
does the judge think about _____?" In this way, a person can stumble into
pathways of thought much more obscure than those that the original instructions were meant to block. At the very least, the path taken by the jury
member may be convoluted, leading him or her in a direction far distant from
the basic issues of the particular trial. A perplexed juror does not make a
well-calibrated instrument of justice. And although the best interests of a
conscientious judge will often be served by remaining silent, instructions to a
jury are expectations of the judge's role. The problems referred to in this
brief essay can only suggest a possible source of confusion in this complex
interaction between the judge who must be fair and the jury who must be
just. The main point is that observation of this alliance from the vantage of
psychotherapy can be of value to both partners. If answers to the questions
raised here are sought in order to make changes in the process of jury
instruction, part of knowing what must be done will be knowing what cannot
be done.[17]

Common law can change with time, as exemplified by the newly accepted interpretation of the obligations that a man has to a common-law
wife. So, too, the procedures that are applied in a court of law can be
improved by modification. Even though the court system must retain its
sovereignty in a democratic state, its methods are not sacred.

PSYCHOTHERAPY AND THE COURTS

One would imagine the relationship of psychotherapy to the courts to be
in tattered disarray, especially considering the recent trend by which therapists are either being kicked out of the courtroom or themselves are asking to

---

[16] This occasionally vexing but ultimately inspiring human propensity was noted in a dictum attributed to Albert Camus, namely "That which bars my path only increases my desire to
travel along that path."

[17] In recent years, extremely valuable research efforts have been made toward investigating
the thought processes of jury members and their reactions to instructions by a judge and other
court practices. Two excellent examples are the contributions of Greene and Loftus (1985) and
Kagehiro and Stanton (1985).

withdraw. This may be a period of transition, says the optimist, or, at the very least, a welcome interregnum. The gulf between legal and therapeutic systems is a real one, but such ideological straits have been known to bridge themselves in time.

Why is the depth of differences so great? One reason is that the court's role is to protect society (greater good for the greater number), and that of psychotherapy is to enhance individual well-being (personal adjustment). Another reason is that the two factions approach a trial from differing viewpoints: The court seeks the facts that describe a person's actions, whereas a therapist wants the person's motives to be understood. Finally, there are differing views of the nature of cogitation in a jury's deliberation. A judge looks upon the juror as a self-regulating mechanism that requires only occasional guidance from an outside source to make a decision. By contrast, the therapist views decision making by a juror as extremely sensitive to changing stimuli in the environment—including those introduced to the courtroom by a judge.

In spite of the many differences of interpretation and emphasis and profound variance in values and goals, law and psychotherapy remain purposefully intertwined. The importance of one discipline to the other will reaffirm itself as their relationship improves with understanding.

REFERENCES

American Bar Association. (1983). The insanity defense: ABA and APA proposals for change. *Mental Disability Law Reporter, 7*(2), 136, 139–147, 210.

American Psychiatric Association Task Force on Nomenclature and Statistics. (1980). *Diagnostic and statistical manual of mental disorders: III.*

Cocozza, J. J., & Steadman, H. J. (1976). The failure of psychiatric predictions of dangerousness: Clear and convincing evidence. *Rutgers Law Review, 29,* 1084–1101.

Committee on Standard Jury Instructions, Criminal, of the Superior Court of Los Angeles County, California. (1970). *California Jury Instructions, Criminal (CALJIC).* St. Paul, MN: West Publishing.

Dix, G. E. (1980). Clinical evaluation of the "dangerousness" of (normal) criminal defendants. *Virginia Law Review, 66*(523), 523–581.

Dorsey, T. P. (1982). Guilty but mentally ill: GBMI verdict. State of New York Mental Hygiene Bureau Report to the Attorney General.

Ennis, B. J., & Litwack, T. R. (1974). Psychiatry and the presumption of expertise: Flipping coins in the courtroom. *California Law Review, 62,* 693–752.

Everstine, D. S., Bodin, A. M., & Everstine, L. (1977). Emergency psychology: A mobile service for police crisis calls. *Family Process, 16*(3), 281–292.

Everstine, L., Everstine, D. S., Heymann, G. M., True, R. H., Frey, D. H., Johnson, H. G., & Seiden, R. H. (1980). Privacy and confidentiality in psychotherapy. *American Psychologist, 35,* 828–840.

Everstine, D. S., Everstine, L., & Bodin, A. M. (1981). The treatment of psychological emergencies. In J. R. Hays, T. K. Roberts, & K. S. Solway (Eds.), *Violence and the violent individual.* (pp. 391–407). New York: SP Medical and Scientific Books.

Everstine, D. S., & Everstine, L. (1983). *People in crisis.* New York: Brunner/Mazel.

Greene, E. & Loftus, E. F. (1985). When crimes are joined at trial. *Law and Human Behavior,* *9*(2), 193–207.

Hall, H. V. (1983). Guilty but mentally ill: Feedback from State Attorney General Offices. *Bulletin of the American Academy of Forensic Psychologists, 4*(1), 2, 7, 8.

Hays, J. R., Roberts, T. K., & Solway, K. S. (Eds.). (1981). *Violence and the violent individual.* New York: SP Medical and Scientific Books.

Hinsie, L. E., & Campbell, R. J. (1970). *Psychiatric dictionary* (4th ed.). New York: Oxford University Press.

Kagehiro, D. K. & Stanton, W. C. (1985). Legal US. quantified definitions of standards of proof. *Law and Human Behavior, 9*(2), 159–178.

Keisling, R. (1983). Turning back the clock: A response to Szasz [Comment]. *American Psychologist, 38,* 343.

Kozol, H., Boucher, R., & Garofalo, R. (1972). The diagnosis and treatment of dangerousness, *Crime and Delinquency, 18,* 371–392.

Martin, J. P. (Ed.). (1978). *Violence and the family.* Chichester, England John Wiley & Sons.

Megargee, E. I. (1976). The prediction of dangerous behavior. *Criminal Justice and Behavior, 3*(1), 3–21.

Monahan, J. (Ed.). (1980). *Who is the client?* Washington, DC: American Psychological Association.

National Commission on the Insanity Defense. (1983). *Myths and realities: A report of the National Commission on the Insanity Defense.* Arlington, VA: National Mental Health Association.

Raiders' judge says to disregard the Hitler quote. (1981, June 19) San Francisco *Chronicle,* p. 6.

Roche Report. (1981). The violent patient: Predicting the probability. *Frontiers of Psychiatry,* 4–5, 11.

Rubenstein, L. S. (1983). Mental Health Law Project responds to proposals to change insanity defense. *Mental Disability Law Reporter, 7*(2), 147.

Slovenko, R. (1973). *Psychiatry and law.* Boston: Little, Brown and Company.

Stone, A. A. (1975). *Mental health and law: A system in transition. Crime and Delinquency Issues Monograph Series.* U.S. Department of Health, Education, and Welfare.

Szasz, T. S. (1963). *Law, liberty, and psychiatry: An inquiry into the social uses of mental health practices.* New York: Macmillan.

Szasz, T. S. (1970). *The manufacture of madness: A comparative study of the inquisition and the mental health movement.* New York: Harper & Row.

Szasz, T. S. (1976, March 13). Mercenary psychiatry. *The New Republic,* pp. 10–12.

Teplin, L. A. (1984). Criminalizing mental disorder: The comparative arrest rate of the mentally ill. *American Psychologist, 39*(7), 794–803.

Trial opens in kidnap-killing of Sacramento State couple. (1982, November 16). San Francisco *Chronicle,* p. 46.

PART I

Trauma Caused by Injury or Assault

Diana Sullivan Everstine

2

Psychological Trauma in Personal Injury Cases

Some of the various psychological phenomena that are associated with being traumatized are discussed in this chapter, and some of society's responses to traumatized persons are described. When people become traumatized, they are psychologically "inundated" by the reality of personal vulnerability (a seeming helplessness in the face of life's events), a loss of trust in persons or institutions once considered safe or nurturing, the possibility of permanent physical impairment, and perhaps, the fear of impending death. The life experiences of few persons will have prepared them for the trauma of personal injury; and few, if any, are capable of facing the enormity of such an event without considerable help and support.

People have many fantasies about what they would do, or should do, were they to be threatened by trauma. Some believe that they would be able to avoid injury by using their wits to escape or in some other way preventing the trauma from taking place. But, in fact, these common fantasies are far from reality. In most cases there is no real prospect of escaping or of preventing the damage from occurring. And, despite all our "rugged individualist" fantasies, most people respond to trauma by sinking into a state of shock and disbelief.

Following a trauma, the psyche enters the Trauma Response and Recovery Cycle, a process that serves to protect one's ego during and after acutely traumatic events. (This cycle is fundamentally similar to the "grief response," which was identified and described by Lindemann [1944].) One of the primary roles of a psychotherapist in treating a traumatized person is to assist and encourage the person to proceed through the Trauma Response and Recovery Cycle in a manner that will facilitate healthy, adaptive behav-

PSYCHOTHERAPY AND THE LAW
ISBN 0-8089-1780-3

ior. The purpose is to help the person recover from the "invisible psychological wounds" (Everstine & Everstine, 1983, pp. 163, 164) that, if left un-
tended or untreated, may result in lifelong psychological problems.

Each of us lives with our problems, fears, and sorrows, but usually
there is a perceived underlying logic or reason to our lives. Suddenly, an
inexplicable, devastating event takes place that occurs beyond the compass
of our usual conceptual framework. In most cases of trauma, a person has
been going about his or her daily life and the trauma occurs in a totally
unexpected way. If the trauma is violent, such as an assault or crash in a
vehicle, the traumatized person will be overcome by disbelief, and the mind
will reel in a desperate attempt to come to terms with the situation. This
sensation of disbelief occurs because the person's mind, in a primitive way,
tries to dispel the trauma by pretending that the event was not real. But when
cold reality descends upon the injured person, a stage often occurs during
which the person's affect (emotional state) becomes quite frozen or "flat."
During the actual trauma, the person's cognitive functions are concentrated
upon one issue: survival. Should a therapist have the rare experience of
encountering a person immediately after a traumatic event, he or she would
be wise to accept (or pretend to) initially the logic of the person's actions,
even if they are bizarre. By doing so, the therapist will be able to enter the
person's frame of reference, which is likely to be extremely rigid immediately after the event. Once one has entered the traumatized person's frame
of reference, it will be easier to redirect him or her toward more appropriate
behavior.

Being traumatized can be brutally destructive to a person's sense of
personal integrity and basic trust of others. If physical, the trauma can be an
assault upon the person's sense of wholeness, self-image, and competence,
because the body is a person's ultimate "territory." We are extremely territorial beings, expressing and experiencing our sense of territoriality in hundreds of everyday situations. It is so basic that we rarely think consciously
of "territory" as such. People have a region of very private "space" around
them, encompassing a radius of about a foot and a half to two feet. (In other
cultures, people have differing critical areas of space, some larger and some
smaller.) A profound source of conflict in a physical trauma is that there
occurs a devastating breach of, and temporary destruction of, the person's
basic sense of territorial boundaries. People who have been robbed experience a similar breach of their territoriality, but to a much lesser extent. The
emotional state of someone who has been physically traumatized is like the
person who has been robbed, compounded a hundred times. Not only has
something intruded into his or her space, but the very skin, the ultimate
personal boundary, has been violated. Instances in which peoples' bodies
are "violated" against their will or consent include stabbings, shootings, car
crashes, rapes; medical malpractice; and injuries caused by defective products. Consider the horrible sense of helplessness and loss that is felt upon

waking from surgery to find that physical damage or disfigurement from the operation has occurred. One can empathize with a person's despair in this situation.

A concept that is helpful in understanding the impact of trauma is that the person's sense of safety, mastery, and physical integrity are at least temporarily destroyed. Basic feelings of strength and self-control are lost. And, with these feelings, one loses confidence in the ability to protect oneself, e.g., forcefully to prevent another person from doing something that one does not want the person to do. Most of us are secure enough within ourselves, and most of us possess a shared fantasy that we have some control over our lives. Suddenly, as a result of a trauma, this sense of security and control can be taken away. This felt devastation may affect every aspect of the person's life. Many even lose their sense of competence to interact with friends and loved ones. As a consequence, many love relationships do not survive after the trauma-induced sequence of events, in part because trauma can greatly damage a person's feelings of trust in others.

The assumption of trust is a vital element upon which personal and professional relationships—as well as society itself—are based. Few of us are consciously aware of how much implicit trust we have in other people with whom we share relationships. We assume that people will not harm us, that the products we use are safe, that the professionals who care for us will make the right decisions, and that our work, home, and recreational environments will be free from danger. Then, in a horrible moment, one is forced to realize how vulnerable to others one has always been.

Although the trauma usually has a physical aspect, a traumatized person may suffer equally severe psychic wounds, namely "invisible" wounds. These psychological effects, combined with the physical assault, leave the traumatized person in a profound state of shock, which may last for days or weeks or months. During this period, the person attempts to deal with the immediate realities of the trauma. This response may range from vividly reliving the event ("flashbacks"), to obsessional attention to details of the traumatic event, to total denial. It will usually be 3 months to a year and a half before the person will begin the process of working-through the trauma in psychotherapy. The length of time required for treatment varies, depending upon the degree of trauma; in some cases, 4 or 5 years will be required. Some persons may never fully recover. Some must learn to adapt or cope with permanent emotional problems—not to mention crippling physical injury or disfigurement and their attendant psychological sequelae.

Treating the traumatized person is often not a simple task because he or she may at first resist participating in the emotional struggle that will lead to recovery. Initially, traumatized people spend considerable time in a state of denial. In the author's view, this period of denial permits the psyche some time to heal, so that it can begin to cope with the reality of loss. Attempting to break through the denial period in order to make the person "face the reality" of what has taken place is usually pointless; it may cause him or her to flee from treatment and view the therapist as another tormentor.

After the denial phase, a traumatized person is likely to internalize his or her anger; as a result, he or she will be depressed. Some people may be too enervated or debilitated by this depression to work actively toward recovery. In some cases, they may become angry at their bodies for "failing" them and resist taking proper care of themselves; in severe cases, they may act in a self-destructive manner. This self-destructive behavior may vary from not complying with their medical doctors' instructions to pushing themselves into activities that may be physically damaging or retard recovery. At the extreme end of this spectrum may lie a suicide attempt. A therapist needs to bear in mind that, in such situations, the client is usually completely unaware of the internal forces causing his or her behavior.

In many cases, even the friends and family of the traumatized person may behave in an unsympathetic manner, which can make it difficult or impossible for the person to work through the trauma. Others who are close to the victim may choose to rationalize why he or she was traumatized, in this way convincing themselves that there was a specific reason for what happened (e.g., "She never should have been there in the first place" or "He asked for it"). And because there was a reason, it could not have happened to them. Frequently, these friends and relatives ascribe the victim's emotional trauma to a prior emotional weakness. In that way, they rationalize that psychological problems of this magnitude could never occur to them, because they suffer no such predisposition. Such self-protecting rationalizations only serve to reinforce the unfortunate victim's propensity for self-blame or self-destructive acting-out. Even though the actual events were absolutely beyond their control, many people who are traumatized feel responsible for what has happened, and this feeling may arise even at an early stage of the posttrauma period. Traumatized people typically spend hours dwelling on the "if I only" aspects of what happened. And when the person's family members or friends or acquaintances indulge in the kind of thinking that shifts responsibility for a trauma onto its victim, it can only serve to deepen the self-blame and depression, and hence retard recovery. This thinking may also lead to the chilling answer "It was your own fault" in reply to the patient's question "Why did this happen to me?" Traumatized people ask, of themselves and others, questions such as "Why me?" for a long time after the assault. These questions are frequently put forth very subtly, and the person carefully scrutinizes the responses of others for their answers.

This issue of "Why me?" needs to be *cautiously* explored by a therapist to discern whether or not the client believes that the trauma is punishment for real or imagined misdeeds. It is very difficult for people to accept the randomness of sudden personal catastrophes, and thus they often search for reasons such as divine punishment for prior misdeeds or an evil force at

work. Even if the victim did contribute in some way to the traumatic event, a therapist should wait until the person is well along in the recovery cycle before attempting to bring this to his or her attention. If possible, the client should be past the angry phase and into the philosophizing period before this subject is broached.

A similar mistake that people close to the traumatized person may make, which will retard or prevent his or her recovery, is advising the victim to "just forget about it," "put it out of your mind," or "pretend it didn't happen." These are examples of classic problem mismanagement, in that belittling a problem can cause it to become more serious. A person who is in a posttraumatic state simply *cannot* put the event out of his or her mind, and such a comment may further alienate the person at a time when he or she deeply needs support and understanding.

It is worth noting that people who are close to the victim (including some therapists) are sometimes unsympathetic toward the idea of the victim suing for damages. There may be two reasons for this. One, if the person who caused the trauma has been found guilty in a criminal proceeding, they may feel that this person has paid his or her dues to society and that the victim's suit against the criminal or a third party goes beyond what society requires. This notion may also become blended with the concept, described earlier, of the need people have to blame traumatized persons for their suffering. It is the author's experience that many people cling to the notion that ours is a "just" world in which one can influence one's own fate. But when they try to assimilate the thought of someone being an innocent victim of random trauma, this thought may clash with their personal conception of the world. So they condemn the victim to justify their belief system. Rather than give up their world concept, and acknowledge their own vulnerability at the same time, they may sacrifice the idea of the victim's innocence. This is not always the reaction of a traumatized person's significant others, but the author has observed it often enough to warrant comment. It suggests that therapists should prepare traumatized clients for the possibility that the responses of significant others toward the idea of suing the person responsible may not always be sympathetic (even though the suit may, in fact, be a just one, and even though it will be resolved on its merits by traditionally accepted methods of the civil legal system).

Those who are close to a traumatized person can mismanage the situation—and block recovery—in another way: by overreacting in a hysterical or outraged manner. This can cause the person to mask his or her feelings, for fear of further upsetting a loved-one. Traumatized people need to feel that the people around them are self-controlled and capable of protecting them. Often they desperately need to regain a sense of order in their own environment while they attempt to cope with the chaos that the trauma has brought to their lives. Hence it is part of the task of a therapist to include in treatment not only the traumatized person but also the significant other people in his or her life, so that the others will not inadvertently say or do things that could impede the person's recovery. Further, a victim's significant others may need treatment merely because they are sharing their lives with a person who is emotionally wounded and because their behavior may serve to exacerbate the wounds. One need only consider the high rate of divorce among rape victims to confirm the necessity of treatment for significant others of a traumatized person.

ASSESSING THE DEGREE OF TRAUMA

It has been the author's experience that the degree of psychological trauma is related to an interaction of several factors, the first of which is the degree to which the body was violated, altered, or disfigured. Assaults in which the body is damaged in some way, or in which the victim believes it to have been damaged, can be especially traumatic, particularly if the damage relates to one's feelings of competence or self-image. The loss of a hand by a factory worker or a police officer, for example, can be far more psychologically disabling than the same loss to someone whose occupation does not require manual dexterity. Another factor is the extent to which the person has feared death. Further, the traumatized person's preinjury relationship with the person (or persons) who were involved in the traumatic event, (i.e., the assailant or perpetrator) can be vital. This phenomenon includes products or situations or circumstances that may have been responsible for the event. Contrary to common belief, trauma caused by a person or object or situation that was known, familiar, and possibly trusted by the victim is often *more* complex and severe than trauma caused by a stranger, an unfamiliar object, or a situation in which the person could have expected danger to exist.

It should not be overlooked that a person's past experiences, as well as currently available coping skills, affect the amount of psychological disability that an injury causes. For example, those who dwell in an idyllic or protected world where they normally feel safe may be more susceptible to trauma than someone whose concept of the world contains the ever-present possibility of danger lurking about; the person whose perception of reality rests upon an illusion of safety may suffer more acutely when his or her conceptions are shattered. Hence a clinician needs to assess the degree to which a person's ability to trust his or her environment has been damaged by the trauma.

The location of the assault itself can play a role in the degree of trauma experienced. The person who is suddenly awakened in bed by someone who holds a gun to the person's head and puts a knee to the person's throat is usually more traumatized than someone who is injured or attacked on the street, where one might expect violence.

There are places in which people assume that they are safe and protected, and when one of those places is violated it is a shattering experience. Typically, a traumatized person may develop some form of phobic reaction to the site of the trauma, depending upon the intensity of the other factors cited above. The clinician should assess how much the person's phobic reaction to the location of the trauma has damaged his or her private life.

Finally, a clinician should take into consideration the traumatized person's emotional condition prior to the event. Those who have rigid personality structures or who were emotionally fragile beforehand may suffer more severe posttraumatic reactions than others who were less fragile.

TREATING TRAUMATIZED PEOPLE

From the beginning of treatment, it is vital that the clinician attempt to create a nurturing atmosphere in which the traumatized person can feel safe, protected, and supported. There are schools of psychotherapy that view defense mechanisms in a negative light and use particularly confrontive and/or intrusive therapeutic methods to break down a client's defenses in order to reach "the true feelings." This approach cannot be opposed too strongly for several reasons. Many traumatized people have been through terrors that others, in their worst nightmares, can only imagine. During the traumatic event, their accustomed defense mechanisms very likely served to insulate and protect them from disintegrating into madness. If the therapist attacks (or is perceived to be attacking) what the traumatized person feels was a source of strength that protected him or her in an hour of deepest need, the person may well decide to leave the therapeutic relationship. The person may feel that the therapist has traumatized him or her as violently as did the person who caused the trauma.

During the first stages of treatment, it is vital for a therapist to (1) take a nonjudgmental approach in which the victim is permitted to express feelings freely; and (2) provide the person with as much information as he or she can tolerate about the reality of the traumatic event and the true roles and motives of various participants in it. Moreover, the therapist should advise the person's significant others to avoid pushing him or her to "get back on the horse." Instead, a realistic process of desensitization is advised. (This insistence that the traumatized person prematurely "face" the traumatic event before he or she is emotionally prepared to do so can lead to the kind of "second injury" that is referred to later in this chapter.) In cases of serious trauma, desensitization techniques should be conducted with great care. They should begin, for example, with the use of stimuli that are perceived as safe and benign, then move forward in smaller increments than would be tried with most other phobic clients.

As indicated above, most people enter a state of shock directly after a traumatic event, which serves to "insulate" them from the event to some extent. This state of shock, in which the affect is dull, is often misinterpreted as meaning that the victim is not upset about what has just happened or is feeling "all right." Shock can last from a few hours to several days, depending upon the severity of the trauma. After this stage, many people slip into a depressive state, chiefly because very few are capable of expressing their anger overtly at this time. Toward the end of this depressed phase, the traumatized person usually experiences severe mood swings. During these early stages, the person may also experience considerable anxiety about his or her mental stability and whether or not he or she will ever be "normal" again. Throughout this period, the clinician needs to reassure the person that what he or she is suffering is part of a normal recovery process and that it will pass more quickly if he or she tries not to resist it.

Following the depressive phase, the person usually enters an actively angry phase, which can be quite destructive if the person (institution or whatever) who was responsible for the trauma has not yet been held accountable for it. At this time the person may displace his or her anger onto some "safe object," such as a loved one or friend (perhaps even a therapist). These significant others will need considerable help to understand why they are being attacked by the traumatized person—especially since this phase usually begins a while after the traumatic assault has occurred. The traumatized person may also benefit from an explanation of the defense of displacement, in which anger is vented upon another (the "object"). A clinician might explain, for example, that the person may not wish to be "nice" toward people—or even want to be close to them—for a while, because he or she has been so terribly hurt. Some version of this comment may prove helpful: "You have a right to be angry about what happened, and some of your anger may be directed toward a loved one or someone who is 'safe.' " The clinician should keep in mind that much of this anger may represent unconscious resentment of a loved one for not having "been there" for protection or for not having been able, in some way, to prevent what happened. A therapist must help the person understand the origins of such feelings, as well as balance this need to ventilate anger against the necessity of preserving the significant relationships in his or her life. The best way to present the concept of displacement to the significant others is to schedule a session when the patient will not be present, so that each may vent some of his or her own feelings (Silverman, 1978).

Anger often emerges in another way. The client becomes angry with his or her body for failing to prevent the trauma. The person may express such anger by not taking care of himself or herself or by not following the physician's orders. Such behavior should be dealt with in a direct but sensitive way, by explaining to the client that his or her anger has taken this form and by directing him or her toward more appropriate and healthy expressions.

Following the angry phase, many traumatized people enter a somewhat "philosophical" period in which they review what the event has meant to them. During this reflective phase, the person realizes (if the rest of the cycle has occurred in good order) that he or she is no longer the same person as before the trauma. Reflection concerns how he or she has changed and what this will mean for the future. The person attempts to accept the extent to which his or her life has been transformed by this unfortunate event.

Those who work in the helping professions need to be careful not to cause what Symonds (1980) called the "second injury." This form of injury can occur when one does not realize how vulnerable and needy a person is after experiencing a trauma. In many cases, the person is unable to express his or her needs—even though, at the same time, he or she expects these needs to be met. This often places a therapist in the difficult position of having to guess at the person's needs. In such a case, the clinician can help prevent a second injury by trying to create an atmosphere in which the person feels safe to ask, eventually, for what he or she wants.

From the beginning of the therapeutic process, a therapist needs to help the traumatized person regain his or her feelings of competence and control over his or her life. One result of the loss of these feelings is an overwhelming sense of helplessness, which needs to be countered by giving the person a measure of control over the therapy situation itself. Traumatized people are extremely sensitive to any intrusiveness, insensitivity, or perceived coercion in their therapist's approach. Consequently, the clinician needs to be sensitive to the issues of power or authority in the transference relationship. As therapy evolves, a therapist can exert considerable authority in the relationship; and, even if a therapist's intentions are totally benevolent and humanitarian, he or she must take care that the victim does not project onto the therapist aspects of his or her trauma. If this occurs, the client will either develop a neurotic, dependent transference to his or her therapist or flee from the therapy experience. In effect, the usual limits concerning permissible levels of inquiry in therapy do not apply with such people. Some traumatized people need simply to be allowed to talk for a while; some need to go over and over what occurred in the traumatic event. A clinician should, initially, be quite patient with traumatized people until a solid trust relationship has been established.

During the first sessions of treatment, a therapist needs to help the person realize that he or she is not alone in having suffered this trauma and that his or her feelings and experiences are consistent with those of other traumatized people. One should be cautious not to demean the person in any way or to imply that his or her experience was less devastating or horrible than someone else's. Soon the person should be assisted in accepting his or her behavior during and after the traumatic event. The person requires assurance that he or she was (and is) reacting normally to an abnormal situation. It will help to know that he or she is accepted by the therapist, even if others do not fully understand or accept what has happened or is happening now.

A clinician should be aware that the patient may eventually be interrogated or deposed by those who are involved in the apprehension, prosecution, and/or civil litigation of the person(s) allegedly responsible for the trauma. In fact, he or she may be questioned by what appears to be an endless stream of people. These people may be less than sensitive to the victim's feelings, and thus there may be additional trauma resulting from the criminal or civil proceedings themselves. Both of the latter will require detailed reporting of the event in an environment that may be perceived as hostile.

When the clinician starts working with a traumatized person, he or she should take a more directive and educational approach than is taken with most clients. The rationale for this approach is that the person usually has a need for basic information and for answers to questions about what he or she has experienced. Many traumatized people can be helped, for example, by an explanation of what ego-defense mechanisms are, how these mechanisms are acquired, and how they work. After the person's shock wears off, he or she will probably make use of some of these defense mechanisms as vital components of the recovery cycle. The responses of most traumatized people are, as mentioned above, similar to those of people who are in the process of grieving after the death of a loved one (Lindemann, 1944). They exhibit similar periods of denial, mood swings, and sleep loss, with a day of elation followed by a day of depression. They wonder "Am I crazy?" or "Am I losing my mind?" Because the recovery process is often confusing, traumatized people need many explanations, as do their family members. The purpose of this educational approach is that the person gains some perspective on the total process, and the loved ones gain an understanding of the person's thoughts—even though they may not be able to change them.

An explanation of the basic defense mechanisms of repression, denial, projection, and displacement can be useful in helping the person gain a perspective on what he or she is experiencing. Sometimes these mechanisms can be described to a person by analogy with physical defenses, for example: "Just as your body has a defense against bacteria called 'antibodies,' so your mind has defenses against too much physical or emotional pain; during and after a trauma, your mind uses these mechanisms to protect itself."

Many traumatized people do not realize that they were in a state of shock during their traumatization, and hence they may misunderstand their seemingly strange behavior. This doubt may find expression in such questions as "Why didn't I stop it or do something?" Some people describe the trauma in terms such as these: "It was like I was under water; everything was going in slow motion; I couldn't even speak." Quite frequently one hears a traumatized person say something like that and then express guilt for

Table 2-1
Trauma Response and Recovery Cycle

Trauma Response
  Shock
  Disbelief (attempt to deny the reality of the event)
  Realization of reality of the event
  Survival state
Posttrauma Recovery Cycle
  Posttraumatic shock
  Posttraumatic attempt to deny reality
  Depression
  Mood swings
  Anger
  Philosophical period
  Laying to rest (or coming to terms with) changes resulting from the trauma

not having been able to do something to prevent the trauma. A good way to resolve this guilt is to explain to the person that because he or she was in shock during the trauma there was no way whatever to stop it. Military training has long relied upon repetitive drill to ensure that, in the terror of battle, reactions will be automatic. Without that training, the soldier might react in combat much as any other victim of trauma does—and despite such training many do.

A clinician can clarify other aspects of the recovery cycle by explaining, for example, that "Each crucial event in our life carries emotions with it that need to be expressed. A wedding has a quantity of emotion attached to it, a birthday or anniversary has feelings that go with it, and so, too, trauma has an intense emotional component. No matter what event has occurred, the relevant emotions must be worked through." Some of the personality changes that a traumatized person experiences, such as depression, anger, or sudden bursts of exhilaration and energy, represent the psyche's attempts to survive this recovery process and, eventually, put to rest the traumatic event. A traumatized person should be encouraged not to fight these vital processes, although for various reasons some will vigorously resist allowing their feelings about the trauma to show. Table 2-1 illustrates the major stages in the Trauma Response and Recovery Cycle.

Traumatized people experience several stages that resemble acute grief because of the severe psychological losses they have suffered. They need to go through the recovery cycle of shock, depression, mood swings, anger, philosophizing, and, finally, "laying to rest." The order of these stages may vary somewhat, but it is basically one unified process. What takes place in this cycle involves dynamic processes that will function to reconstruct the ego after loss or personal tragedy.

Unfortunately, a trauma victim can often be incorrectly labeled by others as a difficult, irrational person who keeps "hanging on" to the problem and licking his or her wounds—consequently, not moving on to "the business of living." As stated earlier, this cycle may last for a long time. It will be useful for the clinician to help those around the client to allow a reasonable period of time for recovery, so that they will not show their impatience when the client does not respond as quickly as "common sense psychology" would expect. The authority of such folk wisdom should not be underestimated, because many people invest it with the power of universal truth.

By no means should one push the posttrauma client into doing what he or she does not want to do. Try to convey the message that a therapist's first role is to help him or her regain a sense of personal integrity and independence. This advice may seem to contradict previous suggestions about being directive, but there is a difference between being directive and supportive (while giving a clear explanation of the psychological processes that the client is experiencing) and pushing a person to deal with thoughts he or she may be ill prepared to assimilate. Of course, in psychotherapy it is sometimes necessary to "confront" a client, but one should be extremely cautious about doing so with a traumatized person. One may say, for example, "I think you need to face the fact that you are avoiding dealing with [an issue]"; later, one may say, "I am not going to force you to do so at this time, but eventually you need to look at some of these issues in your life. . . ." Such statements clearly tell the client that there are significant issues to deal with but permit him or her to maintain a measure of control.

THE LEGAL PROCESS

Although the decision of whether or not to prosecute or whether or not to bring a civil suit must be left to the client, I usually support the person's right to proceed with one or both of these processes for several reasons. There is a certain symbolic value in a victim's reestablishing control by attempting to bring the wrongdoer to justice. There is also value in asking for compensation for one's financial and personal losses.

The potential significance to the recovery process of reestablishing control should not be overlooked, even though many of us tend to discount the significance of symbolic or ritualistic activities in our own lives.

THE CRIMINAL PROCESS

One outcome of a criminal case is that, even if the assailant is not caught or slips through the justice system by some means, the victim will know he or she did what could be done to right the wrong. The experience of watching the person or persons responsible for the trauma being brought to justice may aid in recovery and help the victim restore a sense of rationality to his or her life.

After the traumatic event has ended and the police have intervened, most trauma victims are taken to the nearest hospital or medical clinic for an examination and treatment and for the collection of physical evidence. Questioning by a police officer will take place either at the scene of the event or in the hospital emergency room. The police officer may make a tape recording of this initial statement. On the following day or shortly thereafter, depending upon the type of case, the victim will be interviewed by a detective. This officer will have to ask questions necessary to the investigation of the case. A trauma victim may find that some of the many questions the detective asks do not make sense. They may, however, eventually provide technical evidence for the case. The victim has a right to ask the reasons for the detective's questions if he or she feels that they are improper or intrusive. A therapist may be able to prepare the victim for this questioning, and his or her presence during the process may encourage a trauma victim to be more frank about details. In addition, a clinician's skills in communication and the expression of empathy may assist the investigator in obtaining necessary information with minimal additional trauma for the victim. During this interview session, the investigator will replay a tape recording of the victim's original statement and ask if there is anything he or she wishes to change or to add. Most investigators are aware that the statement was given while the person was in a state of shock and that information could, therefore, have been omitted or confused.

The victim may subsequently meet with the investigator to clarify details of the incident as certain leads are followed to a conclusion. If the assailant was unknown to the victim, he or she may also be asked to assist in making a composite picture of the attacker's face, by means of an Identikit. (As used by the investigator, this consists of specimen drawings of parts of the face from which a victim selects those features that most resemble those of the assailant.) The victim may also be asked to look at photographs of suspects (which, in itself, can be an unnerving experience) and probably to witness a lineup (usually through a one-way-vision screen), which will consist of one or more of the suspects. Going to a lineup can be a frightening and even traumatic event for the person in many ways—some straightforward and some symbolic. It may be the first time the victim has seen the assailant since the attack. This experience can cause shock and profound pain.

Many victims feel that an attacker is omnipotent and that they are helpless. In some cases, the clinician will need to reassure the victim that an assailant cannot escape from the lineup and attack again because a victim has reported the crime to the police. Some victims fear that, if they point out their attacker in the lineup, he (or she) will in some way escape from jail and find them. These victims need to be reassured, frequently, that plenty of people will be around for protection and that they will never be left alone during this necessary procedure. It is worth noting that a husband, lover, or parent should not accompany the victim to the room where the lineup will take place because the victim's emotional reaction to seeing the attacker again can be quite strong; the loved one may misunderstand this reaction and become angry. A victim may have tried, for example, to be brave and maintain his or her pride in front of the family, yet the sight of the assailant may cause the victim to become obviously shaken or hysterical. Watching this may upset a loved one; in turn, when the victim realizes how much the loved one has been upset, he or she may become even more distraught. A therapist will find that victims usually want family members to be *nearby* but not actually present at the lineup. They will much more willingly accept an offer from a therapist than a loved one to accompany them to the lineup. Although a few victims may not accept this offer, it is well worth making. On occasion, a victim has expressed relief at the offer because he or she was too afraid or embarrassed to invite someone other than a family member.

After each contact with the police, and especially such significant occasions as a lineup, it is a good idea to schedule some time alone with the victim, or, if one has not accompanied the person to the lineup, to arrange an appointment for that day or evening. Several key issues may arise in this session: for example, if the assailant was not in the lineup, the victim will probably be depressed that he or she was not there. Memories of the attack will surface again, and the victim's fears of the attacker's omnipotence will be renewed because the police have not been able to catch him (or her). In addition, there may be recurring fantasies about the assailant returning for revenge because the victim called in the police. Conversely, if the attacker *was* in the lineup, another issue may arise: now that he or she has identified the assailant, will that person be able to get out of jail and try to murder or assault him or her again for revenge? Victims sometimes ask, even though they have just seen their assailant in a jail uniform and in handcuffs, questions such as "Are you sure there isn't some way he [she] can get out and get us before we leave?" Sometimes such questions are stated in an embarrassed, half-joking manner, but, in fact, the person is not making a joke at all. It takes considerable time (in some cases long after conviction) for many victims to feel safe from revenge in the form of another assault by the same person.

Many people who have committed violent crimes and have a history of violence are released on bail. In some cases, the assailant or person responsible for a trauma knows the victim or where the victim lives and may threaten or attempt to dissuade him or her from pressing charges. If such harassment does occur, a therapist is well advised to suggest that the client contact the police immediately (as well as his or her personal attorney), so that legal action can be taken to stop it.

If the person who committed the crime is never apprehended or is found but for some reason not convicted, the fears described above will persist even longer. It is difficult for a victim to comprehend that such a terrible personal affront could go unpunished. Regardless of whether the person or persons who caused the trauma are apprehended, a therapist will do well to devote a significant amount of time to helping the victim reestablish a basic feeling of inward security and protection.

If a victim has been successful in identifying the person who committed an assault, the assailant will be arrested and charged. Later, the suspect will be arraigned (i.e., he or she will appear before a judge and plead guilty or not guilty to the charges that have been brought). At the arraignment, a date for the preliminary hearing of the evidence will be set. (A defendant has the right to have a hearing within 10 days of arraignment, but he or she may waive this right.) For a victim, the next step in the court process will be this preliminary hearing of the evidence, and the required waiting period is likely to be filled with disquieting fears and concerns about what will happen at the hearing. During this time in therapy, assertiveness training, as well as role-playing of potential situations and questions that will be asked, can be most helpful. It is also advisable to make sure the client is aware that the preliminary hearing is not a trial but a review of evidence that will enable the judge to decide whether or not a trial should take place.

It is appropriate to give considerable reflection to whether a member of the victim's family (or a friend or other associate) should be invited to the preliminary hearing. The reason is that the victim will be put on the stand and asked—in detail and under oath—about what took place during the crime. The victim should be assured that there are limits to the personal questions that can be asked about his or her past history. A defense lawyer may try to ask personal questions, but they will often be objected to and disallowed. The victim can prepare for this first court experience by learning, through role-playing, to answer slowly and after a pause, thus permitting the district attorney enough time to object if necessary. During the hearing, the judge will also examine any medical evidence and question any other witnesses who pertain to the case. A victim's therapist is the most suitable person to help the victim become as psychologically ready for the hearing as possible. If the victim is psychologically prepared and given support through the preliminary hearing phase, the actual trial will, in most cases, be easier for the victim because he or she has been somewhat desensitized to the vexing courtroom process.

The presence of relatives and loved ones at a preliminary hearing or trial, as at the previously discussed lineup, should be carefully thought through. No matter how psychologically prepared a person is, the trial or hearing for any form of assault will not be a pleasant experience. Once more, the victim will have to see his or her assailant or the person who was responsible for the trauma, and this time without a shield of one-way glass. Moreover, both the victim and his or her loved ones will find themselves in close proximity to that person for an hour or more. So, when considering whether or not a parent, wife, husband, or lover should be present during a hearing or trial, reflect on the following: he or she may have to sit near a person who injured or beat or threatened someone whom they love. The victim must also be present, and will be expected to keep a calm composure and to behave rationally. The family members will also be required to keep their emotions in check while they listen to a graphic description of what was done to their loved one. And both they and the victim may face harassment by the defense lawyer, the defendant, or the defendant's family or friends.

Following the preliminary hearing, should proof against the defendant be compelling, the district attorney and the defense lawyer may conduct plea bargaining, and the defendant may plead guilty to some of the charges. Most enlightened district attorneys will discuss this maneuver with the victim before attempting to negotiate a disposition by plea bargaining. If the defendant does not plead guilty to some charge at this time, another waiting period will ensue before the trial occurs. Most trials for assault last from 3 days to 2 weeks; the duration varies according to how difficult jury selection is, the number of witnesses who are to be called, the complexity of the evidence to be presented, and the straightforwardness of the case. Usually a victim will be on the witness stand from 1 to 4 hours, but the questioning may take longer in more complex cases—and he or she may be called back.

Being on a witness stand is difficult in the best of circumstances, but it is far more painful when the victim has experienced a crime of an intensely personal nature. The worst part is that he or she must face the person who caused the trauma. A victim should be prepared for the possibility that the assailant may attempt to upset and confuse him or her by smiling, grimacing, or making gestures while he or she is testifying. To help a victim get psychologically ready for the trial, a clinician may wish to teach some relaxation techniques before he or she takes the witness stand. These exercises will differ according to the psychological needs of the victim. They may range from breathing and muscle-relaxation exercises to fantasies of the attacker being sentenced to jail or scenes that are beautiful and relaxing—such as walking through a meadow or sitting in front of a cozy fireplace. The therapist can also tell the victim that if he or she needs time to regain composure while on the stand, it is possible to ask for a drink of water or to be excused for a moment because he or she is too upset, feels ill, or needs to go to the restroom.

If their assailant is convicted, most victims experience a feeling of great relief. A successful trial can represent an important symbolic event that will assist the reconstructive or therapeutic process on many levels. It amounts to a clear demonstration that social institutions will protect and avenge people who have been violently attacked. Most victims with whom I have worked, especially those who have had strong support systems, later reported that the court process was worth going through (provided the assailant was tried and convicted). More and more, those who work in the criminal justice system (e.g., district attorneys, police officers, and judges) are beginning to recognize the value of providing support services to victims. These professionals realize that one result of such programs is that they make it possible to obtain a higher percentage of convictions.

What happens when an accused assailant is not convicted? This distinct possibility exists and must be confronted realistically. Note that even if there is no conviction on the principal charge, there may be, instead, a conviction on another, lesser count; or the victim can decide to bring a civil suit for damages. In many cases, even the lesser punishment provides some solace to a victim, expecially if it enables him or her to overcome the feeling of helplessness and, possibly, recover some damages. And even if the accused person is not convicted of anything, a therapist can reaffirm that the victim took a step toward regaining control over his or her life by attempting to right a wrong.

If the person or persons who caused the trauma are neither caught nor convicted, a victim's recovery cycle will probably last longer and may be accompanied by recurrent nightmares and strong fears relating to the trauma. Especially during this period of anxiety and fear, it will be wise for the clinician to recognize the victim's needs and to try to strengthen the existing support network. In therapy it will be a good idea to proceed slowly in a structured, stepwise manner, encouraging the victim to attempt to do more and more on his or her own. Meanwhile, the clinician can encourage a victim to explore practical tasks that he or she can perform, thus helping the person to achieve a better sense of safety and competence.

CIVIL LITIGATION

In many cases of personal trauma, the victim may have an opportunity to seek compensation in a civil suit, even though the injuries suffered were caused by a criminal act. Of course, there are many other instances in which a traumatized person may sue for personal injury that arises as a result of, for example, an industrial accident, a car, train, or boat crash, professional malpractice, or a defective product. Any decision to sue should not be made lightly. One needs to consider that many aspects of the person's personal and professional life that are not admissible in criminal proceedings are, in fact, admissible in civil proceedings. Court protection is available to prevent the dissemination of personal information before the trial, but once the trial begins the person's private life could become quite public.

In the process of deciding whether or not to proceed with a civil case, the victim should be advised to interview several attorneys who specialize in personal injury litigation and to evaluate carefully their expertise. The traumatized person also will need an assessment from a qualified personal injury lawyer as to what the recoverable damages would be in his or her case.

Although some attorneys have had experience in personal injury litigation, a thorough inquiry should be made to determine whether or not the prospective attorney's expertise has been recognized by the National Board of Trial Advocates, the American Board of Trial Advocates, the State Trial Lawyers' Association, or one of the certified specialist programs of the various state bar associations. Reputable attorneys are not offended by such inquiries concerning their backgrounds and their actual trial experience, including jury verdicts obtained and the like, with respect to personal injury work. During this critical decision-making phase, a therapist can act as a sounding board to help the client weigh the wisdom of civil litigation.

A person who seeks compensation for injury will need to prove the nature and extent of the damages that he or she has suffered. This usually requires that the person be examined, by attorneys and experts on both sides, on the subject of the alleged traumatization. Someone who claims psychological damage, for example, will most likely be examined by at least one psychologist or psychiatrist employed by the opposing sides. The therapist should help a traumatized person prepare emotionally for these examinations. The person needs to be aware that he or she is not being judged. Further, if the person feels that this examination is upsetting or inappropriate in any way, it can be reported to his or her attorney. In a case in which the traumatized person is extremely fragile, a therapist can request that (1) the examination be postponed or limited in its length; (2) he or she be present during the examination; or (3) the entire examination be audiotaped or videotaped. The purpose is to make sure that nothing is done that would be additionally traumatic or intrusive in any way.

Repeated examinations such as these can be difficult for the traumatized person because they may force him or her to go over the event in question time and time again. Following these examinations, a deposition of the person who is suing for damages will be taken. Deposition is a pretrial process in which a person is questioned under oath by an attorney, and the entire process of questioning is recorded by a court reporter. The attorneys for both sides are usually present during a deposition, although only the attorney who requested the deposition normally does the questioning. Because these depositions are taken in private, they can be extremely grueling. Hence, if one's client is especially vulnerable, a therapist may request that the victim's lawyer ask the court to protect the client from an aggravating deposition. The court could order that (1) limitations be placed on the attorneys' questions; (2) the therapist be present during the deposition; or (3) the deposition be taped. After a deposition, the client should always request a copy of the deposition transcript to check it and correct any errors. After all the evidence on both sides has been compiled, the court will schedule a settlement conference, in which the two sides will attempt to come to a negotiated settlement without having to go to trial. If that is not possible, the case will proceed to the courtroom stage of the civil process.

A psychotherapist can have one of two roles in a civil proceeding, namely that of treating therapist or that of an independent expert witness who is called upon to determine the degree of trauma suffered by a victim. In many situations, a clinician will be asked to perform both roles. In the latter role, he or she will evaluate the client's pretrauma condition, emotional trauma suffered, and how the trauma has affected the client's personal and professional life.

When a therapist is called upon to testify as an expert witness, he or she should be prepared to present an opinion concerning the case in terms that a lay person (e.g., a member of the jury) can understand. The clinician as expert witness should be aware that it is useful to present a certain amount of educational foundation to help jury members formulate their decision. After all, the therapist represents a profession that the average person may not fully accept or understand, or jury members may hold stereotyped conceptions of psychotherapy that must be dispelled. It is vital to make clear the basic principles and supporting facts on which an opinion is formulated, so that the testimony of the clinical witness will not be dismissed as esoteric "mumbo-jumbo" or "purchased" evidence.

In summary, the role of a psychotherapist in a civil case involving personal injury is a complex one. When one's client is in the process of making the often difficult decision of whether or not to sue for damages, a clinician should assist the client to choose what is in his or her best interests. Once a decision to proceed is made, a therapist may be placed in the dual roles of provider of treatment and expert witness. During the ensuing court process, the clinician will be called upon to help the victim cope with the often arduous demands of civil litigation. Further, in some severe cases, a therapist may have to protect the client from situations that could be a source of additional trauma.

Above all, both clinician and client will need to prepare themselves for the experience of deposition and/or court testimony. Despite much improvement toward more humane treatment of the injured person, testifying can be a painful ordeal. But when a traumatized person is awarded a judgment or is able to negotiate a favorable settlement—just as in those cases in which a criminal assailant is successfully prosecuted—the outcome serves to convey a message that society recognizes the person's loss. One learns that there are forces attempting to right wrongs and to compensate those who have suffered.

REFERENCES

Everstine, D. S. and Everstine, L.: (1983). *People in Crisis*. New York, Brunner/Mazel.
Lindemann, E. (1944). Symptomatology and management of acute grief. *American Journal of Psychiatry, 101,* 141–156.

Silverman, D. C. (1978). Sharing the crisis of rape. *American Journal of Orthopsychiatry, 48,* 166–170.
Symonds, M. (1980b). The second injury to victims. *Evaluation and Change* (Special Issue).

David G. Miller

3

The Legal Right to Recover for Emotional Trauma Sustained as a Result of Physical Injury to Oneself or to Others

Many jurisdictions permit personal injury lawyers to question potential jurors concerning their qualifications to serve. When this occurs, one seldom hears the plaintiff's attorney whose client has suffered fractures of the fibula and tibia inquire as to the panel's willingness to accept (and believe) the testimony of the expert examining orthopedist who will testify on the plaintiff's behalf. Even when that testifying orthopedist has not actually examined the plaintiff, but instead relies upon undisputed objective diagnostic tools such as x-rays, scans, or other nonclinical material, virtually no attorney worries about the jury's uncritical acceptance of the orthopedist's diagnosis of the injury sustained. Prognosis, as distinguished from diagnosis, usually constitutes the litigable issue in a simple broken leg case, but even here the trial lawyer worries not about the willingness of the jury to accept orthopedic testimony; he or she worries about whether the jury will accept the testimony of the particular orthopedist who is to testify.

But take that very same case with different shading. Assume that the plaintiff, call him Larry B., was a college student of some intellectual promise and athletic prowess who suffered serious physical injury when a runaway truck climbed the sidewalk and crushed his leg against a dormitory wall. Sufficient time has now elapsed to enable fairly clear definition of the orthopedic injury (i.e., intermittent pain when there are weather changes and potential or actual traumatically induced arthritis, but nothing of a serious or crippling nature). The personal injury trial lawyer and orthopedist may have worked together on these cases for years. Putting together and

PSYCHOTHERAPY AND THE LAW
ISBN 0-8089-1780-3

presenting the medical proof to a jury's satisfaction, although different in every case, nonetheless rests on a great deal of past practice and experience.

Larry B.'s problems, however, are not merely orthopedic. His college performance has markedly fallen off. He stays in his room a lot. He is fearful of leaving the dormitory and is unwilling even to try to engage in the sports he once loved. Fear of college, crowds, trucks, the streets, and physical activity combine to present a serious, emotionally crippling syndrome; furthermore, an expert psychotherapist is prepared to so opine from the witness stand and to attribute causation to the accident.

Jury selection day approaches. Does the personal injury lawyer treat his *voir dire* of the panel, as to the upcoming psychiatric testimony, with the same equanimity as he does the testimony of the broken-bone specialist? The negative answer is obvious, but the underlying reasons for that answer are perhaps less clear.

We are living in cynical times. Jurors are not especially prone to believe that which is not readily perceptible to the five senses. The credibility of lawyers in general is unfortunately at an ebb, particularly in large urban centers. X-rays, myelograms, and CAT scans, although capable of varying expert interpretations, are at least visible and touchable. The public's general exposure to psychiatrists has been on television—they are "shrinks." Jurors wonder, even if they do not articulate their concern, Can a mental health expert truly render an accurate diagnosis and prognosis for the injured victim, who may or may not be dissembling and whose fears and anxieties are inevitably subjective?

Larry B. is entitled, under the law, to monetary compensation for his mental and emotional pain and suffering, past, present, and future, as well as for his physical impairment. To help achieve this societally worthwhile objective, and to overcome the skepticism with which such claims are often met, the mental health specialist[1] and the personal injury attorney must first learn to deal with and understand each other's problems; they must also learn to understand and work together within the parameters of existing legal rules.

A few hypothetical cases are set forth here as examples of how the psychic injury[2] case might be presented, as well as suggestions, from the lawyer's point of view, for the testifying therapist. The attitude of courts and legislatures to civil personal injury litigation does not yet suffer from the post-Hinckley apprehension that currently threatens to overwhelm the insanity defense in *criminal* trials. The view created by that case—that charla-

---

[1] "Mental health specialist" as used here encompasses psychiatrists, psychologists, and others qualified to give professional opinions as to the diagnosis and prognosis of traumatically caused emotional harm. The term is used here synonymously with "psychotherapist," "therapist," and "clinician."

[2] The terms "psychic injury," "emotional injury," "psychic harm," "emotional harm," and "psychological injury" are used interchangeably here.

tans abound in the legal and psychiatric professions—fortunately does not yet prevail on the civil side of litigation.

Recent developments in the law show an increasing willingness to recognize the seriousness of negligently caused emotional harm to one who is either physically injured or in the "zone of danger" of physical injury. There is also a willingness to recognize the need to compensate the victim. Although to a certain extent we still sail an unchartered course, there are certain patterns by which courts traditionally permit recovery or are now beginning to do so. But, first, some basic stumbling blocks, real or perceived, to a good working relationship between lawyer and psychotherapist must be acknowledged.

No self-respecting personal injury lawyer would dream of asking the mental health specialist to testify that his or her malingering client has been emotionally injured by trauma when such is not the case, and no mental health specialist should expect otherwise. This is not to suggest that all lawyers have sufficient self-respect. Some do not. But it is unfair and unnecessary for the mental health specialist to regard a patient's lawyer as an antagonist; and this, too often, is the specialist's perception. The increase in medical malpractice suits is a frequently proffered explanation for this antipathy; in reality, the roots may be deeper and require a touch of self-analysis.

From a lawyer's perspective, the initial difficulty that is encountered in dealing with the clinician—ironic as it may appear at first blush—is professional ego. Too often the treating specialist (and this is not limited to those who treat emotional injury) truly believes that his or her expert therapy will lead to full recovery for the injured patient. Hence this practitioner becomes unwilling to project the long-term or permanent impairment that a nontreating expert might have predicted from his or her own experience, the literature, some examinations, and a battery of tests. But if the treating specialist recognizes that the caring personal injury lawyer wishes to present only legitimate injury and wants to be told if a client is malingering or dissembling, and if the specialist can approach the case from a relatively objective viewpoint, much of the initial antagonism will be dissipated.

A psychotherapist must also accept that the one degree missing from that wall filled with diplomas, licenses, and certificates is an Ll. B. Lawyers and the medical and psychological professions do not speak the same language. Words such as "insane" or "competence" are rooted more in law than in medicine. The first obligation of the lawyer and the therapist in working together is to find a common language, and because it is the lawyer's language that is spoken in the courtroom, the clinician must become familiar with the legal prerequisites, tests, and language that pertain to a claim for the victim's psychic harm. The personal injury lawyer will usually want to know, for example, the client's preexisting disposition to emotional injury or whether or not a phobia, until now healthily submerged, has been aggravated. In effect, has a dormant emotional vulnerability now been activated and caused emotional injury; or has this formerly (apparently) functioning client now become nonfunctioning because of the emotional effects of a physical injury? If Larry B. can walk normally again but is seriously psychologically impaired in whole or in part as a result of his physical injury, would anyone question his right to recover for the additional injury he has suffered?

No one doubts that the proof of psychological injury is difficult and complicated, particularly in cases in which prior emotional problems are known to have existed. But therapists are often legitimately frustrated by what they perceive to be impossible legal requirements. Consider the cases that follow.

A patient who had previously been discharged from psychotherapy sustains a serious physical injury and requires renewed mental health care; a child whose nervous tic disappeared a year before is exposed to bodily harm through another's negligence, and the tic reappears; the car of a patient who had been in therapy necessitated by a bad marriage is hit in the rear. She witnesses her infant sustain serious injury and is required to resume therapy. Who is to separate the numerous preexisting potentialities from the immediate trauma as the cause of postevent psychological injury? The lawyer tells a mental health specialist that he or she must do so and the specialist is dumbfounded. But these are, too often, the ground rules. Hence lawyer and clinician must both be flexible enough in approach to recognize each other's problems and to maximize the potential recovery for the injured victim. If the law requires an expert to testify within "a reasonable degree of professional certainty," he or she must do so. The expert's quarrel with this requirement is not with the personal injury lawyer, who shares his or her distaste for such an obviously artificial, ill-defined (and therefore meaningless) test, but with the law itself. And here, at least, the law appears to be mistaken. It is impossible for clinical testimony to be given with the same degree of assurance or credibility as an interpretation of the x-ray of a fractured fibula, and the courts are beginning to recognize this basic truth.

Recognition comes belatedly, and sometimes as the result of ludicrous events. Attorney Thomas B. Almy has reported (1984) a recent case in which a 6-year-old child claimed brain damage as a result of an airplane crash. The plaintiff's expert, a psychologist by training who had not examined the child, predicted from his review of documents that when the child reached high school, he would strike his teacher and be expelled. Of course, this type of unsupportable speculation does credit neither to the legal nor the mental health professions, would not be permitted by most knowledgeable trial courts, and should be avoided by the legitimate therapist regardless of the implorings of counsel.

When, then, do the courts allow a plaintiff to recover for emotional trauma caused by accident or injury? The laws differ, but certain basic concepts appear to be achieving general acceptance. Typically, there are three types of personal injury cases in which the testimony of a therapist may become important: when there is an alleged emotional injury (1) to the accident victim himself or herself (2) as a result of witnessing an accident to another person; and (3) as a consequence of loss of parental care and guidance. These are discussed in reverse order.

PARENTAL CARE AND GUIDANCE

All states recognize the right of the child to be compensated if he or she has lost one or two parents through someone's fault. Differing measures of recovery exist from jurisdiction to jurisdiction, but almost all states permit recovery for loss of parental care, guidance, and nurture. By contrast, most deny the right to recover for loss of love and affection or for grief. This represents a fine line for the trial lawyer and the therapist to walk together.

A recent case provides a good example of psychiatric testimony in a situation involving the simultaneous death of two parents of three children in a terrible explosion. The accident and deaths had occurred some 10 years before this trial. (The legal proceedings were extremely complicated, and two full liability trials and appeals were conducted before the medical trial.) The plaintiffs were two young men, 26 and 24 years of age, and their 20-year-old sister. (They had been 16, 14, and 10 when their parents died.) The plaintiffs' testifying psychiatrist had examined the two younger children on only one occasion, shortly before the trial. He was a board-certified psychiatrist, a graduate of Harvard Medical School some 30 years before, and the author of numerous articles and textbooks on children, stress, and the death of a parent. His qualifications were established to the court's satisfaction in the following dialogue.[3]

Q: Following your graduation from medical school, have you specialized in any particular field of medicine?
A: In the field of psychiatry.
Q: Where did you go following your internship?
A: I went to New York City, to the Payne Whitney and the VA Hospital psychiatry training program.
Q: And was it there that you studied psychiatry at that time?
A: I did.
Q: How long were you there?
A: I was there for about 6 months before I was drafted.
Q: In which branch of service?
A: In the United States Navy.
Q: And how long did you spend in the Navy?
A: Two years.

---

[3] Whether or not an expert is initially qualified is for the judge to decide. What weight is given to his or her testimony is for the jury to decide.

Q: And did you work as a physician in the Navy?

A: I did. I was a psychiatrist in a naval training center and then Chief of Neuro-psychiatry at the United States Naval Hospital.

Q: What is neuropsychiatry?

A: It's a combination of neurology and psychiatry.

Q: And could you tell us, doctor, in a general way, the parameters? What is the field of psychiatry? What does it encompass?

A: It encompasses the study of behavior and the treatment of disorders of behavior, emotion, thought.

Q: Following your discharge from the Navy, what was your next training?

A: At the Albert Einstein College of Medicine I studied adult psychiatry.

Q: How long did you study adult psychiatry?

A: Another year and a half.

Q: Now, are there specialties or subspecialties within the field of psychiatry?

A: There are.

Q: And did you, at some point, develop an interest in one of the subspecialties?

A: Yes, I did, in child psychiatry.

Q: And is that a recognized subspecialty?

A: Definitely.

Q: Is child psychiatry the same as you've described before as psychiatry but applied to children?

A: That's correct, children and families.

Q: How long was that training program?

A: That was an additional 2 years.

There followed additional questions inquiring into the doctor's qualifications, board certifications, teaching appointments, published works, and areas of specialization. The questioning then moved into the more specific subject of loss of parental care and guidance.

Q: Have there been studies that psychiatrists have accepted dealing with a problem where children are faced with the death of a parent?

A: Yes.

Q: Have the studies showed the effect of the loss of parental care and guidance where one parent is removed from the home?

A: Yes.

Q: For how long have these studies been undertaken?

A: These studies go back, at least, to the early 1900s.

Q: Have you participated in any of these studies yourself?

A: Yes.

Q: How many different ones?

A: Perhaps six.

Q: And did I ask you today, when I met you, to limit your testimony in this case to the issue of parental care and guidance as opposed to any other problems that may arise from death?[4]

---

[4] This testimony, required in most jurisdictions, excludes from the expert's and jury's consideration legally uncompensable damage testimony, such as mourning and grief.

A: Yes, you did.

Q: Now, let me start with the studies. These are studies upon which other doctors have to base certain conclusions, right?

A: Yes.

Q: And there are things that you have to read and learn and assimilate in your care and treatment of the patients at the Center?

A: Yes.

Q: Do you treat children who have had the death of one or two parents?

A: Yes, regularly.

Q: How many times have you dealt with this situation?

A: Certainly hundreds.

Q: Do the studies reflect whether it's more significant, be it the mother or father, that passed away?

A: They do indicate that, but the answer is not one or the other; it varies.

Q: It would depend on the sex of the child?

A: And the age of the child.

Q: You know the ages of the children involved in this particular case, do you not?

A: Yes.

Q: Are there studies reflecting the effects of the loss of parental care, guidance, and nurture when two parents are suddenly removed from the home?

A: Yes.

Q: Do some of these studies dealing with the loss of parents cover a lot of children?

A: Yes.

Q: Do the studies show a significant effect on children where one parent is removed when the child is of the age of 10, 14, or 16?

A: In the case of one parent, there are many more systematic scientific tests which have been performed.

Q: Do they study a great deal of people, a large number of patients?

A: Tremendous number.

Q: How many are you talking about in any one study?

A: Ten thousand children were studied, of whom approximately 500 had lost a parent by death.

Q: And the other 9,500 had their parents?

A: Yes, the 9,500 were a comparison group.

Q: Where was that study performed?

A: In Minnesota.

Q: When?

A: It was a 10-year study, starting in 1954, going to 1964.

Q: Based upon your own work with children and your review of the regularly accepted psychiatric literature that's been published, what, in your opinion, is the effect on children where one parent has died?

A: Specifically, in regard to my opinion of the study I just cited, to begin my answer, I have published my opinion, which is that that study, as I reviewed it, indicates that the children who lost one parent by death differ from the controlled demographically comparable children (which means that they are from a similar economic, racial background) they differ from the control or comparison children very strikingly in the following ways:

They fail one or more years of school 200 percent more often than the controlled children who are not orphaned of one parent; they are arrested by the police four or more times at a rate of, approximately, 200 percent greater than the other 9,500 children. They drop out of school prematurely at a rate also about double the controlled population of comparable (that is, from the same class economically, racially, ethnically comparable) children.

There was another factor, and that was truancy was about double the rate in these Minnesota one-parent orphans.

Q: Now, was that due, in your opinion, to the lack of parental care, guidance, and nurture?

A: I believe that was the cause of the differences.

Q: In your opinion, does the effect of loss of two parents double that or what? You tell us.

A: It's not only my opinion, which it is, it's my experience that the loss of two parents is far more severe than the loss of one parent in those forms of behavioral outcomes that I just mentioned.

Q: What do the studies that you yourself have conducted show?

A: They show that not only are there quantitative or numerical or arithmetic differences which make the doubly orphaned children worse off, but there are what I call qualitative differences; there are entirely different and worse kinds of things that happen to the children who lose both parents.

For example, they become hospitalized for mental illness more often, they become psychotic more often, they develop sexual deviations more often than the one-parent orphan or the child who has both parents living. They also have very special forms of mental illness, which my findings confirm.

For example, there have been findings that there is a special form of illness which is hallucinatory; that is, there are real breaks with reality and things are seen which aren't there. Also, paranoid illnesses are more common.

Q: Have you done any study of children in foster homes?

A: I've done a great deal of study with foster parents and children in foster homes.

Q: Now, assuming a good foster home—by "good," I mean good people who are caring and desirous of helping. Can that replace the parent in care, guidance, or nurture?

A: I'm impressed with how very often people who are foster parents, who seem in good health mentally, well motivated, seem to be good parents, have the desire to be good parents, are utter failures in giving guidance, support, training to their foster children.

Q: Is there a reason scientifically that that's true?

A: In my opinion, the reason has to do with the breaking, often has to do with the breaking of the attachment and bonds with the previous parent's supportive functions that in a child (particularly under the middle teens) that the best of us parents who want to take over (like foster parents) are at a tremendous disadvantage because the child is psychologically unable to transfer the attachments involved in being guided and educated and trained and supported, and rebels or withdraws from those efforts of the very well meaning and even sometimes very gifted foster parent.

Q: You used the word "bonding" or "bonds"; is that a psychiatric term?

A: It is, yes.

Q: What do we mean when we say "the bonding between people"?

A: Well, psychiatrically, in child psychiatry, it refers specifically to a concept of being a psychological parent; that is, when a bond develops between a child and a parent, the parent—I imagine—is in the child's mind and becomes quite permanent, even if the parent isn't present, even if the parent dies, that parent is still psychologically there in the child's mind.

If the child wants to take a bath or go to school or be fed or be given religious instruction or guidance about an ethical problem, the child will turn to the psychological parent with whom the bond exists and will reject substitution of a parent in the real world for a very long time and, sometimes, forever.

Q: Is it typical, doctor, for the child to, in a foster home, resent or complain about the foster parent, maybe not objectively but, nonetheless, feel that way?

A: It is very typical.

Q: In other words, that's the way the child sees it, whatever the realities are?

A: That's correct, it's very typical and common and very painful to the foster parents.

The foregoing testimony is, of course, very general. Its utility is in (1) demonstrating the witness's expertise in the subject matter as a whole; (2) further impressing the jury with the witness's credentials; and (3) most important, perhaps, giving the impression that psychiatry is just a bit more scientific and precise than it is typically believed to be.

This foundation having been laid, the testimony now proceeds to the specific.

Q: I want you to assume, doctor, that two people died. The man was a police officer, a high school graduate, had gone to college for a year; his wife was a homemaker, age 36, and their three children had always lived with the parents at home. I want you further to assume that they then went to live with very nice people: an uncle, who was the brother of the deceased woman, and his wife, married about 8 years at the time, who had no children. And they took the three children in and did everything that they could to help, and they grew up in a certain way, which I'm going to get to. Now, at my request, recently, did you examine both Linda and Charles Rose [the younger children]?

A: I certainly did.

Q: And were you given a history concerning the older boy, Hank, whom you did not examine?

A: Yes.

Q: I want you to assume that Hank went through college and is an actuary, married, and doing well, okay?

A: Yes, sir.[5]

Q: I want you to assume that Hank graduated from high school, attended col-

---

[5] The reader will recall that the three children were 10, 14, and 16 at the time of their trauma. Unlike the younger children, the oldest boy (Hank) exhibited few problems. It was essential that the trial lawyer and the expert clinical witness explain, eventually, this differing "status" to the lay jury. The seeds are planted here.

lege for a year and half, but didn't do well for the year and a half; is that somewhat consistent with the pattern?

A: Yes.

Q: But then he moved to an apartment on campus and did quite well for the remainder of the school year, got married, got a responsible job as an actuary. Why would Linda have more problems than Hank?

A: He was so much further along in his development that he was almost a whole person. He didn't have to learn as much, how to take care of himself, what his morality should be, his ethics, his work habits. He was pretty well set when this loss occurred of parental function.

Q: What did your examination of Linda consist of?

A: I spent 2 hours with Linda in private.

Q: After your examination, did you form a medical opinion with a reasonable degree of medical certainty pertaining to Linda? And, if you did, could you explain it in lay language and not technical language so that even I could understand it?

A: Yes, sir. I formed an opinion that she suffered from a medical disorder of a psychiatric type called pathological reaction with resultant anxiety and self-punishing tendencies. That was my diagnosis.

Now, what it means in nonmedical terms is that, in reaction to loss (specifically she alleged that both of her parents had been "lost" to her), it was my opinion that in reaction to that loss, there had been a disorder set in of adaptation to the absence of some of the functions those parents had performed in her life.

To be technical for a moment and then to explain it, those functions are called by psychoanalysts self-functions, ego functions, and narcissistic support functions. In nonmedical terms they refer to the guidance that—the functions of guidance that are provided by care-giving persons, particularly parents, the functions of education that parents provide to a growing child, particularly training in how to behave (i.e., training in moral issues, which analysts call super-ego issues, nonmedical people call moral issues or religious issues or ethical issues); training the parents provide as models of industriousness, how to study, how to work, how to approach a task in an efficient, effective, successful way in school or out of school, or socially, or as a mother, or as a lover; task-oriented functions which one ordinarily acquires by the side-by-side learning of them through the guidance of the parent. So, it was my impression that her difficulties were a response or pathological reaction to the loss of those functions provided by her parents.

The testimony next elicited demonstrates how the trial lawyer can make use of psychiatric expertise to help alleviate what he or she regards as a potential problem in the case. Linda had already testified, apparently not altogether to the attorney's liking. If her lawyer could persuade the jury that her apparent personality problems were caused by the loss she sustained as a result of the defendants' negligence, so much the better. The examination resumes.

Q: Doctor, Linda testified here. I want you to assume that her responses were similar to those of a spoiled child. Did you note that when you interviewed her?

A: Yes.

Q: What, in your opinion, caused that in her personality?

A: My opinion is that that's part of her disorder, which is called a disorder of attachment and empathy. She doesn't realize, I think, how she's coming across to an older person or even to a peer, I think, but particularly she lacks the training in how to relate to other people, how to understand what other people are feeling. She doesn't seem to know when she's being obnoxious. I don't think she knows she comes across as a spoiled person or that it's reasonable for her guardians, her aunt and uncle, to ask her to clean the house or take care of their baby or to help out under difficult circumstances.

She comes across as complaining she's entitled to an entirely different set of circumstances, and as if I wouldn't be listening as somebody who might have gone through hard times myself. She seems unschooled in what a parent would ordinarily teach a child as to how to deal with another.

Q: It should be taken as attached to the loss of parental guidance?

A: I think that's the probable cause. I'm reasonably certain of that. And there are other things of that nature that impressed me.[6]

After some questions and answers concerning Linda's religious training before and after her parents' deaths, the attorney elicited Linda's history from the doctor, which included, *inter alia,* leaving home during high school, living with a store clerk, conceiving, giving birth, and never marrying. As most lawyers recognize, such a nonproductive and checkered history does not typically generate jury sympathy in large quantities. Because there was no way to exclude these facts, the best approach was to use them in a positive manner by attributing blame for Linda's situation to her loss of parental care and guidance. The following then occurred.

Q: Is that something which is somewhat typical of people who don't have a parent to guide them?

A: There are two parts to your question. One is the having of the baby under any circumstance very quickly—that is, married or not—is very characteristic of people who have experienced a childhood death of a parent or foster care situation. In this case it was something of both.

The other part of your question about the "not being married," in a family where that's not an acceptable pattern or tradition, that is also more common among children who have lost the guidance, training of the parent than it is in the general population, although it's a common problem. It's more common in situations of deprivation of the parent's presence.[7]

---

[6] This entire testimony is of questionable admissibility in most states. A witness's demeanor and credibility are traditionally for juries to evaluate and are not the proper subject of expert opinion.

[7] Here, the attorney and psychiatrist take a problem, namely the jury's potential displeasure with the concept of awarding a large sum to an unwed mother and apparently ungrateful young lady, and successfully reverse the possible prejudice by attaching blame for Linda's situation to the loss of parental care and guidance caused by the defendant's negligence.

In every jurisdiction, the wrongfully killed person's next of kin are entitled to recover for pecuniary loss, i.e., the monetary damage sustained as a proximate result of the defendant's negligence. Indeed, in a majority of states, wrongful death damages are *limited* to economic losses. These may include, in the context of loss of parental care and guidance, the child's depressed earning capacity. In the following exchange, the lawyer and mental health specialist combine to put this element of damage to the jury for its consideration.

Q: In your opinion, doctor, based on your findings and those that relate from the loss we're discussing, do you think Linda's loss will have any effect on her economic functioning in the future as a member of society?
A: My opinion is very strong on that. I believe there is a substantial economic detriment to her from the consequences of the loss of parental functions.

The next problem to be confronted was Linda's testimony that, notwithstanding all her problems, she had never consulted or been treated by a therapist. Both attorney and witness had a fine line to walk. Obviously, the therapist could not take the position that therapy would have been useless, and thus the failure to seek treatment irrelevant; such a stance would not accord with his or his profession's beliefs. Nor, as is often the case with rejected elective surgery, could an argument of fear of potential hazards be mounted. So the problem was handled in this way.

Q: In your opinion, doctor, would psychiatric care be of help to Linda at this point?
A: My opinion is also very strong on that. I not only think it would be helpful, I have advised her to get it.
Q: Are people with this kind of problem reluctant to get a consistent pattern of care?
A: Yes.
Q: Is that part of the problem they have?
A: Yes.

The plaintiffs' attorney can now make an effective closing to the jury. He may fairly argue that Linda is very much in need of therapy as a result of her terrible loss—a loss caused by the defendant's negligence. He can then build on that need by explaining that her loss has been exacerbated by her inability to seek or accept therapy—an inability also caused by the defendant's negligence.
Finally, the testimonial denouement in the case of Linda:

Q: Is there a higher incidence of accidents . . . of people who have deaths, especially multiple deaths, in the family?
A: It's remarkably so, yes.
Q: Did Linda give a history of having automobile accidents?
A: She had three in the past 12 months, all on the same street. I don't think she

has any awareness that she's contributing to these accidents. But I don't think she's taking care of herself, I think she's neglectful of her welfare.[8]

The testimony then turned to the subject of Linda's brother Charles.

Q: You examined Charles also, correct?

A: Yes, sir.

Q: And did you form a medical opinion with a reasonable degree of medical certainty pertaining to Charles?

A: Yes, sir.

Q: And what was that?

A: My opinion of the diagnosis in Charles's case was that he has two disorders: the first is a schizoid personality characterized by difficulty initiating, sustaining, and maintaining closeness in occupational, social, sexual, and familial activities. The second was a gender identity conflict disorder characterized by distress over homosexual versus heterosexual interests and an inability to settle with comfort into one gender identity.

Q: In layman's talk, what does that mean?

A: Well, the first thing is almost self-explanatory by the terms I've used; that is, a schizoid person is a person who cannot maintain a closeness without taking serious efforts to defend himself against the continuation of any intimacy, whether it's on the job (having to deal every day with the same boss could be a tremendous problem for a schizoid person); being married is often hell for a schizoid person, being a parent is often very poorly performed, having a lover is very difficult for a schizoid person, being intimate in any way is very difficult.

Now, the second thing, the second disorder, a gender identity conflict commonly called bisexuality in this form; and that is, this young man has very strong and clear conscious interest in people of both sexes. He's unable to be intimate with people of either sex in a continuous fashion, but he has a small number of experiences, a very limited number of experiences, with people of both sexes and, in fact, feels, to his dismay, an agony that he likes men better than he likes women sexually and wants very much to like women better.

Q: Did he indicate a tremendous admiration for his late father to you?

A: All out of proportion, I think, to what an adult at his age would ordinarily say.

Q: Do you think that this sexual problem—I guess it's a problem to resolve, isn't that true?

A: It's a problem if it hurts him. It hurts him very much.

Q: Is that, in your view, related to the loss of his parents insofar as the care and guidance and nurture?

A: I believe that's the most reasonable medical explanation.

Q: Can you give us a medical explanation?

A: Well, I think he was 14 when his father and mother died. As he gives the history, he was very close with his father in certain ways, trying to model himself on

---

[8] It would be as improper to proffer speculation that this particular plaintiff would die in an accident as to elicit the opinion that a child would one day strike a teacher and be expelled (See p. 50). The testimony here makes the point just as effectively.

the father. The father was quite strong physically. I think that there was some ordinary adolescent admiration for this tough, brave man, his father. I picked that up.

My opinion is based . . . my formulation about his homosexuality includes the fact that he, when his father was missing, for example, which he was for some period of days before the body was found, he said, "The minute my father didn't come home I knew he was dead because my father was so tough nobody could kill him, he couldn't get lost; only something like an earthquake could kill my father, he was like John Wayne."

So what I gather is that in retrospect, as many, many orphaned people do, there is a retrospective overidealization of the strength of this father and, at another level, he feels this man let him down. If he would become like this man he might get killed, too; he might be broken to pieces, he might be burned up, he couldn't live.

I can't carry it into detail, my formulation, but it has to include that if this father-admiring boy had the advantage of a continuation of the father's educational functions and support and training, that heterosexuality is more moral than homosexuality, this boy probably would have successfully put down the homosexual part of his identity and proceeded to be more like his father, who appeared, by the history I've heard, appeared to have been a heterosexual person.

Every lawyer is understandably nervous (some would say paranoid) about possibly offending any juror. Lawyers are not privy to the jurors' sexual preferences. In a proper exercise of caution, the lawyer then asked:

Q: You're not saying (just to clarify) that homosexuality in itself is any kind of psychiatric disorder if one accepts it and understand it?

A: I'm not. In fact, that's the official position of the Society to which I belong.

Q: It's the refusal to accept it is the problem?

A: No, it's the suffering over it that's a problem.

Q: In your opinion, with a reasonable degree of medical certainty, had he had the guidance of his parents, would he have been able to handle the situation without any psychiatric problem?

A: Yes, if you include under "guidance" the educational example of the heterosexual couple, of his parents, the moral training. Probably the religious training would have helped.

These questions and answers, which have been substantially abbreviated for inclusion in this chapter, are exemplars of how the trial lawyer and therapist, working together, can accomplish a worthwhile result for the victim of a terrible loss: the simultaneous, violent deaths of two parents.

PSYCHIC TRAUMA AS A RESULT OF WITNESSING INJURY OR DEATH TO A LOVED ONE

Whether or not a person has the right to recover for an emotional injury that was sustained because he or she observed someone causing physical injury or death to a loved one has long been debated in legal circles. As has often been the case, California led the nation in recognizing such a right in 1968 (*Dillon v. Legg,* 68 Cal.2d 728, 441 P.2d 912).

Because such a right to recover is a relatively new jurisprudential concept, it is essential that the therapist who is called upon by the lawyer for aid and assistance understand the factors that the courts have held necessary to sustain such a recovery, as well as the standards of medical proof that are developing. These are not universal.

Prior to *Dillon,* courts occasionally permitted a litigant to recover for emotional harm, but only to the extent that the person feared for his or her own safety because of actually being in the "zone of danger" created by the defendant's negligence or because he or she actually suffered some physical injury or impact, no matter how slight. These preconditions to recovery are necessarily artificial and present grave difficulties to both lawyer and therapist when they attempt to explain such fine distinctions to a jury. The *Dillon* court, given the unusual facts presented in that case, was able to discard these prior, unnatural limitations and to carve out a legally cognizable claim of emotional injury resulting purely from observation.

In *Dillon,* the plaintiff mother saw her infant daughter killed by a car as she crossed at an intersection. Also present at the scene, but closer than the mother to the actual point of impact, was another daughter—the dead girl's sister. An action was commenced seeking recovery for the emotional trauma sustained by both mother and surviving daughter. The lower court in California, following precedent, initially dismissed the mother's claim while permitting the surviving daughter's to remain. It did so based upon its understanding of the "zone of danger" rule: although both mother and daughter saw the accident and death, only the daughter could reasonably have feared for her own safety because she was in the zone of physical danger.

The California Supreme Court reinstated the mother's claim, holding

That the courts should allow recovery to a mother who suffers emotional trauma and physical injury from witnessing the infliction of death or injury to her child for which the tortfeasor is liable in negligence would appear to be a compelling proposition. As Prosser points out, "All ordinary human feelings are in favor of her [the mother's] action against the negligent defendant. If a duty to her requires that she herself be in some recognizable danger, then it has properly been said that when a child is endangered, it is not beyond contemplation that its mother will be somewhere in the vicinity, and will suffer serious shock. [Prosser, *Law of Torts* (3d ed., 1964) p. 353, 441 P.2d at 914]

The relative uniqueness of the facts in *Dillon* gave the court an opportunity to expose "the hopeless artificiality of the zone of danger rule":

We can hardly justify relief to the sister for trauma which she suffered upon apprehension of the child's death and yet deny it to the mother merely because of a happenstance that the sister was some few yards closer to the accident. [441 P.2d at 915]

I believe that this attitude was due, in some measure, to the increased respect afforded the profession of psychotherapy. As noted in *Dillon,* one of the concerns that had previously led to legal denial of a witness's right to recover for emotional injury resulting from watching a loved one's accidental injury or death was the fear of fraudulent or undefinable claims. The rationale, as the court noted, was that "juries, confronted by irreconcilable expert medical testimony, will be unable to distinguish the deceitful from the bona fide" (441 P.2d at 917). California's decision to permit recovery in such cases is due, at least in part, to a greater willingness to accept the testimony of qualified therapists as to this largely subjective area of suffering.

In fact, damages have traditionally been allowed for mental suffering, which, as the *Dillon* court stated, is a "type of injury, on the whole, less amenable to objective proof than physical injuries" (441 P.2d at 919). Notwithstanding this, we have seen the specter of courts permitting recovery for emotional injury if the plaintiff feared for *himself* or *herself,* while denying recovery for the fright, fear, and consequential injury caused by witnessing the death of one's own child. The *Dillon* court soundly criticized this anomaly:

> Moreover, it is inconguous and somewhat revolting to sanction recovery for the mother if she suffers shock from fear for her own safety and to deny it for shock from the witnessed death of her own daughter. To the layman such a ruling must appear incomprehensible; for the courts to rely upon self-contradictory legalistic abstractions to justify it is indefensible . . . . [To] hinge recovery on the speculative issue [of] whether the parent was shocked through fear for herself or for her children would be discreditable to any system of jurisprudence. [441 P.2d at 919,fn.]

Dillon refers to the possibility that laypersons may find artificially structured legal doctrines logically incomprehensible. But the legal and psychotherapeutic professions are not manned by laypersons and they too have had, at times, problems in communicating. No doubt a substantial contributing cause of this difficulty has been the too frequent willingness of the courts to "rely upon self-contradictory legalistic abstractions" (see above). If such contradictions are incomprehensible to laypersons, they must appear equally obtuse to the well-trained, qualified clinician who examines or treats a truly depressed and anxious mother and then is asked, in a court of law, to distinguish between the depression and anxiety caused by witnessing her daughter's death versus that caused by fear for her own safety at the moment in question.

Unfortunately, the therapist who is confronted with this dilemma tends to blame the lawyer (rather than the law itself), and instead of two professions working together to change some anachronistic legalisms, too often frustration and bitterness ensue. Cooperation here carries the potential for effective social change. Instead of debating about legalisms and the choice of technical language with each other, the attorney and therapist should concentrate their efforts on achieving a successful result. When enough juries return favorable verdicts in cases of emotional injury, both courts and legislatures will take note. The eventual outcome will, one hopes, be a body of statutes and case law reflective of the sophisticated state of modern psychotherapy and law, which recognizes the very real existence of traumatically induced emotional harm.

In the case of *Dillon,* the plaintiffs alleged that emotional trauma resulted in physical injury. Such a reaction, however, does not always occur. To *require* physical harm as well as emotional injury again makes for superficially structured pleadings; and it makes what should be an obvious right to recover a more nebulous one requiring psychiatric testimony that, at best, is stilted and structured to "fit the facts."

A good example is the case of *Shanahan v. Orenstein* (52 A.D.2d 164, 383 N.Y.S.2d 164 [1st Dept, 1976]), which was a case with a fiction writer's catalogue of facts. In *Shanahan,* the plaintiff was returning home from church with her two infant children and her mother on Mother's Day when a building parapet, which had long threatened to topple, did so as the family passed below. Bricks rained down, and in front of her eyes the plaintiff's 2-year-old son and 62-year-old mother were struck. They both sustained severe injuries from which they soon died. The New York Intermediate Appellate Court affirmed this plaintiff's right to recover, but *only* because she alleged physical ailments as *sequelae* of the stress that she herself had suffered; i.e., not as a result of witnessing the deaths of her loved ones, but only because of her fears for her own safety. Again, the testifying therapist and the plaintiff's lawyer faced a difficult problem of proof.

Sophisticated courts have, fortunately, taken a more trusting view of the clinician's ability to diagnose and predict psychic reaction to trauma that is negligently inflicted on others who were in close proximity to, or closely related to, the plaintiff. Demonstrative is the case of *Leong v. Takasaki,* 55 Hawaii 398, 520 P.2d 758, 94 ALR3d 471 (1974), in which a 10-year-old boy sought to recover damages for the nervous shock and psychic injuries he sustained when he saw the defendant's automobile strike and kill his step-grandmother. The Hawaiian Supreme Court addressed the legal and medical problems of proof in a manner instructive to lawyer and therapist alike, as follows:

From a medical perspective, negligently-inflicted mental distress may be characterized as a reaction to a traumatic stimulus, which may be physical or purely psychic. Traumatic stimulus may cause two types of mental reaction, primary and secondary. The primary response, an immediate, automatic and instinctive response designed to protect an individual from harm, unpleasantness and stress aroused by witnessing the painful death of a loved one, is exemplified by emotional responses such as fear, anger, grief, and shock. This initial response, which is short in duration and subjective in nature, will vary in seriousness according to the individual and the particular traumatic stimulus.

Secondary responses, which may be termed traumatic neuroses, are longer-lasting reactions caused by an individual's continued inability to cope adequately with a traumatic event. Medical science has identified three frequently occurring forms of neuroses resulting from trauma. In the first, the anxiety reaction, the trauma produces severe tension, which results in nervousness, weight loss, stomach pains, emotional fatigue, weakness, headaches, backaches, a sense of impending doom, irritability, or indecision as long as the tension remains. The second, the conversion reaction, is a reaction to trauma in which the individual converts consciously disowned impulses into paralysis, loss of hearing or sight, pain, muscle spasms, or other physiological symptoms which cannot be explained by actual physical impairment. The third, the hypochondriasis reaction, is characterized by an over-concern with health, a fear of illness, or other unpleasant sensations. Thus only secondary responses result in physical injury.

Traumatic neuroses are more susceptible to medical proof than primary reactions because they are of longer duration and usually are manifested by physical symptoms which may be objectively determined. While a psychiatrist may not be able to establish a negligent act as the sole cause of plaintiff's neurosis, *he can give a fairly accurate estimate of the probable effects the act will have upon the plaintiff and whether the trauma induced was a precipitating cause of neurosis, and whether the resulting neurosis is beyond a level of pain with which a reasonable man may be expected to cope. . . .* [Emphasis added.]

In a situation where only the primary response to trauma occurs, the defendant's negligence may produce transient but very painful mental suffering and anguish. Because this reaction is subjective in nature and may not result in any apparent physical injury, precise levels of suffering and disability cannot be objectively determined. The physician or psychiatrist must rely on the plaintiff's testimony, the context in which the trauma occurred, medical testing of any physical ramifications, the psychiatrist's knowledge of pain and disability likely to result from such trauma, and even the framework of human experience and common sense to determine the amount of pain resulting naturally as a response to defendant's act, and whether it is beyond the level of stress with which a reasonable man may be expected to cope. [520 P.2d at 766-67]

It may therefore be concluded that in those jurisdictions that permit recovery for pure emotional harm, the "accurate estimates" of the qualified therapist are a *sine qua non* for recovery. But just how "accurate" those estimates are remains a matter of considerable controversy, and this holds true even in those jurisdictions where the law has historically led.

The highest court in New York has only recently, and in modified fashion, recognized that there is a right to recovery in "witness" cases, and has done so by a bare majority (*Bovsun v. Sanperi,* 61 N.Y.2d 219, 473 N.Y.S.2d 357, 1984). New York has joined the majority of states in adopting a "zone of danger" approach. It now holds that when a defendant's negligence has created an unreasonable risk of bodily harm to a plaintiff, *and* when the plaintiff suffers emotional injury resulting from observing serious physical injury or death to an immediate family member, the plaintiff may recover damages for such injuries.

A vigorous dissent in this case raised the ancient concern about claims for indirect or tenuous emotional injuries. That concern was disposed of by imposing a requirement that the emotional disturbance suffered be "serious and verifiable" (473 N.Y.S.2d at 363) and by reliance upon "the contemporary sophistication of the medical profession" (473 N.Y.S.2d at 363).

The battle to win public acceptance of the reality of psychic injury continues to be waged. One would not imagine great reluctance on the part of either the courts or laypersons to accept that compensable emotional distress might justly ensue from watching one's child die because of the act of a reckless driver—the facts in *Bovsun*. But the spate of critical editorials and the outpouring of public comment following *Bovsun* make clear that the legal and psychiatric professions are still a long way from achieving general acknowledgment of the validity of such contentions.[9]

EMOTIONAL TRAUMA TO THE ACCIDENT VICTIM

The most currently accepted compensable psychological injury in the law is that of emotional harm not to the close relative standing by but to the victim of the accident himself or herself. Negligent infliction of psychological distress is now recognized as actionable, even without actual physical impact (e.g., *Battalla v. State,* 10 N.Y.2d 237 [1961]). When physical impact and injury occur simultaneously, emotional injuries often result, and here the dual roles of psychotherapist and lawyer are more clearly defined. And in those instances when organic brain damage is suspected, psychological testing has traditionally played a major role.

For years, organic impairment as a result of accident has been established, at least in part, by means of the testing and testimony of psychologists or psychiatrists. Results of Grassi procedures may demonstrate serious intellectual impairment caused by organic encephalopathy. Responses to the Wechsler Adult Intelligence Scale, particularly on the arithmetic reasoning, object assembly, and picture arrangement subtests can show impaired intellectual functioning, especially when scaled, graphed, and contrasted with

---

[9] Illustrative of the difficulty referred to here is a letter that was written to the editor of a major New York newspaper after *Bovsun,* which said, "The whole concept of financial compensation for a psychological trauma is an affront to my personal values, and is a sad testimony to the morally casual attitude present in society today" (*Newsday,* March 15, 1984).

premorbid functioning. Absence of logical memory or an inability readily to learn paired associates (as seen in learning any new set of skills)[10] are probative of organicity.

Testimony by the psychologist or psychiatrist in such cases often has the added utility of explaining a victim's emotional responses to his or her neurological injury. Examples may include unrealistically high levels of aspiration, sharply varying levels of motivation, or a sense of total frustration with his or her inability even to approach preaccident levels of functioning. All of these by no means typical reactions fall within the sphere of the psychotherapist, and the ability to articulate them may well mean the difference between success and failure at trial.

Moreover, the development of CAT scans and their more advanced nuclear progeny do not obviate the need for the proper preparation and presentation of clinical testimony in cases of traumatically caused organic brain damage. A negatively read CAT scan does not rule out the possibility of such injury: Neither the test itself nor its interpretation is infallible. And even the positively interpreted CAT scan must be correlated, not only neurologically but causally, with the psychic injury sustained. Just as rightsided brain injury will not explain rightsided paralysis, not all damage shown by a CAT scan will necessarily be connected causally, to ensuing emotional harm. Many personal injury lawyers routinely have their nonparalyzed, organically brain-damaged clients tested by psychometrists. The bottom line is that, regardless of the advances made in neurological diagnostic medicine, the role of the mental health specialist in organic brain injury cases has not diminished. In fact, it has increased.

Most cases, such as that of the hypothetical Larry B., which was discussed at the beginning of this chapter, do not involve organicity. Yet they do present the commonly observed accident sequelae of anxiety, depression, and/or phobia. Further, when these emotional injuries are substantial, the therapist must be able to help both the plaintiff's lawyer and jury understand the present seriousness and likely prognosis of the plaintiff's condition. In cases of posttraumatic depressive illness, the lawyer must accumulate and present—from the plaintiff, his or her relatives, friends, co-workers, teachers, neighbors, and others with personal knowledge—hard evidence of the plaintiff's fears, as well as objective observations of the plaintiff's behavior. From the mental health witness must come a description of the causal relationship of symptoms with the accident, in addition to the

---

[10] It is not generally acceptable to the lawyer that the expert merely interpret test data without having actually administered the tests. It is important to observe a test taker's reactions while answering questions or doing test tasks, and the clinician who fails to do so may expose himself or herself to probing and effective cross-examination. On those occasions when a clinician is asked only to interpret test data, he or she would do the attorney a great service by asking to administer the tests as well.

psychological meaning of those fears and that behavior. The plaintiff's predisposition to depression will always be relevant. Other possible symptoms that the lawyer must find out about and the clinician explain include anorexia, loss of sexual drive, loss of ambition, insomnia, psychotic delusions, inability to make decisions, infantile behavior, seclusiveness, instability, suicidal ideation, poor job performance, and general deterioration of the plaintiff's prior social, family, and economic structures.

One reason why the depressed, anxious, or phobic patient is more likely to have his or her neuroses accepted by a jury (after careful explanation by the clinician) may be that many people personally, or by way of the media, have been exposed to these reactions. It is no longer rare for the lay juror to have sustained periods of acute anxiety, or at least to have been in the presence of those who have. Fright, periods of panic, difficulty in breathing, nightmares, unexplained sweating, chronic chest pains, agraphobia, nausea, fainting, headaches, backaches, and fatigue—these symptoms are more understandable today than formerly and thus are more easily explained and attributed to traumatic origin by the testifying clinical expert.

Nothing that has been written here is meant to imply in the slightest that the personal injury lawyer who represents a severely impaired patient has some God-given expertise in the etiology, diagnosis, or prognosis of emotional injury occurring as a result of physical injury or assault. The mental health professional must recognize that there is an obligation—when treating anybody from the victim of rape to the innocent witness/bystander to a relative's accident—not only to advise the patient to consult with an attorney but, when appropriate, to educate the attorney about the subtlties of how the patient's psyche became so deleteriously affected by the trauma.

In my view, therapists do not have the right (much less the duty) to decide for themselves that legal action is not in a patient's best interest, unless they first consult with both the patient and the lawyer. Psychotherapy and the law both recognize the existence of a syndrome of reactive depression to a relatively minor accident, which usually disappears upon settlement of the ensuing lawsuit. The skeptic assumes, therefore, that some complaints of emotional impairment have been fraudulent. The true professional, whether psychotherapist or lawyer, if sufficiently unburdened by his or her own emotional baggage (and this must never be eliminated from the equation), recognizes the legitimacy of this suspicion. Nevertheless, he or she is not afraid to go forward and prove, in the appropriate case, the individual's need to feel justified or revenged or to have his or her anger recognized. The Bible's "eye for an eye" tenet has been explained on such grounds; why not also the need for pecuniary compensation to the physically injured victim who has sustained emotional impairment?

I recognize the controversy. Panaceas do not exist, but at least the two professions should be working together for a common cause, namely the welfare of the patient/client, and not antagonistically or from postures of distrust.

REFERENCES

Almy, T. B. (Winter, 1984). Psychiatric testimony: Controlling the "ultimate wizardry." *Personal Injury Actions, 19* pp. 233, 234.

PART II

Criminal Responsibility

David L. Shapiro

4

Criminal Responsibility: An Integrative Model for Assessment

There is a growing body of literature suggesting that the insanity defense be totally abolished or replaced by concepts such as "guilty but mentally ill" or "diminished capacity." For instance, in the state of Illinois, officials have proposed that the insanity defense be replaced by two alternative concepts, one called "culpable and mentally disabled" and a second, which in essence replaces the insanity defense, referred to as "mentally disabled but neither culpable nor innocent." This concept is very similar to a statute in Michigan that evoked the concept of guilty but mentally ill and was subsequently upheld constitutionally.[1] Several states have recommended that the insanity defense be abolished and replaced with a concept of diminished capacity. Under this diminished capacity ruling, evidence of mental disorder would be admissible only to determine the seriousness of the crime for which the defendant could be tried. For example, murder which by definition requires intent or knowledge, could be reduced by a jury to a crime requiring only recklessness, such as manslaughter or criminal negligence. Such a jury finding could, at least in part, be based upon psychiatric or psychological input. Of course, the furor that surrounded the acquittal of John Hinckley by reason of insanity has also stimulated many people to advocate an abolition of the insanity defense.

An implication of this trend is that expert witnesses, e.g., psychotherapists, should stay out of the arena of criminal law altogether because their

---

[1] Michigan Compiled Laws Annotated, section 768.36[3]: Michigan Statutes Ann., Section 28.1059; see also *Michigan v. Bazzi,* 318 N.W. 2d 484 (Michigan Court Appeals, 1981).

PSYCHOTHERAPY AND THE LAW
ISBN 0-8089-1780-3

analyses of issues such as criminal responsibility are no more accurate than those of a lay person. Such critiques generally fall into two categories, the theoretical and the practical. The first critique deals with the opinion that it is presumptuous to assume that one can infer a person's state of mind at some prior point in time. The second, more practical objection is that such examinations are inadequate, that a poor foundation is laid for the conclusions, and that there is a general lack of reliability among different experts who view the same case.

This chapter will address primarily the first issue, that is, the theoretical one, although many implications of that issue will be reflected in the second, namely the adequacy of the examination. There are, to be sure, many situations in which it is virtually impossible to render an informed or educated decision about a person's state of mind at some time in the past. Not *all* situations, however, are like this. The danger of overgeneralizing from such cases is that it rapidly becomes a completely nihilistic approach in which psychotherapists basically tell the courts that they have nothing at all to say about such matters.

It is my contention that if certain conditions or criteria can be met, valid inferences can indeed be made regarding a person's state of mind at the time of a criminal offense. There are six important criteria that should be fulfilled before an expert witness makes a statement on the issue of criminal responsibility. Each of these criteria will be presented, along with some case illustrations from my practice.

THE PATIENT'S ABILITY TO RECONSTRUCT

The first criterion is whether the patient appears able to reconstruct his or her mental and emotional experience around the time of the offense. This is frequently not possible, and in such cases many difficulties can ensue; when such reconstruction is impossible, the expert should not offer any opinion. When the patient is able to perform such a reconstruction, however, it can be of great benefit.

EXAMPLE 1: A patient who was already in the hospital and who had been diagnosed as suffering from a schizophrenic thought disorder was observed by his therapist to be drinking a great deal of coffee and chain-smoking cigarettes. His therapist mentioned to him that he was smoking too much and drinking too much coffee. This behavior, the therapist said, would diminish if the patient could have a satisfying relationship with a woman. Subsequent to that time, because of a behavioral infraction on the ward, the patient was placed on coffee and cigarette restrictions by the ward staff. By his schizophrenic logic, he regarded this as an indication on the part of the ward staff that they wanted him to comply with his therapist's advice. He went over to the women's ward and attempted sexual intercourse with a 72-year-old woman.

EXAMPLE 2: A patient had a serious thought disorder but showed no evidence of assaultiveness and was being treated as an outpatient. One one occasion, when seen by his physician, he was found to be seriously physically ill. His doctor felt that the patient needed some laboratory work. Knowing the patient's propensity for noncompliance with medical directives, he gave his suggestions to the patient in very strong terms, telling him to get to the laboratory "as soon as possible and by any means necessary." Convinced of the sense of urgency, the patient took the nearest car to the clinical laboratory and was charged with unauthorized use of a motor vehicle. When arrested, the patient was exceedingly bewildered, indicating that he had committed no crime but was only following the doctor's orders.

One can see from these examples that the logic each patient followed in carrying out his criminal activity was clearly related to his mental disorder.

RETROSPECTIVE FALSIFICATION

The second criterion for valid assessment of criminal responsibility consists of evaluating the degree of retrospective falsification in the patient's presentation. Retrospective falsification refers to the tendency of an individual to appear either more disturbed or less disturbed at the time of the evaluation than he or she did at the time of the offense. In many cases, an individual may well possess excellent ego controls at the time of the offense, then deteriorate or disintegrate psychologically while incarcerated in jail and look acutely psychotic at the time of the psychological examination.

EXAMPLE 1: Because many jails and correction facilities are stressful environments, a patient may appear acutely psychotic in that setting. After being admitted to a hospital, however, his or her behavior may very rapidly and dramatically improve. One of the common features of jail life, in addition to the "sensory deprivation," is homosexual acting out. Frequently, a patient is transferred from jail to hospital in an acute homosexual panic with many paranoid fears. Once in the more secure setting, he or she may undergo a spontaneous remission of symptoms. One needs to evaluate the patient's history carefully, taking note of the presence or absence of psychosis in the past. One should determine whether or not it is merely an acute situational stress reaction to the conditions in the jail or, perhaps, to the fact that he or she was sexually approached or assaulted in the jail. One should not fall into the trap of inferring that behavior observed at the time of an examination is the same behavior that occurred at the time of the offense. Very likely it could be postarrest behavior due to some sort of deterioration or decompensation. Alternatively, a certain restitutive process may occur beginning when the patient is placed in the hospital. That is, he or she may have been psychotic at the time of the offense but be psychically intact at the time of the evaluation. Whenever possible, as noted above, one should attempt to obtain jail records, interview the jail staff regarding the patient's behavior within that setting, and compare that behavior with statements from family members, witnesses to the offense, and police reports.

EXAMPLE 2: A patient had been charged with assault with intent to kill, as well as a bank robbery that occurred several days after the assault. A psychologist who was retained by the defense completed an initial evaluation of the patient, finding him to be overtly psychotic. The psychologist reasoned that because psychosis represents a breakdown in the person's ability to control impulses and exert appropriate judgment, the two crimes (committed 9 months earlier) were causally related to the psychosis. No witnesses to either offense were interviewed.

An expert who was retained by the government also examined the patient and concluded that he was overtly psychotic, but that inferring 9 months back to the time of the offense was unwarranted. This expert proceeded to interview many witnesses to the patient's behavior around the time of the offense. First, the patient's mother was interviewed. She indicated that her son's prior psychotic episodes were consistently characterized by withdrawal, seclusiveness, fearfulness, and a sense of preoccupation; *at no time were his actions during the psychotic episodes characterized by aggressive behavior.*

The victim of the assault was then interviewed. He was a retired police officer who, in his career had transported "hundreds" of patients to the local state hospital for treatment. He was well aware of the variety of symptoms acutely psychotic patients manifest, and indicated that the defendant was angry but that in no way did he manifest any signs of psychosis.

Two bank tellers who were present at the scene of the bank robbery indicated that the patient appeared "nervous" at the time of the robbery but did not seem preoccupied, distracted, or as though he was responding to imaginary forces.

A variety of hospital records were reviewed, which revealed that the patient's manner, during psychotic episodes was confused, "drifty," (i.e., seemingly dazed), and at times manifested inappropriate sexual behavior (i.e., exposing himself and masturbating in the presence of female staff members). Once again, no aggressive or hostile behavior that would be consistent with assault was ever documented.

An interview with the patient's treating psychiatrist (The patient was on a one-day pass at the time of the first offense and had been expelled from the hospital because of inappropriate sexual behavior at the time of the second offense) revealed, again, no evidence of assaultiveness or that any apparent "command hallucinations" might have precipitated aggressive behavior. In fact, the psychiatrist noted that the patient was not on medication at the time the offenses occurred (because several side effects had been noted) and that he appeared to be far more alert, coherent, and goal-oriented when he was off medication. According to the doctor, the only continuing symptom was the patient's inappropriate sexual acting-out.

Following the patient's arrest, he was "bounced around" among approximately six hospitals and correctional facilities. He appeared to deteriorate grossly during that time and was diagnosed at one of the hospitals as suffering from schizophrenia, catatonic type.

The government-appointed expert concluded, based on the above analysis, that there was no evidence of psychosis at the time of the offenses that could be consistent with the behavior noted. Instead, the bizarre symptoms had manifested themselves following the commission of the offenses; therefore, under the law, the patient was criminally responsible, although currently psychotic.

This case highlights the necessity for careful investigatory work in forensic evaluations to determine whether or not the behavior observed in the current examination is consistent with the behavior occurring at the time of the offense. In this case, because the patient had been hospitalized previously, it was also noteworthy that none of the symptoms he manifested in the past was consistent with his criminal behavior. This case also points to the dangers of inferring backward in time from current clinical impressions.

In contrast to the above example, one frequently encounters cases in which the person was flagrantly psychotic at the time of the offense but has, over the course of months, gone into remission from his or her psychosis. Hence he or she may well look psychically intact at the time of the clinical examination.

EXAMPLE 3: A patient suffered an acute psychotic episode as the result of a homosexual panic and murdered his girl friend. There was ample evidence of a well-delineated paranoid system surrounding his relationship with his girl friend, concerning the "powers" that she had over him. At the time of the examination, several months later, the patient appeared rational and coherent and could only express bewilderment at the offense—he could not understand his motives at all. The issue of his psychotic motivation for the offense was reconstructed through interviews with family and friends, as well as the results of psychological testing; the latter suggested a potential for deterioration when themes relating to sexual identity were stirred up.

One must therefore compare, very carefully, the results of a current psychological examination with descriptions of the patient's behavior at the time of the offense and at the time of the arrest. If possible, one should review descriptions of his or her behavior during the whole period of time from the commission of the offense to the time of the examination.

CONSISTENCY OF BEHAVIOR

A third criterion for assessment of responsibility involves the necessity of correlating long-term observations of a patient's behavior with the behavior at the time of the offense. This is most ideally achieved when one has the opportunity to observe a patient for a substantial period of time within an inpatient setting. In the absence of such observation, one must have available, at the time of the examination, complete records of the patient's behavior while in the hospital or while incarcerated in a correctional setting. The following example illustrates how critical such observations can be.

EXAMPLE: A patient, who had had a prior history of acute psychotic episodes, especially while incarcerated, was admitted for pretrial examination to an inpatient forensic facility. During the course of the evaluation, he was noted to be withdrawn, preoccupied, and very silent; he frequently stood off, hallucinating, in the corner of his room. There was no evidence of violent behavior or of acting-out of any sort accompanying the psychotic behavior. In fact, on his previous admission to the hospital, the same pattern had been noted, namely that when he deteriorated into a psychotic condition, he became withdrawn, moody, and preoccupied. An interview with family members confirmed this picture exactly. At the time of the offense, however, the patient was described as aggressive, belligerent, and hostile. It was said that he told the victims of the armed robbery in which he was involved to lie still on the floor or he would blow their brains out.

It became rather clear that although the patient had had a history of acute psychotic episodes and was indeed psychotic at the time of his present evaluation, the behavior that characterized his psychosis was not consistent with the behavior manifested at the time of the offense. Therefore, in this case a decision was rendered that, despite the patient's underlying mental disorder, there was no evidence that the mental disorder was related to the offense as charged.

PSYCHOLOGICAL TEST INFERENCES

Somewhat correlated with the previous criterion is a situation in which the patient's responses to psychological testing provide a paradigm for his or her behavior in various situations of stress. These responses, in turn can be correlated with his or her behavior at the time of the offense.

EXAMPLE 1: Psychological testing of a patient suggested a relatively intact neurotic facade that could, given a relatively amorphous or ambiguous situation, deteriorate abruptly into very violent and explosive rages. The situation regarding the offense was precisely that: just prior to the patient's assault of a woman, which resulted in her death, he had experienced an acute depersonalization and derealization in which he reported a sensation of not knowing where he was and of not recognizing the woman, who in fact had been a friend of his, and a feeling that the woman's apartment "looked different and smelled different" to him.

It goes without saying that in following such an approach one must at this point analyze the tests and the inferences from the tests in a "blind" fashion, without having the details of the criminal offense in mind.

EXAMPLE 2: A patient who was charged with murder was given a complete battery of psychological tests. His responses to a series of projective techniques were basically intact—with notable exceptions in respect to his perception of older men, authority figures, and "father figures." At such times, the patient's thought processes became loose and illogical, and his reality testing was grossly impaired. In actuality, his mother had been murdered several years before, and the patient often felt that his father had been involved. The patient was charged with murdering a total stranger, a man who was the same height, weight, and body build as his father, in a setting virtually identical to the father's place of business. The murder occurred during the early hours of the morning, when it was dark outside. The parallel between the inferences from psychological testing and the facts of the offense were very striking, leading to the opinion that the patient misperceived the victim as his father and had been acutely psychotic at the time of the shooting.

THE USE OF SECONDARY SOURCES

In addition to the sources referred to above, one needs to have access to a comprehensive description, from secondary sources, of the defendant's behavior before and during the time of the offense. Police reports are certainly very helpful in such circumstances, but one also needs to request statements of witnesses, family members, and others who observed the patient's behavior around the time of the alleged offense. These statements need to be compared with other behavioral evidence in family, school, and occupational histories, as well as hospital reports, if any. The expert witness should not allow himself or herself to be placed in a position of being cross-examined with comments such as "Then you based your opinion just on what the patient told you!"

THE PHYSICAL EVIDENCE

A very critical aspect of a comprehensive evaluation for criminal responsibility is a comparison of the behavior that is typical of the particular mental disease or defect with the physical evidence in the case. This often goes beyond reading a police report and involves review of, for example, the medical examiner's report. Frequently, the novice forensic psychiatrist or psychologist is made quite uncomfortable by the necessity to consider carefully the physical evidence involved in the offense. Often the expert feels that his or her work should somehow take place in a more rarefied atmosphere than that of a police investigation.

In many cases, however, the physical evidence must be clearly evaluated and considered for an effective forensic evaluation to be done and an opinion rendered.

EXAMPLE 1: A person who had recently been released from jail went to a bar, where he then allowed himself to be solicited by a homosexual—for money. The man was promised that he would be paid if he would perform a homosexual act on the other person. At the homosexual's apartment, they apparently got into a fight, during the course of which the defendant threw the homosexual out a three-story-high window; the man was killed in the fall. One of the pieces of the physical evidence that was very striking was that there were bite marks all over the victim's body. During the course of the examination of the defendant, there was no evidence whatever of any mental disorder. The patient appeared to be best described as having a character disorder, most likely antisocial or passive-aggressive. At the time of the trial, the defense, presented through a defense psychiatrist, was "acute homosexual panic." In theory, of course, an acute homosexual panic occurs in a person who has deeply repressed homosexual feelings and for whom the arousal of these feelings is so threatening that he acts-out in violent ways. That is, if he loses behavioral control, he may be capable of exceedingly violent activity. The teeth marks noted above were accounted for by the defendant, who stated that during the course of the fighting, he had bitten the other man a number of times. Regarding the physical evidence, a forensic dentist, who had examined the teeth marks, offered the expert opinion on the witness stand that the marks represented passion bites rather than the aggressive bites that might have been sustained in the course of a fight. Hence, by combining physical evidence with results of the evaluation and with theoretical background on the personality of someone who would experience a homosexual panic, the following became clear.

If the patient voluntarily engaged in a homosexual act, which he obviously did by contracting with the other man, and if he bit the man out of passion, it is clear that he could not have experienced a homosexual panic. Moreover, his personality structure was inconsistent with that of a person who is subject to such panics. The man therefore was regarded as responsible for his actions because he voluntarily engaged in the homosexual act and was not in any "panic" state. His throwing the individual out of the window had nothing to do with panic.

EXAMPLE 2: A rather difficult and involved case had to do with a patient who was charged with murder and who had a history of epileptic seizures and chronic alcoholism. The patient was charged with stabbing a man (many times) in the man's apartment. The cause of death was listed as exsanguination. His defense was based on his having had some form of seizure activity precipitated by alcohol. It was either a temporal lobe seizure, in which he lost control and killed the other person; or, consistent with some earlier medical records, an episode of postictal violence—that is, in the phase immediately following the seizure. It has been observed that if one tries to move a patient too rapidly before he or she emerges from the comatose, stuporous state following seizure activity, he or she has the propensity for exploding into rather violent and aggressive behavior that may take a variety of forms. The defense was trying to establish this as the grounds for a lack of criminal responsibility. During the previous hospitalization, when the hospital staff had tried to move him too soon after his seizures, he had indeed gone "absolutely wild." There was documentation in the clinical record of this patient's unusual strength (e.g., pushing the doctors aside, holding the nurses at bay, and throwing chairs, waste baskets, and his hospital bed around the room).

The physical evidence in this case became very critical because there was a pattern to the stab wounds. Also important was the trail of blood in the apartment. The pattern of blood was not at all random or scattered in the way that a person who was attacked by someone experiencing a temporal lobe seizure might have bled; rather, there was clear physical evidence that the defendent chased the man from room to room. In addition, of course, is the well-documented fact that violent behavior associated with seizure activity is exceedingly rare.

The interplay of knowledge of behavior which is typical of a temporal lobe seizure or in the postictal state with the physical evidence and the inconsistency of the pattern of blood stains was very critical in this case. Another aspect was that the police report contained a statement that the defendant made to the police very shortly after the stabbing. The statement was exceedingly coherent, and had the patient indeed been in a stuporous state following a seizure, he would not have been able to make such a coherent statement. Therefore, by process of elimination, the

Table 4-1
Criteria for Criminal Responsibility Evaluations

1. Evaluate the patient's ability to reconstruct his or her experience.
2. Evaluate the extent of retrospective falsification and the reasons for it.
3. Observe the consistency, or lack of consistency, of disturbed behavior in different settings.
4. If available, consider inferences from psychological testing and whether or not they coherently "fit" the events of the offense.
5. Gather and integrate all secondary sources of data.
6. Gather and integrate the physical evidence with the inferred behavior and its relationship to the diagnosis made and behavior typical of that diagnostic grouping.

opinion rendered to the court was that, most likely, the patient was not experiencing a seizure at the time of the offense. In this case, although there was a documented history both of a seizure disorder and of severe alcoholism, there was no apparent relationship between the mental defect (that is, the seizure disorder) and the offense. It appeared, instead, that the patient's excessive consumption of alcohol, rather than any seizure activity, may well have been the precipitating factor in the stabbing.

If all six of the criteria in Table 4-1 can be satisfied, then the psychiatrist or psychologist has a reliable and valid basis for rendering inferences about a person's state of mind at the time of the offense—even if the offense occurred some time in the past. An important point is that if these criteria cannot be satisfied, the expert witness has the option of notifying the court that not enough data are available to render an informed decision. This will not only enhance the credibility of the expert witness but serve to heighten reliability among the several experts who are involved in the evaluation and obviate the so-called "battle of the experts."

Once these underlying criteria are met, one may then move to a conceptual schema for the assessment of criminal responsibility, which can further heighten reliability in the assessments made of a person by different expert witnesses. The basic assumption underlying this conceptual schema is a simple one: The closer the mental illness is in logical sequence to the person's actual criminal behavior (i.e., the fewer intervening variables), the greater is the likelihood that the mental illness is producing the behavior.

For example, a patient fears that a man walking toward him on the street has come to get him and that he has to kill him to protect himself. This would be regarded, in this conceptualization, as a Stage One Relationship. In other words, there is a direct sequential relationship between the delusional system and the behavior.

A Stage Two Relationship is characterized by a situation in which the delusional system affects the behavior but somewhat more indirectly (i.e., there are relatively more intervening variables).

EXAMPLE: A young man, who was examined several years ago, felt he had heard God's voice telling him that there were devils in the United States Senate. He had written a series of exceedingly delusional letters to senators, and their lack of responsiveness convinced him of the truth of God's "message." He left his home state and went to Washington. He then attempted to enter the Senate chamber with a machete, threatening to cut off a senator's head unless everyone in the Senate listened to his proclamations of the kingdom of heaven on earth. This would be regarded as a Stage Two Relationship, in that it is not quite as direct as that of a patient who assaults a person because of a paranoid delusion. In this example, the idea of using a machete was the patient's reconstruction of what God's voice instructed him to do, and the lack of responsiveness to his letters "convinced" him of the veracity of his hallucinations. Nevertheless, the reconstruction itself was certainly grounded in this patient's mental disorder.

A Stage Three Relationship, within this conceptual system, involves somewhat more intervening variables; also, some experts would no longer be of the opinion that there is a lack of criminal responsibility. Here, many volitional elements intervene between the delusional system and the criminal act.

EXAMPLE: A patient had developed a delusional system in which the Republican Party had been persecuting him for the past 10 years; in fact, the party invented a mind-control machine that was implanting obsessive thoughts of self-destruction in the patient's mind. The patient decided that he was going to expose the leaders of the Republican National Committee. He therefore robbed a bank, with the intention of using the money to obtain a lie-detector machine. With this machine, he was going to test the leaders of the Republican National Committee and make them confess on national television their heinous plot against him. Here, although the motivation was clearly a delusional one, there were many volitional "choice points" along the way.

Finally, in a Stage Four Relationship, the mental disorder does not appear to bear any direct relationship to the crime. For example, a person who has some self-destructive tendencies robs a supermarket in his own neighborhood without any attempt to disguise himself. He could clearly be identified, and one might hypothesize that there was an unconscious desire to be punished involved in his committing such a blatant act. The relation-

Table 4-2

Mental Illness and Criminal Activity

Stage 1:	A one-to-one correspondence exists between the illness and the crime.
Stage 2:	The illness has a significant impact on the crime but intervening variables are present (e.g., criminal activity based upon an interpretation of a delusion).
Stage 3:	Mental illness is a factor, but there are many more "choice points" regarding expression of behavior.
Stage 4:	There is an indirect relationship between crime and illness, or illness is related to peripheral activity.

ship here between the emotional problem and the crime is so distant, however, that one cannot refer to the person as lacking in criminal responsibility.

In summary, using the six criteria and the conceptual schema outlined in Table 4-2, it is my contention that expert witnesses can indeed perform valid and reliable assessments of criminal responsibility, maintain high credibility in the courts, render decisions on cases in which an insanity defense would be appropriate, and at the same time avoid the criticism that criminal responsibility examinations are superficial, ambiguous, and/or speculative.

Leonard S. Rubenstein

5

Making Decisions about Criminal Responsibility: The More Things Change . . .

People who have exercised free will should be held accountable for their acts. Those who lack free will, however, should not be considered responsible, even if their acts are crimes. These simple principles, central to Anglo-American justice, seem, among all legal principles, uniquely difficult to apply. The insanity defense has been the focus of that difficulty; more than any other aspect of the law, it forces society to attempt to define its own notion of what free will is, who is blameworthy and who is not, and where free will ends. It is not an easy task. And, strangely enough, the growth of psychiatry has made the task even more difficult.

Throughout this century, discussion of the insanity defense has focused on the effort, as Sheldon Glueck put it, "to bring the criminal law more into harmony with modern psychiatric views."[1] This meant that the legal system asked psychiatry to help it devise a way to decide who is sane and who is not. And psychiatrists have been willing to oblige. One could even argue that the many variations in the insanity defense in this century amount to a rough intellectual history of psychiatry. First came the influence of Freud, with the argument that unconsciously motivated behavior ought to be considered a reason for an insanity acquittal.[2] This was followed by post–World War II optimism and the belief that with vast advances in clinical knowledge, the therapy profession could use its skills to separate the guilty from the innocent. And today, we see virtually every personality disorder and syndrome

---

[1] S. Glueck. (1928). Psychiatry and the criminal law. *12 Mental Hygiene* 569.

[2] S. Glueck. (1925). *Mental disorder and the criminal law*. Boston, Little Brown pp. 315.

Editors' note: In this chapter, the terms "psychiatry" and "psychiatrist are synonymous with the terms "psychotherapy" and "psychotherapist." The term "psychiatric" is synonymous with the term "psychotherapist."

PSYCHOTHERAPY AND THE LAW
ISBN 0-8089-1780-3

embraced by the *Diagnostic and Statistical Manual: III* used as a basis to avoid or lessen responsibility for one's conduct.[3]

Neither the enormous growth in the belief of the psychiatric explanation of behavior nor the growth of "psychohistory," has resulted in an intellectually satisfactory and judicially workable test for criminal responsibility. The reason lies in a premise of the task, namely a mistaken notion that the law can look to psychiatry for answers to moral and legal problems. This premise has led not only to a confusion of roles but to substantive standards for criminal responsibility which bring arbitrary, inconsistent, and unpopular results. These difficulties will continue until legal decisions are no longer submerged in clinical issues and until a very sharp line is drawn in the courtroom between the role of medicine and the role of the law in determinations of criminal responsibility.

INSANITY: A LEGAL OR PSYCHIATRIC CONCEPT?

The acquittal of John Hinckley, Jr., triggered debate anew, this time fueled by the attorney general of the United States, who blamed the insanity defense for crime in the streets.[4] The usual suspects—liberals soft on crime, corrupt psychiatrists, and rich defendants—were rounded up. These were soon let go because statistics showed that a miniscule number of defendants are acquitted as insane and that fewer still go free.[5] Quickly the reforms, i.e., proposed verdicts of "guilty but mentally ill" or "guilty but insane," were shown to be intellectually specious.[6]

Strong and legitimate objections remain. Perhaps more than any other rule of law, the results of the insanity defense seem anarchic. The momentous question of innocence or guilt turns on clinical theories that are not widely accepted, sometimes not even within the psychiatric profession itself. This abdication of responsibility to clinicians demeans the proceeding and subverts the very idea of the rule of the law. The results of a *successful* insanity plea are more problematic still: When is a person who, though innocent, may be violent to be let free?

---

[3] W. Gaylin. (1982). *The killing of Bonnie Garland*, New York: Simon & Schuster pp. 255–265.

[4] See (1982, June 23). High U.S. Officials Express Outrage. Ask for New Laws on Insanity Plea. *New York Times,* p. B6.

[5] A 1978 national study showed that the insanity defense was successful in only one-tenth of one percent of criminal prosecutions. H. Steadman, J. Monahan, E. Hartstone, S. Davis, & P. Robbins. (1982). Mentally disordered offenders: A national survey of patients and facilities. *Law and Human Behavior 6,* 31.

[6] The "guilty but mentally ill" verdict would offer a jury another choice when the insanity defense is raised. It does nothing to address the issues that underlie the insanity defense and tends to mislead the jury. "Guilty but insane" is a verdict that requires conviction even if the jury finds a person not criminally responsible.

There does seem to be a surprising consensus on the most fundamental question, namely whether or not the insanity defense should exist at all. Lawyers, therapists, judges, and the public appear to agree that, under some circumstances, mental illness can render a person not responsible for his or her conduct. Reasons for this consensus have little to do with mental illness and everything to do with the moral basis of the criminal law. Criminal law is based upon the premise that an individual is capable of abiding by the rules of society and is subject to blame and punishment when he or she does not. But if he or she lacks the ability to obey the law, for whatever reason, we do not consider his or her actions blameworthy. However difficult the application of this principle, to abandon it would be to condemn the moral basis for criminal law. Arguments for abolition of the insanity defense are rarely persuasive, even when based upon claims regarding the personal dignity of the defendant. The insanity defense is likely to remain a part of the criminal law, however infrequently it is used and however bizarre are its occasional consequences.

The insanity defense, however, is not well understood. Its invocation amounts to a claim that, because of an impairment of the mind, society ought to refrain from placing moral and legal responsibility upon an individual for behavior it otherwise would judge criminal. It is not the only defense that can relieve a person of responsibility for acts otherwise considered criminal. Others, such as duress, mistake,[7] or self-defense, all derive from the setting of the act and from the extrinsic circumstances under which the criminal act occurred. The insanity defense, however, looks inward—to skewed qualities of mind and thought. The difference between the "outward" and "inward" circumstances are, of course, very significant, but the conceptual similarities between these defenses to legal responsibility (as opposed to the conventional defense to the *act,* i.e., "I didn't do it") are far more important. The central similarity is that, in each case, a judgment must be made by a juror (a lay person) about responsibility under a given set of circumstances. The judgment is not just about the nature of the threat in a duress case or the nature of the psychosis in an insanity case, but about whether the jurors, as society's representatives, believe it is just and reasonable to hold the person responsible in those circumstances.

This point can be illustrated by a familiar case: the participation of Patricia Hearst, some years ago, in armed robberies after being kidnapped by the Symbionese Liberation Army. Without relying upon the specific facts of her case (and, for purposes of argument, taking some liberties with them), it is possible to envision two separate defenses. One is a conventional de-

---

[7] Traditionally, "duress" is the submission of the will of the defendant under fear (e.g., one forges a signature while there is a gun to one's head). Mistake of fact occurs when a person honestly and reasonably believes a condition to exist that would make his or her conduct lawful (e.g., in defense to a charge of theft, a defendant says that he thought he had paid for the item).

fense of duress, the argument being that a person who is kidnapped, held captive under severe conditions, and threatened with reprisals if she fails to commit a crime cannot be held responsible for her acts.[8] The other might be insanity: that the extraordinary stresses of Ms. Hearst's captivity led to a dramatic break with reality, so that, at the time she engaged in criminal conduct, she had completely lost all normal control or capacity for moral judgment.

Each defense would require different proof. But, ultimately, a judgment must be made by a finder of fact: Given the facts that we know about Ms. Hearst's condition or her mind, are we prepared to hold her responsible for what she did? In each case, it will be a lay judgment, a question for a jury. The jury's decision concerning an insanity defense claim would be no more a professional judgment than it would be concerning a duress claim. Instead, it would be a moral, social, and legal decision about free will, about which psychiatry has nothing to say. The expert testifies about an impaired mind; then the jurors must decide whether, in view of those facts, they believe the defendant capable of exercising his or her free will. Accordingly, although psychiatrists can testify about a defendant's pathology, they cannot say whether he or she is responsible (i.e., whether he or she is innocent or guilty).

The jurors' choice would only be a relative judgment, in that a defense against responsibility is socially acceptable only to the extent that it is limited to a very few cases. To be sure, we want an insanity defense that achieves what we perceive as "correct" results; that is, those who are acquitted should be the same persons whom we as a society believe ought to be acquitted. But acquittal on grounds of duress or insanity must be a rarity, or else the criminal law itself has no force. This is a matter of social necessity, not science; the number of acquittals cannot acceptably rise to a level at which every aberrant defendant could be found not guilty for his or her acts.[9] If an entire community became insane, the legal result would likely be a revision of standards, not mass acquittal.

In principle, the relativity of the defense is easy to abide, and most clinicians and lawyers agree that the insanity verdict is a legal and moral one that psychiatrists are no more expert to make than are geologists. But this distinction, although often articulated, has proven very hard to accept and even more difficult to apply. It conflicts with another, even stronger desire: the quest for scientific certainty. We seek scientific identification of those

---

[8] This was the defense actually raised in the case *United States v. Hearst*, 563 F.2d 1331 (9th Cir. 1977). The jury rejected the defense and convicted Ms. Hearst.

[9] Indeed, there is evidence that a huge percentage of inmates in the nation's prisons have a mental disorder. An analysis performed in litigation concerning the Texas prison system, one of the largest in the country, found that approximately 17,000 (68 percent) of the inmates needed treatment for a mental disorder. It was estimated that from 5 percent to 20 percent of the inmates had psychoses. *Ruiz v. Estelle*, 503 F. Supp. 1265, 1332 (S.D. Tex. 1980).

who should not be found guilty as insane. This is especially so in a culture in which psychological explanation has become commonplace. The way we think about the insanity defense has reflected this attitude—the product of a belief that the determination of guilt or innocence is, after all, a matter of science or medicine, for resolution by experts.

This attitude is often expressed when one considers the critical question of causation, i.e., whether or not a mental impairment *caused* the defendant to commit acts that constituted a crime. Such "cause" is usually understood in a "but for" sense, viz., but for the impairment, the defendant would not have committed the illegal act. This form of causation is familiar to the law and is deeply embedded in the law of torts. It comes up in run-of-the-mill personal injury cases (the defendant drove his car too fast, causing him to lose control and hit the pedestrian) and in more sophisticated matters involving, say, medical malpractice (the doctor's failure to order the test indicated by the patient's symptoms caused the misdiagnosis and resulted in injury to the patient). The issue even arises in criminal prosecutions (the gunshot wound caused the victim's death).

But causation has a more problematic place in the determination of moral responsibility, such as in the defenses of duress and mistake discussed above. In those cases, the question of causation is inextricably connected to a judgment about responsibility, which cannot be addressed in scientific, cause-and-effect terms. Take the Patricia Hearst example again, assuming that a defense of duress is asserted. At one level, the question is simply whether or not the external pressure, isolation, and threats "caused" the defendant to commit a crime. But that question, even if phrased in strictly causal terms, involves an issue of how much the jury expects the defendant's moral judgment to hold up under the pressure placed upon it. The decision on cause and effect, in other words, includes an assessment of the defendant's judgment of the risks *to him or her*, his or her level of resistance to the risk, his or her courage, and the jury's belief concerning a reasonable response—none of which can be objectively measured. Even more important, society may subject the defendant to moral standards independent of the severity of those risks.[10] In the Hearst case, the jury had to decide whether, even if the stresses on Ms. Hearst were real and her fears were real, the fears plus the stresses gave moral legitimacy to her acts.

The concept of causation carries an equally heavy burden in the insanity defense. At the simplest level, the insanity defense is about causation—whether or not the impairment caused the act. But that question cannot be answered in clinical terms. We think of actions as governed by free will, and no psychological evidence can say whether someone "lost" his or her free

---

[10] For example, there is a very long tradition of failure with respect to the duress defense in cases involving cooperation with the enemy by prisoners of war. The objective, "scientific" factors are subordinated to a very strict moral standard.

will. It is a moral judgment, on which clinical facts may be relevant but not definitive. Science cannot tell us when free will, a nonscientific concept, has been impaired.

Unfortunately, this distinction is obscured in very extreme cases—those that seem to dominate the debate about the insanity defense but, in fact, occur infrequently. For example, it is easy to conclude that a person who thinks he is a messenger of God is psychotic and that his behavior can be explained by the psychosis. We may also conclude that his loss of touch with reality has deprived him of his free will. But the two conclusions are not identical. Psychiatry cannot say that this person's impairment deprived him of moral responsibility for his act.

This point is evident in less clear-cut cases, even those in which the clinician has a fair degree of insight into the person's diagnosis and behavior. Take the example of a man who suffers paranoid delusions. He believes that the CIA is persecuting him, that his phone is tapped, that his mail is being opened, and that his neighbors are spying on him. He is afraid to go out and is terrified of the police, who, he believes, have joined the CIA in conspiring against him. One evening a local police officer, on routine business, rings his doorbell. The man opens the door and shoots the officer.

Psychiatrists could diagnose this man's condition, describe his agitated state, and discuss his feeling that he needed to defend himself or be killed. They could describe his history, which might reveal that the fellow's feelings had been under control with medication but that, at the time of the incident, he had been off drugs for a week. They might conclude that the defendant's paranoia led to impaired judgment and irrational behavior, particularly an inflated sense of danger to himself. They could also "explain" his act in terms of his impairment. But could they advise whether to acquit on grounds of insanity? Could clinicians say that the impairment was so severe as to prevent the defendant from making the moral judgments that would enable him, despite impairment, to obey the law? Surely not. For such a conclusion concerns free will—a philosophical, not a psychological, concept—which must be based upon common sense and lay understanding. To the extent that a clinician draws conclusions about whether or not the behavior in this case deserves exoneration, he or she is not making a clinical judgment at all. Certainly, it is not one that he or she would make it in the ordinary course of practice.

The distinction drawn here is not new, but it has proven extraordinarily difficult to apply in practice. Both clinicians and lawyers have demonstrated a tendency to reduce the question of insanity to a matter of psychological knowledge. The mystery of mental illness appears to bring with it a desire to confer the issue upon the psychiatrists—a pattern that will continue for as long as psychiatrists willingly (or unwillingly) control who will be convicted and who will be acquitted.

Scholars have argued that the particular insanity-defense standard that is applied in a given jurisdiction or case has little bearing upon the jury's verdict.[11] The conclusion often drawn is that the test or standard for determining insanity does not matter. This is probably true, but only because each of the tests studied asks the experts to testify about innocence or guilt. If the standard invites or permits testimony on innocence or guilt by the expert, results are likely to be determined by what the experts say (i.e., whether the defendant's conduct meets the standard), rather than by what test is applied. A test for the determination of legal insanity must be devised to delineate sharply between the jury's and the expert's role. Most experience with the insanity defense has done precisely the opposite.

MORAL QUESTION/CLINICAL ANSWERS

Over the past 100 years, the destiny of the insanity defense has followed the psychiatry profession's beliefs concerning the scope of its knowledge about the connection between mental illness and behavior. Psychiatrists have been assigned the task of conveying that knowledge to juries. Although the profession's conclusions concerning the extent of that knowledge have changed over the years, the consequences have not. The insanity defense, both in its form and in the method of proof, has been handed to the psychiatrists. The moral question, which can be illuminated by clinical knowledge but cannot be made dependent upon it, has been submerged in the process.

In 1843, Daniel M'Naghten attempted to assassinate Sir Robert Peel, prime minister of England, but instead shot Peel's private secretary. After his acquittal as insane, public furor, fueled by the views of Queen Victoria, demanded change. The judges in the case were summoned to the House of Lords. The result of this tumult was a rule that bears M'Naghten's name, although it was not applied to M'Naghten himself: One is found guilty only if, as a result of mental disease, one does not *know* what one has done or does not *know* that what one did was wrong. Its most common formulation is stated as follows:

> A person is not guilty if at the time of the committing of the act, the party accused was laboring under such a defect of reason, from disease of the mind, as not to know the nature and quality of the act he was doing; or if he did know it, that he did not know he was doing what was wrong.

By the 20th century, this emphasis on cognitive functioning had become criticized as irrelevant (even positively harmful) to the criminal law, because it embodied a view of behavior that departed from what was then known about the mind. As early as 1930, Justice Benjamin Cardozo, who was enlightened on modern science, wrote that the *M'Naghten* rule'' has little

---

[11] See, for example, A. Goldstein. (1967). *The insanity defense.* New Haven: Yale University Press. pp. 62–63.

relation to the truths of mental life.''[12] In the 1940s and 1950s, psychiatric opinion generally regarded the *M'Naghten* test as outmoded because it did not reflect prevailing knowledge concerning the causes of criminal behavior or the nature of the mind. The prestigious Royal Commission on Capital Punishment (1949–53) argued that the test was "based on an entirely obsolete and misleading conception of the nature of insanity."[13]

This attack had two principal grounds. First, the test itself precludes acquittal if *cognitive functions* were unimpaired, even though the defendant was unable to control his or her *conduct*. Particularly with the growth of Freudian dynamic psychology, the notion of focusing on cognitive impairment alone seemed a form of quaint psychology unsuited to the 20th century. Sheldon Glueck, one of the leading scholars of law and psychiatry early in this century, argued, for example, that dynamic psychology did not view cognitive impairment (i.e., impairment that prevents one from knowing the "nature and quality" of an act) as the sole component of mental disease—nor even as an important one—and that it certainly was not the sole determinant of criminal responsibility.[14] Second, psychiatrists complained that the terminology of *M'Naghten* (i.e., its focus on knowledge of right and wrong) represented a moral, not a clinical, concept about which clinicians could not testify fruitfully (although testify they did).

Both criticisms have the same origin: the departure of the insanity determination from the province and language of psychiatry. Expert communication of clinical knowledge was hampered, it seemed, by concepts such as knowledge of right and wrong, which were not clinical concepts at all, and by limitations in the theory of cognitive functioning. Psychiatrists wanted to be able to tell jurors how to decide cases based upon their own discipline, with its own language and explanations. One early result was the "irresistible impulse" test, which gained prominence early in the century as an expression of dynamic psychology. This test provides for a finding of insanity if the defendant, though understanding that what he was doing was wrong, "lost the power to choose between right and wrong" and if his or her "free agency was at the time destroyed"[15] This test, however, continued to be expressed in moral, and hence unsatisfactory, terms.

By the late 1940s and early 1950s, the ascendancy of psychiatry was complete, and displeasure with *M'Naghten* was widespread. Both *M'Naghten* and the irresistible impulse test, though expressing the two fundamental grounds on which someone could be held not responsible ("He didn't understand what he was doing" or "He couldn't control his conduct") were seen as inadequate, particularly in their reliance on language

---

[12] B. Cardozo. (1930). *What medicine can do for the law*. New York, Harper & Brothers p. 32.

[13] Quoted in *Durham v. United States*, 214 F.2d 862, 871 and n.28 (D.C. Cir. 1954).

[14] S. Glueck. (1928). Psychiatry and the criminal law. *12 Mental Hygiene* 569.

[15] See, for example, *Parsons v. State*, 2 So. 854, 866–67 (Ala. 1887).

such as "free will" and "right and wrong." The notion was that the mental health profession would tell us when a person's act should be excused because of a diseased mind. Although lip service continued to be paid to the distinction between clinical diagnosis and moral responsibility, this distinction was lost in the drive to modernize the law of insanity to make it clinically respectable.

One result of this tendency appeared in the famous case of *Durham v. United States.*[16] In that case, the U.S. Court of Appeals for the D.C. Circuit, a pioneer in matters of law and psychiatry, introduced the rule that legal insanity meant that the criminal act was the cause or "product" of a mental disease. No reference to free will, right or wrong, or any other moral concept would intrude upon the psychiatrist's freedom to testify in his or her own terms. On the contrary, the question of causation left the moral realm entirely and became, instead, a scientific question. Clinicians would have complete leeway to describe the defendant in the fullest, most complete way, unencumbered by any restriction on the scope of their testimony. They would go on to explore the connection between the mental defect and the defendant's antisocial behavior. And finally, triumphantly, they would pronounce whether the person's act was a "product" of the disease or defect.

The problem with *Durham* now seems all too obvious, namely a complete abdication of law to psychiatry. In *Durham*'s defense, it must be said that its intent was to fashion a standard that would be in harmony with clinical knowledge but would not be swallowed up by it. Although the *Durham* court was criticized (like *M'Naghten*) as depending unrealistically on "defects of reason," it also saw the rule it was establishing as enhancing the *jury's* function. The court wished to assign to the expert the role that he or she played in any other case (i.e., to describe technical facts and explain their significance). Unlike *M'Naghten,* which encouraged psychiatrists to testify about moral issues (the defendant's knowledge of right and wrong), *Durham* was seen as delineating the respective roles of expert and jury according to their proper functions: Psychiatrists would testify about clinical issues, and the jury would decide moral matters. This approach could be analogized to proof of proximate cause in the civil law of torts.[17]

But *Durham* was doomed from the start, for the very reason that it treated the connection between the impairment and the act as a clinical one, to be drawn by the psychiatrist. By asking a clinical question, it demanded a clinical answer. The moral question was suppressed. Two decades later, another judge of the D.C. Circuit, Judge Leventhal, put his finger on it:

There is, indeed, irony in a situation under which the *Durham* rule, which was adopted in large part to permit the experts to testify in their own terms con-

---

[16] 214 F.2d 862 (D.C. Cir. 1954).

[17] This interpretation of *Durham* was offered by its author, Judge David Bazelon, in *United States v. Brawner,* 471 F.2d 969 (D.C. Cir. 1972).

cerning matters within their domain which the jury should know, resulted in testimony by the experts in terms not their own to reflect unexpressed judgments in a domain that is properly not theirs but the jury's. The irony is heightened when the jurymen, instructed under the esoteric "product" standard, are influenced significantly by "product" testimony of expert witnesses really reflecting ethical and legal judgments rather than a conclusion within the witnesses' particular expertise.[18]

The fundamental problem of *Durham,* namely the inadequacy of a clinical/causal test of insanity, contributed to the unhappy spectacle of psychiatrists arguing for exoneration based upon their own idiosyncratic notions of behavior and responsibility. When it became clear that the "product" rule had led to clinical control of the insanity defense, the court ruled that psychiatrists could not testify in "conclusory" terms on whether the act was the "product" of a disorder—the ultimate question of innocence or guilt.[19] But this rule was impossible to apply. Who but psychiatrists could answer the question demanded by the "product" rule?

About the same time that *Durham* was decided, the American Law Institute recommended a different test for the insanity defense which represented an attempt to avoid the pitfalls of *Durham* yet was considered in harmony with contemporary mental health knowledge. It provided two alternative reasons for relieving someone of criminal responsibility: either (1) because the person did not understand what he or she was doing or (2) because the person could not control his or her conduct. So far so good. These two concepts appear to define the moral universe of the insanity defense; all those who are not blameworthy because of their impaired mental state seem to fit into one of these categories. The test was stated thusly:

> A person is not responsible for criminal conduct if at the time of such conduct as a result of a mental disease or defect he lacks substantial capacity either to appreciate the criminality of his conduct or to conform his conduct to the requirements of the law.

This test was eventually adopted by all federal courts of appeal[20] and by about half of the states.

Even so, it was the American Law Institute (ALI) test that led to the very results that inspired cries for reform. That standard, like *Durham,* opened up the courtroom to every psychiatric theory imaginable, from alcohol-induced psychosis to the most recently fashionable ailment, posttraumatic stress disorder, as a basis for acquittal. Especially in high-visibility

---

[18] *United States v. Brawner,* 471 F.2d 969, 983 (D.C. Cir. 1972).

[19] *United States v. Washington,* 390 F.2d 444 (D.C. Cir. 1967).

[20] Until recently, Congress had not established an insanity defense standard applicable to the federal courts. As a result, this task fell to the 12 U.S. courts of appeal. In the aftermath of the Hinckley verdict, Congress enacted an insanity defense standard for the federal courts along the lines suggested by the American Psychiatric Association and the American Bar Association, as discussed below.

cases, psychiatrists were hired by both defense and prosecution and, inevitably, became advocates. Each clinician not only battled to establish his or her own credibility but to tell the jury whether or not the defendant should be found blameworthy. Worse, communities developed a stable of "defense" and "prosecution" psychiatrists, each holding strong views about questions of culpability, who shaped the local version of the insanity defense by their frequent appearances. This has become a source of embarrassment to both the legal and mental health professions.

The root of the problem is the same as in the case of *Durham*. Too much faith was placed in the clinicians' ability to make appropriate judgments, and too little effort was made to confine psychiatric testimony to its proper sphere. In fact, the ALI test is really nothing but a more refined version of *Durham*. Instead of asking whether or not the conduct was the "product" of a mental disease, the ALI standard asks a jury whether or not certain conduct was "a result of" a mental disease—hardly a meaningful distinction. And instead of saying that a criminal *act* was the product, the ALI test simply describes the possible characteristics of that act (i.e., the defendant did not appreciate what he or she was doing or could not conform his or her behavior to law at the time of the act). Hence the only real difference between ALI and *Durham* is that ALI stated the possible exonerating characteristics of the defendant's insane behavior. It still asked psychiatrists to draw the proper conclusion as a clinical judgment. And like *Durham,* the moral question—the place where science leaves off—was hidden behind a scientific cause-and-effect analysis.

In this context, it is difficult to understand the ferment that arose during the 1950s and 1960s concerning *Durham* and the growing enthusiasm for the ALI test among so many legal scholars and forensic psychotherapists. For whatever advantages the ALI test had over *Durham* (primarily its explicitness), it had adopted *Durham*'s worst features.

OLD QUESTIONS, FAMILIAR ANSWERS

With the Hinckley verdict, a furor was raised anew, this time with the prevailing ALI test the principal object of attack. The anarchy of ALI test verdicts only led to a search for firmer scientific ground wherein psychiatry would offer more sure causal judgments and would, in the future, prevent the acquittal of a man who seemed, in the minds of many, completely responsible for his attempt to kill the president. The professional associations of both lawyers and psychiatrists each provided the same answer, namely a virtual return to *M'Naghten*.[21]

---

[21] American Psychiatric Association (1982), *Statement on the insanity defense* (hereafter "APA Statement"); American Bar Association (1983), *Policy on the insanity defense* (hereafter "ABA Policy").

Both the American Bar Association and the American Psychiatric Association found that therapists were being continually asked to make moral judgments based upon clinical facts. The ALI test, once offered as a solution to this very problem, was particularly criticized for using such nonclinical terms as "appreciate" and "substantial capacity to conform his [or her] conduct to the requirements of law," about which clinicians were expected to testify. Some psychiatrists told congressional investigators, during committee hearings on the insanity defense, that they refused to testify in insanity defense trials because they objected to supplying the opinions on innocence or guilt that were demanded by lawyers and by the courts. Of course, the ALI test itself required such opinions and was meant to elicit clinical opinions on innocence or guilt. Psychiatrists, not lay people, were expected to draw the connection between impairment and the defendant's ability to "appreciate" what he or she did or his or her capacity to conform to the law.

One proposal, by the American Psychiatric Association, was to exclude expert opinion on the "ultimate" question, that is, whether or not the clinician believes that a defendant meets the prevailing legal test for insanity:

> Juries . . . find themselves listening to conclusory and seemingly contradictory psychiatric testimony that defendants are either "sane" or "insane" or that they do not meet the relevant legal test for insanity. This state of affairs does considerable injustice to psychiatry and, we believe, possibly to criminal defendants. These psychiatric disagreements about technical, legal and/or moral matters cause less than fully understanding juries or the public to conclude that psychiatrists cannot agree. In fact, in many criminal insanity trials, both prosecution and defense psychiatrists do agree about the nature and even the extent of mental disorder exhibited by the defendant at the time of the act.[22]

This observation concerning testimony on innocence or guilt by experts does not altogether proscribe psychiatric participation. On the contrary, the psychiatrist's role would continue much as before; however, it would be appropriately limited to matters within his or her expertise.

> Psychiatrists, of course, must be permitted to testify fully about the defendants' psychiatric diagnosis, mental state and motivation (in clinical and commonsense terms) at the time of the alleged act so as to permit the jury or judge to reach the ultimate conclusion about which they and only they are expert. Determining whether a criminal defendant was legally insane is a matter for legal fact-finders, not for experts.[23]

The latter assertion is hardly new, but psychiatric domination is not easily defeated. In the same breath that the American Psychiatric Association recognized that psychiatrists should not give opinions on legal and moral questions, it urged adoption of a standard that could only encourage

---

[22] APA Statement, at 19.
[23] Id.

psychiatrists to testify on those questions, and that amounts to a virtual return to *M'Naghten,* namely: a person will not be held responsible if "as a result of mental disease or mental retardation he was unable to appreciate the wrongfulness of his conduct at the time of the offense"[24] In other words, one of the two possible grounds for acquittal is eliminated, as follows: A person who does not understand the wrongfulness of what he or she has done will be acquitted; a person who cannot control his or her conduct will be convicted.

As with the *Washington* decision 25 years before, the proposed prohibition on psychiatric testimony on innocence or guilt contradicts the substantive rule. Although the role of psychiatrists appears to be restricted, the test itself demands clinical testimony on the matter of causation. The APA's own explanation demonstrates this continuing paradox. While purporting to limit psychiatric testimony, it justifies the return to *M'Naghten* precisely because psychiatric testimony on whether a person understands the nature of his or her act and of its wrongfulness "is more reliable and has a stronger scientific basis" than whether a defendant is able to control his or her conduct.[25] Furthermore, "the concept of volition is the subject of some disagreement among psychiatrists."[26] Accordingly, testimony about volition "is more likely to produce confusion for jurors than is psychiatric testimony relevant to a defendant's appreciation or understanding."[27] In short, by limiting the scope of the defense, the result will be a higher degree of clinical accuracy.

The American Bar Association has embraced similar logic, arguing that the volitional prong of the insanity defense was too difficult to rely upon scientifically:

> Of even greater importance is the fact that our proposed test eliminates the "volitional" part of the ALI test. This is a noteworthy aspect of our proposal for it would do away with the impairment of "normal" behavioral controls. And, we submit, it is just this volitional or behavioral part of the ALI test that has brought the insanity defense under increasing attack. During the 1950's a wave of clinical optimism suggested that scientific knowledge concerning psychopathology had expanded to the extent that informed judgments could be made regarding impairment of behavioral control. That optimism was reflected in the volitional portion of the ALI test. Yet, experience confirms that there is still no accurate scientific basis for measuring one's capacity for self-control or for calibrating the impairment of such capacity. There is, in short, no objective basis for distinguishing between offenders who were undeterable and those who were merely undeterred, between the impulse that was irresistible and the

---

[24] In addition, the APA defines "mental disease" to include "only those severely abnormal mental conditions that grossly impair a person's perception or understanding of reality." The definition seems redundant.

[25] APA Statement at 14.

[26] *Id.*

[27] *Id.*

impulse not resisted, or between substantial impairment of capacity and some lesser impairment. Whatever the precise terms of the volitional test, the question is unanswerable or, at best, can be answered only by "moral (and not medical) guesses." In our opinion, to even ask the volitional question invites fabricated expert claims, undermines the equal administration of the penal law and compromises the law's deterrent effect.[28]

A contradiction is obvious here between the yearning for scientific "accuracy" and the recognition that insanity is not exclusively a scientific issue.[29] How, on the one hand, can one assert that the insanity defense involves matters of "moral faith rather than scientific fact" and then criticize the volitional test because it is unscientific and calls for "moral guesses"? Why are "medical guesses" implicitly approved?

The answer, I suggest, lies simply in another variation on the same theme, namely an inability to take the moral issues seriously because of the quest for scientific certainty. The current solution is to eliminate all cases in which the moral issue must be faced by the jury *as a moral issue*. Why, in the judgment of the American Bar Association, will the volitional test invite "fabricated expert claims"?[30] That would only be possible if the expert were permitted to give opinions on the ultimate moral issue. Similarly, the desire for "a more objective basis for evaluating the exculpatory weight of legitimate psychiatric testimony" only makes sense if that "objective basis" can serve to inform a jury whom to convict and whom to acquit—which is exactly what led to the problems in the first place. If expert opinion is excluded on the ultimate issue, these objectives are baseless.

Despite these problems, Congress enacted an insanity defense standard for the federal courts, modeled closely on these proposals, in the Insanity Defense Reform Act of 1984.* The results of this change though, will likely, more than ever, encourage clinical control over decisions to acquit or convict. Most decisions on legal insanity are not made in a trial at all. Both under federal practice and in many states, any defendant who intends to raise the defense of insanity is required to notify the court and to undergo a psychiatric examination by the government. As a practical matter, the conclusions of the appointed psychiatrist on legal responsibility determine not only whether the insanity defense is to be raised at all but what the outcome will be.

---

[28] ABA Policy at 4–5.

[29] Indeed, earlier in the text, the ABA Policy said flatly, "The basis for the insanity defense is a moral one. And questions regarding the defense are moral rather than scientific questions. The ethical foundations of the criminal law are rooted in beliefs about human rationality, determinability and free will. *These beliefs represent articles of moral faith rather than scientific fact.*" ABA Policy at 3; emphasis added.

[30] *Id.* at 5.

* Pub. L. 98–473, 18 U.S.C. § 20 (a) Federal Rules of Evidence 704 (b).

Often the only clinical evaluation is the one done by court order at government expense. If the psychiatrist concludes that a defendant is insane, the case may never go to trial or may be tried on stipulated facts for an agreed-upon disposition.[31] If he or she concludes that the person is not insane, the defense usually evaporates, for financial if not other reasons. Under the new standards for federal courts, this practice will be exacerbated, because the decision on criminal responsibility is so closely tied to generally accepted notions of clinical evaluation. And, as before, clinicians will be asked to answer moral and legal questions in psychological terms. Eventually, the same outcry against clinical control of the decision on responsibility will probably recur.

There may be another agenda here: fewer acquittals. By eliminating the control test, Congress has eliminated a large number of cases, perhaps including that of Hinckley, in which the insanity defense would be likely to succeed. But it is not clear that even this purpose would be achieved. A strong case was made, years ago, that *M'Naghten* need not be interpreted as the narrow, cognitive test that it appears to be—indeed, that all the *volitional* elements of the irresistible impulse and ALI tests could be construed as part of it.[32] If that turns out to be the case, the furor will be raised anew after the next spectacular insanity acquittal.

What is to be done? How can the moral issue regain its proper role and the clinical testimony be placed in perspective? A test for the insanity defense must be developed which, itself, discourages professional domination—not as a rule of evidence, but as a substantive rule of law. Judge David Bazelon, the author of *Durham,* has suggested that the causal question, namely the relationship between the impairment and the act, is simply the wrong question.[33] He contends that, because the question for the jury is one of *responsibility,* the standard for conviction or acquittal should address that question explicitly and exclusively and demand no inferences about cause and effect. This would end both the domination by experts and the misleading emphasis that is placed on causality. His standard is as follows: "A defendant is not responsible if at the time of his unlawful conduct his mental or emotional processes were impaired to such an extent that he cannot justly be held responsible for his act."[34] This proposal has the advantage of focusing the jury upon responsibility and virtually foreclosing clinical testimony

---

[31] A study of insanity cases in New Jersey found that of 46 acquittals, 40 involved either agreed dispositions or instances in which only one clinician testified, signifying an agreement between prosecution and defense. In only 3 cases did opposing therapists testify. A. Singer, (1978), Insanity acquittal in the seventies: Observations and empirical analysis of one jurisdiction, *Mental Disability Law Reporter 2,* 406.

[32] A. Goldstein. (1967). *The insanity defense.*

[33] *United States v. Brawner,* 471 F2d. 969, 1031 (D.C. Cir. 1972).

[34] *Id.* at 1032.

about the ultimate issue, because that issue is squarely posed as concerning justice—a matter on which mental health professionals have no expertise to testify.

Yet even Judge Bazelon's approach seems problematic. No matter how difficult it is to show, clinically or scientifically, the relationship between mental illness and criminal conduct seems grounded in ideas of causality. The foundation of an insanity defense is the idea that the defendant could not have acted otherwise, that he or she was not able to follow the laws that everyone must obey. To eschew causation altogether appears too extreme a solution (e.g., destroying a village in order to save it). Further, the test seems too open-ended. Judge Bazelon has himself written that his proposal would allow evidence of environmental, cultural, educational, economic, and hereditary factors.[35] Hence the new insanity defense could also be a defense based upon poverty, deprivation, or bad genes. That is not likely to be a socially acceptable resolution unless the idea of criminal responsibility itself is rejected.

An alternative is possible, suggested by a minority of the American Law Institute 30 years ago and all but forgotten since. It permits relevant medical evidence, preserves a causal test, and focuses the attention of a jury on the two possible grounds for acquittal: lack of understanding or lack of control. But it also realistically poses the moral question in explicitly moral terms. It provides that a person . . . "[is] not responsible for criminal conduct if at the time of such conduct as a result of mental disease or defect his capacity either to appreciate the criminality of his conduct or to conform to the requirements of law is so substantially impaired that he cannot justly be held responsible.[36] With this standard, the focus of the jury's attention would be placed on the ultimate issue, which is whether or not someone should be held responsible. Unlike all tests that have been tried in the past, this one would make it difficult (even impossible) for a psychiatrist to testify on the "ultimate" question, insofar as it is ludicrous to ask an expert whether, in his or her judgment, a person can justly be held responsible. Thus the test itself would result in a proper allocation of roles in the trial.

It has been objected that the "justly be held responsible" standard is either too vague or not a standard at all. According to this objection, asking a jury to "do justice" provides no guidance at all and leaves to the jury a decision concerning what the law is. That criticism, however, misperceives what is happening at present. Under the guise of medicine and science, an expert is being asked to answer that very question. No matter how much the answers given by therapists to questions about cause are couched in diag-

---

[35] D. Bazelon (1976). The morality of the criminal law. *Southern California Law Review 49*, 389, 396.

[36] American Law Institute *Model Penal Code* §4.01 (Alternative (a) to ¶ (1) (Tent. Draft No. 4, 1955).

nostic terms, they are themselves making the judgments that this test simply renders explicit.

This test would not solve all the problems in the administration of the insanity defense; for example, lawyers spinning theories of nonresponsibility, inconsistent verdicts, and public outcry. But these continuing difficulties would inevitably arise, simply by virtue of the immense difficulty of sorting out the guilty from the innocent, under the best of circumstances. Indeed, the generality of the latter standard is an acknowledgment that there are severe limitations to the hoped-for precision that is entailed in devising any insanity test. The ambitiousness of the insanity defense has repeatedly led to abuse and failure. Perhaps setting our sights lower would yield more acceptable results.

PART III

Competency to Stand Trial

Ralph Slovenko

6

The Developing Law on Competency to Stand Trial

The issue of an accused's competency or fitness to stand trial has become one of high visibility. As a consequence, the use of the plea is subject to greater scrutiny than ever before. It has become one of the more controversial issues in criminal law.[1]

It has frequently been alleged that the issue of competency is used for legal maneuvering by both sides in criminal trials. The plea brings "flexibility" to the administration of the criminal law. The defense may use it to lay a foundation for the introduction of mitigating circumstances or to avoid the lengthy, difficult, and usually unsuccessful trial of an insanity plea. The prosecution might raise the question to preclude any pretrial release of the accused. In either event, the demonstrated effect of raising the plea has been to delay or interrupt the trial process. Although indefinite or prolonged delay is no longer permissible, the plea continues to be used, and increasingly as a device to procure an otherwise unobtainable psychiatric examination for consideration in plea bargaining or sentencing. Thus psychiatric evaluation

---

[1] See, for example, T. S. Szasz, *Psychiatric Justice* (New York: Macmillan, 1965); D. B. Wexler, *Criminal Commitments and Dangerous Mental Patients: Legal Issues of Confinement, Treatment, and Release* (Washington, D.C.: U.S. Government Printing Office,): *Misuse of Psychiatry in the Criminal Courts: Competency to Stand Trial* (New York: Group for the Advancement of Psychiatry, 1974); C. Foote, "A Comment on Pre-Trial Commitment of Criminal Defendants," *University of Pennsylvania Law Review, 108,* 832 (1960); A. L. Halpern, "Use and Misuse of Psychiatry in Competency Examination of Criminal Defendants," *Psychiatric Annals 5,* 4 (1975); L. McGarry, "Demonstration and Research in Competency for Trial and Mental Illness: Review and Preview," *Boston University Law Review, 49,* 46 (1969); B. J. Winick, "Incompetency to Stand Trial," in J. Monahan and H. J. Steadman (eds.), *Mentally Disordered Offenders: Perspectives from Law and Social Science* (New York: Plenum Press, 1983).

© Federal Legal Publications, Inc. 157 Chambers St. New York New York, 10007, The Journal of Psychiatry & Law, Summer, 1977 Vol. V:2, pg. 165–201.

PSYCHOTHERAPY AND THE LAW
ISBN 0-8089-1780-3

remains a part of the process, and, in some jurisdictions, the raison d'être of the triability plea. It is estimated that for each defendant found not guilty by reason of insanity, at least a hundred defendants are determined to be incompetent to stand trial.[2]

Since the mid-17th century, the common law rule has been that one cannot be required to plead to an indictment or stand trial when so disordered as to be incapable of putting forth a "rational" defense. Presence of mind as well as presence of body is required at trial. Unlike a student, who may be unprepared, fast asleep, or just a body in a classroom, much more is demanded of a criminal defendant. For triability, the accused must have the ability to cooperate with counsel in his or her own defense (a communicative ability) and the ability to understand the proceedings against him or her (a cognitive ability).[3]

Virtually every court opinion nowadays on competency to stand trial quotes the standard of competency set forth in the 1960 United States Supreme Court two-paragraph per curiam opinion in *Dusky v. United States,*[4] which established the test of whether or not the defendant "has sufficient present ability to consult with his lawyer with a reasonable degree of rational understanding—and whether he has a rational as well as factual understanding of the proceedings against him."[5] To apply this legal standard adequately, according to some opinion, "the court must thoroughly acquaint itself with the defendant's mental condition."[6]

---

[2] D. L. Bacon, "Incompetency to Stand Trial: Commitment to an Inclusive Test," *Southern California Law Review, 42,* 444 (1969).

[3] Properly speaking, the test ought to be ability to understand the "accusation" rather than the "proceedings." What lay person understands legal proceedings, be they civil or criminal! In a recent study by the Fund for Modern Courts, one of the most frequent observations made by the family court monitors was that the participants did not appear to understand what was happening in court. Lawyers and judges have a "peculiar cant and jargon of their own, that no other mortal can understand," said Gulliver of the people he met in his travels. See T. Goldstein, "Lawyers Now Confuse Even the Same Aforementioned," *New York Times,* April 1, 1977, p. B-1.

[4] 362 U.S. 402 (1960).

[5] The case involved an interpretation of the federal competency statute, which provides: "Whenever after arrest and prior to the imposition of sentence or prior to the expiration of any period of probation the United States Attorney has reasonable cause to believe that a person charged with an offense against the United States may be presently insane or otherwise so mentally incompetent as to be unable to understand the proceedings against him or properly to assist in his own defense, he shall file a motion for a judicial determination of such mental competency of the accused." 18 U.S.C. § 4244 (1970).

[6] *United States v. Makris,* 535 F.2d 899, at 907 (5th Cir. 1976). See also Anno., 100 L.Ed. 412, 4 L.Ed.2d 2077, 142 A.L.R. 961, 32 A.L.R.2d 434. "Evaluative" reports, falling under the public records exception to the hearsay rule, may be used without the expert's presence at the hearing. Federal Rules of Evidence, Rule 803(*); see also 18 U.S.C. § 4245; Michigan Mental Health Code § 330.2030 (1975). Generally see, C. T. McCormick, "Can the Courts Make Wider Use of Reports of Official Investigations?" *Iowa Law Review, 42,* 363 (1957); E. R. Yates, "Evaluative Reports by Public Officials—Admissible as Official Statements?" *Texas Law Review, 30,* 112 (1951).

The test is generally considered to represent a substantive constitutional test of competency which is binding on the states. In any event, state rules regarding competency are generally consistent with the *Dusky* test. Although *Dusky* purportedly established the competency standard only for federal courts, it has been held that when a federal court reviews a habeas corpus petition filed by a state prisoner, it must assess the mental competency of that prisoner at the time of his or her trial in state court in accord with the *Dusky* test.[7] Thus it appears to be widely recognized that *Dusky* establishes a minimal constitutional standard on competency. In 1975, in *Drope v. Missouri*,[8] the Supreme Court stated that it is a violation of due process to require a person to stand trial while incompetent, but the Court once again declined to spell out the precise meaning of "incompetent." The logical inference is that, although the test of incompetency is vague, the states may not abolish the rule of incompetency to stand trial, even though such action has been recommended.[9]

Some jurisdictions have attempted, with varying success, to spell out with more particularity the test for triability. Extensive criteria, for example, have been adopted by statute in New Jersey and by court decision of the U.S. District Court for the Western District of Missouri.[10] The state of Florida by court rule adopted, slightly paraphrased, a list of 13 "qualifiable clinical criteria" for assessing competence that were formulated by the Laboratory of Community Psychiatry at Harvard University.[11] Still another list of 20 similar yet somewhat differing criteria was proposed in a Nebraska

---

[7] *Noble v. Sigler*, 351 F.2d 674 (8th Cir. 1965).

[8] 420 U.S. 170 (1975).

[9] R. Slovenko, *Psychiatry and Law* (Boston: Little, Brown, 1973) p. 92; N. Morris, *Madness and the Criminal Law* (Chicago: University of Chicago Press, 1982) p. 35; R. A. Burt and N. Morris, "A Proposal for the Abolition of the Incompetency Plea," *University of Chicago Law Review, 40,* 66 (1972); R. Slovenko, "Competency to Stand Trial: The Reality behind the Fiction," *Wake Forest Law Review, 8,* 1 (1971); R. Slovenko, "The Criminally Insane Unit," American *Criminal Law Quarterly, 7,* 96 (1969).

[10] N.J.S. 2C:4-4; *Wieter v. Settle*, 193 F. Supp. 318 (W.D. Mo. 1961). These specific criteria include: (1) That the defendant has the mental capacity to appreciate his presence in relation to time, place, and things; (2) that his elementary mental processes are such that he comprehends: (a) that he is in a court of justice charged with a criminal offense; (b) that there is a judge on the bench; (c) that there is a prosecutor present who will try to convict him of a criminal charge; (d) that he has a lawyer who will undertake to defend him against that charge; (e) that he will be expected to tell to the best of his mental ability the facts surrounding him at the time and place when the alleged violation was committed if he chooses to testify and that he understands the right not to testify; (f) that there is or may be a jury present to pass upon evidence adduced as to guilt or innocence of such charge or, that if he should chose to enter into a plea negotiations or to plead guilty, that he comprehends the consequences of a guilty plea and that he be able knowingly, intelligently, and voluntarily to waive those rights that are waived upon such entry of a guilty plea and (g) that he has the ability to participate in an adequate presentation of his defense.

[11] Laboratory of Community Psychiatry, Harvard Medical School, final report, *Competency to Stand Trial and Mental Illness* (1973); *Florida Review Criminal Proceedings, 3,* 211 (1980).

opinion.[12] Arizona has directed examining experts to file with the court reports addressing seven specific matters.[13] Professor Gerald Bennett observes that insofar as the compilation of numerous specific findings may lead to an overall picture of the defendant's mental state, such criteria can significantly aid the expert and the court in reaching a determination of competence, but insofar as each separate finding is mandated to support a finding of competence, the list becomes counterproductive, substituting particularized judgments on superficial aspects of the defendant's mental state for the more important ultimate conclusion of competence.[14] The Supreme Court, in *Dusky* and in *Drope,* established a minimum standard, understandably and necessarily imprecise, in order to permit individual judges to evaluate each case in the light of the individual defendant's level of functioning in relation to the complexity of that case.

Curious as it may seem, prosecutors raise the issue of competency more often than the defense. In most cases, the prosecutor and defendant have a joint commitment to the success of the motion. When initiated by the prosecutor, the process is often labeled "preventive detention." When raised by the defense, it is called "medical immunity" from trial. The prosecutor is allowed to raise the motion on the ground that he or she has a responsibility to seek justice and to protect society. Indeed, a defendant may not oppose an inquiry into competence. In a number of well-known cases in England in the latter part of the 19th century the prosecutor was allowed to raise the

---

[12] Chief Justice A. Krivosha of the Nebraska Supreme Court, concurring in *State v. Guatney,* 207 Neb. 501, 299 N.W.2d 538 (1980), set out the following factors for consideration in determining competency: (1) that the defendant has sufficient mental capacity to appreciate his presence in relation to time, place, and things; (2) that his elementary mental processes are such that he understands that he is in a court of law charged with a criminal offense; (3) that he realizes there is a judge on the bench; (4) that he understands that there is a prosecutor present who will try to convict him of a criminal charge; (5) that he has a lawyer who will undertake to defend him against the charge; (6) that he knows that he will be expected to tell his lawyer all he knows or remembers about the events involved in the alleged crime; (7) that he understands that there will be a jury present to pass upon evidence in determining his guilt or innocence; (8) that he has sufficient memory to relate answers to questions posed to him; (9) that he has established rapport with his lawyer; (10) that he can follow the testimony reasonably well; (11) that he has the ability to meet stresses without his rationality or judgment breaking down; (12) that he has at least minimal contact with reality; (13) that he has the minimum intelligence necessary to grasp the events taking place; (14) that he can confer coherently with some appreciation of proceedings; (15) that he can both give and receive advice from his attorneys; (16) that he can divulge facts without paranoid distress; (17) that he can decide upon a plea; (18) that he can testify, if necessary; (19) that he can make simple decisions; and (20) that he has a desire for justice rather than undeserved punishment.

[13] D. Wexler, et al., "The Administration of Psychiatric Justice: Theory and Practice in Arizona," *Arizona Law Review, 13,* 1 (1971).

[14] American Bar Association Report on Criminal Justice Mental Health Standards (1983). It may be added that the extensive criteria give the impression that what is involved is the measure of the competency of a person to be a lawyer rather than the competency of the accused to be put to trial.

issue of fitness to proceed, a practice subsequently confirmed in the United States by the Supreme Court.[15]

Indeed, according to some recent rulings, incompetency, however defined, may not be waived, even with the consent of the court. The trial judge is obliged to raise the issue sua sponte and to convene a hearing on the question at any time during proceedings when the evidence before the court raises a "bona fide doubt" as to the defendant's competence.[16] In the leading case of *Pate v. Robinson,* setting the precedent firmly, the undisputed facts were that the defendant, Robinson, had committed shocking acts of violence—killing his common-law wife and infant son. He had also attempted suicide. Given "the uncontradicted testimony of Robinson's history of pronounced irrational behavior," the Supreme Court said that the trial court could not dispense with a hearing on competency, even though the defendant appeared alert and rational at trial.[17]

Some states provide for a jury hearing on the issue, but it is not required

---

[15] See *Pate v. Robinson,* 383 U.S. 375 (1966). The same is true in some countries with regard to the not-guilty-by-reason-of-insanity plea. (Competency to stand trial relates to the accused's mental condition at the time of the hearing, whereas the insanity defense concerns the accused's mental state when he or she allegedly committed the crime.) In a recent Canadian case, defense counsel argued that the prosecution did not have the right to decide what defense should be put forward or what defense is in the best interest of the accused. The Ontario Court of Appeal rejected the proposition that "the accused has the right to choose to be found guilty and punished, even though not criminally responsible, rather than to risk detention in a psychiatric facility." The prosecution accordingly was allowed to show that the accused was insane at the time of the act. *Toronto Globe and Mail,* April 30, 1977. p. 5.

In the United States, the prosecutor may raise the incompetency but not the insanity plea. The defendant has the sole option on pleas of substance (as distinguished from procedural objections). Substantive pleas to an indictment are (1) guilty, (2) not guilty, and (3) not guilty by reason of insanity. R. Slovenko, *Handbook of Criminal Procedure and Forms* (Baton Rouge, La.: Claitor, 1967), p. 371.

[16] When the circumstances warrant, the trial court sua sponte must order a psychiatric examination on present mental illness or mental illness at the time of the commission of the offense. *United States v. Street,* 557 F.2d 574 (6th Cir. 1977).

[17] See also *People v. Chambers,* 345 N.E.2d 119 (Ill. 1976). In 18 U.S.C. § 4245, a duty is imposed on the director of Federal Prisons to raise the issue when there is probable cause to believe that the convicted person was mentally incompetent at the time of his or her trial and the issue was not raised at trial. It provides: "Whenever the Director of the Bureau of Prisons shall certify that a person convicted of an offense against the United States has been examined by the board of examiners [18 U.S.C. § 4241], and that there is probable cause to believe that such person was mentally incompetent at the time of his trial, provided the issue of mental competency was not raised and determined before or during said trial, the Attorney General shall transmit the report of the board of examiners and the certificate of the Director of the Bureau of Prisons to the clerk of the district court wherein the conviction was had. Whereupon the court shall hold a hearing to determine the mental competency of the accused in accordance with the provisions of section 4244 above, and with all the powers therein granted. In such hearing the certificate of the Director of the Bureau of Prisons shall be prima facie evidence of the facts and conclusions certified therein. If the court shall find that the accused was mentally incompetent at the time of his trial, the court shall vacate the judgment of conviction and grant a new trial."

on the theory that the question is procedural, i.e., it is not a substantive one that involves guilt or innocence. Putting the developing statutory requirements aside, no duty rests upon the court to impanel a jury on the issue, but the court must consider and determine it in a judicial manner.[18]

In the past, serious difficulties arose when, on arraignment, the accused did not plead at all, or, in the ancient legal phrase, "remained mute." As joinder of issue (*litis contestatio*) was essential, it made possible a legal maneuver by which the defendant would attempt to block the proceeding by not pleading. Prior to the 19th century this difficulty was harder to overcome, because at that time the accused was not entitled to legal representation in court if the charge was treason or felony. There was then no one to act on his behalf, and the court had no method of proceeding. When the court came to the conclusion that the accused remained obstinately mute, or "mute of malice," he was subjected to a form of judicial torture to compel him to plead. Increasingly heavier weights were placed on his chest—he was literally "pressed for his answer."

This *peine forte et dure* was abolished in England in 1772, and by an act of 1827, a plea of not guilty was entered whenever an accused person remained mute of malice. Prior to the beginning of the 19th century, it was not for the court to decide whether an accused who stood mute was mute of malice or mute by visitation of God. In this period, a jury was impaneled to try the issue. In such proceedings, witnesses were called to give evidence of the defendant's condition. If the accused was found unfit to plead, the judge would have no alternative but to order his detention.

Modern advances in medication, science, and technology might be expected to affect the status of persons otherwise deemed incompetent. An analogue might be considered. Rabbinical courts have refused conversion to deaf-mutes on the ground that according to Jewish religious law, the Halacha, "deaf-mutes are like persons not in full possession of their faculties and hence are incapable of observing the *mitzvot*," the religious commandments. The question now before religious courts in Israel is whether or not modern advances in science and technology which have helped deaf persons to hear and mutes to speak have not changed their status under the Halacha. In Judaism, "conversion is not merely a formal ritual—the proselyte must understand the basic elements of the faith and be fully cognizant of the duties he is to undertake." Therefore, rabbis in the past have always refused to convert persons who would not meet these requirements, such as the feebleminded. Throughout history it has not been possible to establish a rational communication with the deaf, so they too have been put into the category of those who should not be converted. Considering that many deaf-mutes in modern times can read lips or have mastered some degree of speech, they

---

[18] *Youtsey v. United States*, 97 F. 937 (6th Cir. 1899).

may be able to comply with Halachic strictures.[19] As a dictum in law puts it, each case must be studied on its merits.

To compare, what happens now when an accused in a criminal case cannot or will not speak, hear, or even read the charges against him or her? In the case of the apparently competent defendant, a plea of not guilty is automatically entered at arraignment, and at trial, like most defendants, he or she may rest mute on the basis of the privilege against self-incrimination. What about the allegedly incompetent defendant? Like some cases of amnesia, an illiterate deaf-mute may never meet the triability standard. That was the situation, among others, of Donald Lang, a young Chicago black—deaf, mute, illiterate—linked by circumstantial evidence to the brutal killing of a prostitute. In his book *Dummy* (which has been made into a film), Ernest Tidyman describes the background and trials of the defendant, as well as the story of the deaf lawyer who came to his defense.[20] The lawyer urged that Lang be allowed to waive his constitutional rights and his unfitness for trial, and thus be allowed to proceed with trial. The trial court refused, committing him to an institution. On appeal, however, the Illinois Supreme Court held:

> This defendant, handicapped as he is and facing an indefinite commitment because of the pending indictment against him, should be given an opportunity to obtain a trial to determine whether or not he is guilty as charged or should be released.[21]

As precedent for its decision, the Illinois court relied on an English decision, *Regina v. Roberts,*[22] which is, it may be noted, no longer the law in England. This case held that it was legally permissible to try an incompetent individual. Another basis for the Illinois decision was that, under its law at the time, Lang would be subject to an indefinite or lifetime commitment without a determination of guilt. The Illinois Supreme Court's order permitting Lang to be tried, for the crime that occurred in 1965, finally came down in 1970. By then, two key witnesses had died and a third had disappeared. The state was forced to drop the charge, and Lang was free. But within 5 months Lang was arrested again, charged with strangling to death another prostitute. Once again the evidence against Lang was strong. The day before the body was discovered, he and the victim registered at a hotel; Lang left alone. Again, police found bloodstains on his clothing. In 1972 he was tried, convicted, and sentenced to 14 to 25 years, but in 1975 the Illinois appellate court reversed that conviction on the ground that it was "constitutionally impermissible" because it was impossible during the trial to compensate for Lang's inability to communicate. The court said:

---

19 *Jewish Week-American Examiner*, February 27, 1977, p. 9.
20 E. Tidyman, *Dummy* (Boston: Little, Brown, 1974).
21 People *ex rel. Myers v. Briggs,* 46 Ill.2d 281, at 288 (1970).
22 [1953] 2 All E. R. 340.

[If] a person is handicapped to the extent that modifications in trial procedure cannot be devised, he cannot be constitutionally tried. Implicit in this finding is that if special trial procedures can be devised to compensate for a defendant's handicap, a trial can be held consistent with due process.[23]

After another hearing Lang was declared unfit to stand trial, and again was sent to a mental institution. Under the criminal law on triability, as now limited, Lang could not be held indefinitely; and under the mental health law on civil commitment, he could not be confined. He was not "mentally ill"; he had nothing to treat and would not benefit from treatment. The Chicago public was outraged, and in fear. Chicago newspapers carried editorials on the "gaping void where the criminal code and the mental health statutes fail to meet."[24]

In late 1976, on the basis of testimony from doctors and therapists who observed the accused murderer over a 7-month period, Cook County Circuit Judge Joseph Schneider found that although the defendant had "manifested dangerous behavior," he had at least an average intelligence and was not insane. Furthermore, for the first time since his initial arrest in 1965, Lang seemed ready to learn sign language, quickly picking up basic symbols for words like *eat, cigarette, sad* and *happy.* Sign language experts, however, stated that it could take Lang as long as 5 years to master the abstract concepts necessary to stand trial. To that end, Judge Schneider ordered the Department of Mental Health to come up with a special education program for Lang.[25]

What intensity of effort, what expenditure of funds, and what level of patience is required to "shape people up" for trial? There is the case of the individual who from early childhood carried the nickname "non compos mentis" (NCM for short). He was given that name by his peers, though psychiatrically he may not have been labeled mentally ill. He was, literally speaking, a person of few words. For some psychological reason, he either did not wish to or could not speak. He would, however, grunt when sufficiently enraged. (He was like the mute swan—a swan capable of producing a trumpeting sound but mostly silent, only hissing when alarmed or angered.) Even as a child, he had been extremely violent. He was known to attack with little or no provocation. When criminally charged, he refused to cooperate with counsel and was committed as incompetent to stand trial. The institu-

---

[23] *People v. Lang,* 26 Ill. App.3d 648, at 699 (1975). In another unusual case in Cook County, the defendant was a deaf-mute, and the victim and most of the state witnesses were also deaf-mutes. No fewer than three interpreters trained in deaf-mute sign language were used at all times. In such cases it is necessary to have jurors with more than the usual amount of patience. C. Mount, "Attorneys Prepare 'Silent' Rape Trial," *Chicago Tribune,* May 30, 1977, p. 5.

[24] See, for example, *Chicago Daily News,* November 12, 1976, p. 12.

[25] *Time,* January 17, 1977, p. 74.

tion tried to "shape him up" for trial. It took many months of concentrated effort before he managed to say his first words, "Mother, F - - - - -."[26]

In 1972, in the much discussed case of *Jackson v. Indiana*,[27] the United States Supreme Court set out a durational limit for the length of confinement for pretrial commitment for incompetency to stand trial, though it did not

---

[26] See M. Rabinowitz, *The Day They Scrambled My Brains at the Funny Factory* (New York: Scorpio, 1977), p. 98. In the Brothers Grimm's fairy tale "The Three Languages," an old count had an only son who was stupid and was unable to learn anything. So the father said, "Listen, my son, I can't get anything into your head, as hard as I try. You've got to get away from here. I'll turn you over to a famous master; he shall have a try with you." The son studied with this master for a year. When he returned, the father was disgusted to find that all his son had learned was "what the dogs bark." Sent out for another year of study with a different master, the son returned to tell that he had learned "what the birds speak." Angry that his son had again wasted his time, the father threatened, "I'll send you to a third master, but if again you learn nothing, I shall no longer be your father." When the year was over, what the son had learned was "what the frogs croak." Furious, the father cast out his son, ordering his servants to take him into the forest and do away with him. The servants though had pity on him and simply left him in the forest. B. Bettelheim, *The Uses of Enchantment: The Meaning and Importance of Fairy Tales* (New York: Random House, 1975), p. 97.

Then there is the individual who for "religious" reasons refuses to talk with an attorney or examiner. In one case the accused made it clear that the reason he could not communicate or cooperate with the attorney or examiners more adequately was because they refused to inform him of their religious backgrounds and affiliations so that they would know the "holy" position from which he was attempting to address them. He indicated that he needed "Jesus' permission" to talk with them, and that he could not obtain this permission without their willingness to inform him of their own religious backgrounds. He also made it clear that if their questions were "human questions," he also could not cooperate as he was only able to answer "holy questions." Moreover, he did not see the need for an attorney as his "lawyer is inside my heart." Any efforts at talking with him about pleas and dispositions had him constantly translating the word "guilty" to "healthy." The examiners concluded that the accused, because of the poor quality of his responses, did not have the ability to cooperate with counsel. Report of February 22, 1977, of Courts Diagnostic Clinic, Hartford, Conn., Szasz argues that coerced personality change, by medication or other procedures, affects religious belief or conduct, and thus conflicts with the First Amendment guarantee of freedom of religion. T. S. Szasz, *Psychiatric Slavery* (New York: Free Press, 1977), p. 111. Compare S. I. Shuman, *Psychosurgery and the Medical Control of Violence* (Detroit: Wayne University Press, 1977), chap. 6 (psychosurgery and freedom of thought).

And then there is the case of the individual who is able to communicate and cooperate with counsel and understands the proceedings against him but has a tendency to go "off the track" into irrelevancies. In one case of this sort, the evaluation report to the court stated: "In the course of his digressions, it became evident that the accused is delusional, a fact which we mention because of the possibility of its becoming disconcerting in the courtroom. His delusions, for example, involve the idea that he is being stimulated sexually by people a great distance from him, of others "drawing out" energy and goodness from his body while he sleeps, and of people using their minds to irritate his skin. He also claims to have a relationship and engage in telepathic communication with Susan Ford (the [former] President's daughter). [But] the accused's disturbance does not impinge upon his ability to stand trial. He was quite capable of bringing his attention to bear on the questions we were asking, and responded in a way which demonstrated that he is aware of his current legal situation, and has a totally adequate under-specify an exact time limit. Prior to this decision, the pretrial commitment procedure was widely used as a method for final disposition of a defendant's case. Commitment for incompetency was tantamount to confinement for life, especially when the accused was permanently retarded. In this case, Theon Jackson, a 27-year-old mentally defective deaf-mute who could not read, write, or communicate intelligently, had been charged in 1968 with robberies of two women. The case in many ways paralleled that of Donald Lang. The testimony at the competency hearing indicated that Jackson's condition precluded his comprehension of the nature of the charges against him or his effective participation in his own defense. The prognosis was "dim" that he would ever develop the necessary communicative skills. Nevertheless, following the usual practice, the state court, finding Jackson incompetent, ordered him committed until such time as he could be certified by the health department as "sane" and possessing "comprehension sufficient to understand the proceedings and make his defense."

The Supreme Court ruled that such prolonged commitment violates the due process clause of the 14th Amendment. It stated that a person committed on account of incapacity to proceed to trial cannot be held more than the "reasonable period of time necessary to determine whether there is a substantial probability that he will attain that capacity in the foreseeable future." The Court further stated:

> If it is determined that this is not the case, then the State must either institute the customary civil commitment proceeding that would be required to commit indefinitely any other citizen or release the defendant. Furthermore, even if it is determined that the defendant probably soon will be able to stand trial, his continued commitment must be justified by progress toward that goal.[28]

In oft-quoted language, the Court said, "At the least, due process requires that the nature and duration of commitment bear some reasonable relation to the purpose for which the individual is committed."[29] Inasmuch as Jackson was committed because he was incompetent to stand trial, the Court concluded that the purpose of such commitment must be to make the defendant competent. The Court in *Jackson* did not address the issue of the disposition of the criminal charge in the case of one for whom restoration of competency was not a foreseeable possibility. It stated only that if such a defendant was to be further confined, the confinement would

---

standing of legal issues and procedures, courtroom protocol, the differential roles of the main actors in the courtroom (judge, prosecutor, defense attorney), the facts relevant to his case, and the possible pleas, dispositions and penalties should he be found guilty." Report of October 8, 1976, of Courts Diagnostic Clinic, Hartford, Conn.

[27] 406 U.S. 715 (1972).

[28] 406 U.S., at 738.

[29] 406 U.S., at 738 See also *McNeil v. Director,* 407 U.S. 245 (1972).

have to be based on the criteria for civil commitment applicable in that jurisdiction.[30]

Following the *Jackson* decision, various states either by judicial decision or legislation have limited the term of commitment to either a "reasonable period"; or a term of 12, 15, or 18 months; or not to exceed a maximum sentence for the offense charged.[31] Some say that having a maximum period encourages malingering, since with the passage of time the situation usually cools and witnesses may disappear or forget. It is to be noted, however, that the *Jackson* limitation on the length of confinement is not faithfully followed in all places. Decisions of the High Court are not self-executing. There is no one to seek out the inmate and represent him or her. Not infrequently, no one wants the inmate out on the streets, including the inmate. Unlike the case of physical disability, the mentally disabled defendant is not as a matter of prevailing practice released on bail or on recognizance while awaiting trial.[32]

How is evidence to be preserved for the actual trial of the case? As illustrated by the first Lang trial in Illinois, one of the problems facing prosecutors is that a case may become stale during the treatment period. Witnesses may die or leave the jurisdiction. Memories of the witnesses to the event fade or become confused. To resolve this problem, the Illinois code provides for a hearing to be held within one year of the date of the original incompetency finding. The transcripts of the testimony taken at that hearing may be used to refresh the memory of witnesses who are still available. If a

---

[30] 406 U.S., at 738.

[31] See J. J. Gobert, "Competency to Stand Trial: A Pre- and Post-Jackson Analysis," *Tennessee Law Review, 40,* 659 (1973). Connecticut now has an 18-month limit (the Connecticut statute states that the "maximum shall not exceed the longer of eighteen months or the maximum period to which the accused may have been sentenced," Connecticut Public Act. No. 76-353, 1976), but in practice the minimum of these two periods is apparently used as the maximum). Florida has a 1-year period. (The Florida Bar, 343 So.2d 1247 Fla., 1977). Michigan in 1975 amended its law to limit confinement to 15 months or one-third of the maximum sentence, whichever is lesser. (Michigan Mental Health Code § 330.2034, 1975). Michigan settled on a 15-month period, amending the 18-month limitation that it had just recently enacted, apparently on the theory that 15 months is the average time of imprisonment. Michigan, a state of approximately 9 million population, one year had 1,200 triability pleas, a 5 percent increase over the previous year. As around the country, motions for a competency hearing are almost uniformly granted by the court, but fewer than 10 percent are now found incompetent on examination and hearing.

[32] A number of states now provide for release on bail or on recognizance during the period of examination. (Connecticut Public Act No. 76-353 (1976); *Report of the Governor's Commission for Revision of the Mental Health Code of Illinois,* 1976, p. 178.) The statue of limitations on the criminal charge is stayed during the period of incompetency on the theory that the prosecutor is unable to move the case. (Art. 579, Louisiana Code of Criminal Proceedings.) Legislation sometimes specifically provides that time spent in custody shall be credited against any sentence imposed on the defendant in the pending criminal case or in any other case arising from the same transaction. Michigan Compiled Laws Annotated § 330.2042 (1975).

witness is legally unavailable at the time of trial, the transcript of his or her testimony may be introduced as evidence under the "previously recorded testimony" exception to the rule against hearsay.[33]

Some states provide that an incompetent defendant, through his or her counsel, may first test the merits of the state's case, thus limiting the right of the prosecutor to manipulate the issue. Most semiliterates make good witnesses; jurors believe that they are too stupid to lie convincingly. The Model Penal Code of the American Law Institute suggested adoption of a provision whereby: "The fact that the defendant is unfit to proceed does not preclude any legal objection to the prosecution which is susceptible of fair determination prior to trial and without the personal participation of the defendant."[34] In *Jackson*, the Supreme Court stated:

> Both courts and commentators have noted the desirability of permitting some proceedings to go forward despite the defendant's incompetency. . . . We do not read this Court's previous decisions to preclude the States from allowing, at a minimum, an incompetent defendant to raise certain defenses such as insufficiency of the indictment, or make certain pretrial motions through counsel.[35]

In an 1876 English case, *Regina v. Berry*,[36] it was decided that defense counsel could choose to address the general question of the accused's guilt without abandoning the right to fall back upon the question of unfitness to plead. In this particular case, the jury decided that the accused was guilty but that he was incapable of understanding the nature of the proceedings, so he was detained under the Criminal Lunatics Act of 1800.[37] In this country, Justice Warren Burger, speaking for a unanimous court in *Drope v. Missouri*,[38] said that "a procedure [deferring a competency evaluation until after trial had been completed] may have advantages, at least where the defendant is present at the trial and the appropriate inquiry is implemented with dispatch."[39] That observation is taken to indicate approval of provisional trials of incompetent defendants. Illinois has an "innocent only" trial, called a

---

[33] *Report of the Governor's Commission for Revision of the Mental Health Code of Illinois* (1976), p. 186.

[34] *Model Penal Code* §4.06 (Proposed Official Draft, 1962).

[35] 406 U.S., at 740-41.

[36] 1 Q.B.D. 447 (1876).

[37] See "The Accused Retardate," *Columbia Human Rights Law Review, 4,* 239, 242 (1972).

[38] 420 U.S., at 182.

[39] Reserving decision on a defendant's competence until the trial is completed is said to have particular advantage when the defendant waives counsel, represents himself, and bungles his defense. B. J. Ennis and C. Hansen, "Memorandum of Law: Competency to Stand Trial," *Journal of Psychiatry & Law, 4,* 491, at 509 (1976). A defendant may represent himself without the assistance of counsel ["Fools in Court," *Time,* May 9, 1977, p. 44], provided the trial court first determines, after inquiry, that the waiver of counsel is "intelligent and competent." *Johnson v. Zerbst,* 304 U.S. 458, 465 (1938).

discharge hearing, which provides for a full trial at which the defendant may not be convicted but only acquitted.[40] This form of dispositional hearing has been criticized on the grounds that it can involve duplication of expense and effort if the defendant is not acquitted and has to be retried.

The Supreme Court in *Jackson* also compared Indiana's procedures for indeterminate commitment of incompetent defendants with its procedures for commitment of the feebleminded and for involuntary civil commitment, and found these standards substantially different. The Court thus held that subjecting a defendant who is mentally incompetent to stand trial "to a more lenient commitment standard and to a more stringent standard of release than those generally applicable to all others not charged with offenses [denies him] equal protection of the laws under the Fourteenth Amendment."[41] Thus mandatory commitment of those found incompetent to stand trial or those found not guilty by reason of insanity has been supplanted by the requirements of civil commitment procedures and criteria.[42]

Hearing and speech defects and illiteracy do not constitute mental illness, however, and they are thus not grounds for commitment under civil commitment statutes. Moreover, in a civil commitment, the hospital has control over discharge, and the courts are concerned about the discharge of certain individuals. The triability issue, before it became one of high visibility, did not literally mean what it said. The court, in calling on a psychotherapist for an opinion, did not really want to know whether or not the accused was capable of standing trial. The court itself could decide that issue by a few simple questions. The judge really wanted to know whether the accused was likely to be dangerous or unduly bothersome in the community. In other words, labeling a person "incompetent to stand trial" signified that he or she was either dangerous or a nuisance and should be confined. That was then and remains to some extent today the hidden agenda. The consequence of a decision is often the unarticulated major premise of the decision. Sir Thomas More poked fun at his fellow lawyers, calling them "people whose profession is to disguise matters."

Saying one thing but meaning another was clearly demonstrated by the difficulties formerly encountered by the superintendent of the criminally insane unit who certified to the court that a defendant was "competent to stand trial" under a literal interpretation of the test though he was still being maintained on medication.[43] Just as an athlete may not use drugs to improve

---

[40] D. Paull, "S. B. 133: The Near Resolution of a Major Problem: Fitness in the Criminal Law," *Chicago-Kent Law Review, 56,* 1107 (1980).

[41] 406 U.S., at 730.

[42] See *People v. McQuillan,* 392 Mich. 511, 211 N.W.2d 569 (1974); *Matter of Torsney,* 47 N.Y.2d 667, 394 N.E.2d 262, 420 N.Y.2d 192 (1978); *People v. Escobar,* 90 A.D.2d 322, 456 N.Y.S.2d 766 (1st Dept. 1982).

[43] For a literal study of competency to stand trial, see A. Robey, "Criteria for Competency to Stand Trial: A Checklist for Psychiatrists," *American Journal of Psychiatry, 122,* 616 (1965).

performance, an accused had to come to trial *au naturel*. Refusal to accept a defendant for trial who is only "synthetically competent" strikingly indicates that the judge is concerned not with the defendant's capacity to undergo trial but with his or her ability to get along in the community without medication. In these cases the judge is concerned that the accused, an individual who has already shown himself or herself—albeit allegedly—to be troublesome to the community, may not continue pharmacological treatment in the event of release and may again become a threat to society.

The competency rulings based on the use of psychotropic medication not only have been inconsistent, they have also been one-sided. Although it was usually held that a defendant had to be in a natural state when competency was raised by the prosecutor or the judge, a plea by the defendant that he or she should not be put to trial when on medication has been rarely successful. In some cases defendants have contended that they have an absolute right not to be tried while under medication. For example, in certain cases tranquilizing drugs may be necessary to control a defendant's disruptive behavior during trial. Some defendants seeking trial immunity have argued for a "right to appear in court with mental faculties unfettered." In allowing the defendant to be tried, one court justified its decision in this way:

> There is no evidence that [tranquilizing drugs such as Thorazine] affected defendant's thought processes or the contents of defendant's thoughts; the affirmative evidence is that Thorazine allows the cognitive part of the brain to come back into play. The expert witnesses declined to call Thorazine a mind altering drug. "Rather, Thorazine allows the mind to operate as it might were there not some organic or other type of illness affecting the mind."[44]

Another problem is presented if one supposes the accused, though able to cooperate with counsel and understand the proceedings against him or her, alleges that the stress of trial or the televising of the trial will cause a physical or mental breakdown. In other words, the accused is claiming that he or she is not strong or fit enough for trial. In common law, the issue of incompetency could be raised not only as a bar to arraignment but also to trial, judgment, or execution. In Hale, it is said:

> If a man in his sound memory commits a capital offense, and before his arraignment he becomes absolutely mad, he ought not by law to be arraigned during such frenzy, but be remitted to prison until that incapacity be removed. The reason is, because he cannot advisedly plead to the indictment. . . . And if such person after his plea, and before his trial, become of nonsane memory, he shall not be tried; or, if, after his trial, he becomes of nonsane memory, he shall

---

[44] *State v. Jojola*, 553 P.2d 1296, 1299 (N.M. 1976). See A. Brooks, "The Constitutional Right to Refuse Antipsychotic Medications," *Bulletin American Academy Psychotherapy & Law, 8,* 179 (1980); B. Winick, "Restructuring Competency to Stand Trial," University of California at Los Angeles Law Review, 32:922–985 (1985). *Am. Bar Foundation Res. J.* 769 (1977).

not receive judgment, or, if after judgment he becomes of nonsane memory, his execution shall be spared; for were he of sound memory, he might allege somewhat in stay of judgment or execution.[45]

It is to be recalled that at this time in history there were many capital offenses, some 170 in number. The incompetency plea was allowed at any stage of the proceedings to undercut the penalty.[46]

Contemporary defendants or witnesses may feel that a trial is just as harrowing an ordeal as the ancient ordeal by battle, though their feelings often change when they are relegated to prison to wait out their incapacity. In various ways a witness or the accused who chooses to testify at trial is placed under stress: it is believed that stress aids in the ascertainment of truth, be the witness shy or bold. The idea that a witness "breaks" under heavy pressure or skillful cross-examination and finally tells the truth is depicted in countless tales, of which *Mutiny on the Bounty* is a particularly memorable example. At one time in the United States, and still the practice in most other countries, the accused or witness had to stand up while testifying (hence the term "witness stand"). The occasional physical strain of prolonged standing increased the anxiety. And, of course, he or she may be subjected to a vigorous cross-examination—"one of the principal and most efficacious tests which the law has devised for the discovery of truth."[47] Apparently, polite cross-questioning of one seated in a comfortable sofa is not considered effective except for minors and idiots. The chapter titles in one book on cross-examination are illustrative of the practice: "Break Your Witness," "Step by Step Attack," "Witness on the Run," "The Kill," "Shock Treatment."[48]

Direct examination of the accused or witness is often gentle (the attorney and witness are fellow travelers), but the adversary must probe to get at the facts. To accomplish this, the adversary has the right to lead a witness, with his or her questions, and to rip the witness apart if possible. Suppose a

---

[45] Hale, 1 *Historia Placitorum Coronae* 34, 35 (1736). To the same effect are all the common law authorities. See *Youtsey v. United States,* 97 F. 937, 940 (6th Cir. 1899); see also *Hayes v. Florida,* 343 So.2d 672 (Fla. 1977) (issue of probationer's competency to stand trial in probation revocation proceeding). Michigan's "guilty but mentally ill" statute has been challenged because, in practice, it provides not treatment but punishment of the insane. It was designed to fill the gap left by limitations on the incompetency and insanity pleas. *Detroit Free Press,* May 12, 1977, p. 3.

[46] R. Slovenko, *Psychiatry and Law* (Boston: Little, Brown, 1973), chap. 7 (competency to be executed). In Hungary, a convicted man on his way to the gallows smiled amiably and stroked his neck, but he collapsed at the sight of the ladder. Two minutes before the sentence could be carried out, he died of heart failure. G. Konrad, *The Case Worker* (New York: Harcourt Brace Jovanovich, 1974), p. 6.

[47] Wigmore, the leading commentator on the law of evidence, also said: "Cross examination is the greatest engine for getting at the truth," J. Wigmore, *Evidence* (Boston: Little, Brown, 3d ed. 1940), vol. 6, § 1885.

[48] *Trial Diplomacy* (Chicago: Court Practice Institute) (n.d.).

witness, suffering from profound shock, is able only to blink, thus identifying the assailant? Is the right to cross-examine a witness effectively denied
because of the witness' poor condition? A direct examination may be accomplished by one question (e.g., "Did he shoot you?"), but on cross-examination the evidence may have to be dragged out of the witness. There are
numerous cases in which the lack of opportunity for cross- examination has
resulted in the striking of the direct examination.[49] On the other hand, there
is authority to the effect that if a witness dies or becomes incapacitated prior
to cross-examination under circumstances wherein no responsibility can be
attributed to either the direct examiner or the witness, the evidence given
before the witness became incapable is allowed to stand.[50]

When is an accused or witness able for trial? It becomes the type of
sensitive question faced by many parents in deciding whether to push their
child another step or to wait. At the wrong time, the ordeal will upset one's
equilibrium. Given a particular stress, of whatever kind, anyone can break
down. Can a given person's stress threshold be measured? Are stress and its
effect predictable? That is, are the parameters known and fixed? In the case
of the criminal defendant, is it the accusation, the pretrial wait, the trial, the
decision, the sentence, or the lawyer's fee that will prove overwhelming?
Will it make a difference whether the accused will take the stand to testify on
his or her own behalf?

In attempting to deal with these questions, it may be helpful to consider
the New Orleans case of Nick Karno, a 65-year-old nightclub operator in-
dicted by the grand jury for the murder of a former employee. He was
granted numerous continuances because of his poor health; he suffered from
gout, anemia mellitus, and angina pectoris. For this reason the case remained dormant for nearly 3 years, until again, apparently prompted by
newspaper publicity, the district attorney's office compelled Karno to show
cause why he should not stand trial.[51] At the hearing both state and defense
physicians testified that Karno could not stand the stress of a trial which
"might cause" him to suffer a heart attack. Because Karno was suffering
angina pectoris (chest pains) and had only recently been discharged from a
hospital, the trial judge ruled that he could not be brought to trial. The

---

[49] For example, in *People v. Cole,* 43 N.Y. 408 (1871), the witness at the close of her direct
examination was stricken with fainting fits and convulsions and could not be cross-examined.
The trial court was reversed for its refusal to strike the testimony given on direct examination.
See also *Kemble v. Lyons,* 184 Iowa 882, 169 N.W. 117 (1918).

[50] *Kubin v. Chicago Title & Trust Co.,* 307 Ill. App. 12, 29 N.E.2d 859 (1940); J. Wigmore,
Evidence (Boston: Little, Brown, 3d ed. 1940), vol. 5, § 1390.

[51] In the case of Meyer Lansky, reputed financial wizard of organized crime, the court
dismissed the 4-year-old indictment because Lansky, 77, suffering from a heart ailment, diabe-
tes, and ulcers, would "never be well enough to stand trial," UPI news release, October 2,
1976. See also M. Schumach, "Queens Urges Court to Try Heart Patient," *New York Times,*
May 3, 1977, p. 41.

question thus became, Do people with a heart condition or other disability have a license to commit crime?

The district attorney took writs to the Louisiana Supreme Court asking it to establish guidelines so that Karno could be brought to trial. The district attorney contended that Karno's heart condition would not get any better, noting that the doctors all agreed that his condition would only worsen with time.[52] The Louisiana Supreme Court ruled in a rather summary manner that the "lifestyle and activities" of the accused should be considered in determining whether he was able to stand trial. The ruling also said a continuance might be avoided if steps were taken, such as shortening the trial day and having medical aid available.[53]

Thereupon, the district attorney called in an out-of-state psychiatrist who had conducted research on "life changes and illness onset," a field of study that tries to determine from a person's lifestyle how much stress he or she will suffer from a certain experience and how to mitigate the effect.[54] To the dismay of many, the psychiatrist was asked to evaluate Karno's stress scale and the amount of stress he would suffer if he stood trial. In a press interview, the district attorney commented, "If we can possibly evaluate Karno's stress scale, then we can see how we can mitigate the life change and mitigate the illness." He further observed:

> In any change in our life, there is a certain amount of stress. Divorce, marriage, watching your dog die, all cause stress. Of course, that's just a general

---

[52] In *Youtsey v. United States,* 97 F. 937 (6th Cir. 1899), the accused was a confirmed epileptic and his counsel and medical advisers apprehended that the excitement and strain of a prolonged trial might induce another epileptic attack. The application did not show any present inability to attend the trial and promised no hope that any future trial would be attended by any less risk to the health or life of the accused. Under such circumstances, the court ruled, the trial could proceed.

[53] W. Philbin, "Is Karno Fit to Stand Trial?" *States-Item* (New Orleans), March 24, 1977, p. D-3. Can one be competent to serve as governor yet be unfit for trial? This question was presented in the political corruption trial of Governor Marvin Mandel of Maryland and five associates. Five neurologists testified that Governor Mandel was suffering from a circulatory problem in his brain. The trial was postponed. The prosecution, objecting, asked, "If the Governor can continue to exercise his duties of Governor, why can't he sit in the courtroom in a passive role?" *New York Times,* April 14, 1977, p. 16.

[54] To recall, Judge John Sirica ordered a panel of independent medical experts to examine former President Richard Nixon to see if he was fit enough to participate in the Watergate coverup trial of five former aides. (News release, November 8, 1974.) One cartoon depicted President Nixon's physician stating, "He's coming along nicely unless you want him to testify, in which case he's dead." In another high profile case, Patty Hearst was declared fit for trial, physical and neurological examinations showing that she has "no significant debilitating physical or neurological disorders." A dire psychiatric report, however, claimed that she was too fragile to be put to trial. She was portrayed as a pathetic, crushed, battered child. She survived the trial. Then the question became whether she could survive imprisonment. L. Fosburgh, "Patty Today," *New York Times Magazine,* April 3, 1977, p. 19: *Daily News* (New York). November 8, 1975, p. 1.

analogy. Karno may be a person who takes on more stress just waiting for a situation (the trial). He could even be like an actor who throws up every night before going on stage.[55]

Following nearly 5 hours on the witness stand, the psychiatrist was qualified as an expert in the field of "life-change (stress) analysis," and Karno was ordered to submit to a 3-hour examination at his home. During the qualification hearing, the psychiatrist testified that, after administering a series of questions amounting to a test of Karno's lifestyle and ability to deal with stress, he should be able to give an evaluation as to how sitting through a murder trial would affect Karno. During the hearing Karno's attorney asked the psychiatrist to administer the test (consisting of 42 questions about changes in lifestyle) to him from the witness stand. The attorney said he would answer as if he were Karno. During the "run-through" the attorney-as-Karno explained that the defendant's life had been falling apart in almost all areas following the incident. The psychiatrist concluded, however, following the hypothetical examination, that Karno suffered "less risk of falling seriously ill now" than he did 2 years ago. "He has entered into a stable period . . . and is probably in pretty good shape." "I would not predict a heart attack or death on the horizon for Mr. Karno," the psychiatrist said. The doctor testified that by using the same test he had in the past been able accurately to predict who would fall ill on an aircraft carrier cruise and what players on a football team would be injured in a particular season.[56]

Earlier in the hearing, Karno's attorney noted that several doctors had speculated that a trial might cause another heart attack. "Only one man can testify to that," said the trial judge, pointing to the heavens. "And I can't subpoena Him."[57] A few days before the scheduled testing, Karno (now age 68) suffered another heart attack.[58] Was he frightened by the psychiatric examination? In general, is waiting for trial more stressful than the trial itself? It could be that the answer lies only in the stars. The judge signed another continuance in the case, putting the matter off indefinitely.

Medication may alleviate anxiety, as we all know. In Michigan, there is no bar to the use of medication provided there is a statement from the treating physician that medication "will not adversely affect the defendant's understanding of the proceedings or his ability to assist in his defense."[59]

---

[55] P. DeGruy, "Karno Stress Study Set," *Times-Picayune* (New Orleans), March 23, 1977, p. 4.

[56] J. D. Murphy, "Karno To Face Psychiatrist," *Times-Picayune,* April 20, 1977.

[57] *Supra.*

[58] "Karno Trial Again Delayed," *Times-Picayune,* May 26, 1977.

[59] Michigan Compiled Laws Annotated §330.2020(2) (Supp. 1976). There is a fundamental difference between involuntary hospitalization for treatment of mental illness under civil commitment and commitment of a criminal defendant for treatment to restore competence to stand trial. The function of the former is to provide a benefit to the patient—to restore the patient to health and to a productive life; the function of the latter is to permit the state to try a criminal

But as previously noted, a number of cases are reported in which the defendant urged a right not to be tried while under medication. A defendant may claim that medication will make him or her appear glassy-eyed or drugged and that appearance would prejudice him or her in the eyes of the jury. Another claim is that courtroom demeanor may be relevant to the theory of defense. Demeanor is affected by medication. Professor B. J. George says that medication may be barred as a matter of procedural due process if it will impede an adequate presentation of the legal insanity defense by concealing, for example assaultive tendencies of an untranquilized defendant.[60] Assuming that a due process issue exists, the courts though tend to respond that due process is not violated when a defendant is given an opportunity to inform the jury as to the fact of medication and its effect upon the defendant.

> The defense can introduce any prior unusual behavior of the defendant as evidence at the trial and, in addition, can introduce at trial as evidence the fact that he is using Thorazine and the effect that the drug medication has on the defendant by expert testimony.[61]

Likewise a claim made by a defendant of general inability to reconstruct the events of the period in question (when the claim is opposed by the state) has generally been held insufficient to establish denial of due process. A general claim of being unable to remember events for the period in question is insufficient, the courts say, because if such a claim had to be accepted, almost every defendant could successfully assert such a defense.[62] In the

---

defendant. Its benefit is primarily to the system, incidentally to the defendant, hence the right to refuse treatment doctrine that prevails in civil commitment is inapplicable in commitment to provide triability.

   [60] "Due process can be denied by . . . producing such a calming effect on a defendant that he or she cannot through conduct or mode of testifying demonstrate to a jury the irrationality or lack of control under pressure important to establish the insanity defense." B. J. George, "Emerging Constitutional Rights of the Mentally-Ill," *National Journal of Criminal Defense, 2,* 35, at 38 (1976). To quote Dr. Emanuel Tanay, then chairman of the Committee on Psychiatry and Law of the American Psychiatric Association: "It can be reasonably concluded that the presence of psychosis is not a handicap but an asset where the only defense is insanity. If the defense was that Mr. Berkowitz did not commit the acts which gave rise to the charges, his mental illness could interfere with his ability to help his lawyer to prove his claim. In the case of 'Son of Sam,' the only available defense is that at the time of the commission of these acts he suffered mental illness and therefore should not be held legally responsible for the crimes he committed. The presence of mental illness at the time of the trial might help his lawyer to establish this particular claim in court." E. Tanay *New York Times* [Letter], September 14, 1977, p. 32.
   [61] *State v. Jojola,* 553 P.2d 1296, 1300 (N.M. 1976).
   [62] *State v. Crump,* 82 N.M. 487, 484 P.2d 329 (1971): *United States v. Atkins,* 487 F.2d 257 (8th Cir. 1973). In an Arizona case involving a charge of murder, the prosecution's evidence indicated that approximately 5 hours after the defendant had purchased a rifle while on a trip with his ex-wife, he was found on the ground outside his car, suffering from an apparently self-inflicted head wound, and she was found inside the car, dead from a single bullet. At a hearing to determine triability, the trial court found he was sane, rational, and competent in all respects

film, *Silver Streak,* Gene Wilder says at one point that he always loses his memory when he falls in love.[63] Less frivolous but more credible excuses are not difficult to imagine. Furthermore, there are other problems, such as a catatonic who is unable to communicate an alibi to counsel.

One application for a continuance by counsel for a defendant, supported by affidavits of reputable physicians, alleged that the defendant was suffering from the effects of epileptic seizures and that the attacks had so impaired his mind and memory that he fell below the standard of triability.[64] Like almost every psychological disability, there are two types of amnesia— organic and functional, and a "gray area" in which the organic and functional seem to overlap. Narcosynthesis may facilitate some incomplete memory return in only about 30 percent of hysterical amnesias, and is virtually useless in organic cases. Except for hysterical amnesias and fugue states, emotional stress can also interfere with memory. And who is not frightened, who does not feel overwhelmed, by a criminal trial? As a paradigm of everyman, Joseph K. in Franz Kafka's *Trial* "stands terrified before the court. Incapable of understanding what law he has violated or the

---

except that he had amnesia and could not recall the facts and circumstances immediately surrounding the alleged crime. It was also found that he understood the nature of the charges against him. The trial court then certified for determination by the state supreme court the question of the defendant's competence to stand trial. The Arizona Supreme Court held that, although it is a reproach to justice to try a man suffering from amnesia of an uncertain type and extent when it appears that reasonable continuance of the trial may provide the time needed to effectuate a limited or full recovery from the amnesic state, especially when the amnesia blots out the facts of the crime alleged, this particular defendant was competent to stand trial without violating his right to due process. The court emphasized that each case concerning amnesia must be considered on its own merits and that no absolutes may be justified without investigation. *State v. McClendon,* 103 Ariz. 105, 437 P.2d 421 (1968). See *Anno.,* 46 A.L.R.2d 544 (amnesia as affecting capacity to commit crime or stand trial). Generally, courts give little weight to amnesia in support of an incompetency plea when they want to put the defendant on trial. A. L. Halpern, "Use and Misuse of Psychiatry in Competency Examination of Criminal Defendants," *Psychiatric Annals, 5,* 4 (1975). The D.C. Circuit in *Wilson v. United States,* 391 F.2d 460 (D.C. Cir. 1968), outlined in some detail the mechanism of post facto review of fairness. The court suggested that the trial judge should, before imposing sentence, make detailed findings, after taking any additional evidence deemed necessary concerning the effect of the amnesia on the fairness of the trial. The practical objection to the procedure outlined in *Wilson* is based on the possibility that a lengthy trial, carried to a verdict, would be a nullity. Nonetheless, the procedure provides a mechanism to test the prosecution's case and thereby determine the strength of the evidence on which the criminal charges and the consequent continued pendency of the criminal action are based.

[63] "[Amnesia] is nothing more than a failure of memory concerning facts or events to which an individual has been exposed. Every individual's memory process is marked by some distortion which may occur at any point. . . . As a result, no one's memory is in fact complete, even under ideal conditions . . . every one is amnesic to some degree." "Amnesia: A Case Study in the Limits of Particular Justice," *Yale Law Journal, 71,* 109 (1961). See also D. Koson and A. Robey, "Amnesia and Competency to Stand Trial," *American Journal of Psychiatry, 130,* 588 (1973).

[64] *Youtsey v. United States,* 97 F. 937 (6th Cir. 1899).

charges against him, he does not know the identity of his accusers, how the trial will be conducted, or what the sentence might be. Unable to defend himself or to assist his attorney, Joseph K.'s terror derives from his helplessness and uncertainty in the face of the omnipotent power of the state seeking to destroy him in the name of justice." Nevertheless, the prevailing view is that of the Louisiana Supreme Court when it said of an alleged case of "nerves," that it does not make the defendant incapable of understanding the proceedings against him or of assisting in his defense even if his emotional state impairs his recollection of the crime.[65]

The Illinois Mental Health Code provides a single hearing in which the issues of both fitness to stand trial and commitment for treatment are considered. Psychotropic medication is specifically authorized in order to render a defendant fit. The statute has detailed special provisions designed to compensate for the disability of an incompetent defendant so as to render him or her fit to stand trial. Under the Illinois code, psychotropic medication is considered to be essentially the same as any other necessary medication prescribed by a physician for a defendant. The choice of proceeding with or without medication is left to the defendant. Other special provisions to render the defendant fit to stand trial include "appointment of qualified translators who shall simultaneously translate all testimony at trial into language understood by the defendant" and "appointment of experts qualified to assist a defendant who because of a disability is unable to understand the proceedings or communicate with his or her attorney."[66]

Studies indicate that a majority of mentally disordered defendants who are unfit can, with active treatment, attain fitness within a relatively short period of time, often less than 90 days. As a consequence, on site (*in situ*) examination is increasingly required, and this procedure prevents stowing the accused in some remote facility. On-site examination is also recommended as a less expensive procedure. Statutory changes in Connecticut in 1975 disallowed commitment to a state hospital for the purpose of determining competency and made provisions for on-site examinations by a mental health team. The Illinois code, in selecting a placement for treatment, employs the principle of "least restrictive alternative" to the extent it is consistent with the defendant's pretrial release status. Like the defendant with a physical disability, the defendant with a mental disability may be placed in any appropriate public or private facility that agrees to accept him or her or with the Department of Mental Health on a "no decline" basis.[67]

Does it really matter *why* the accused is unable to cooperate with counsel or to understand the proceedings against him or her or to endure the stress of trial? Is psychiatric diagnosis always necessary? Is it necessary to

[65] *State v. Pellerin*, 286 So.2d 639 (La. 1973).
[66] *Illinois Report*, p. 184.
[67] *Illinois Report*, p. 181.

know if the accused is "schizophrenic" or "schizoid"? What difference does it make whether the cause of the disability is organic or functional? In the case of a physical disorder (e.g., a heart condition), the accused may be able to assist counsel or understand the proceedings against him or her but be unable to withstand the stress of trial. On the other hand, in the case of mental disorder (whether the cause is organic or functional), the accused may not have the necessary communicative and cognitive ability to plead or go to trial. With the bar on the use of the triability issue to detain mentally disordered offenders indefinitely, the current trend may be away from the ancillary issue of the accused's "mental condition."[68]

A purely operational procedure would ask simply whether the person understands the charges and can assist counsel, or whether he or she can undergo trial or punishment.[69] A clinical evaluation, however, follows from a "mental illness" interpretation of competency to stand trial.[70] One of the early cases involving mental health professionals in the process of determining triability is *Youtsey v. United States* in 1899,[71] in which the defendant alleged that epileptic seizures affected his memory. The competency statutes of many states refer to "mental disease or defect." For example, the North Carolina statute provides, similar to the wording in Hale:

> No person may be tried, convicted, sentenced, or punished for a crime when *by reason of mental illness or defect* he is unable to understand the nature and object of the proceedings against him, to comprehend his own situation in reference to the proceedings, or to assist in his own defense in a rational or reasonable manner. [Emphasis added.][72]

---

[68] Accordingly, the Courts Diagnostic Clinic of Hartford, Connecticut, reportedly is using an interview approach that attempts to elicit responses from the accused that reflect whether or not he or she meets the aforementioned criteria of competency. It is the quality of these responses to questions, all of which relate to the accused's ability to stand trial, along with observations of behavior, that form the basis of an opinion. Considering that "medical" expertise is not necessary, any of the three mental health professionals (psychiatrist, psychologist, social worker) can perform such an evaluation. Over the protest of a number of judges, the "finding" is unrelated to the "need for hospitalization." (Correspondence of October 19, 1976, and March 11, 1977, from John F. Fitzgerald, Administrator, Courts Diagnostic Clinic, Hartford, Connecticut.) This is in accord with the view that problems in living are not to be seen necessarily as an "illness." These reports of the Courts Diagnostic Clinic are called "psychosocial reports."

[69] R. Slovenko, *Psychiatry and Law* (Boston: Little, Brown, 1973), p. 93.

[70] There is, at times, a confusion of triability with criminal intent or *mens rea* at the time of the offense. That is, the test on competency to stand trial is sometimes confused with that of competency to commit crime, which is linked to "mental disease" or "mental defect." Criminal responsibility traditionally has not been related to other conditions—such as economic or educational deprivation—that might affect intent. On the other hand, as noted, continuances may be granted when there is a physical disability such as a heart condition.

[71] 97 F. 937 (6th Cir. 1899).

[72] North Carolina G.S. 15A-1001; discussed in R. Roesch and S. L. Golding, *A Systems Analysis of Competency to Stand Trial Procedures: Implications for Forensic Services in North Carolina* (Urbana: University of Illinois, 1977) p. 21. The Connecticut law on competency to

A number of courts in various states have recently ruled that evidence regarding triability may consist of lay observations as well as expert clinical testimony.[73] The duty of the court to acquaint itself thoroughly with the defendant's mental condition may be satisfied by lay or clinical witnesses. In *United States v. Makris*,[74] the bulk of lay testimony pointed to competency, whereas the expert clinical evidence suggested incompetency. The trial court gave more credence to the lay evidence. Though a determination of triability affects substantial constitutional rights, the beyond-a-reasonable-doubt standard of proof is not required. An element of the crime not being involved, the preponderance standard is sanctioned for judging triability.[75] In *Makris*, the defendant challenged on appeal the trial court's apparent disregard of the medical experts' conclusions. The federal appellate court observed:

> Especially where the medical expert applies legal standards to arrive at a competency conclusion, he is performing a task at which only a judge is truly an expert. In the final analysis, the determination of competency is a legal conclusion; even if the experts' medical conclusions of impaired ability are credited, the judge must still independently decide if the particular defendant was legally capable of reasonable consultation with his attorney and able to rationally and factually comprehend the proceedings against him.[76]

A number of commentators have urged abolition of the incompetency-to-stand-trial plea (a theoretical proposal in view of the Supreme Court's indication that it may be only provisionally waived). Those commentators seem to question whether or not we are prisoners of the past, adhering to old rules in the face of wholly changed circumstances. Without the assistance of counsel, as was the case in early common law, the defendant's physical and mental presence is essential if he or she is to use the right to cross-question witnesses and make a defense; but today, given the assistance of counsel, the defendant's presence would seem to be less important.[77] Actually, from a

---

stand trial makes reference to such accused "so insane or so mentally defective" (Public Act No. 76-353 [a] [1976]), but in practice this language is reportedly ignored. John F. Fitzgerald, Administrator of the Courts Diagnostic Clinic in Hartford, advises: "In our examination we do not become focused on the 'why' behind the accused's difficulties. The exception to this is when in the course of the examination there is a question that it is the accused's low level of intellectual functioning that is the primary underlying factor behind his inability to meet the legal criteria for competency. Then we will attempt to ascertain that level of functioning more adequately to be sure our recommendation or commitment to the Department of Mental Retardation is reasonably accurate." (Correspondence of April 4, 1977.)

[73] *State v. Fischer*, 231 N.W.2d 147 (N.D. 1975).

[74] 535 F.2d 899 (5th Cir. 1976).

[75] *United States v. Makris*, 535 F.2d 899, at 906 (5th Cir. 1976). In *Lego v. Twomey*, 404 U.S. 477 (1972), the preponderance standard was sanctioned for judging the admissibility of confessions.

[76] 535 F.2d, at 908.

[77] *Snyder v. Massachusetts*, 291 U.S. 97, 107 (1934).

practical point of view, the crucial question is not the competency of the accused but rather the competency of his or her attorney. In the course of upholding the trial court for excluding the defendant from the courtroom when his behavior was contumacious, Justice Hugo Black in *Illinois v. Allen* in 1970 wrote:

> Although mindful that courts must indulge every reasonable presumption against the loss of constitutional rights . . . we explicitly hold today that a defendant can lose his right to be present at trial if, after he has been warned by the judge that he will be removed if he continues his disruptive behavior, he nevertheless insists on conducting himself in a manner so disorderly, disruptive, and disrespectful of the court that his trial cannot be carried on with him in the courtroom.[78]

Is an exception to the prohibition against trials in absentia to be made only when the defendant has apparent control over his or her behavior? In factitious incompetency it may be said that, if the defendant wants to be present, he or she has an easy choice: he or she can decide to behave, but such an option is not available to the person who is mentally "out of it." The Supreme Court in *Allen* ruled as it did in spite of the questionable mental competence of the defendant. In condoning trial in absentia, the Court may have implied that there are no longer any substantial societal interests underlying the defendant's ancient right to be present and that exceptions to the general prohibition against trials in absentia might be developed or expanded. Professors Robert Burt and Norval Morris suggest that an incompetent's trial could be conducted under procedural rules that in some measure redress the incapacities suffered by a particular defendant, much like the aforementioned Illinois code procedures. They particularly suggest requiring that the prosecution afford complete pretrial discovery of its case; that it meet a particularly heavy burden of proof; that a corroborating eyewitness establish some or all elements of the alleged offense; and that special instructions be given to the jury.[79]

Moreover, should not a distinction be drawn between competency to stand trial and competency to plead?[80] The practical question is really not whether the accused is able to undergo trial, but rather whether or not he or she is fit to plead. It is common knowledge that, in the vast majority of cases, there is no trial. A criminal trial is in fact a rarity. With few exceptions, virtually all criminal convictions are entered by a guilty plea after plea bargaining. A trial, on the other hand, is open and public, and the state is put to

---

[78] 307 U.S. 337, at 343 (1970).

[79] R. A. Burt and N. Morris, "A Proposal for the Abolition of the Incompetency Plea," *University of Chicago Law Review*, 40, 66, at 71 (1972).

[80] The argument that there is or ought to be a different (higher) standard of competency for plea proceedings has been rejected by a number of courts. *United States v. Harlan*, 480 F.2d 515 (6th Cir. 1973), *cert. denied*, 414 U.S. 1006 (1973); *People v. Belanger*, 252 N.W.2d 472 (Mich. App. 1977).

its proof beyond a reasonable doubt. Theoretically, in plea bargaining or in the acceptance of a guilty plea, the plea must be entered voluntarily, with an understanding of the charge and consequences of the plea; and the judge must satisfy himself or herself that a factual basis exists for the plea. But because the proceeding is clandestine, it might be suggested that only incompetency to plead ought not be waivable. A number of courts have recently stated that the standard for competency to plead guilty is more exacting than the triability standard.[81] Holding a defendant incompetent to plead but competent to stand trial would result in forcing the defendant into a trial that the defendant would rather avoid to obtain a more favorable negotiated sentence.

But the question still remains: What is to be done with the troublesome and possibly dangerous person who is unfit to stand trial?[82] One should first ask whether he or she is indeed troublesome or dangerous and whether he or she would be responsive to treatment in a hospital setting. Moreover, how

---

[81] *Sieling v. Eyman,* 478 F.2d 211 (9th Cir. 1973); *State v. Robinson,* 526 P.2d 396 (Ariz. 1974); *Anno.,* 31 A.L.R.3d 375 (1977); Note, *Wayne Law Review, 22,* 1463 (1976). The informal plea of guilty (confession or admission) made to a police officer is, for all practical purposes, usually excluded as evidence, much to the dismay of the general public. Theoretically, the evidentiary use of incriminating statements made by an accused to the police while in police custody is permissible when "the statements are the product of a rational intellect and a free will, and when the statements are given voluntarily, knowingly, and intelligently, after the required *Miranda* warnings have been given." See *Miranda v. Arizona,* 384 U.S. 436 (1966); *State v. McDonald,* 195 Neb. 625, 240 N.W.2d 8 (1976). A number of courts have ruled in effect that an accused who makes incriminating statements in the face of the *Miranda* warnings is either an imbecile or insane, and have excluded them as evidence. *People v. Markiewicz,* 348 N.E.2d 240 (Ill. 1976); *Interest of Ruth,* 360 A.2d 922 (Pa. 1976); J. D. Murphy, "Glover Goes Free," *New Orleans Times-Picayune,* April 5, 1977.

Of course, the rulings have some variation. In *People v. Cleveland,* 251 Mich. 542, 232 N.W. 384 (1930), a pre-*Miranda* case, a defendant accused of arson was interrogated in his hospital room. He was suffering from a skull fracture and was in pain. The testimony established that he was rational, although at times he would become confused. The Michigan Supreme Court held the statements taken from him were correctly determined to be voluntary and said: "The mere fact that a defendant was suffering from severe physical injuries, and was under great excitement and strain, does not of itself render a confession inadmissible." See also *People v. Cutler,* 251 N.W.2d 303 (Mich. App. 1977). A determination of the effect tranquilizers or sedatives have on the voluntariness of an accused's statement is based on the same criteria as that used to determine the voluntariness of a statement made by one under the influence of alcohol. The rule as generally stated is that intoxication short of mania (such an impairment of the will and mind as to make the person confessing unconscious of the meaning of his words) will not in itself render a statement inadmissible. *Ex parte* Lowery, 342 So.2d 802 (Ala. 1977).

[82] Blackstone said: "[I]n the case of absolute madmen, as they are not answerable for their actions, they should not be permitted the liberty of acting unless under proper control; and, in particular, they ought not to be suffered to go loose, to the terror of the king's subjects. It was the doctrine of our ancient law, that persons deprived of their reason might be confined till they recovered their senses without waiting for the forms of a commission or other special authority from the crown: and now, by the flagrant acts, a method is chalked out for imprisoning, chaining, and sending them to their proper homes." U. Blackstone, COMMENTARIES 9:24–25 (9th ed., 1978).

can he or she be kept under the control of the court? As a general principle of Anglo-American procedure, it is deemed irrelevant prior to determination of guilt for the court to inquire about what kind of person is before the bench. Apart from youthful offender laws that have a built-in provision for psychiatric evaluation, the only other way that the criminal law provides a means of getting this type of evaluation is when the accused pleads insanity at the time of offense. The presentence report that is possible following conviction often comes too late; the options open to the court at that time are more limited. As anthropologist Edward T. Hall puts it, the Anglo-American trial system is a low-context one.[83]

In contrast, courts in other countries allow great leeway in the testimony admitted as evidence. In these higher-context systems, the court seeks to find out as much as possible about the circumstances behind the acts that brought the accusation. To circumvent the anticontext bias to get at data, courts in the United States often turn to the incompetency motion. Under the guise of obtaining a triability evaluation, the court is able to obtain a psychiatric evaluation of the offender, and it wants the evaluation of the offender to be related to the need for institutionalization. Many defense attorneys, too, want a psychiatric report that they might use in litigation or as material for defense, and so they resort to the incompetency plea.

But now that the use of the incompetency plea to confine an individual is restricted, new questions have been posed. For example, should there be a moratorium on the construction of special buildings for the criminally insane? What shall be done with the troublesome and possibly dangerous person? What shall be done with the untried accused whose trial is impeded, or the defendant who is found not guilty by reason of insanity? Consider for a moment, a true story. A man kills seven children in a little over a year. The suburban neighborhood is in shock. Children are not allowed outside; many of them are having nightmares. A newspaper editorial says: "What all of us want is that the killer be identified for certain and put away so that the children will be safer."[84] Competent or no, that killer has to be put away to satisfy the public as well as to protect the killer from a lynch mob. Such is often the case, depending on the community and the notoriety of the offense.

One way or another, when someone causes such an outrage, society demands, and rightly so, that something be done to atone for the misdeed and to protect the populace. The Criminal Lunatics Act of 1800 in England provided for the detention in Broadmoor of both the untriable and the acquitted insane. To retain jurisdiction in the criminal system, Michigan in 1975, and later a number of other states, adopted a "guilty but mentally ill" statute.[85] A statute enacted in the District of Columbia, the constitutionality of

---

[83] E. T. Hall, *Beyond Culture* (New York: Anchor Books, 1977), p. 108.

[84] *Detroit Free Press,* March 25, 1977, p. 10.

[85] M.C.L. §738.36; M.S.A. §28.1059, discussed in R. Slovenko, "Guilty But Mentally Ill," *Journal of Psychotherapy & Law* (in press).

which has been upheld by a D.C. circuit court, provides for judicial review and hearing when a mental health facility proposes to discharge a defendant who has been charged with a serious crime, found not guilty by reason of insanity, and committed to the facility for treatment.[86] Georgia, too, recently adopted legislation giving the court similar control over discharge.

CONCLUSION

Perhaps the single lesson that can be derived from a examination of the current cases and legislation in the area of fitness to stand trial is that one can no longer use labels of incompetent or competent, fit or unfit, as black and white distinctions that separate a certain class of "triable" persons from the "untriable." Thinking in terms of absolute capacity or incapacity has only produced the unsatisfactory results illustrated by the *Lang* and *Karno* cases. Rather, the realistic approach of the Illinois Mental Health Code, which strives to compensate for the physical or mental handicap of the accused by providing various special considerations, seems to be the inevitable and fairest course. It is inevitable because the public will stand for neither the indefinite incarceration of those allegedly unfit for trial whose guilt is not yet determined nor the failure to try and sentence an accused whose guilt is settled in the public eye.

Moreover, the approach of the Illinois code is the fairest because only by an open trial within a reasonable time (whether the accused has to be drugged or is deaf, mute, or schizoid) can the incompetent get the equal protection of the law, namely a just and speedy trial, routinely afforded to the competent. It is time that the law face up to the fact that every criminal defendant is to a certain degree "unfit" for trial and to a certain degree "fit."[87] Rather than draw an arbitrary line between two fixed categories, the law should try to see that each individual, regardless of his or her physical or mental state, is afforded a fair and speedy trial, or a fair and speedy plea. It is apparent that the indeterminate detention in hospitals for the criminally insane and interminable delays of trial that marked the pre-*Jackson* period did not afford such equal rights. That day has pretty much ended.

---

[86] 24 D.C. Code § 301(e), upheld in *United States v. Ecker*, No. 75-1074 (D.C. Circ., April 2, 1976).

[87] In a Seattle jail study, Dr. John Petrich of the University of Washington School of Medicine found that prisoners in jail for misdemeanors have a higher incidence of psychiatric morbidity than a comparable unselected population of jail inmates and convicted felons. In the Seattle study, the psychiatric morbidity figures of 10.5 percent for men and 12 percent for women convicted of misdemeanors were found to be roughly twice that of the overall psychiatric morbidity of the jail population taken as a whole. *Clinical Psychiatry News*, August 1977, p. 47.

Paul D. Lipsitt

7

Beyond Competency to Stand Trial

Competency for trial referrals by criminal courts are the most common procedure for the transfer of people from the criminal justice system into the mental health system. The origins of the legal rationale for the competency evaluation have a great deal of importance for the integrity of legal due process and are of very little concern in the diagnosis and treatment of the mental illness or mental defect. The concept, as first enunciated in the Anglo-Saxon common law in 1746 (Kinloch's Case), held that no man should be obligated to defend himself who did not possess the mental faculties to meet the due process considerations of a fair trial. Lacking the capacity to participate adequately in one's own defense in court in response to a criminal charge would be tantamount to a trial *in absentia*.

The specter of a trial without the opportunity to confront one's accusers, to be represented adequately by counsel, and to testify in one's own defense raises fundamental due process issues for a fair trial. The requirement of competency for trial was to assure that a defendant could muster the cognitive and affective resources to defend himself.

Paradoxically, in this country, focus upon the competency issue arose, not because incompetent individuals were subjected to trial, but because of the status and condition of those who, instead, were committed to hospitals as incompetent for trial. The increasingly large numbers of persons hospitalized for extended periods of time raised questions regarding the appropriateness of the commitments (*Commonwealth v. Druken,* 1969), length of time hospitalized (*Jackson v. Indiana,* 1972), and adequacy of treatment (*Nason v. Superintendent of Bridgewater State Hospital,* 1968). The due process concerns were now of a different order than merely a determination

PSYCHOTHERAPY AND THE LAW
ISBN 0-8089-1780-3

of fitness for trial. It appears that the cure was more threatening to the rights of the accused than was the potential of being unfairly tried.

ROLE OF THE MENTAL HEALTH PROFESSIONAL

The introduction of the mental health professional into the judicial process, usually occurring at the arraignment or pretrial stage, addresses the mental health status of the defendant insofar as incompetency must be the result of mental illness or defect. A caveat is that mental illness or defect is a *necessary* condition; it is not sufficient to conclude that one is incompetent to stand trial. Prior to the 1960s, little attention was paid to this distinction (Laboratory of Community Psychiatry, 1973). Without the awareness of the legal concept of competency for trial as the basis for evaluation, mental health professionals were likely to evaluate on the basis of the diagnostic criteria for mental illness and the need for treatment.

Neither the courts nor the mental health system (individually or collaboratively) focused on the nice distinctions between mental illness and the more circumscribed issue of competency for trial. Major conceptual changes regarding involuntary hospitalization during the 1960s were to have a profound impact upon mental patients hospitalized through the criminal justice system as incompetent to stand trial. Two general movements developed impetus during this period. One was a growing interest in the civil rights of patients, and the other was a strong movement toward deinstitutionalization, encouraged by federal funding of community mental health centers and the promise that psychotropic drugs would facilitate this transition.

Legal action brought on behalf of patients committed to hospitals by the courts as incompetent for trial was first based on the doctrine of right to treatment, contending that the exchange, or *quid pro quo,* for involuntary deprivation of freedom through hospitalization was that treatment would be forthcoming (*Rouse v. Cameron,* 1966). Bolstering this argument for patients who had competency status was the fact that, although they were in the criminal justice system, they had not yet been tried, and the presumption of innocence should place their status as closer to civil commitments (*Commonwealth v. Druken,* 1969). The absence of treatment results in a condition indistinguishable from incarceration (*Nason v. Superintendent of Bridgewater State Hospital,* 1968). The purpose of commitment as incompetent for trial was not necessarily to "cure" mental illness, or even to return to a state of remission, but only to reach the minimal level of competency needed to proceed with the trial.

A survey of mental hospital records in 1967 revealed that most persons committed through the criminal justice system were under the status of incompetent to stand trial (Scheidemandel & Kanno, 1969). Until such issues as the civil rights of patients and the civil liberties of the involuntarily committed came into focus, little attention was paid to the vagueness (or complete lack) of standards and guidelines for determining competency for trial.

Investigations during the 1960s revealed that a commitment for incompetency for trial was likely to extend indefinitely; at one institution, it was often equivalent to a life sentence (McGarry, 1965). Examination of random samples of cases, as well as among the most severely mentally ill, resulted in a finding of a high frequency of inappropriately committed cases. Through ignorance and confusion regarding the legal basis for competency for trial, many defendants who carried a diagnosis of mental illness, but were in fact competent for trial, remained hospitalized long after the evaluation period.

Hospitalization for competency observation or commitment as incompetent for trial could legitimate the use of the mental health system. The legal status of incompetency was enough to transfer primary responsibility for the defendant/patient from the court to the hospital. In many cases, after commitment as incompetent, the criminal charges were dropped without notification to the hospital, leaving the hospitalized person in a state of legal limbo. With the advent of the first legal challenges to the circumstances of the patient/defendant in involuntary hospitalization, there developed a recognition of the need for improved standards and guidelines for the determination of incompetency for trial, as well as the treatment issues involved.

The statutory procedure for the evaluation of competency for trial and its implications for assuring due process and fairness to the defendant provided superficial justification for transferring responsibility for cases that the court was ill equipped to handle to the mental health system. In effect, the courts were asking for assistance in the disposition of cases, not in the preparation of people for trial. The underlying agenda was a request for care and treatment of many persons who went before the court and were perceived by judges and probation officers as "strange," "weird," or "bizarre." The deviance that brought them before the court was usually a misdemeanor, and responsibility for social control in such cases was often viewed by the courts as primarily a mental health rather than a judicial function.

Research at the Laboratory of Community Psychiatry (1973), funded by the National Institute of Mental Health in the mid-1960s, was a response to turbulence felt in both the mental health and judicial systems. At this time, reviews appeared that reflected changing perspectives in law and psychiatry regarding the civil liberty and mental health concerns surrounding the issue of competency to stand trial ("Incompetency," 1967; Bennett, 1968). With the increasing sophistication of forensically trained mental health professionals in an atmosphere that pressed toward reduction of hospital censuses and the deinstitutionalizing of patients, long-term commitments as incompetent for trial sharply decreased. Toward the goal of avoiding unnecessary hospitalization, research at the laboratory selected as its primary product the development of protocols and tests to aid in the standardization and quantification of the concept of competency for trial.

The research on competency to stand trial highlights a problem that has always been present in experimental research. The need to draw inferences and make generalizations from research findings to performance in the natural setting raises the issue of ultimate validation. Competency to stand trial requires that a person possess the capacity and ability to play adequately the role of a defendant in a court. Observations and measurements in court would be the best validating data. The methodology for controlled research would require that people who were already assessed as either competent or incompetent be sent to trial and independent measures be taken through observations of their courtroom performance. Such research is highly unlikely, especially for a sample considered incompetent. There are social limitations to the forms our research can take.

As the criteria for involuntary commitment narrowed, allowing fewer persons to be hospitalized against their wishes, more attention was paid to criteria for the determination of competency for trial. In the mental health system, psychiatrists and others responsible for the assessment of competency for trial did not have the objective methods for making a determination of competency and, more likely than not, had no understanding of the legal concept of competency for trial. In most cases, incompetency for trial was considered the equivalent to mental illness for purposes of hospitalization.

The situation was no better on the judicial side. Many state statutes were vague or confusing or provided no guidelines at all. Lawyers often confused competency to stand trial with criminal responsibility, and many judicial decisions further compounded the problem by failing to make clear whether the issue in the case dealt with competency to stand trial or with other issues of mental illness and criminal responsibility.

As a result of the trend toward deinstitutionalization, as well as increasing attention by the courts to the conditions in mental hospitals and the rights of the mentally ill, large mental hospitals were beginning to decrease their censuses dramatically. Patients who were civilly committed were involved in these discharges disproportionately. This was because the channeling of accused offenders into the mental hospitals through the process of competency for trial evaluation was a practice over which the mental health system had no control. The decisions were being made by lawyers, probation officers, and judges. Guidelines to place both the legal and mental health systems on the same communication "wavelength" were missing in the competency assessment process. There was a clear need for a functional test.

Among the products of research was the construction of two instruments designed to measure competency to stand trial (Lipsitt, Lelos, & McGarry, 1971; Laboratory of Community Psychiatry, 1973). One was called the Competency Screening Test (CST), and the second was called the

Competency Assessment Instrument (CAI). These tests were designed to be used in a two-step fashion: (1) the CST as an initial screening instrument, administered preferably in the court or original place of detention, to avoid hospitalization of individuals who are clearly competent for trial; (2) the CAI as an open-ended interview checklist for cases in which the question of competency still remained after the CST was administered. The purpose of these tests was to offer more objective and measurable guidelines to the assessment of competency for trial. One assumption was that if an operational definition of ''competency for trial'' could be established, based upon the common law criteria, there would be a common language for communication between the legal and mental health systems.

Whether the CST or another method for the pretrial evaluation of competency is used, it is important not only to determine the understanding and awareness of the defendant vis-a-vis his or her circumstances before the court and in relation to his or her attorney, but also to heighten understanding and awareness between the judicial system and the mental health system. Both systems must meet the requirements of due process and equal protection of defendants charged with offenses and appearing before the court.

Since the publication of the original research, several investigators have conducted replication studies with the CST (Shatin, 1979; Shatin & Brodsky, 1979; Nottingham & Mattson, 1981; Randolph, Hicks, & Mason, 1981; Randolph, Hicks, Mason, & Cuneo, 1982). Findings by each of these investigators have been consistent with those of the original study, indicating that the CST is effective as a screening instrument for patients referred to a forensic center for evaluation for competency to stand trial. Two studies modified the test for female subjects because the original research used male samples (Shatin, 1979; Shatin & Brodsky, 1979). In each of these studies, the control evaluation was conducted by a forensic psychiatrist or a forensic evaluation team. In one study (Shatin, 1979), a 5-item brief form of the CST developed in the original research was compared with the full 22-item scale and found to be highly correlated. The consistent findings among these studies raise the level of confidence with which forensic mental health evaluators may rely on test results in support of their conclusions regarding the competency of a defendant.

Paradoxically, with the increased level of confidence by which a defendant's competence may be ascertained without hospitalization, a dilemma may then confront the court. Absent vagueness in an initial competency evaluation, the court may be dealing with a defendant with a substantial mental illness who is nevertheless competent to stand trial. When the criteria for competency for trial are less well defined and the clinical findings are not supported by ''hard data,'' the use of the statutory route to a hospital through evaluation for competency is less likely to be challenged. Although civil commitment procedures could be invoked at this point, judges are reluctant to use that parallel route to involuntary commitment because control of the defendant/patient then belongs to the mental health system rather than to the judicial system.

Standardized and quantifiable measures used to assess competency for trial can rule out large numbers of defendants who otherwise would be transferred to hospitals for evaluation. Even so, the care and treatment of competent but mentally ill persons still presents a dilemma for the courts. At the pretrial stage, there is no other justification for a hospital commitment in the criminal justice process.

An initial competency screening examination may uncover pathology that may lead the clinician to recommend either hospitalization or outpatient treatment. Unless the referral is accomplished by a competency for trial evaluation, however, the court may lose control of the case to the mental health system. Judge David Bazelon, reflecting upon the relationship between the court and behavioral scientists, has said: "I have tried to open the courthouse doors, but never hand over the keys" (1982, p. 115).

Perhaps, as social scientists, we can go only so far with the competency issue. The rest is up to the courts. As Judge Bazelon (1982) observed, the ultimate conclusions of law regarding competency for trial must be the responsibility of the judge. What has been achieved has been a heightened awareness of the meaning of competency for trial. The development of operational tests that focus specifically on the criteria for competency for trial has had the salutory effect of keeping the system honest. The competency route to hospitalization is reserved for those for whom fitness for trial is the real issue. The hospitalization of defendants merely because they behave strangely, or for the purpose of restricting their freedom for other reasons than evaluation for competency for trial, has been reduced because of the factors discussed above.

CROSSOVER BETWEEN THE CRIMINAL JUSTICE AND THE MENTAL HEALTH SYSTEMS

Blurring of the constituencies of the mental health and criminal justice systems has complicated the tasks of both systems. Mental health practitioners are treating a clientele whose clinical problems are confounded by past and present engagement with the criminal justice system. Defendants in criminal court more often arrive before the judge with a history of diagnosis and treatment in a mental hospital or other psychiatric program. The "mad" and "bad" categories are likely to overlap.

The enhancement of due process through well defined standards and measures of competency for trial has been paralleled by marked changes in the mental hospital population. In contrast to research findings of the 1940s, mental patients hospitalized today in public institutions are more likely to have been charged with offenses or found guilty of crimes. Early research found no significant difference between the rate of criminal behavior among the mentally ill in hospitals and that of the general population (Pollock, 1938; Brill and Malzberg, 1962). More current research clearly demonstrates that these findings no longer prevail (Zitrin, Hardesty, Burdock, & Drossman, 1976; Sosowsky, 1978; Steadman, Cocozza, & Melick, 1978). Patients who are involuntarily hospitalized are more likely to have a prior criminal record and are more likely than the general population to commit criminal offenses after discharge, even when controlled for age, sex, and socioeconomic status.

Although some interpretations supported the belief that mental patients were more dangerous than the general population, more plausible explanations have been forthcoming. Steadman and his colleagues (1978) have found, in a detailed analysis of patients admitted and discharged from mental hospitals, that the percentages of patients having prior arrests have increased significantly. These investigators compared data from 1968 to 1975 and found that in the patient sample the arrest rate per 1,000 population increased from 73.5 to 98.5, whereas the rate in a comparable stratified sample of the general population increased from 27.5 to 32.5 during the same period. Because the best predictor of subsequent deviant or criminal behavior is prior criminal behavior, it follows that patients with preadmission criminal records are more likely to be arrested after discharge. When patients with prior arrests were compared with those in the community who had arrest records, rates of rearrest were not significantly different, thus supporting the conclusion that mental illness alone does not add to the risk of rearrest. These findings reflect the increasing responsibility of the mental health professional in assisting the courts in framing decisions for hospitalization of defendants, whether the issue is competency for trial or other treatment issues.

It is useful for the clinician to learn as much as possible about the referral from a court. Was the court motivated to refer strictly on the competency for trial issue, or were there other potential strategies on the agenda? Perhaps the defense attorney or the prosecutor initiated the request for an evaluation as a pretrial maneuver. If so, what was the purpose? Was it purely a tactic to delay the trial, or was there a desire to transfer responsibility for the defendant to the mental health system, with the hope that charges would be dropped or that the case would be continued without a finding until a later date? All of these possibilities are important for consideration by the clinician in understanding the implicit—if not explicit—reasons for referral. This background will be relevant in aiding the clinician to make an appropriate recommendation based on his or her evaluation of the defendant. If the defendant *is* competent for trial, thus ruling out hospitalization for further observation and restoration of competency, the court must consider alternatives pending trial. The judge then is participating in decisions that go beyond the narrow legal options. This tendency to move beyond the rigid, formal legal process and to consider the "whole person" has been observed by one researcher (Feely, 1979, p. 25). Such procedures are much more discretionary and time-consuming and require an available network of community resources as well as a flexible orientation in the court (Hiday, 1981). Critics of this extended concern for defendants by judges and probation officers state that it is not the role of the court to serve as "social workers."

A competency for trial evaluation will aid the court in making recommendations for treatment, but only as a tangential aspect of the judicial process. Close cooperation is necessary between those offering mental health resources and personnel in the court. The establishment of a link by which to establish a feeling of trust and credibility on both sides will aid in successful implementation of treatment modes that go beyond the strictly legal aspects of the court process. If the individual is to be released from jail or place of detention during the period while awaiting trial, the judge must either set bail or release on trust that the defendant will appear on schedule before the court. Many factors that go beyond the mental health of the individual will enter into the judge's decision: (1) the seriousness of the offense, (2) the perceived dangerousness of the defendant to the community, and (3) the degree to which the judge is confident that the mental health resources will make a good-faith effort in managing and treating the case.

Any recommendation for treatment should be presented to the court as a suggestion, recognizing that the original referral was for the purpose of a competency for trial evaluation. The clinician must be prepared to explain clearly the reasons that the defendant may be competent to stand trial and yet be mentally ill. Much of the inappropriate hospitalization resulting from competency for trial examination has been because lawyers and judges, as well as clinicians, have been confused over this distinction. The use of instruments, such as the Competency Screening Test, that offer an operational dimension can aid the clinician and the court in distinguishing mental illness issues from the narrower consideration of competency for trial.

TREATMENT AT AN EARLY STAGE

Evaluation in the court by mental health professionals can offer a service that goes far beyond the immediate legal problems of the accused. The offense may be circumstantial or self-limiting; or it may reflect a symptom of much more extensive mental health implications. In the latter situation, the finding—whether guilty or not guilty—and subsequent sentencing within the criminal justice system may be more ritualistic than effective in reducing recidivism or offering a rehabilitative opportunity. The mental health professional can see this opportunity, presented in the atmosphere of the court process, in a crisis intervention context. The alleged offense provides an opening to the mental health system through the *status* of defendant, but the therapeutic opportunity is much more far-reaching. By exploring the behavioral and the dynamic issues that go beyond the court's concern with a specific offense, the status may change from defendant or offender to client or patient.

Reports of competency for trial commitments to hospitals have ranged from about 39 percent to 52 percent of all cases referred by the criminal justice system. The variation in these figures is caused by the differing definitions of the status of patients hospitalized as incompetent to stand trial. The higher percentage includes those defendants referred for a short observation period for evaluation, and the lower percentage contains only those cases in which there was a true commitment (Steadman & Hartstone, 1983). Steadman and Hartstone observed that it is inappropriate to include among "mentally disordered offenders" defendants who are being evaluated—because a diagnostic decision has not yet been made. Although technically correct, persons who are not yet committed may remain hospitalized for as long as 40 days.

Changes in commitment criteria, periodic reviews of hospitalized mental patients by the courts, and the increased awareness among forensic specialists and other clinicians of standards for competency for trial have dramatically contributed to the *reduction* of commitments as incompetent for trial. The frequency of referral for observation and evaluation, however, has remained at least at the level prior to changes in the law.

CONCLUSION

From the point of view of the mental health professional, referral for evaluation of competency can offer an opportunity either for treatment and rehabilitation (Mowbray, 1979) or be limited to strict adherence to the guidelines for evaluation for fitness for trial. In most instances, the probation department can play an integral part in coordinating links between the judicial and mental health systems. In courts that have in-house clinics, probation officers can enhance their effectiveness with probationers through consultation with clinicians over supervision issues.

In contrast to the strictly legalistic use of the mental health professional for evaluation of competency for trial, a more generalized focus on the broader mental health needs of the person may be thought of as humanistic. This approach is not without its critics and detractors, who believe that the introduction of mental health services will divert from the main purpose of the court, i.e., to determine guilt or innocence and to sentence. The possibility of abuse through coercive treatment merits serious consideration. The danger of overly zealous persuasion to accept treatment is balanced by the recognition among mental health professionals that prognosis is usually poor for one who strongly resists the need for treatment. Many do accept the invitation to participate in therapy, however, even though they would not have voluntarily attended a clinic prior to involvement with the court.

In summary, many cases first come to the attention of a court clinic or a mental health professional through the competency for trial evaluation. If these persons are found to be competent for trial through a routine screening or are hospitalized, many will remain at risk after the case is disposed of. Steadman (1979) found that 44 percent of short-term hospitalized incompetent defendants were rehospitalized within 2 years and 9 months. By looking beyond the competency for trial evaluation, the broader mental health needs of many of these defendants/patients may be addressed with early intervention, thus benefiting both the person and the legal and mental health systems.

REFERENCES

Bazelon, D. L. (1982). Veils, values and social responsibility. *American Psychologist, 37,* 115–121.

Bennett, D. E. (1968). Competency to stand trial: A call for reform. *Journal of Criminal Law, Criminology and Police Science, 59,* 569–582.

Brill, H., & Malzberg, B. (1962). Statistical report based on the arrest records of 5354 male ex-patients released from New York State hospitals during the period 1946–1948. In *Mental Health Service Supplement 153.* Washington D.C.: American Psychiatric Association.

Commonwealth v. Druken, 356 Mass. 503, 254 N.E.2d 779 (1969).

Feely, N. M. (1979). *The process is the punishment: Handling cases in the lower criminal court.* New York: Russell Sage Foundation.

Hiday, V. A. (1981). Court discretion: Application of the dangerousness standard in civil commitment. *Law and Human Behavior, 5,* 275–289.

Incompetency to stand trial. (1967). *Harvard Law Review* [Note], *81,* 454–473.

Jackson v. Indiana, 406 U. S. 715 (1972).

Kinloch's Case, 18 How. St. Tr. (Eng.) 395 (1746).

Laboratory of Community Psychiatry, Harvard Medical School. (1973). *Competency to stand trial and mental illness* (DHEW Publication HSM 73-9105).

Lipsitt, P. D., Lelos, D., & McGarry, A. L. (1971). Competency for trial: A screening instrument. *American Journal of Psychiatry, 128,* 105–109.

McGarry, A. L. (1965). Competency for trial and due process via the state hospital. *American Journal of Psychiatry, 122,* 623–630.

Mowbray, C. T. (1979). A study of patients treated as incompetent to stand trial. *Social Psychiatry, 14,* 31–39.

Nason v. Superintendent of Bridgewater State Hospital, 353 Mass. 604, 233 N.E.2d 908 (1968).

Nottingham, E. J., & Mattson, R. E. (1981). A validation study of the competency screening test. *Law and Human Behavior, 5,* 329–335.

Pollock, H. H. (1938). Is the paroled patient a threat in the community? *Psychiatric Quarterly, 12,* 236–244.

Randolph, J. J., Hicks, T., & Mason, D. (1981). The competency screening test: A replication and extension. *Criminal Justice and Behavior, 8,* 471–481.

Randolph, J. J., Hicks, T., Mason, D., & Cuneo, D. J. (1982). The competency screening test: A validation study in Cook County, Illinois. *Criminal Justice and Behavior, 9,* 495–500.

Rouse v. Cameron, 373 F.2d 451 (D.C. Cir. 1966).

Scheidemandel, P. L., & Kanno, C. K. (1969). *The mentally ill offender: A survey of treatment programs*. Washington, D. C.: Joint Information Service, American Psychiatric Association.

Shatin, L. (1979). Brief form of the competency screening test for mental competence to stand trial. *Journal of Clinical Psychology, 35,* 464–467.

Shatin, L., & Brodsky, S. H. (1979). Competency for trial: The competency screening test in an urban hospital forensic unit. *Mount Sinai Journal of Medicine, 46,* 131–134.

Sosowsky, L. (1978). Crime and violence among mental patients reconsidered in view of the new legal relationship between the state and the mentally ill. *American Journal of Psychiatry, 35,* 33–42.

Steadman, H. J. (1979). *Beating a rap? Defendants found incompetent to stand trial*. Chicago: University of Chicago Press.

Steadman, H. J., Cocozza, J. J., & Melick, M. E. (1978). Explaining the increased rate among mental patients: The changing clientele of state hospitals. *American Journal of Psychiatry, 135,* 816–820.

Steadman, H. J., & Hartstone, E. (1983). Defendants incompetent to stand trial. In J. Monahan & H. J. Steadman (Eds.), *Mentally Disordered Offenders*, (pp. 39–62). New York: Plenum.

Zitrin, A., Hardesty, A. S., Burdock, E. I., & Drossman, A. K. (1976). Crime and violence among mental patients. *American Journal of Psychiatry, 133,* 142–149.

Duty to Report and
the Confidentiality Privilege

Gary M. Heymann

8

Mandated Child Abuse Reporting and the Confidentiality Privilege

Once upon a time, not so terribly long ago, it was reasonably realistic for psychotherapists to assure their clientele that whatever was told in the course of the professional work together would remain confidential, protected by law and tradition from the eyes and ears of the world. Not so today. Things have changed and continue to do so. In the 1970s we were given the "duty to warn" by the California Supreme Court decision in the *Tarasoff* case. The 1980s were off to a rousing start when the California Legislature handed us the "duty to report." That is, California's child abuse reporting laws were revised in 1980 (California Penal Code, Sections 11165-11174) to require clinicians of various professional disciplines to report any instance of known or "reasonably suspected" child abuse to a "child protective agency" at the city or county level of government. The law provides no money or specialized personnel or training to carry out this mandated work. Under this law, it is the duty of the clinician to make an *immediate* report, without the opportunity to exercise professional judgment regarding either the appropriateness or the implications of doing so; it is the agency being reported to that has the function of deciding what to do in the way of investigation and/or intervention. Ours is not to reason why, ours is but to report. This constitutes the most far-reaching, legally mandated breach of the professional confidentiality privilege, in an ever-broadening course of gradual erosion.

A look at some of the details of this situation is in order. The 1980 law applies to any child under the age of 18 years. The concept of "child abuse" has been expanded to include unjustifiable mental suffering and a variety of

PSYCHOTHERAPY AND THE LAW
ISBN 0-8089-1780-3

specific and general sexual behaviors, in addition to the usual concepts of physical injury, cruelty, and neglect. "Unjustifiable mental suffering" is not defined in this law. Some examples of specific sexual behaviors that are subject to mandated reporting are rape, incest, sodomy, oral copulation, and genital and anal penetration; those of a vaguer nature are lewd or lascivious acts and child molestation. Who are these "child protective agencies," and what is their function? The law specifies them to be a police or sheriff's department, a county probation department, or a county welfare department. These designated agencies have the function and power to investigate and intervene with the aim of protecting a child from further abuse. The reporting requirement is automatic and swift: at once by telephone, followed by a written report within 36 hours of learning of the incident. The psychotherapist–patient privilege does not apply to information reported pursuant to this law, and the reporting clinician is specifically protected from incurring any criminal or civil liability for making this required report. On the other hand, failure to report leaves the clinician vulnerable to criminal as well as civil prosecution. Failure to report constitutes a misdemeanor that can result in a jail term up of to 6 months and/or a fine of up to $500. In addition, on the basis of the California benchmark court case in this field (*Landeros v. Flood,* 1976), failure to report may leave the clinician civilly liable if there are repeated incidents of such child abuse soon after the unreported incident. This leaves us pretty much between the proverbial devil and the deep blue sea.

The reporting statute, per se, functions as an all-or-none law that leaves unaddressed a host of issues and considerations that are unavoidably part and parcel of reporting the real-live child abuse situations that come to the attention of clinicians in the course of their professional work. An example would be the time and circumstances under which reportable behavior has occurred. It certainly makes a meaningful difference (1) whether someone's loss of control over aggressive or sexual impulses was an isolated instance or is an ongoing behavioral pattern; (2) whether it happened several years ago or just started now; and (3) the circumstances under which this behavior was revealed to the therapist. In one instance, the parents may have come to therapy for the very *purpose* of getting help in overcoming their aggressive behavior toward their children. In another instance, the therapist may learn about ongoing brutality from a third party. Ignoring important differences such as these, in fulfillment of an indiscriminate reporting duty, is hardly likely to serve the best interests of anyone.

Further, what are the likely consequences of this sort of reporting to the parties involved—the child, the adults, the therapist—or to the treatment process itself? Imagine a child who has been enticed to trust his or her therapist and who has revealed some sexual behavior that took place at home (with all the open and not-so-open feelings about that), coming home from school the next day to a family still reacting to a surprise visit by the police. Imagine that child's sense of betrayal, of shame and guilt for inadvertently triggering this family disaster. And what if the reported behavior is based on *fantasy* or emotionally loaded misperception? We see this sort of thing all the time in the course of our work; and it is part of our work to explore this to the point at which fact and fiction gradually emerge so as to help lead the patient to a better understanding of her or his internal workings. Yet the law would bid us suspend our professional training and blunder straight into mindless reporting. Along similar lines, suppose that our patient is an adolescent who, for reasons of complex internal motivation, is "setting up" one of the parents to experience the distress such reporting would predictably bring about. It has been known to happen.

There are still other considerations. How likely will reporting, in fact, protect a child from further harm? What consequences will the reporting and its unpredictable sequelae have for the child's psychological welfare and personality development? By reporting to these child protective agencies, we trigger events and processes over which we have no influence or control. The law does not require us to be responsible participants in the resolution of the reported situation, and the public agencies are not bound to consider any caveats or recommendations we might propose. As a practical matter, who would pay the therapist for the time required to see things through in a therapeutically appropriate manner?

All these considerations, and then some, are currently in a kind of legal limbo. There is no systematic way of knowing what is in the works at the trial level; and it takes several years before court cases reach the appellate or Supreme Court level, where court rulings can be made to address what was left out of the California legislation.

REVIEW OF STATE REPORTING LAWS

It is instructive to review similar reporting laws of other states.[1] State reporting laws first made their appearance in the early 1960s; 20 states had them by 1964, and 49 states by 1966. Today, all states have such laws, as well as the District of Columbia, Samoa, Guam, Puerto Rico, and the Virgin Islands. Their collective *purpose* is explicitly stated in the laws of 43 states and is generally declared to be the protection of children. More specific purposes are the identification of the child in peril, the designation of agencies to receive and investigate reports, and the offering of services and treatment. *Reportable circumstances,* in most states, now include these four

---

[1] The sources are Irving J. Sloan, Ed., *Protection of Abused Victims: State Laws and Decisions* (Dobbs Ferry, NY: Ocean Publications, 1982); and Herner and Company for National Center on Child Abuse and Neglect, *Child Abuse and Neglect, State Reporting Laws* (Washington, D.C.: Department of Health and Human Services, 1980).

major categories: (1) physical abuse, (2) neglect, (3) sexual abuse, and (4) exploitation, mental and emotional maltreatment, or harm. All states require reporting on a "reasonable basis for belief or suspicion" that such abuses have occurred. The *definitions* of "reportable abuse" and "neglect" vary widely, each jurisdiction defining them differently. These definitions are found (or cross-referenced) in such varied sources as the reporting laws themselves, juvenile court laws, criminal codes, and welfare laws. No state prohibits reasonable corporal punishment, and 26 states specifically include provisions approving "justified use of force," but this does not lessen the duty to report even though this provision precludes a judicial finding of child abuse. The *age limit* is 18 years in all states except Wyoming, where it is 16 years; some states extend the age limit to 21 if the avowed victim is physically or mentally handicapped. The lists of *those who must report* also vary widely. Physicians must report in all states, nurses in 47 states, social service workers in 46, coroners and medical examiners in 27, clergymen in 7, and attorneys in 4. It is not clear whether these reporting laws are intended to overturn the "clergy-penitent" privilege, which in California is immune from breach by the clergy on any legal ground whatsoever. Thirty-two states also provide for *permissive reporting* by any person, in addition to that mandated for the just enumerated occupational categories.

Two states, Maine and Maryland, provide for *discretion not to report*. Maine permits this discretion if the information emerges in a course of treatment and, in the opinion of the person required to report, i.e., the therapist, the child's life or health is not immediately threatened. Discretion is permitted in Maryland if efforts are being made, or will be made, to alleviate the condition and if the person required to report believes that these efforts will indeed alleviate the abuse situation; or if the potential reporter believes that such reporting would inhibit the child, parent, guardian, or custodian from seeking assistance in the future and thereby be detrimental to the child's welfare.

All states provide *immunity* from civil or criminal liability for reporting; a majority of the states require that the report be made "in good faith." In California, only a medical or nonmedical practitioner or child care custodian is immune should the report be false, i.e., if the "person knew or should have known that the report was false" (Penal Code, Section 11172[A]). Forty-four states provide for *religious exclusion,* in that neglecting to provide a child with medical treatment on religious grounds does not constitute reportable child abuse, should this be the sole reason for the failure to provide medical care. *Failure to report* will incur criminal penalties in 45 states. In most of these states it is a misdemeanor; the penalty ranges from 5 to 30 days in jail and/or a $10 to $100 fine to one year in jail and/or a $1,000 fine. The legal basis for such a penalty is "knowing" or "willful" failure to report. It is very difficult to prove this in court, and there are no reported cases of such criminal prosecution to date. In five states, there is additional exposure to *civil liability* if subsequent abuse is proximately caused by failure to report.

The *reporting procedure* in nearly all states requires immediate oral reporting, followed by a written report to the designated authorities. The oral report is to permit immediate protective action to be taken if the child's life or health is in danger. The written report must be forwarded within a specified time frame ranging from 1 to 7 days and provides the basis for a detailed investigation. *Mandated action,* in the majority of states, requires initiation of an investigation immediately or within 48 hours, as well as appropriate action to protect the child. The aim of this investigation is to determine the factual basis for the reported abuse and, if necessary, to recommend appropriate action and services; removal from the home is authorized if the child is in immediate danger.

A *central registry* is mandated in 44 states, to be maintained by departments of welfare or social services in all states except California, where it is maintained by the Department of Justice. This register contains data about the maltreated children and the persons responsible for their condition, all reports received, and case disposition information. Only two states have arrangements for separating "unfounded" reports from "founded" ones. Only 18 states have provisions for the amendment, expunction, sealing, or destruction of registry records. Only 4 states destroy unfounded records; 10 states expunge the names on unfounded reports. Only two states mandate destruction of the registry record when the child reaches the age of 21. Only five states require that persons in the registry data bank be informed to that effect. *Release of information* procedures vary widely. Twenty-eight states specifically exempt registry information from the confidentiality privilege and are empowered to release information, with all identifying data, to a variety of specified agencies or individuals. It is not clear whether this information could become accessible to the press or general public once it is released to the police or other agency, whose files can constitute a matter of public record.

The original intentions of the laws and court rulings concerning child abuse were undoubtedly good, thoughtful, and humanitarian. The idea was to protect children from further bodily injury or harm by removing them from the environment in which such abuse was being inflicted upon them. This extreme form of intervention may well have been an appropriate attempt to deal with an extreme and desperate situation, and it can certainly be considered as serving to protect a hapless child from further physical damage. The revised law apparently strives to prevent, through early intervention, a possibly incipient situation from developing into an extreme and desperate state of affairs. Although few clinicians would argue against such a laudable objective, it seems that retaining this putting-out-the-brush-fire mechanism of social intervention is likely to be counterproductive to the good intentions of the law.

IMPLICATIONS OF THE LAW

As chair of the California State Psychological Association's Committee on Confidentiality from 1981 to 1985, I have gained an overview of the issues and dilemmas that result from implementation of the duty to report law in the daily workplace of psychologists. I assume that these experiences are similar to those of psychiatrist and clinical social worker colleagues, and I hope that extended dialogue on these issues by our respective professional organizations will shed more light on this subject in the near future. The following are some exemplary cases.

The client is an 18-year-old woman, hospitalized for the past 2 monhts, who now reveals that she was sexually molested by her father since the age of 6. Her parents were divorced when she was 7 years old, and she lived with her father while she was growing up. She states that he has been peeping at her in the bathroom, and that 2 years ago there was one incident of vaginal penetration when she was drunk. She now hates her father, who is currently living with a girl friend. The client was living alone prior to her hospitalization. Question: considering the time frame, present age, and mental condition of the patient, does the therapist need to report this molestation to the designated authorities? Answer: according to the law, as written, yes. But what kind of sense would it make to do so? The incidents occurred years ago; the "child" is now 18 years old, and she is not now living with her father. How well does that achieve the avowed purpose of reporting, namely to prevent *further* abuse? Then there is the matter of the reliability and/or validity of the information. Certainly what she claims may indeed have happened, but as clinicians we also know the role that fantasy and underlying dynamics can play in a situation like this. How professionally ethical would it be for us to ignore such considerations? And what would be the likely effects upon the treatment situation if the therapist (1) reports without informing the woman or (2) requests her authorization to release the information? We have not yet exhausted the dilemmas that this kind of case can pose for a therapist.

A little girl was referred to a psychologist for treatment by a pediatrician, who had already informed the authorities that child abuse had occurred in her family. The abuse occurred once or twice, some 6 to 9 months before, and the parents were outraged when they learned that their pediatrician had reported them. Question: do considerations of time passage, frequency of occurrence, or the fact of previous reporting affect the therapist's duty to report? Answer: the law does not address any of these considerations, and there are no known court cases in California dealing with the law; therefore, there is a legal duty to report.

In the following case, all three adults involved were clients of a psychologist: a woman (age 38), her mother, and the woman's boyfriend (age 40). Some months before, the mother had discussed her suspicion that her daughter's boyfriend was a "queer sort." Now the daughter reveals that the boyfriend confessed to her that he had been sexually molesting a 10-year-old girl and that he was convicted of child molestation 2 years ago. The parents of the young girl have been friends, of long standing, with all three of the therapist's patients, and they continue to let the girl go out with the man and to stay overnight at his place. The therapist intends to comply with the law and to deal with the clinical consequences of doing so with her clients, but she needs clarification of some specific legal, i.e., confidentiality, issues to guide her course of action. Question: does she *have to* tell the man that she will be reporting him? Answer: no, the law is silent on this point. Question: because she plans to discuss with the man what she suspects and what the law requires her to do, must she tell him how and where she got her information? Answer: no, the law is silent on this point, but he could certainly figure it out easily enough. Question: because she told the girl friend that she would have to report the boyfriend's molesting behavior but did not tell her that she would be discussing this with the boyfriend first, is she violating the girl friend's confidentiality? Answer: yes. Question: because of the timing involved in the therapist's sequential plan of action, she will not be able to report to the authorities within the 36 hours specified in the law; will this make her legally vulnerable? Answer: no, for all practical purposes; under the circumstances, the therapist would likely be covered by the "substantial compliance" concept. In sum, one can see the implications of trying to act in a clinically responsible manner while pursuing one's duty to report obligation.

Even these few cases show that it can be a pretty cold and lonely world "out there" when the duty to report arises. Few attorneys are readily knowledgeable about confidentiality issues in general, and the lack of court cases specifically involving this law leaves them with little more than the bare bones of the penal code on which to base their counsel. When all is said and done, however, it still comes down to each therapist having to make his or her own decision and living with it.

At a slightly different level of analysis, a bit removed from the immediate statute versus clinical case interface, there are still other dilemmas for the clinician. These broader implications for confidentiality have to do with social roles and sociopolitical forces. The primary social role of a professional therapist is to help people with their intrapersonal and/or interpersonal problems and to perform this work in a very special setting of privacy and confidentiality. That is how the public perceives psychotherapists, and that is how they see themselves. This special condition of confidentiality has evolved over centuries along with the social role, from priest to physician to psychotherapist, and it is currently defined by the psychotherapist–patient privilege in our laws. Therapy and the confidentiality privilege are highly interdependent entities but if, in the course of this trust-induced interaction, someone says the "magic" words, e.g., reveals child abuse, the therapist becomes instantly deputized into a police agent. The client is still the same person, but there has been a sudden and drastic switch in social roles, whereby the therapist exits and the informer bursts in at the door.

The quality of life is, to a considerable extent, a function of the social and political forces that prevail at any given time. We create forces in the world that favor trust, tranquility, and growth, but, in addition, those that promote distrust, fear, and destruction. I personally have terrible memories of Nazi Germany, where the informer function became a part of daily life, with dreadful consequences for the entire social fabric. The reported utterances of children were turned against their parents, and those of friends against friends. People soon learned to use this vehicle in the service of their own needs of ambition, fear, revenge, and the like. The similarity here is not that farfetched. The line between "good" and "bad" use of unevaluated reporting to government agencies can be very thin indeed, and can always be subject to shift. A quick replay of our own relatively recent history of the FBI, CIA, and the McCarthy era will suffice to make that point. The duty to report asks us to transfer unconfirmed information, entrusted in confidence, from that context into one of investigation and intervention with police power, without the knowledge or permission of the client or control of its use by the therapist. Even if nothing comes of one specific report concerning a person, the police and similar agencies do keep, cumulate, and share dossiers—it's part of their job. This duty to report legislation has us feeding into such a system. And thereby, we may be contributing to those forces that tend to rend our country's democratic social fabric. I don't want to do that.

The concept of all-or-nothing mandated reporting is a complete antithesis of the role-appropriate confidentiality concept that was embodied in the Hippocratic oath. There must be a better way of dealing with this genuinely complex social issue. The sensible approach embodied in the Maine and Maryland laws, providing mental health professionals discretion not to report, seems to be a step in the right direction. I think our profession should find a way to light a candle rather than just curse the darkness.

A CASE IN POINT

Splashed all over the San Francisco newspapers recently was the case of a 12-year-old seventh-grade girl who was caught up in a Kafkaesque consequence of the mandated child abuse reporting law. Throughout the case this girl was called "Amy" to protect her and the family from publicity. In the summer of 1983, Amy's family was composed of her 31-year-old mother, a former nurse; her 32-year-old stepfather, a physician; and a 6-year-old sibling. They lived in a medium-sized town in the San Francisco Bay area. Amy had been telling her mother that her stepfather was "fondling" her, and when the mother became convinced of the truth of the matter she insisted that her husband move out of the house for the time being and that both parents and Amy seek professional help for their family problems from a local counselor. Having heard their story, the counselor, in compliance with the law now in effect since 1981, duly informed the local child protective services agency that the stepfather had allegedly fondled Amy. This agency reported the information to the district attorney's office. The parents were stripped of custody, and Amy was placed in the home of her maternal grandparents. The district attorney filed charges against the stepfather, thereby plunging the entire family into the criminal justice system.

At a preliminary municipal court hearing, Amy declined repeatedly to testify against her stepfather, whereupon the judge found her guilty of civil contempt and ordered her held in a four-by-eight windowless, solitary confinement cell of juvenile hall. She was allowed outside her cell only when no other children were around, thus adding to her isolation from the rest of the world. When Amy again declined to testify at the hearing after 5 days of this punitive confinement, the judge ordered her held over the weekend and barred further visits from her mother. After 8 days of juvenile hall confinement, Amy's attorney finally obtained her release from a superior court judge, and she was transferred to a foster home. Another superior court hearing took place 2 days later to rule on possible permanent foster home placement for Amy. When the dust had settled, Amy was made a ward of the court and returned to her mother; the stepfather was ordered not to see Amy, and the family was ordered to undergo treatment and report back to the court 6 months later. The mother and stepfather continued to live in separation, reportedly trying to work out a reconciliation.

Reported retrospective comments by two of the attorneys in the case are of interest. The prosecuting attorney stoutly justified and defended his actions, claiming that he "had no choice" about the way the case was handled and that he followed "the only remedy the law gives me." Our laws, however, are seldom ever so cut and dried. Indeed, both the child protective services agency and the district attorney's office ignored those provisions in the law that are designed (1) to prevent psychological harm to the child and (2) to promote helpful social service and treatment approaches to the problem.

In this case, several options immediately are apparent to any experienced clinician. The family could have continued seeing their original counselor or any qualified mental health professional; or it could have received help from such available self-help programs as Parents United. The stepfather could have received a psychodiagnostic evaluation from a clinical psychologist that would have focused on his impulse control status. On the basis of this evaluation, his professional practice as a physician could, if warranted, have been appropriately modified for the time being—such as seeing adults only, peer supervision of his practice with child patients, and so forth. Evidently, the people responsible for implementing this law were not open to such considerations. The stepfather's attorney expressed the belief that "the reporting laws were enacted with the best possible intentions, but at the same time any family sitting at home wondering what to do about this problem—and hearing about this—is certainly not going to seek counseling."

What, then, went wrong? The law that was avowedly designed to protect and promote children's welfare certainly did not achieve that purpose in this instance. In looking back at the reported events, there appear to have been three major policy decision issues. One was the general perception of what was most important to accomplish. The choice here was between doing something constructive that could have been helpful to all concerned or implementing the belief that the behavior of the girl warranted punishment to bring it to a halt. Those in the child protective services agency and the criminal justice system evidently opted for the latter alternative.

Another decision seems to have been inherent in the workings of the criminal justice system. Once the decision to bring a felony prosecution was made by the district attorney's office, Amy's testimony became essential to the successful prosecution of the case. I believe this to have been a most crucial juncture in the whole process, because it was at this point that all consideration for Amy's welfare went out the window in exchange for society achieving "justice." Thus the stated reasons for, and purposes of, the law were superseded by forces that were set loose in its implementation.

A third issue relates to the task of protecting other potential "victims" from this physician's behavior in the future. The prosecuting attorney was reported as feeling confronted by a situation in which a "confessed molester of a female minor" was in a position of trust in the community, which would bring him into intimate contact with other female minors in course of his work as a practicing physician. Given the nature of the attorney's professional training and his position in a public agency, it is little wonder that he chose to "proceed with the prosecution to achieve justice" as the preferred way of responding to this problem. Some of the alternative options mentioned earlier do not, alas, seem to fit this frame of reference. No doubt, each participant in the case had multiple personal motivations for their actions, but that is really beside the point. Any law that can allow such blatantly counterproductive events to occur is, I conclude, an ill-conceived one that should be revised or rescinded.

CONCLUSIONS

We need confidentiality as a necessary condition to help people sort out the thoughts and emotions that lie behind the problems in their lives. Conversely, we need legal safeguards that can be invoked to protect the safety and welfare of our clients, their families, and other persons. There is a delicate balance between these two basic requirements. Who is best suited to decide what to do—psychotherapists or police or social service workers? I believe that our professional judgment, imperfect as it is bound to be, is yet preferable to the present approach, which attempts to gain one desirable end at the expense of another. We are addressing issues that involve value judgments, for "truth" in this regard is not scientifically demonstrable. So, in the final analysis, one will be guided by one's value system. I believe it is more important to preserve the certainty of professional confidentiality in our society than to attempt to protect vulnerable persons by processes that could not conceivably approach a level of certain success.

REFERENCES

1. *Tarasoff v. Board of Regents of the University of California,* 17 C 3d 425; 131 Cal Rptr. 14, 551 P. 2d 334 (1976).
2. *Landeros v. Flood,* 17 Cal. 3d 399; 131 Cal. Rptr. 69, P 2d 389 (1976).

Robert Weisberg
Michael Wald

9

Confidentiality Laws and State Efforts to Protect Abused or Neglected Children: The Need for Statutory Reform

Child protection agencies investigate more than 1 million reports of child abuse or neglect each year.[1] These agencies institute approximately 150,000 court proceedings yearly to establish state supervision over children alleged to be abused or neglected.[2] If a court determines that a child has suffered abuse or neglect, it must decide whether to leave the child with the parents or place the child in foster care.[3] When a child is removed from the parents' physical custody, the court must later decide whether to return the child to

---

A more detailed treatment of this subject by the same authors appeared in *Family Law Quarterly, 18* (Summer, 1984), pp. 143–212.

This research was supported, in part, by funds from the Stanford Center on Youth Development and from the Stanford Legal Research Fund, made possible by a bequest from the estate of Ira S. Lillick and by gifts from Roderick M. and Carla A. Hills and other friends of the Stanford Law School. We thank Doug Besharov, David Chambers, Sam Gross, John Kaplan, Mark Kelman, Wallace Mlyniec, and Saul Wasserman for their comments on earlier drafts, and Lewis Lazarus, Robert Woll, and Nancy Goodman for their research help.

[1] *Study Findings—National Study of the Incidence of and Severity of Child Abuse and Neglect, U.S. Department of Health and Human Services* (DHHS Pub. No. [OHDS] 81-30325) at 11 (1981) (hereafter *Study Findings*).

[2] National Center for Juvenile Justice, *Juvenile Court Statistics 1980*, pp. 20–21 (1982).

[3] For a description of the decisions agencies and courts make regarding whether and how to intervene, *see* Wald, *State Intervention on Behalf of "Neglected" Children: A Search for Realistic Standards*, 27 STAN. L. REV. 985 (1975); Wald, *State Intervention on Behalf of Neglected Children; Standards for Removal of Children from their Homes, Monitoring the Status of Children in Foster Care, and Termination of Parental Rights*, 28 STAN. L. REV. 625 (1976) (hereafter Wald I and Wald II); for a description of the process *see* D. BESHAROV, JUVENILE JUSTICE ADVOCACY 114–53 (1974).

the parents. If the child cannot be returned to his or her parents, the agency may institute court action to terminate the parents' ties to the child so that the child may be adopted by another family.[4]

In making decisions involving abused or neglected children, agencies[5] often request information from medical and mental health professionals who have treated or counseled the parents or the child. In some cases the professional has directly observed evidence of the abuse or neglect; for example, the professional may be a physician who treated an injured child and learned that the parent inflicted the injury. In many cases, however, a professional who has no direct evidence of abuse or neglect has information that may be useful to the investigating agency. For example, a mental health professional who treated the parent in psychotherapy or in a drug or alcohol abuse program may have obtained information about the parent, such as evidence about violent behavior, which would help in determining whether the child has been abused or neglected or whether the parent is able to care for the child.

To ensure that professionals from medicine, psychology, and clinical social work assist in identifying abused or neglected children, all states have passed "child abuse reporting laws," which require medical and mental health professionals to report to a child welfare agency any child whom they know or suspect to be abused or neglected.[6] These laws, however, mandate reporting when a professional has specific information indicating that a child may have been abused or neglected. They do not require professionals to report other information that might be useful to courts or agencies making decisions regarding abused or neglected children.[7]

Although most professionals accept the need to report their knowledge or suspicion that a child has been abused or neglected,[8] many are reluctant to

---

[4] *See infra* note 35 and accompanying text for a description of termination laws.

[5] We refer in the text to agencies. Most of the information we discuss in this article will first be sought by a child protection agency deciding whether to bring a court action. We are also concerned about the use of the information in the actual court proceedings. We believe that the same standards should apply during investigations and at court proceedings. Therefore, unless the context indicates otherwise, when we use the term "agency" we also mean "court." We generally use only one term to make the chapter more readable.

[6] For an overview of reporting laws, see S. COHEN & A. SUSSMAN, REPORTING CHILD ABUSE AND NEGLECT (1975). The most timely summary is M. ALDERMAN, CHILD ABUSE AND NEGLECT: STATE REPORTING LAWS (DHHS Pub. No. [OHDS] 80-30265) (1979).

[7] The exact scope of mandatory reporting laws is very unclear, as is their relationship with confidentiality laws. The statutory language is generally vague. *See e.g.,* KAN. STAT. ANN. § 38–717 (1980) (requiring reporting of "injuries inflicted as a result of physical or mental abuse or neglect"). The few civil or criminal proceedings brought against professionals for failure to report involve egregious situations of physical abuse and thus do not help define the contours of these laws. Lack of clarity in the laws is a major complaint of professionals.

[8] While many professionals resisted the idea of reporting laws when the laws were first introduced during the 1960s, the predominant attitude appears to have changed. *See* COHEN & SUSSMAN, *supra* note 6 at 127–48: Contemporary Studies Project, *Iowa Professionals and the*

share any other information.[9] Although they are concerned with protecting children, most professionals believe that safeguarding the confidentiality of information received from their clients is both essential for successful treatment and ethically required. Their beliefs find support in laws that expressly constrain professionals from disclosing confidential information.

Two types of laws recognize confidentiality between doctors or therapists and their patients. Most prevalent are those that create *evidence privileges*.[10] These laws bar the use, *in court proceedings*,[11] of certain information obtained by a professional during the course of treatment or therapy unless the patient authorizes disclosure. A second type of law, far less well understood than privileges, we call *nondisclosure* laws. These statutes, which generally apply when a patient receives treatment in a psychiatric facility or a state-run drug or alcohol abuse program, or when a welfare client receives social services, prohibit anyone connected with the treatment or service agency, including a professional, from revealing any information regarding a client, even the fact that the person is a client. These laws apply both *inside and outside court proceedings*. Both types of statutes, which we shall call generally "confidentiality" laws, are designed to protect personal privacy as well as to encourage and help maintain relationships between clients and professionals. In addition to such public laws, many professions have written standards of professional conduct that address the need to provide confidentiality to patients or clients.[12] Professionals often look to those standards in deciding when to preserve particular confidences. These standards are sometimes the basis of civil actions against professionals who violate them.[13]

Iowa Child Abuse Reporting Statute—A Case of Success. 65 IOWA L. REV. 1273 (1980); Nell and Rosen, *Privacy, Confidentiality and Informed Consent in Psychotherapy*, in PSYCHIATRIC PATIENT RIGHTS AND PATIENT ADVOCACY 176–78 (B. Bloom and S. Asher eds. 1982). There are still dissenters who believe that such laws contribute little to protecting children and needlessly interfere with doctor–patient relations. *See* J. GOLDSTEIN, A. FREUD, & A. SOLNIT, BEFORE THE BEST INTERESTS OF THE CHILD 71 (1979). There is substantial debate about the proper scope of reporting laws. *Compare* Solnit, *Too Much Reporting, Too Little Service: Roots and Prevention of Child Abuse*, in CHILD ABUSE: AN AGENDA FOR ACTION, 135–46 (G. Gerbner, C. Ross, E. Zigler, ed. 1980) *with* Besharov, *Putting Central Registers to Work*, 6 CHILDREN TODAY (1977); HERNER & COMPANY, IMPACT OF FEDERAL LAW ON PROVISION OF CHILD PROTECTIVE SERVICES 9–10 (DHHS Report No. 117, 1981).

[9] In fact, professionals still substantially underreport where the laws mandate reporting. *See Study Findings, supra* note 1, at 34–35. Ironically, professionals also overreport. *See infra* note 20 and accompanying text. The problem, in part, lies in the vagueness of reporting laws.

[10] These laws are described more fully in the section on "Privilege Laws" below.

[11] They may also bar revealing information outside of court. *See infra* notes 53–54 and accompanying text.

[12] *See e.g., Principles of Medical Ethics with Annotations Especially Applicable to Psychiatry*, 130 AM. J. PSYCHIATRY 1058 (1973). The ethical standards of various professional groups are reproduced in B. SCHUTZ, LEGAL LIABILITY IN PSYCHOTHERAPY 98–184 (1982).

[13] *See e.g.,* Martin v. Family Serv. Agency, 112 Ill. App. 3d 593,445 N.E.2d 6 (1983).

Unfortunately, in most states the laws regulating the withholding or disclosure of information are unclear or inconsistent. A professional may be confronted with laws *requiring* him or her to report certain information, laws *allowing* him or her to report or disclose information at his or her discretion, and laws *forbidding* disclosure of some information. As a result of the vagueness and inconsistencies in these laws, professionals bound by them often are confused about what information relating to past abuse or neglect or the possibility of future abuse or neglect they must, can, or cannot reveal to child protection agencies or courts.[14] Agency personnel and courts may be equally uncertain.[15] This confusion impedes the agencies in obtaining information relevant to abuse and neglect charges. Some professionals who want to provide information to agencies are afraid of liability if they do so. Other professionals who do not want to share information—and many professionals do not[16]—rely on these unclear laws as a justification for maintaining the confidentiality they believe important. In fact, confidentiality laws may bar professionals from providing information that may be crucial to agency or court decisions regarding abused or neglected children.[17]

In this chapter we address the question of when, if ever, information that is known to a medical or mental health professional, but that is not covered by abuse reporting laws, should be available to agencies investigating, or courts adjudicating,[18] cases of child abuse or neglect or termination of parental rights. We conclude that the benefits derived from full disclosure outweigh the costs of requiring disclosure in all *civil*[19] proceedings brought by the state relating to abused or neglected children. Therefore, we propose that professionals have a legal *duty* to disclose information not already covered by a mandatory reporting law when a child protection agency or a court

---

[14] One of the authors (Wald) frequently receives questions about the meaning of these laws in the course of training programs he conducts. A leading manual on abuse and neglect indicates that even experts are confused. *See* Snyder, *Child Abuse Reporting and Release of Information,* in 2 CALIFORNIA CONTINUING EDUCATION OF THE BAR, CALIFORNIA JUV. CT. PRAC. 279 (1981).

[15] *See* HERNER & CO., *supra* note 8, at 11. *See also* the opinions and dissents in Edward D., 61 Cal. App. 3d 10, 132 Cal Rptr. 100 (1976); *In re* Collins v. Superior Court, 74 Cal. App. 47, 141 Cal. Rptr. 273 (1977); *In re* S. W. 79 Cal. App. 3d 719, 145 Cal Rptr. 143 (1978). Confidentiality and child custody proceedings cause similar confusion. *Compare* Roper v. Roper, 336 So.2d 654 (Fla. App. 1976) *and* Critchlow v. Critchlow, 347 So. 2d 453 (Fla. App. 1977).

[16] *See supra* notes 8, 9. One of the authors (Wald), in conducting training sessions for social workers, frequently encounters mental health professionals who are reluctant to cooperate with child protection agencies.

[17] *E.g., In re* Westland 48 Ill. App. 3d 172, 362 N.E.2d 1153 (1977).

[18] The term "adjudicating" is meant to cover all phases of abuse/neglect proceedings: the initial determination as to whether the child is abused or neglected, the dispositional hearing at which it is decided how to handle the case, review proceedings, and termination hearings. These stages are described at notes 30–36 *infra* and accompanying test.

[19] As we discuss later we would not apply these rules to criminal proceedings.

requests the information. We do not, however, recommend expanding the scope of mandatory reporting laws.[20]

The first part of this chapter examines the problems of child abuse and neglect and the types of information professionals often obtain that might bear on abuse or neglect but that might also fall within some confidentiality law.

The second part surveys the state of the law of confidentiality, examining the diversity and inconsistency of laws requiring, permitting, and forbidding professionals to disclose information.

The third part examines the policies promoted by confidentiality laws.

The fourth part considers the weight to be given the various goals in resolving the conflict between the need for information and the need to protect confidentiality.

The fifth part proposes a new legislative scheme restricting confidentiality laws so that agencies and courts can obtain all the information they legitimately need in protecting children from abuse and neglect.

CHILD ABUSE AND NEGLECT: THE NATURE OF THE HARM AND THE NEED FOR INFORMATION

Child Abuse and Neglect: The Harm

Parents harm their children in a variety of ways. At the extreme, at least several thousand children are killed or permanently incapacitated by parents each year.[21] Another 20,000 to 50,000 children receive less severe, but still very serious, injuries, including broken bones or beatings that impair their bodily functions. In addition, in 1981 child protection agencies received approximately 40,000 reports of parents engaging in sexual activity with their children, activity ranging from fondling to intercourse. Children who have been sexually involved with parents often experience severe emotional problems, both during childhood and as adults.[22]

---

[20] In fact, we believe that many current statutes are too broad and require reporting of situations which do not justify intervention. Broad, vague reporting laws are harmful in several ways. First, they make professionals hostile to the entire reporting system. Second, they lead to more reports than the system can or should process. Approximately half of all current reports, including those from professionals, prove to be unfounded or not to require any action. *See Study Findings, supra* note 1, at 12. In investigating these reports, agencies use resources that they ought to conserve for helping people who have seriously abused or neglected their children. Reporting laws need to be clarified so that mandated reporters know what is, and is not, expected from them.

[21] *See* AMERICAN HUMANE ASSOCIATION HIGHLIGHTS OF OFFICIAL CHILD NEGLECT AND ABUSE REPORTING (1983). The statistics in the rest of this paragraph also are taken from *id.* at 7 and from *Study Findings, supra* note 1, at 18.

[22] *See generally* K. MEISELMAN, INCEST 194 (1978).

Parents harm children through inattention as well as through physical or sexual abuse. A parent may leave young children unattended or unsupervised for lengthy periods of time, exposing them to risk of injury. The family home may be in such dangerous condition that it threatens the child's health or physical safety. Finally, some parents fail to send their children to school or to obtain medical care necessary to prevent the child from suffering severe physical harm.

Without some type of coercive intervention by state child protection agencies, many children face repeated abuse or neglect. In fact, abuse and neglect often recur even when the state does intervene.[23] Without state intervention the majority of *seriously* abused or neglected children would likely face substantial risk.[24]

In addition to the actual harm from abuse or neglect, children sometimes face risk by being placed in foster care for an indefinite time, often for many years. It is now widely accepted that children need permanent homes and that long-term foster care ought to be avoided whenever possible.[25] If an abused or neglected child is placed in foster care and cannot thereafter be returned home safely, termination of parental rights may be necessary to prevent the harms associated with long-term foster care.[26]

We do recognize that, at present, not all cases of abuse or neglect that agencies investigate or bring to court involve life-threatening or serious harm. Unfortunately, vague, broadly worded laws have led the state to intervene where parents pose little, if any, harm to a child.[27] To the degree that the state intervenes unnecessarily, it adds to the costs of such intervention by abrogating confidentiality laws as well. Vague, overbroad laws defining abuse and neglect or mandating reporting ought to be repealed and replaced with new laws that carefully define the type of harm to children that justifies intervention. Because one of the authors has written extensively about the need for revised laws,[28] we will not develop the issue in this

---

[23] *See* Cohn, *Essential Elements of Successful Child Abuse and Neglect Treatment,* 3 CHILD ABUSE AND NEGLECT 491 (1979); Herrenkohl, Herrenkohl, Geech, Egolf, *The Repetition of Child Abuse: How Frequently Does it Occur?* 3 CHILD ABUSE AND NEGLECT 67 (1980). Studies in states show that more than 25 percent of all child fatalities attributed to abuse or neglect involve children who already have been brought to the attention of a child protection agency. *See* Anderson, Ambrosino, Valentine, and Lauderdale, *Child Deaths Attributed to Abuse and Neglect: An Empirical Study,* 5 CHILDREN AND YOUTH SERVICES REV. 75 (1983).

[24] We assume that if up to half the parents receiving agency services reabuse their children, the rate would be higher without services. Although services are not uniformly successful, they do make some difference. *See* Cohn *supra* note 23.

[25] *See* Wald II, *supra* note 3, at 645–46.

[26] *See* Wald II, *supra* note 3, at 660–700. To end long-term, unstable foster care, Congress adopted the *Adoption Assistance and Child Welfare Act of 1980,* Pub. L. No. 96–272, which requires states to provide permanent homes for children in foster care.

[27] *See* Wald I, *supra* note 3, at 1004–36.

[28] *See* Wald I and II, *supra* note 3; AMERICAN BAR ASSOCIATION, STANDARDS RELATING TO ABUSE AND NEGLECT (1977).

chapter. In the latter sections, however, we attempt to balance the agencies' and courts' need for information and clients' need for confidentiality; in so doing, we are assuming a system with specific and narrow definitions of abuse and neglect, so that coercive state intervention occurs only to prevent serious harm.[29]

The Importance of the Information from Professionals

In deciding whether to limit confidentiality laws, a legislature must do more than merely determine whether children suffer harms as a result of abuse, neglect, or long-term foster care. It must also consider the courts' and agencies' need for the information that confidentiality laws protect. To show how information known to professionals, but not covered by mandatory reporting laws, is useful in abuse or neglect proceedings, we first describe how agencies and courts establish that a child has been abused or neglected, and how they determine by which means the state should intervene to protect such children, and whether the state should terminate parental rights. We then describe the types of information professionals may have and which, because of confidentiality laws, may not be available to agencies or courts.

The Child Protection Process

Public social work agencies in all states are charged with receiving reports that a child has been abused or neglected and with investigating these reports to determine what response, if any, is appropriate.[30] The initial information may come to the agency from such diverse sources as doctors, nurses, or teachers who have known the child; friends or relatives who know the family; or mental health professionals who have treated or diagnosed the parents.[31] Some reports come from police, children, or agency workers themselves. More than half the reports come from nonprofessionals.

After the agency receives the initial report, it must determine whether the report is well-founded. Agency workers may interview the parents and child; question neighbors, relatives, or teachers about how the parent cares for the child; and contact any doctor, mental health professional, or social

---

[29] An uncoordinated legislative scheme will fail, whatever its content. The legislature cannot create sensible limits to confidentiality rules without regard to the definitions of abuse and neglect which determine how much private information professionals can disclose. If the legislature defines "neglect" too broadly, we would propose broader confidentiality laws to prevent professionals from sacrificing their clients' privacy unnecessarily. The problem of overbroad intervention arises less in abuse cases, since under virtually all legal definitions of abuse, the state child protection systems must closely examine whether the child faces serious harm.

[30] *See* BESHAROV, *supra* note 3, for a fuller description of the process.

[31] *See* AMERICAN HUMANE ASSOCIATION, *supra* note 21, at 8.

worker who has treated the parents or child. If the agency believes the child is endangered, it can offer services to the family on a voluntary basis,[32] or it can initiate a civil proceeding in juvenile court, alleging that the child has suffered harm falling within the statutory definition of abuse or neglect and that court supervision is needed to protect the child. When the parents contest the allegations, the agency will present evidence trying to establish the abuse or neglect.[33]

If the court determines that the child has suffered abuse or neglect (either by the admission of the parent or after a trial), the court will hold a "dispositional" hearing.[34] At this hearing, the judge determines whether the child can remain with the parents under the supervision of the child protection agency or whether the child should be placed in foster care. The investigating agency generally provides the court with a "social study" describing the background of the parents and recommending an appropriate disposition. This report usually includes a summary of any information provided by professionals to the investigating agency.

If the court removes the child from his or her parents and places her or him in foster care, the court will hold later hearings to determine whether to return the child to the parents. At such hearings, the agency will report on changes in the parents' behavior or home conditions and, generally, recommend whether the child should be returned.

Finally, if a child has been removed from the parents' custody and the agency responsible for the child believes that the child should never be returned to the parents, it may ask the court to terminate the parents' rights to custody of the child so the child may be adopted by another family. The agency usually brings these proceedings only after the child has been in foster care for at least a year. Most states have statutes specifying the

---

[32] In the great majority of cases when an agency believes a child is endangered the case is handled informally, with the family voluntarily accepting services (and surveillance) from the agency. In these situations the child usually remains with the parents. Presumably, the more information the agency has during the initial investigation, the more likely it will make a good decision on the need for court action.

[33] These proceedings are held in juvenile courts before judges sitting without juries, and are usually conducted more informally than most civil trials. For example, some states permit "hearsay" evidence at these adjudications, and virtually all states permit hearsay at the dispositional phase. *See e.g.,* CAL. WELF. & INST. CODE § 355 (West 1983). The court may also consider a social study prepared by the child protection agency, which contains a great deal of background information about the parents and the current allegations *before* it decides whether the child has been abused or neglected. *See In re* Biggs. 17 Cal. App. 3d 337, 94 Cal. Rptr. 519 (1971).

[34] This hearing is often held right after the court determines that the child has been abused or neglected. In fact, in some jurisdictions the state may introduce evidence relating to disposition during the adjudicatory stage. This practice has been criticized by commentators. *See* Walker & Wienerman, *Jurisdictional Hearing,* in CALIFORNIA JUV. CT. PRAC. 101-102 (1982).

grounds for terminating parental rights. California law, which is typical, allows termination if:

(3) [the] parent or parents suffer a disability because of the habitual use of alcohol, or any controlled substance, which renders the parent or parents unable adequately to care for and control the child.

(6) [the] parent or parents are, and will remain incapable of supporting or controlling the child in a proper manner because of mental deficiency or mental illness.

(7) [the child] has been [in foster care] for 12 months, provided the court finds by clear and convincing evidence that return of the child to the child's parent or parents would be detrimental to the child and that the parent or parents have failed during such period, and are likely to fail in the future, to do all of the following:

   (i) Provide a home for the child.
   (ii) Provide care and control for the child.
   (iii) Maintain an adequate parental relationship with the child.[35]

The agency generally conducts a separate investigation on the parents' fitness to resume custody before it begins a termination proceeding. As in the other proceedings, it provides a social study about the parent and child to the court[36] and may include a recommendation.

The Information Professionals Can Provide

Information from professionals may be useful in making any of the four decisions just described. The court or agency obviously needs any *direct* information that a parent has abused or neglected a child, such as when the professional has observed injuries that appear to have been inflicted nonaccidentally, or learns from the parent or child that the child has been physically or sexually abused by the parent. For the most part, such information falls within child abuse-reporting laws. These laws, though not uniform across the states, are all basically similar. They require that certain persons, including doctors and mental health professionals, notify either a social service or law enforcement agency if, in their professional capacity, they come in contact with, or have knowledge of, a child who they know or suspect has been abused or neglected. A professional who fails to report may be subject to criminal penalties or monetary damages.

At first glance, abuse reporting statutes seem to reflect a conclusive

---

[35] CAL. CIVIL CODE § 232 (West 1983). The statute contains other grounds not relevant to our point.

[36] Contested termination proceedings generally tend to be more formal than the other types of hearings. They are often held in a court of general civil jurisdiction, not in a specialized juvenile court. Parents generally are represented by counsel, which often is not the case in other juvenile proceedings. The United States Supreme Court has established some constitutional restrictions on the conduct of such hearings. *See Santosky v. Kramer.* 455 U.S. 745 (1982).

public policy favoring, in fact requiring, disclosure of all information that might be relevant to protecting an abused or neglected child. Yet even under the broadest statutes, professionals may have information relevant to abuse or neglect which they are not required to disclose. Although all reporting laws cover physical abuse, some do not specifically cover sexual conduct or various types of neglect.[37] More important, reporting laws focus on situations in which the professional has information from which he or she can reasonably infer that a child has already suffered harm as a result of abuse or neglect. As we have noted, however, professionals often may have information that does not, by itself, show abuse or neglect and that therefore falls outside the mandatory reporting laws but still might help the agency or court determine the issues that arise in any of the various proceedings. We call this *indirect evidence,* and it is this type of information that we focus on throughout the chapter.

Indirect evidence generally falls into five categories. First, a professional may be aware of *conditions of the parent,* such as drug or alcohol addiction, which might bear on the likelihood that the parent abused or neglected a child or on the parent's ability to provide adequate care for the child.[38] For example, the professional may know that because of her addiction the parent suffers from blackouts or other impairments. Second, a pro-

---

[37] *See* M. ALDERMAN, *supra* note 6. In addition, although all states require the professional to report the specific basis of her or his allegation or suspicion of abuse or neglect, such as his or her direct observation of the child's injuries or unsafe conditions in the home, it is not clear how much collateral information they require. For example, if the reporter is a therapist who has been treating the client for some time, can the therapist reveal anything about the therapy, other than the evidence of abuse? *See* Snyder, *Child Abuse Reporting and Release of Information* in CALIFORNIA JUV. CT. PRACT. Vol. 2, at 279 (1981). In some states it also is not clear whether a professional must report or reveal information once a child has been reported by another person. Reporting laws are designed to identify mistreated children, not to obtain the maximum available information about mistreatment. *See People v. Stritzinger,* 34 Cal. 3d 505, 668 P.2d 738, 194 Cal. Rptr. 431 (1983).

[38] As discussed in note 7 *supra,* the coverage of reporting laws is debatable. At least one expert with whom we have spoken, Douglas Besharov, former director of the National Center on Child Abuse and Neglect in the Department of Health and Human Services, believes that the fact that a parent is addicted or suffers from mental illness might be covered by mandatory reporting laws. We disagree. We believe that such laws require reporting only if the professional has reason to believe that the parents' condition makes the parent unable to care for the child. For example, a hospital might have to report that a mother of a newborn is so retarded that she cannot properly feed or care for the child. The mere fact that the parent is an alcoholic is not reportable unless the parent has shown an inability to care for the child.

Although we believe that the mere fact of the parent's condition is not, and should not be reportable, we would see this information as highly relevant *if the child is later reported* as being left unattended or inadequately cared for. A parent's drug or alcohol addiction may greatly affect her ability to care for the child. *See* Lawson and Wilson, *Parenting among Women Addicted to Narcotics,* 59 CHILD WELFARE 67 (1980); Cohen and Densen-Gerber. *A Study of the Relationship between Child Abuse and Drug Addiction in 178 Patients: Preliminary Results,* 6 CHILD ABUSE AND NEGLECT 383 (1982).

fessional who has helped the parent with addiction or mental health problems can advise the court or agency on the parent's *receptiveness to treatment*. Third, a parent may have made *statements* to a physician or therapist that might help in deciding whether an injury was caused accidentally or intentionally or whether a dispositional plan is likely to be successful. For example, the parent may have revealed aggressive feelings toward her child or expressed concern over her overuse of physical discipline or inability to cope with her child's troublesome behavior. Yet if the professional did not know that the child had been injured, these statements would not be reportable. Fourth, a professional might know of the parent's *violent behavior,* itself unrelated to the child, that would be relevant in abuse or neglect proceedings, as when the professional knows that a parent has a history of spousal abuse. Finally, the professional may be aware that the child has a *history* of suffering minor injuries, none of which alone indicated abuse but which in connection with other information known to an agency tend to help show that the parent has provided inadequate care for the child.

Any of these kinds of information may be relevant to each of the four decisions an agency or court must make. At the initial stage, the agency or court may need such information to determine whether the parent has injured or neglected the child. As previously noted, most reports of abuse or neglect are from nonclinical sources—teachers, relatives of the child, or neighbors. Such reports are often quite sketchy. For example, a neighbor may report that she has frequently seen the child crying, or that the child has bruises and scratches on her face, or that the parent has been seen screaming at the child in public. With only this information, the agency might be uncertain what to do. Has the child been injured enough to require medical care? Did the parent inflict the injuries? Is the parent prone to violence? Is the parent providing adequate protection? If the parent has been under the care of a mental health professional, that professional might have *indirect evidence* that might help answer these questions.[39]

Information from professionals may be even more important in neglect than in abuse cases. In neglect cases, the state generally does not intervene merely because the parents have left the child unattended or denied the child proper care on a specific occasion. The agency generally wants to know whether a parent has exhibited a *pattern* of neglectful behavior. Agencies and courts therefore must examine the parents' entire way of life, not just the current conditions of their home or specific examples of neglect. The

---

[39] We believe that although such information is not direct evidence of abuse, it is probative. A record of previous patterns of behavior often is admissible to show the likelihood that a person did a given act, especially to show intent when the person claims the act was accidental. *See* C. McCORMICK, HANDBOOK OF THE LAW OF EVIDENCE 450 (2d ed. 1972). In light of the difficulties in proving abuse in cases of very young children where there are no eyewitnesses, such information is particularly important. *See* Dembitz, *Child Abuse and the Law*, 24 RECORD OF N.Y.C.B.A. 613, 617–19 (1969).

parents' mental or emotional condition, history of drug or alcohol abuse, or failure to respond to past therapies may be especially relevant when the state evaluates their ability to care for their child or to understand the causes of their poor parenting.

Indirect evidence generally will be even more important at the dispositional stage than at the adjudication stage. In deciding whether to leave a child at home or place the child in foster care, the agency and court is trying to predict the future behavior of the parent. Will the parent abuse the child again? Will a pattern of neglectful behavior continue? Will the parent respond to treatment?[40] The decision whether to remove a child is very problematic.[41] Information about a parent's mental illness, drug or alcohol addiction, responsiveness to past treatment, willingness to take medication, or ambivalent feelings toward the child may help answer these questions. Although the predictions of mental health professionals are far from perfect, they are often the best evidence the court will have.[42]

Of course, the court can order the parents to submit to a mental health examination to aid it in making these decisions. The testimony of a professional who already knows the parents or children is likely to be more helpful, however, than information derived from court-ordered examinations, in which the professional is likely to know little about the parents and in which the parents may not speak candidly.

If a child has been removed from his or her parents, the issue at the review hearing is whether the parents can now provide adequate care so that the child can be returned safely. Because the child has not lived with the parents, the court will not have any direct evidence of continued abuse or neglect (unless this abuse or neglect occurred while the child was visiting the parent during the period of removal). The major questions at these hearings usually are, Have the parents responded to therapy? Does a parent still have a drug or alcohol problem which impairs his or her ability to care for the child? Has an abusing parent come to understand reasons for his or her behavior? Obviously, these questions call for just the types of information that fall outside the reporting law and that may be protected by confidentiality laws.[43]

---

[40] For example, a depressed mother may provide adequate care while taking medication but fall apart if she stops taking the medication. Her history of compliance with medication requirements thus would be very useful to a court in deciding whether to leave a child with her.

[41] *See* Wald, Carlsmith, Leiderman, & Smith, *Intervention to Protect Abused and Neglected Children*, 16 MINNESOTA SYMPOSIA ON CHILD PSYCHOLOGY 207 (1983).

[42] We recognize that clinical prediction is far from a science. *See* J. MONAHAN, PREDICTING VIOLENT BEHAVIOR (1981). We are not asking, however, for predictions but evidence of conditions, behavior, specific statements or the effect of past treatment. While such information might not always lead to better decisions, *see infra* note 113, we can think of no better basis for a court's decision.

[43] The issue of confidentiality is somewhat more complex at review hearings than at earlier hearings. In many cases, the parent will have been ordered by the court or agency to participate

The final type of investigation or proceeding in which the professional may be called upon for information is a termination of parental rights hearing. As is evident from the terms of the California statute previously quoted,[44] a termination decision also requires just the type of information professionals might have but not be required to report. In fact, under termination statutes like California's, a history of mental illness or drug or alcohol addiction often is the factual question at issue. The state must establish these conditions before the court can consider termination. Thus, on these issues the professional does have *direct evidence,* although such evidence falls outside reporting laws.[45] The court must also evaluate the parents' future ability to provide adequate care for the child. The success or failure of past efforts to treat the parent is the most probative evidence on this issue.

Is Such Information Important and Really Unavailable?

There are no systematic data available indicating how often agencies have need of *indirect evidence* of abuse or neglect. Probably, in the majority of cases, the agencies have enough evidence independent of confidential

---

in some type of therapy. Under many evidentiary privilege laws, court-ordered treatment is not treated as confidential, since the parent has no expectation of confidentiality. *See In re* S. W., 79 Cal. App. 3d 719, 145 Cal. Rptr. 143 (1978). Even if privilege laws apply, the parents may be asked to sign waivers of confidentiality. Moreover, a judge may presume that a parent's refusal to waive confidentiality indicates that the requested information is unfavorable and thus will be reluctant to return the child. The parent may then feel great pressure to permit the therapist to testify.

Thus, confidentiality may not pose a significant problem at most review hearings, even though the professionals who perform the court-ordered therapy may be reluctant to share their impressions, fearing that disclosure will impair therapy. Ironically, it is in just this situation that confidentiality may in fact be most important. We argue later, *see infra,* notes 112–113 and accompanying text, that in most situations limiting confidentiality will not have much of an effect on client behavior. As we discuss *infra* note 114 this may not be true in cases of court-ordered therapy.

On the other hand, the information may be most critical at this stage. In general, the therapist treating the parent is in the best position to assess the parent's ability to resume custody. the success or failure of the therapy *is* the issue at the review proceeding.

A parent may also have seen a professional after the state intervenes without having been ordered to do so by the court. For example, the parent may have been involuntarily hospitalized in a psychiatric facility between the time the child was removed and the review hearing or may have sought out private counseling. In these instances the issues are the same as at the adjudication or disposition hearings.

[44] *See supra* text accompanying note 35.

[45] Again, at the time of a termination proceeding the court may have information derived from court-ordered therapy. In such instances the considerations discussed *supra* in note 43 are applicable.

It is also possible that court-ordered *evaluations* at the time of the termination hearing can provide some of the information required by California-type statutes. Since such *evaluations* are not protected by confidentiality, see, *e.g.,* CAL. EVID. CODE § 730 (West 1983), confidentiality laws will not deprive the court of all information.

information to proceed successfully, especially at the adjudication stage. Moreover, agencies have developed many ways to get information from professionals. The agencies may induce parents to sign waivers of confidentiality, and some professionals believe that they are required to reveal information to child protection agencies or acquiesce when a police officer, district attorney, or child protection worker tells them (often incorrectly) that they are required to do so.[46]

Nonetheless, we believe that there remain a significant number of cases in which confidentiality laws prevent agencies from obtaining needed information. We base this conclusion on clinical experience. One of the authors, who has extensive experience in handling abuse and neglect proceedings and training social workers throughout the United States, has often encountered cases in which a court or agency could not make a proper decision regarding adjudication, disposition, or termination without information from professionals that might be unavailable under current laws. The percentage of cases in which confidentiality laws might bar needed information undoubtedly would increase if parents were more often and more aggressively represented by counsel.[47] If counsel for parents successfully kept out such information in the many cases when it is now available because of parental waivers or illegal disclosure, the agencies' need for the information would become more manifest.

Moreover, the information known to a professional may be most important outside of the courtroom, before legal proceedings begin, in helping child protection agencies determine what legal steps, if any, it must take to help the child. Yet professionals most often refuse to cooperate outside the court because under existing laws professionals may be barred, or believe they are barred, from sharing this information with investigative agencies. As a result, investigating agencies may not have enough information to decide whether or not to institute proceedings. An agency might therefore bring improper cases or fail to act when a child needs protection.

To prove that the information is important is not to prove it should be revealed. The law often recognizes that the value of confidentiality out-

---

[46] Professor Wallace Mlyniec informs us that in the District of Columbia many professionals who work for the government normally share information with all other government agencies, including child protection agencies.

The numerous means of obtaining waivers probably account for the limited amount of litigation on the issue. The fact that many parents are unrepresented, or poorly represented, also limits challenges to the use of such evidence. *See* Note, *Representation in Child Neglect Cases: Are Parents Neglected?* 4 COLUM. J. OF LAW & SOCIAL PROBLEMS 230 (1968): Lassiter v. Department of Social Services. 452 U.S. 18 (1981). It is not surprising that most challenges occur in termination of parental rights cases, where parents are more often represented.

[47] The best available manual for attorneys handling abuse or neglect cases on behalf of parents alerts attorneys to the various ways of excluding confidential information. *See* CALIFORNIA JUV. CT. PRAC. 121. 279–335 (1981).

weighs the value of other policies that disclosure of private information might serve. Therefore, we must now examine the legal structure of confidentiality, since neither the legal nor mental health literature spells out, in one place, the various privilege and nondisclosure laws that come into play when a professional has information that may be relevant to an abuse or neglect determination. We then evaluate the importance of the goals underlying confidentiality laws.

REPORTING LAWS, PRIVILEGE LAWS, AND NONDISCLOSURE LAWS: AN UNRULY STATUTORY SCHEME

As previously noted, a professional who obtains information from a client that might prove relevant to an issue of child abuse or neglect is likely to face a confusing scheme of state laws. If the mandatory reporting laws were the only statutes applying to professionals who obtain information about child abuse or neglect, the legal situation would be troublesome enough. A reporting law divides information about abuse or neglect into two categories—information the professional must disclose on his or her own initiative, and information he or she need not, but in some instances may, disclose. Therefore, reporting laws leave disclosure of some potentially relevant information to the unguided discretion of the professional. The professional has no special duty to offer noncovered information in response to questions from child welfare investigators who have already begun an inquiry into charges of abuse and neglect in reliance on some other source of information.

Yet the legal situation in most states is far more complicated. The professional who takes the trouble to study his or her legal duties will realize that the mandatory reporting law in his or her state is just one part of a statutory scheme. Other statutory rules, as well as professional codes of ethics, may demand that the professional *not* disclose relevant information, even if that information is requested by child welfare authorities. We now turn to those laws.

Although privilege and nondisclosure laws are often treated as if they were interchangeable, they actually have very different purposes and applications. In most states the legislatures seem to have drafted these two types of laws without any effort to coordinate them.

Understanding the difficulties the legislatures have imposed, however inadvertently, on professionals and the courts requires a fuller explanation of how privilege and nondisclosure laws differ in their purpose and operation and a survey of the particular types of privilege and nondisclosure laws that affect the disclosure of information about child abuse and neglect.

Privilege Laws

General Considerations

Privilege laws or, more precisely, communications privileges, are older and far more familiar than nondisclosure laws.[48] Privilege law focuses on a relationship between a professional person offering a service to a lay person, the service bearing on intimate medical, psychological, legal, or economic issues in the latter's life and requiring an atmosphere of secrecy and trust. Generally, a privilege law prevents disclosure of *communications* made in confidence between the professional and the client for the purpose of carrying out the professional service.

Of course there would be no need for a privilege law if no one demanded, or threatened to disclose, confidential information arising in the professional relationship. The professional, the immediate recipient of the information, is the person most obviously capable of breaching that privacy. Nevertheless, privilege law traditionally does not view the professional as the enemy of the client's privacy. Rather, privilege law views the professional as sharing the client's interest in privacy as against the rest of the world; indeed, professionals usually see the client's privacy as lying in their own interest.

Privilege law views the chief threat to the client's privacy as the lawsuit. A party in litigation may try to obtain confidential information from a professional to help his or her case, and absent a privilege law, the court can require the professional to reveal it. Though rooted in moral principles of honor and privacy,[49] privilege law has become a branch of the law of evidence; indeed privilege law is essentially a set of exceptions to a major principle of evidence law—that the courts are presumptively "entitled to every man's evidence."[50] The most often noted rationale of privilege law is that the client or patient must feel assured that the professional cannot be forced to reveal any confidential communications in court. Without the assurance, the client will be reluctant to speak as candidly as the success of the professional service requires, or will choose not to seek the professional service at all.[51]

The client, or the professional, normally may invoke the privilege in any court proceeding, in pretrial discovery, or in any situation where he or she is

---

[48] For a general discussion of privileges, *see* C. McCormick. *supra* note 39. §§ 72–113 (2d ed., 1972).

[49] Louisell, *Confidentiality, Conformity and Confusion: Privileges in Federal Court Today,* 31 Tul. L. Rev. 101, 109–15 (1956).

[50] J. Wigmore, Evidence § 2191, at 71 (1961) (quoting Lord Hardwicke. 12 Cobbett's Parliamentary History 675, 693 (1742).

[51] For a fuller discussion of this "instrumental" rationale and of an alternative rationale as well, *see infra* notes 92–128 and accompanying text.

asked for privileged information that may ultimately be relevant in some litigation in the future. Privilege law does not require that the privileged client be a party to the litigation. Nor must the professional or client necessarily claim the privilege out of fear that disclosure will cause the client some legal harm. Privilege law aims at protecting people from the embarrassing disclosure of private information (at least in legal proceedings), not from the loss of lawsuits. Nevertheless, most privilege claims arise when the privileged person is a party. The client's fear of legal harm from disclosure is often the major reason for the claim of privilege; the privacy interest may be secondary or even a pretext.

Although privilege laws assume a general harmony of interest between the professional and the client, one might imagine in the area of child abuse and neglect some professionals wanting to disclose privileged information to protect an endangered child. Nevertheless, the privilege law may still bar the professional's testimony. The privilege statutes usually refer to the client, but not the professional, as the holder of the privilege. In a case in which a professional wanted to breach his or her client's privacy in a court proceeding and the client was in court, the client could request the judge to bar admission of any privileged information. Even if the client was absent, the court might restrain the professional on its own motion.[52]

An important but rarely discussed question regarding privilege laws is their application outside a court proceeding. The language of most privilege statutes, and their typical placement in the state's evidence code, might suggest that privilege laws apply only in litigation. Does this mean that a professional who receives an inquiry about a client who is being investigated for possible abuse or neglect is free to share information with the investigator even if the information would be privileged in a court proceeding? The answer is not clear. Privilege laws, as we have noted, have their source in ethical principles that antedate technical evidence law. Even if the privilege law seems to refer expressly only to litigation, the client may be able to bring a contract or tort suit against a professional who discloses confidential information out of court, citing the privilege law as the source of the governing legal principle. Moreover, the ethical or disciplinary code of the relevant profession is likely to bar all unauthorized disclosure of a client's confidences unless the disclosure is required by law.[53] Therefore, the professional may construe the evidentiary privilege law as a rule against all disclosure; whether or not he or she is technically correct as a matter of law,[54] the

---

[52] *See* C. McCormick. *supra* note 39. § 73, at 152.

[53] *E.g.,* American Psychoanalytical Association, Principles of Ethics for Psychoanalysts § 6 (1975).

[54] Some physician and psychotherapist privilege laws expressly state that the privilege applies in enumerated types of legal proceedings. (*See, e.g.,* Va Code § 8.01-399(1977), perhaps implying that they are meant to apply only in the enumerated proceedings. Other privileges might be construed as applying only in court proceedings simply because they appear as part of

professional is likely to refuse a third party's request for privileged information on the ground that the privilege law requires him or her to remain silent.

Exceptions to Privilege Laws

Abrogation of privileges. Despite the virtually universal legal recognition of professional privilege, legal protection of confidentiality is never
absolute. Courts and legislatures narrowly define or create exceptions to
privilege rules to recognize a variety of other interests. Faced with a privilege law that bars disclosure of information relevant to a charge of child
abuse or neglect, a court could conceivably cite public policy to make an
exception when the usefulness of the information in protecting the child
outweighs the parent's need for confidentiality. Although there are no reported cases under abuse and neglect laws, the willingness of courts to make
such an exception in the analogous area of divorce-custody suits suggests
that they might do the same in abuse and neglect cases brought by the state.[55]
But the incursion on confidentiality in abuse and neglect cases has been
statutory. In recent years, however, the legislatures in all but five states have
enacted some sort of statute abrogating one or more of their privilege laws
for confidential information relevant to child abuse or neglect.[56] These abro-

---

the evidence code or the rules of court in the state's statute books. *See e.g.*, CAL. EVID. CODE
§§ 990. (West 1966), 1010 (West Supp. 1984); N.Y. CIV. PRAC. LAW §§ 4504, 4507 (McKinney
1963 & Supp. 1983-84). On the other hand, some privilege laws appear in the state's special
professional codes, alongside licensing and disciplinary laws, thereby implying that they are not
limited to judicial proceedings. *See, e.g.*, ARIZ. REV. STAT. ANN. § 32-2085 (West Supp. 1983),
LA. REV. STAT. ANN. § 37-2366 (West 1974).

Finally, certain fairly common substantive exceptions to the privilege laws tend to imply
legislative intent, cutting one way or the other on the issue as to whether privilege rules apply
outside litigation. One example is the "dangerous patient" exception, which removes the
privilege when the psychotherapist has reasonable cause to believe that the patient threatens
harm to himself or others. *See, e.g.*, CAL. EVID. CODE § 1024 (West 1966). That exception,
which formed one of the bases of the California Supreme Court's decision in *Tarasoff v. Board
of Regents.* 17 Cal. 3d 425, 551 P.2d 334, 131 Cal. Rptr. 14 (1976), would seem to apply chiefly
outside litigation, when a therapist might have to warn law enforcement authorities that the
patient threatens imminent harm. The exception would likely apply in court primarily in a
proceeding to commit the patient civilly, a situation in which an express exception to most
privilege laws applies anyway.

[55] In private child custody disputes arising in divorce cases, the courts have been willing to
make such exceptions when it serves "the best interests of the child." *E.g.*, State *ex rel Hickox
v. Hickox,* 64 A.D.2d 412, 410 N.Y.S.2d 81 (1978); *Perry v. Fiumano,* 61 A.D.2d 512, 403
N.Y.S.2d 382 (1978). *But see Koerner v. Westland,* 48 Ill App.3d 172, 362 N.E.2d 1153, 1156
(1977).

[56] *See, e.g.*, ALA. CODE § 26-14-10 (1977 & Supp. 1981); ALASKA STAT. § 47.17.060 (1979);
ARIZ. REV. STAT. ANN. § 8-546.04 (Supp. 1983-84). The five states that have not enacted any
statute abrogating a privilege law are Georgia, Maryland, Minnesota, New Jersey, and Ver-
mont. *Cf. In re Q.,* 31 Cal. App.3d 709, 107 Cal. Rptr. 646, 658 (1973) (admitting otherwise
privileged information from physician's examination of child in neglect adjudication, under
statutory exception to privilege for a "proceeding to commit the patient or otherwise place him
in control of another because of his alleged mental or physical condition").

gation statutes themselves are either seriously (and sometimes illogically) limited or extremely vague, creating problems both for the courts and for professionals covered by the privilege laws.

Some abrogation laws apply to privileges rather selectively, often applying to some categories of psychotherapists and not to others.[57] Where they do apply, one might read such laws as removing any confidentiality bars whenever one of the covered professionals wants to, or is asked to, disclose any information about an abuse or neglect issue to an investigating agency or court. Even when a professional is clearly covered, the language of these statutes leaves it unclear whether they wholly abrogate the privilege in all situations in which confidential information might be relevant to an abuse or neglect charge.[58] The most problematic statutes are those that tie abrogation

---

[57] In roughly 29 states, the abrogation laws clearly refer to all the privileges that might apply to psychiatrists, psychologists, psychiatric social workers, or school counselors, either by mentioning them specifically or by referring to all privileges (or all but the attorney-client privilege). *E.g.*, Ariz. Rev. Stat. Ann. § 8-564.04(B) (Supp. 1983-84); Colo. Rev. Stat. §§ 19-10-112 (Supp. 1983), 12-63.5-115(3) (1978); Del. Code Ann. tit. 16, § 908 (1983). That leaves roughly 16 state abrogation laws that abrogate some privileges, such as the physician-patient or husband-wife privileges, but not the psychotherapist privilege, at least with respect to psychotherapists who are not physicians. *See e.g.*, Alaska Stat. § 47.17.060 (1979); Hawaii Rev. Stat. § 350-5 (1976). Significantly, of these 16 states, 13 have a psychologist-patient privilege and 2 have general psychotherapist privileges. *E.g.*, Conn. Gen. Stat. Ann. § 52-146(c) (West Supp. 1981) (psychologists).

Thus, in about a third of the states, the limited scope of the abrogation law is significant since the abrogation law would not require disclosure from licensed clinical psychologists or other professionals covered by privileges other than the physician-patient privilege. Moreover, a psychiatrist covered by both an abrogated physician-patient privilege and a non-abrogated psychotherapist privilege could rely on the latter in refusing to disclose information about abuse and neglect.

Eight states have built directly into their privilege laws, rather than separate abrogation laws, exceptions for disclosure of matters related to child abuse or neglect. *See* Del. Code Ann. tit. 16, Rule 503(d)(4)(1981); D.C. Code Ann. §§ 2-1704.16. 14-307 (1981):Idaho Code § 9-203(4)(a). (6)(Supp. 1983); Neb. Rev. Stat. 27-504(d)(1979);N.Y.Civ. Prac. R.4504, 4507 (McKinney Supp. 1983-84); R.I.Gen. Laws § 40-11-11 (1977); Wash. Rev. Code § 5.60.060(4) (Supp. 1983). But as we will show with regard to the abrogation laws themselves, the scope of these exceptions is often uncertain. One state makes an express exception to both its physician-patient and psychotherapist privileges for *any proceeding* involving allegations of child abuse. *See* Del. Code Ann. tit. 16, Rule 503(d)(4). Other states limit the exception to cases of a doctor observing physical signs of abuse or injury on a child patient, and so merely confirm, and then only partially, that the required reporting law preempts the privilege law. *See e.g.*, Idaho Code § 9-203(4)(a) (Supp. 1983). Two states have an exception to privileges for any information relevant to abuse or neglect but inexplicably apply the exception to some privileged professionals and not others. *See* Neb. Rev. Stat. § 27-504(d)(1979)(doctor only); Or. Rev. Stat. §§ 40.245, 40.250(1981)(social worker only).

[58] Among the states with some sort of abrogation law, 17 appear to abrogate the privileges in any proceeding when child abuse or neglect is at issue. *E.g.*,Ariz. Rev. Stat. Ann. § 8-564.04(b) (Supp. 1983–84); Del. Code Ann. tit. 16, § 908 (1983); Fla. Stat. Ann. § 827.07 (Supp. 1983). Such general provisions are likely to cover any state-initiated suit to declare a child abused or neglected or to terminate parental rights. Two others apply "in any proceeding

to a required child abuse report. Seven states abrogate the privilege in any proceeding relating to the subject matter of a report or in which the report is introduced.[59] But almost half the state statutes abrogate privileges only in a proceeding *resulting* from a required report.[60] There are two potential flaws with these statutes. First, in some abuse or neglect cases and in most termination cases, there may have been no required report at all, or the suit may not have *resulted* from the report. Second, tying the abrogation to the report might lead a court to conclude that the abrogation law serves only to remove the required report itself from the privilege rule, or to remove confidentiality only for statements or testimony from the particular professional who made the report.

Some of these very technical limitations on the scope of the abrogation laws may reflect no more than careless drafting by legislatures, but they, nevertheless, may cause serious confusion for courts and professionals.

Other rules creating exceptions to confidentiality. Abrogation laws aside, many privilege laws contain express exceptions that might apply to information about child abuse or neglect but that remain unclear in their scope or operation.[61] Seven states have express exceptions for any matter that is part of any report that another statute requires a person to make to a government agency.[62] This exception, of course, covers the child abuse and neglect reporting laws but does not by its terms apply to information relevant

---

regarding abuse or neglect." Ark. Stat. Ann. § 42-815 (Supp. 1983); La. Rev. Stat. Ann. § 14:403(F)(1979). That language is somewhat narrower and conceivably would not apply in a termination suit. One state abrogates privileges "in cases of physical injury" to children. Idaho Code § 9-203(1). (4). (7) (Supp. 1983). This law would not necessarily apply in neglect cases. *Cf Dasovict v. A.B.*, 259 N.W.2d 636, 639 (N.D. 1977)(psychotherapist and physician privileges abrogated in neglect or abuse adjudication, but not in termination suit).

[59] *See* Ind. Code § 31-6-11-8 (1979); Iowa Code § 232.74 (Supp. 1983; Mont Code Ann. §41-3-204 (1982); Nev. Rev. Stat. § 200.506 (1979); N.M.Stat. Ann. § 32-1-16(a)(1978); Okla. Stat. Ann. tit. 21, § 848 (West 1983). The California law has been construed to override confidentiality only for the initial required report, not for any later testimony or statements by the professional about the incident that prompted the report. *People v. Stritzinger,* 34 Cal.3d 505, 668 P.2d 738. 194 Cal. Rptr. 431 (1983).

[60] *See, e.g.,* Ala. Code § 26-14-10 (Supp. 1981); Alaska Stat. § 47.17.060 (1979); Colo. Rev. Stat. § 19-10-112(Supp. 1983); Hawaii Rev. Stat. § 350-5 (1976); Ill. Rev. Stat. ch 23 § 2060 (Supp. 1983).

[61] We will not examine here two very common privilege exceptions which might apply in child abuse or neglect cases, but do not raise the difficult questions we address in this chapter: the exception permitting disclosure of confidential information from a psychotherapist in a proceeding leading to the civil commitment of the patient, and the exception for any court-ordered psychiatric evaluation or treatment. *But see supra* note 43 and *infra* note 114.

[62] *See* Alaska R. Evid. 504(d)(5) (1983) (doctor and psychotherapist); Ariz. Rev. Stat. Ann. § 32-2085 (Supp. 1983) (psychologist); Cal. Evid. Code §§ 1006 (doctor). 1026 (psychotherapist or psychologist) (West 1966); Ill. Rev. Stat. ch. 111, § 6324 (Supp. 1983) (social worker); Kan. Stat. Ann. § 60-427 (doctor); N.C. Gen. Stat. § 8-53.1,4,5 (1979 & Suppl. 1983); Pa. Cons. Stat. Ann. § 5945 (1978) (school counselor, nurse or psychologist).

to abuse or neglect that is not contained in a required report, or not required to be in the report.

Three states provide the most flexible—and least defined—of all exceptions, allowing the court to remove the privilege whenever, in the court's discretion, the interests of justice demand disclosure.[63] This exception, in effect, allows the court to engage in ad hoc balancing of the policies favoring disclosure of information relevant to abuse or neglect against the need for confidentiality in the therapist–patient relationship.

Seven states have versions of the so-called dangerous patient exception.[64] Under such a provision, the therapist has no privilege if he or she has reasonable cause to believe that the patient may be dangerous to himself or herself or others. When a therapist *wants* to reveal a confidence that indicates a parent-patient has abused or neglected the child or might do so, he or she would probably have little difficulty in bringing the disclosure under this exception. In some states, the therapist may have a duty to do so, independent of a reporting law.[65] The exception is not without its problems. This exception usually leaves unclear whether the professional *must* disclose information about a dangerous patient or merely *may* do so. Moreover, the professional who honestly wants to know the boundary of the exception, rather than rely on it to rationalize a disclosure he or she in any event wishes to make, will have difficulty. Does danger include just physical abuse of a child, or continuing neglect as well? When a therapist has merely been told that the parent has abused the child in the past but is wary of the difficulty of predicting violence on the basis of past violence, should he or she infer that the patient remains dangerous?

The final potentially relevant exception concerns litigation in which the medical or mental condition of the privileged patient is at issue. Nineteen states have the conventional exception for proceedings in which a patient-party whose confidences are otherwise privileged relies on his or her condition as an element of a claim or a defense.[66] Particularly in the area of child abuse and neglect, the statutory notion of "tendering" the issue is troublesome. Some parents threatened with removal of their children or termination of their parental rights might want to put forth evidence that they are in good

---

[63] *See* N.C. GEN. STAT. § 8.53.3 (Supp. 1983); TENN. CODE ANN. § 24-1-207(2) (1980); VA. CODE § 8.01-399 (1977).

[64] *See* CAL. EVID. CODE § 1024 (West 1966); CONN. GEN. STAT. § 52-146f(2) (Supp. 1984); MASS. GEN. LAWS ANN. ch 233, § 20B(a) (West 1983); N.Y. CIV. PRAC. LAW § 4508 (McKinney Supp. 1983); OR. REV. STAT. §§ 40-245, 40-250 (1981); R.I. GEN. LAWS §§ 5-37.3-6(2)(D) (Supp. 1983); TEX. REV. CIV. STAT. ANN. art. 4495b, § 5.08(h)(2) (Vernon Supp. 1984).

[65] *Tarasoff v. Regents of Univ. of California*, 17 Cal. 3d 425, 551 P.2d 334, 131 Cal. Rptr. 14 (1976).

[66] *See, e.g.*, ALASKA R. EVID. 504(d)(1) (1983); CAL. EVID. CODE § 996 (West 1966); CONN. GEN. STAT. 52-146(b) (Supp. 1984); FLA. STAT. § 90-503(4)(c) (1979); HAWAII REV. R. EVID. 504(d)(3) (1980).

psychological condition or have successfully solved psychological problems, but can only do so at the loss of the privilege.[67] Conversely, it is unclear whether a parent would be putting his or her condition in issue as an element of a defense if he or she tries to rebut state claims of poor psychological condition with some positive proof.[68]

Summary

An examination of the two types of privilege laws that most often involve information about child abuse and neglect—the physician and psychotherapist privileges—reveals two essential points. First, these privileges may block disclosure of a significant amount of information relevant to child abuse and neglect that is not covered by the mandatory reporting laws. Second, the privileges are subject to abrogation laws or statutory exceptions that might provide avenues for disclosure but that often operate so vaguely or selectively as to confuse both professionals and the courts.

Nondisclosure Laws

General Considerations

The laws we group under the title "nondisclosure laws" are much less familiar than privilege laws. Partly because they are new, and partly because their major effect lies outside judicial proceedings, the legal literature has paid relatively little attention to the purpose and operation of these laws[69] and no attention at all to their relationship to evidentiary privileges. Yet the nondisclosure statutes have grown tremendously in number and scope in recent years, and the statutes probably have far more effect on the lives of

---

[67] See Matter of Doe, 98 N.M. 442, 649 P.2d 510, 514 (1982) (mother loses privilege by relying on her mental condition in termination of parental rights case).

[68] But cf. Koshman v. Superior Ct., 111 Cal. App. 3d 294, 168 Cal. Rptr. 558 (1980). This issue has been chiefly litigated in the analogous area of child custody suits and has produced some inconsistent holdings. See Guernsey, The Psychotherapist-Patient Privilege in Child Placement: A Relevancy Analysis, 26 VILL. L. REV. 955, 967–73 (1981).

The essential problem with the "tender" exception is that it confounds the question of waiver with the more important question of relevancy. If the law's concern is whether the need for private information in the case exceeds the individual's need for privacy, the application of the privilege should not turn on the technicalities or accidents of pleading. Significantly, only four states have exceptions wholly or partly removing the privilege in proceedings where the privileged patient's mental condition is relevant, regardless of which party "tenders the issue." See, e.g., MASS. GEN. LAWS ANN. ch. 233, 20B(c) (Supp. 1983); VA. CODE § 8.01-399 (1977). Yet even in these states, of course, it may be unclear whether any confidence bearing on a parent's past or potential infliction of abuse or neglect reflects her "mental condition."

[69] For general discussions of the purposes of nondisclosure laws, see PRIVACY PROTECTION STUDY COMMISSION, PERSONAL PRIVACY IN AN INFORMATION SOCIETY (1977); A. WESTIN, COMPUTERS, HEALTH RECORDS, AND CITIZEN RIGHTS (1976); A. WESTIN. PRIVACY AND FREEDOM (1967).

most people than privilege laws. Although these laws partly overlap with privilege laws in purpose and effect, they arise primarily from different concerns and depend on a different notion of the relationship between the giver and receiver of intimate information.

A few general distinctions between privilege and nondisclosure laws may prove helpful to introduce the latter. First, while privilege laws generally attempt to protect confidential information generated in a relationship between a professional and his or her client or patient from the demands of judicial factfinding, nondisclosure laws focus on a different relationship: the one between a private individual and large institutions and agencies—usually government but sometimes private—that provide such necessities as food, welfare income, medical care, psychiatric care, insurance, and credit. Nondisclosure laws focus on the confidential information that people must give these institutions in order to obtain their services; the laws aim to protect this information from indiscriminate disclosure that might prove harmful or embarrassing to the recipients of these services, and to reduce the collection and distribution of this confidential information to the minimum required by the agency or institution in providing its service.

As a result, nondisclosure laws probably have their primary effect outside litigation—to prevent indiscriminate disclosure of confidential information by the receiving agency to other agencies or institutions. A nondisclosure law, when applicable, will unequivocally operate to bar an employee of the receiving agency from disclosing information about child abuse and neglect, other than information required under a mandatory reporting law, to a child protection agency engaged in a preliminary investigation without any immediate plans to go to court. By their language, most nondisclosure laws would appear to prevent a covered person from testifying in a court proceeding as well. Although most nondisclosure laws contain exceptions to this absolute bar, which we discuss below, these exceptions are often different from those found in privilege laws. Thus confusion may arise when a professional called to testify in court is covered by both a privilege law and a nondisclosure law, and the two laws yield different answers to the judge who must determine whether the professional can be forced to disclose his or her client's confidences.

A second difference is that, although privilege laws on their face normally apply only to specified professionals, nondisclosure laws apply to anyone in the receiving agency or institution who has any access to confidential information.

Third, privilege and nondisclosure laws are enforced differently. A privilege law is essentially enforced by a judge barring questions or testimony about privileged information on the motion of the client or the professional. Because nondisclosure laws apply chiefly outside litigation, and the beneficiaries of these laws may be in no position to block unauthorized disclosure of confidential information, nondisclosure laws rely on publicly enforced civil and criminal sanctions against institutions or persons who disclose confidential information covered by the laws.

Fourth, although privilege laws apply only to information freely and confidentially communicated by the client to the professional for the purpose of obtaining the service, nondisclosure laws frequently apply to any information the institution or agency receives from the client. Thus nondisclosure laws may protect information even if the individual did not knowingly give it in order to obtain services, and even if it arose not from confidential communications but rather from inquiry or observation by the institution or agency.

Finally, although a client may implicitly waive his or her protection under a privilege law by allowing the information to be disclosed to a third party, a client protected by a nondisclosure law will usually not be deemed to have waived that protection except by some formal method of authorizing disclosure established by statute or regulation.

Many people within large institutions and agencies who receive information covered by the nondisclosure laws are professionals who are also covered by the privilege laws. The prime example is the psychiatrist or psychologist on the staff of a public mental health institution. In most states, that psychotherapist will both enjoy an evidentiary privilege and be restrained from disclosing similar information by a nondisclosure statute applying to the entire institution. Nevertheless, the major impetus behind nondisclosure laws appears to be somewhat different from that of privileges. A privilege law assumes that the giver and receiver of confidential information have a relationship of trust and share an interest in retaining the secrecy of that information. By contrast, nondisclosure laws conceive the receiver of information as an impersonal institution that collects detailed records of intimate facts about individuals who have no choice but to provide that information if they want certain necessities of life. The nondisclosure statutes seem to assume that the agents of that institution are indifferent to the client's privacy, or are even inclined to breach it indiscriminately; the institution may even bear an adverse relationship to the individual and might disclose the information to other institutions that might use the information to deny the individual some other service. Nondisclosure laws, unlike privilege laws, do not *assume* trust between the individual and the institution but may aim to *promote* that trust by providing legal enforcement of confidentiality.

Although nondisclosure laws are often part of omnibus privacy of records and freedom of information acts, most jurisdictions have enacted specific nondisclosure laws protecting private information collected in the distribution of particular institutional services. Those most relevant to information about child abuse and neglect include statutes governing public mental health facilities, social welfare programs, drug and alcohol abuse treatment programs, and schools. We now examine these laws in some detail.

Specific Nondisclosure Statutes

Mental health records.   More than 40 states have nondisclosure laws barring the unauthorized disclosure of records of any information concerning a voluntary or involuntary patient in a state mental health facility or, in many states, a licensed private mental health facility.[70] Some statutes also cover people being treated as outpatients in a public mental health system.[71] These laws generally apply to any record or information derived from the treatment, evaluation, or other professional handling of the patient.[72] In fact, they often forbid disclosure of the very fact that a person is or was a patient.[73]

These laws are remarkably uniform across the states. They generally cover more information than psychotherapist–patient privilege laws. The information need not be a confidential communication between a therapist and a patient. The laws cover *any* information generated by the treatment or evaluation of the patient, including the professional's work product, diagnosis notes, or patient's case history.[74] Second, the laws also apply to any employee of the facility with access to these records or information, whether or not an actual therapist.[75] The goal is to keep information confidential, not just to preserve a professional relationship. Thus many employees may be covered by a mental health nondisclosure law who are *not* explicitly covered by a privilege for psychotherapists or doctors.

Some of these laws expressly impose civil or criminal sanctions for unauthorized disclosure.[76] Others do not mention sanctions,[77] apparently leaving enforcement to internal administrative control or private rights of action, or intending merely to be exhortatory. Nondisclosure laws rarely

---

[70] *See, e.g.,* ARIZ. REV. STAT. ANN. 36-509 (1974); CAL. WELF. & INST. CODE § 5328 (Supp. 1984); N.Y. MENTAL HYG. LAW §33.13 (1978 & Supp. 1983).

[71] *See, e.g.,* ALA. CODE § 22-50-62 (1977); ALASKA STAT. § 47.30.590 (1979).

[72] *See, e.g.,* ALA. CODE § 22-50-62 (1977); CAL. WELF. & INST. CODE § 5328 (Supp. 1984).

[73] *See, e.g.,* R.I. GEN. LAWS § 40.1–5–26 (1977); WASH. REV. CODE 71.05.390 (Supp. 1983).

[74] *See, e.g.,* ALA. CODE § 22-50-62 (1977) (covers "any record, report, case history, memorandum or other information, oral or written, which may have been acquired, made or compiled in attending or treating any patient"); HAWAII REV. STAT. § 334-5 (1976) (covering all "certificates, applications, records, and reports" made during treatment or evaluation); IDAHO CODE § 66-348(a) (1980) (same); ME. REV. STAT. ANN. tit. 34, § 1-B (1983) (covers all "orders and commitment, medical and administrative records, applications and reports and facts therein" pertaining to any patient): ILL. REV. STAT. ch. 91½, §§ 802, 803 (Supp. 1983) (detailed definitions of mental health professional's diagnosis notes).

[75] *See, e.g.,* ALA. CODE § 22-50-62 (1977); ARK. STAT. ANN. § 59-1416 (14) (Supp. 1983); N.C. GEN. STAT. § 122-8.1(a) (1981).

[76] *See, e.g.,* TEX. MENTAL HEALTH REV. STAT. ANN. art. 5561h(5) (Vernon Supp. 1984) (providing for both injunctive relief and action for civil damages); UTAH CODE ANN. § 64-7-50 (1978); VT. STAT. ANN. tit. 18, § 7103(c) (criminal sanctions).

[77] *See, e.g.,* ALA. CODE § 22-50-62 (1977); ALASKA STAT. § 47.30.590 (1979); ARK. STAT. ANN. § 59-1416 (Supp. 1983).

contain the "implied" waiver provisions common to privilege laws. Rather, they expressly permit disclosure only with the formal consent of the patient, to people formally named by the patient.[78]

A straightforward reading of the language of these nondisclosure laws suggests that they might bar disclosure of a significant amount of information not covered by a mandatory reporting law but still indirectly relevant to an investigation or charge of abuse or neglect. Moreover, the laws also apply when a child is being treated in a public mental health facility. The records of his or her treatment or diagnosis may contain information about his or her mental and physical condition, or statements the child makes about things the parents have done or said. Even if this information does not itself demonstrate, or even raise a suspicion of, abuse or neglect, it may prove invaluable to an agency or court seeking to corroborate other, more direct, evidence of abuse or neglect. If it is the parent who decides whether to waive the confidentiality of the child's hospital records (and whether parents can do so is unclear under existing law in most states), a juvenile court or investigating agency cannot get this information unless one of the exceptions to these laws applies.[79]

Exceptions to mental health nondisclosure laws.   Although the nondisclosure laws in the mental health area are very broad, most contain provisions that allow release of information under some circumstances. Although these laws vary from state to state, there are certain common exceptions that might apply in cases involving abuse or neglect.

Virtually all statutes permit disclosure of otherwise protected mental health information on the order of a court.[80] Depending on the particular language of the exception and court interpretation, this judicial exception may operate both in litigation and outside litigation. The standard for disclosure in most statutes is vague, usually as "in the interest of justice."[81] When the state calls a professional covered by the nondisclosure law to testify in court, the statutes do not give judges any standards for determining when the interests of justice are served by disclosure. Undoubtedly many courts hearing abuse, neglect, or termination cases will order the professional to

---

[78] *See, e.g.*, ARIZ. REV. STAT. ANN. § 36-509(2) (1974); COLO. REV. STAT. § 27-10-120(6) (1982); DEL. CODE ANN. tit. 16, § 5161(a)(7)(c) (1983); FLA. STAT. ANN. § 394.459(9) (Supp. 1983).

[79] *See Anonymous v. Norton,* 168 Conn. 421, 362 A.2d 532, *cert. denied,* 423 U.S. 935 (1975) (nondisclosure law bars evidence of parents' psychiatric history in termination proceeding).

[80] *See, e.g.*, ALA. CODE § 22-50-62 (1975); ARIZ. REV. STAT. ANN. § 36-509(4) (1974); COLO. REV. STAT. 27-10-120(e) (1982); DEL. CODE ANN. tit. 16, § 5161(a)(7)(a) (1983).

[81] *See, e.g.*, ALA. CODE § 22-50-62 (1975) (court may order disclosure "for the promotion of justice"); CAL. WELF. & INST. CODE § 5328(f) (Supp. 1983) (same). *See also* HAWAII REV. STAT. § 334-5 (1976) (court may order disclosure if nondisclosure "would be contrary to the public interest"); IDAHO CODE § 66-348(a)(3) (1980) (same standard for disclosure).

testify as a matter of course (assuming the testimony is not protected by a privilege law).[82]

The administration-of-justice exception to the mental health nondisclosure laws creates special complications in the investigation stage. Even if this exception permits out-of-court disclosure of confidential information to a child protection agency engaged in a preliminary investigation of child abuse and neglect,[83] the agency would have to get a court order—in effect, a subpoena—before *requiring* a professional to disclose. Neither a mental health professional nor a child protection agency, however, is likely to consider it practical or desirable to go to court to get authorization for disclosure of confidential remarks made by a patient that might vaguely suggest the parent has neglected or abused his or her child. Moreover, even if the professional or agency goes to court, the statutes give the court no specific guidance on whether to authorize disclosure. The likely effect is to deter some agencies from seeking information and some professionals from giving it. Especially in light of the criminal penalties for an unauthorized disclosure, a clearer law is essential.[84]

---

[82] *See In re* S.W., 79 Cal. App.3d 724, 145 Cal. Rptr. 143 (1978) (administration-of-justice exception to mental health and nondisclosure law does not override psychotherapist privilege; evidence barred where no exception to psychotherapist privilege law applies).

[83] The administration-of-justice exception is usually strictly construed to limit disclosure to actual courts, not administrative agencies. *County of Riverside v. Superior Court,* 42 Cal. App. 3d 478, 116 Cal. Rptr. 886 (1974). Some statutory exceptions permit disclosure to other state agencies, but the scope of these exceptions is always limited to disclosure to professionals or agencies that are helping, serving, or treating the patient. *See, e.g.,* ALASKA STAT. § 47.30.590 (1979); ARIZ. REV. STAT. ANN. § 36-509(1) (1974); COLO. REV. STAT. § 27-10-120(1)(2) (1982); HAWAII REV. STAT. § 334-5 (1976); IDAHO CODE § 66-348(a)(2) (1980). These exceptions presumably would not apply to a child protection agency investigating a patient's possible neglect or abuse of her child.

[84] One other type of exception to the mental health nondisclosure laws bears mention. Many states permit disclosure to professionals or employees within the mental health institution when necessary to help treat the patient. In some statutes, the exception seems designed to do no more than to confirm the obvious—to allow the minimum disclosure necessary to carry out the treatment or evaluation for which the patient was admitted. Other statutes are slightly broader, apparently giving anyone in possession of confidential information the power to take the initiative in disseminating the information to other professionals in the facility, so long as the dissemination is in the interests of the patient. A few others are still broader, permitting disclosure even to other state mental health or social service agencies, though under some standard referring to the "interest" or "rehabilitation" of the patient. Some statutes vaguely permit disclosure "among qualified professionals in the provision of services or referrals."

This type of exception, of course, gives little guidance to the professional and does not directly address information revealing child abuse or neglect. When the patient is a child, most information generated in the course of treatment or evaluation and bearing on child abuse or neglect will be covered by a mandatory reporting law that applies to professionals in the facility, and by fairly obvious implication, the nondisclosure law would yield to the reporting requirement in such cases. When the narrow definition of the evidence of abuse or neglect places the information outside the required reporting, a professional might be able to invoke the exception

Two states permit disclosure of information when necessary to prevent serious and imminent harm to the patient and others.[85] These exceptions obviously give the professional broad discretion to reveal information about child abuse. One might also expect that the laws abrogating evidentiary privileges for information about abuse or neglect would apply to the nondisclosure laws as well. Surprisingly, the abrogation laws by their terms generally do not.[86] In most states reporting laws expressly preempt nondisclosure laws, so that professionals must report *direct* knowledge of abuse or neglect,[87] but of course these preemption provisions will not apply to the broader category of *indirect evidence* of abuse or neglect.

The Problem of Overlapping Laws

As this survey of privilege and nondisclosure laws reveals, even if a particular statute is treated wholly in isolation from other statutes, it might well cause the professional or the court difficulty in determining the propriety or necessity of disclosing information about child abuse or neglect. Most of the privilege and nondisclosure laws potentially bar disclosure of a significant amount of information relevant to abuse or neglect, but most also contain vague exceptions that create opportunities for disclosure. More-

---

for disclosure necessary to treatment to give out information bearing on abuse or neglect. Such disclosure requires a very plausible, if somewhat nonliteral, reading of the statutory language concerning the patient's needs or treatment. It would require, however, overcoming the statutory language limiting the disclosures to intra-agency disclosure, when the professional wants to alert a child welfare department.

When a parent is the patient, the nondisclosure law is a greater barrier to disclosure. When, under the statutory exception, disclosure can only be in the interest of the treatment, evaluation, or care of a parent who has revealed that she has abused or neglected a child or might do so, the statutory language must be strained, and indeed perhaps statutory intent directly overcome. Indeed, the patient's fear of legal consequences of child abuse or neglect charges might threaten the treatment of the parent.

[85] ILL. REV. STAT. chap. 91½, § 811 (Supp. 1983-84); MICH. COMP. LAWS § 330.1748 (748)(6)(c) (West Supp. 1983-84).

[86] First, in not a single state does the abrogation statute explicitly remove the bar on disclosure imposed by nondisclosure laws. A few statutes refer to privileges and add a vague reference such as "and other rules against disclosure" or other rules regarding confidential communications. *See, e.g.,* MISS. CODE. ANN. § 97-5-39(5) (Supp. 1983) (refers to "physician-patient privilege or similar privilege or rule against disclosure"); N.M.STAT. ANN. § 32-1-16(A) (1981) (same); OKLA. STAT. ANN. tit. 21, § 848 (West 1983) (same). Such language arguably refers to nondisclosure statutes as well, but not even these statutes make any express cross-reference to the state's nondisclosure statutes. In any event, roughly 40 of the 45 states that lift a disclosure bar in child abuse or neglect cases speak expressly and only of "privileges," after enumerating specific rules from the state *evidence* code. *See, e.g.,* ALA. CODE § 26-14-10 (1975); ALASKA STAT. § 47.17.060 (1979); ARIZ. REV. STAT. ANN. § 8-546.04(B) (Supp. 1983-84); OHIO REV. CODE ANN. § 2151.421(c) (Page Supp. 1983). [*See supra* note 37 and accompanying text.]

[87] *See supra* note 37 and accompanying text.

over, many of the privilege laws must be examined in connection with abrogation laws that explicitly remove the privilege bar for some information about abuse or neglect (but do so only under ill-defined or narrow circumstances) and that do not necessarily apply to nondisclosure laws as well as privilege laws.[88]

Assessing the effect of all the laws becomes more complicated when we address the rarely discussed question of the intersection of a privilege and nondisclosure laws. Many of the health care, social service, or mental health professionals covered by nondisclosure laws are also physicians, psychologists, social workers, or school counselors covered by evidentiary privileges.[89] Thus, in deciding on the propriety or necessity of a particular disclosure, a professional may have to deal with both a privilege and a nondisclosure law, as well as his or her profession's ethical code.

The conflict might not arise if privileges governed only disclosure in litigation and nondisclosure laws applied outside litigation. But as we have shown, though privilege laws are primarily designed as court rules, they affect disclosure out of court, whereas nondisclosure laws nowhere exclude, and sometimes expressly include, disclosure in court proceedings in their coverage.

Of course, if overlapping privilege laws and nondisclosure laws would yield the same result in a particular case, the overlap problem would only be academic. In numerous situations, in and out of court, the privilege and nondisclosure laws may pull in opposite directions. These conflicts can arise in various permutations both within litigation and without. A few examples should suffice to underscore the problem.

Overlaps outside litigation.   First, let us consider problems of the professional outside litigation. A therapist in a public mental health facility is told by her patient that the patient harbors a strong desire to hurt her child. The therapist does not feel that this vague remark by the parent warrants reporting under the reporting law. She consults the evidentiary privilege law and discovers the dangerous-patient exception and plausibly finds it applicable; alternatively, she may discover that the privilege is abrogated for any information about abuse or neglect. But the therapist also consults the state mental health records nondisclosure law. She concludes that this law gives her no discretion to disclose on her own initiative or in response to an informal request from the child welfare authority, unless disclosure would be for the purpose of treating the parent. She feels certain that this disclosure will not aid in the treatment of the parent, and may actually harm that treatment by upsetting her relationship with the parent. On the other hand,

---

[88] *See supra* notes 55–60 and accompanying text.

[89] Some professionals not explicitly mentioned in privilege laws might be covered anyway as "agents" of professionals who are explicitly covered.

she wonders whether the safety of the child is more important. The nondisclosure statute might permit disclosure under court order. But she is not sure if the exception to the privilege rule, which does not mention court orders, overrides the nondisclosure law's court-order requirement. She may also be uncertain whether she can seek a court order allowing her to disclose on her own initiative, or whether that exception only allows the child welfare authority to obtain an order to force her to disclose. She could seek the advice of a local county attorney or other officer or, theoretically, she could go to a local judge, but she may simply be reluctant to undertake the burden of such inquiries.

The converse is also possible. Assume that the therapist in the mental health institution is treating a child, and the child reveals that her parent has left her unsupervised for long periods of time or has uttered vague remarks that the parent harbors violent feelings. The therapist might be inclined to reveal this information on her own initiative, but she plausibly concludes that the mandatory reporting law does not require her to report it. Or, the child may simply have revealed to the therapist some of her emotional difficulties, and the child protection agency, acting on some other report that this child has been mistreated, might ask the therapist to reveal any potentially relevant information about the child's condition.

In this second case, if the mandatory law does not apply, the therapist must once again confront the nondisclosure and privilege laws. The "purposes of treatment" exception to the nondisclosure law would clearly allow her to disclose, but the applicable privilege law might contain no relevant exception, and the state may have no abrogation law that applies to therapists who are not physicians.

Overlaps in litigation.   Similar problems may arise in litigation. A psychologist in a public mental health facility might be called to testify in a judicial proceeding involving abuse or neglect. The psychologist might correctly claim a privilege not to testify—a privilege that contains no relevant exception for abuse and neglect matters and that is not negated in that particular proceeding by an abrogation law. The child protective agency may argue that the professional is covered by a nondisclosure law that permits disclosure upon the order of a court. The question then arises as to whether the court order exception to the nondisclosure law overrides any simultaneous privilege, or merely removes the bar of the nondisclosure rule and allows the normal privilege rules to operate as they would in the absence of a nondisclosure law.[90] If the court holds that the nondisclosure rule with its exception does override the privilege rule, it still faces a question of criteria: Does it admit any relevant evidence of abuse or neglect, or does it weigh the

---

[90] For a holding in favor of the latter view, *see In re* S.W., 79 Cal. App. 3d 719, 724, 145 Cal. Rptr. 143 (1978).

need for disclosure of the evidence against the client's or patient's need for confidentiality?

Resolving the statutory conflict.   On an abstract legal level, these situations present fairly difficult questions of statutory construction. Even when it is the court facing the dilemma—in which the question is one of the professional's obligation to testify in litigation—a confusing range of solutions or theories of statutory construction arises. The court may decide that in cases of conflict between statutes supporting and restricting disclosure in the area of child abuse or neglect, the interest of protecting the child categorically outweighs the need for privacy. Or the court might decide that the statutes effectively cancel each other out, leaving the court with the responsibility to balance the interests in disclosure and confidentiality on the facts of the particular case.

The court might, on the other hand, treat the conflict as a technical problem of statutory construction and invoke some canon of construction for choosing between the statutes. It might try to determine which statute is more "specific" or which is more "general," or it might infer that the later-enacted statute prevails.[91]

The confusion of these choices, resulting from the ill-coordination of the privilege and confidentiality laws, is a serious enough problem for a court that has the opportunity to reflect on the nuances of statutory construction and social policy. That confusion is obviously a greater problem for the professional who tries to discern his or her legal responsibilities in making quick decisions in the daily course of work. To the professional in that situation, the theoretical subtleties of statutory construction are useless.

Summary

This survey of mandatory reporting laws and privilege and nondisclosure laws reveals several important problems. First, there is one fundamental substantive problem. In most states, to the extent that the privilege and nondisclosure laws speak clearly, they permit or require professionals *not* to disclose a significant amount of information that might be relevant in proceedings regarding child abuse or neglect. Therefore, with respect to information that is not covered by the reporting laws, these statutes make it

---

[91] These issues of statutory construction rarely appear in reported cases, because in the relatively few instances where a professional or agency directly confronts a statutory conflict, the parties are likely to resolve them without litigation. The technical questions sometimes appear, however, in such nonbinding form as state attorney advisory opinions. *E.g.,* 57 Cal. Ops. Atty. Gen. 205 (1974) (state mental health disclosure law is "specific" statute that overrides "general" statute providing "dangerous patient" exception to psychotherapist privilege law).

difficult for child protection agencies or the courts to obtain information that might be useful in preventing harm to children.

Second, the current statutes governing confidential information bearing on child abuse and neglect often fail to speak clearly and thereby create further substantive and procedural problems. The privilege and nondisclosure laws, especially when read in relation to each other and to vaguely drawn mandatory reporting laws, impose considerable uncertainty on all the participants in the legal process of child protection. Individual privilege and nondisclosure laws contain vague exceptions that may permit or require disclosure. Moreover, nondisclosure and privilege laws rarely mark their own boundaries clearly, leaving the courts and professionals uncertain as to whether a particular law applies just within litigation, just outside litigation, or both. Finally, the uncertain boundaries and substantive content of particular laws are especially troublesome when a professional or court faces apparently overlapping privilege and nondisclosure laws which yield different results concerning the necessity of disclosure.

Therefore, some type of legislative change is necessary to put forth a consistent state policy and to provide adequate guidance to agencies and professionals. We look next at the factors that should be considered in adopting a clear, consistent statutory structure.

CONFIDENTIALITY—THE INTEREST BEING PROTECTED

The Need for Confidentiality

We have described the types of harms addressed by abuse and neglect laws and the degree to which courts and agencies need confidential information to protect children from these harms. Here, we examine the values promoted by confidentiality laws.

The Instrumental Argument for Privileges

It is easiest to address this question first in terms of the privilege laws. Because privilege laws have existed in America and England for more than two centuries, Anglo-American jurisprudence has produced a good deal of commentary on the reasons for evidentiary privileges. Early in its history, common law privilege, especially the law of attorney–client privilege, was grounded in the demands of honor imposed by the profession. To the extent that the law recognized privilege, it was respecting the professional's sense of vocational self-esteem more than the client's desire for privacy or the larger social interest in maintaining confidential relationships. The conventional wisdom is that this hoary justification for privilege did not survive the 18th century, but it is worth noting that this justification has persisted in somewhat different form. The particular set of privileges the law has recognized at any time probably reflects the political power of particular professions to impose their images of professional authority and honor on the courts and legislatures, as much as it reflects a neutral judicial or legislative decision about which privileges are in the public interest.[92]

In any event, the strongest current rationale for privileges is a primarily utilitarian one, a view that was best articulated by Wigmore. He specified four criteria for recognition of a privilege:

(1) The communications must originate in a *confidence* that they will not be disclosed.
(2) This element of *confidentiality must be essential* to the full and satisfactory maintenance of the relation between the parties.
(3) The *relation* must be one which in the opinion of the community ought to be sedulously *fostered*.
(4) The *injury* that would inure to the relation by the disclosure of the communications must be *greater than the benefit* thereby gained for the correct disposal of the litigation.[93]

Virtually every discussion of privilege begins with Wigmore's famous criteria. These criteria help explain such general matters as why privilege is limited to confidential communications only, and why the privilege is lost if the client discloses the information outside the professional relationship. The Wigmore criteria, however, raise as many questions as they answer about how we choose which communications and which relationships to protect with privilege laws. Yet few judicial and academic discussions of privilege proceed beyond a rote citation of these criteria.

The essential point about the Wigmore criteria is that they are *instrumental*. They do not assert that confidentiality or privacy themselves justify privilege laws. Rather, they assume that society perceives that certain professional relationships serve the common good more than others, and that some of these relationships cannot survive unless the private individuals who form them are sure that the professionals will respect their confidences.[94]

This view assumes a relationship in which the client normally discloses intimate information to the professional and would not seek professional

---

[92] Probably the three professions that most frequently and successfully raise privilege claims today are psychotherapists, attorneys, and journalists (who claim privileges for communications from confidential informants).

[93] S.J. WIGMORE, EVIDENCE § 2285, at 527 (McNaughton, rev. ed. 1961).

[94] Wigmore interpreted the second of his four criteria to intend the promotion and maintenance of prospective relationships. *E.g.,id.* § 2380(a), at 829 (arguing that physician-patient privilege is unjustified because person suffering injury or illness will not consider risk of court disclosure of medical confidences before establishing relationship with physician). Under this view, confidentiality or privacy rules are legal instruments designed to effect important practical social goals.

help or communicate fully and honestly without assurance that his or her confidences would remain private. The relationship, however, between a client's interest in confidentiality and the need for a privilege *law* is not a simple one.

Many clients may not worry at all about confidentiality. Others, perhaps the majority, may be concerned with confidentiality but may not have the slightest idea whether their state has a *law* governing confidentiality or may never rely on the law as protection for their privacy. Rather, most clients probably rely on their personal sense of the trustworthiness, integrity, and empathy of the professional as safeguards for their confidentiality. Finally, even those clients who are concerned with formal legal protection for their privacy might not foresee that the particular threats to confidentiality with which the laws of privilege deal—especially disclosure in litigation—are serious threats to them. If a client cannot imagine his or her confidences becoming relevant in litigation, he or she might not rely on the privilege law in disclosing intimate information to the professional.

Nevertheless, the privilege laws may indeed enhance professional relationships, even though most clients are not evidence scholars. First, even if clients do not advert to the legal rules governing confidentiality, many professionals probably do. A professional who fears that he or she might have to disclose confidential information in a court might be inhibited from eliciting it from the client. Second, even though the client relies largely on the image of the professional's ethics or integrity as protection for his or her privacy, that image in turn will depend on how the law treats confidential communications. If clients, like the general public, learn that professionals sometimes are forced to disclose client confidences in court, they may have a more skeptical image of the ethics and integrity of the profession. Finally, some clients in some professional relationships may indeed foresee the danger of disclosure of their confidences in specific litigation and may therefore require the assurance of a privilege law. A prime example might be the parent separated from her spouse who needs psychotherapy but fears that any intimate information she conveys to a therapist might be disclosed in court when she seeks custody of her children.

The Instrumental Argument for Nondisclosure Laws

Most of our discussion about the instrumental basis for the privilege laws also applies to the nondisclosure laws—those covering public mental health institutions, drug and alcohol treatment programs, and general social services—which also govern the release of information about child abuse and neglect. If the legislature creates health and welfare agencies because it believes they give valuable services, it must ensure the privacy of clients' confidential communications to encourage clients to use these services.

The instrumental argument for the nondisclosure laws might seem weaker than that for privilege laws. The professional relationships governed by the nondisclosure laws might seem less voluntary than those governed by the privilege laws. Some clients protected by the nondisclosure laws are seeking services they are relatively powerless to refuse. The patient in a public mental health institution may have suffered involuntary commitment. The welfare client seeking financial assistance or food stamps might have such a compelling need for the service that no fear of invasion of her privacy could deter her from seeking help. But the difference does not significantly weaken the instrumental argument.[95] Social service programs governed by the nondisclosure laws, like drug or alcohol abuse programs, are essentially voluntary. In the case of other programs, even if the client's fear of invasion of privacy does not or cannot deter him or her from initially *forming* the professional relationship, it certainly might deter him or her from *cooperating* fully and candidly with the professional.

Testing the Instrumental Argument

Measuring the instrumental argument for privileges and nondisclosure laws would seem to call for empirical research, but such research has rarely been attempted. Rather, the laws of privilege and nondisclosure have evolved, or stumbled along, as legislatures and courts have made fairly crude general guesses about social behavior and have responded to an uncertain mixture of unsupported instrumental assertions and the politics of professionalism. The psychotherapist privilege is probably the best example of both the strength and uncertainty of the Wigmore instrumental criteria. Though the mental health professionals have often been a strident lobby, the widespread enactment of the privilege probably reflects the legislators' honest belief that the privilege meets all the demands of the instrumental theory. First, psychotherapy has become very common in modern America, and the public has increasingly recognized its importance. Second, more than any other professional relationship, psychotherapy seems to require the client to disclose intimate personal information. Finally psychotherapy remains the most fragile of professional relationships. The fear of being stigmatized as mentally ill[96] still makes many people hesitant to seek psychotherapy; thus,

---

[95] Many of the professional relationships governed by the nondisclosure laws—such as individual psychotherapy in public mental health institutions or drug or alcohol rehabilitation programs—are simultaneously governed by the privilege laws; in these situations, the instrumental effects of the privilege law will be directly obtained in any event. Moreover, though some clients protected by nondisclosure programs do not view the professionals with the same faith and trust as do, say, private psychotherapy patients protected by the privilege laws, this fact may *strengthen* the instrumental argument: If the client of public welfare does not trust the personal ethics of the professional or view the professional as sharing her or his interest in privacy, she or he may rely even more heavily on a formal *law* barring disclosure of her or his confidences.

[96] *See* Goldstein & Katz, *Psychiatrist-Patient Privilege: The GAP Proposal and the Connecticut Statute,* 36 CONN. B. J. 175, 178 (1962).

disclosure of professional confidences might deter many people from obtaining therapy.[97]

If the instrumental justification for the psychotherapist privilege is sound, restricting or removing the privilege when the therapist has information relevant to child abuse or neglect charges will bring serious social costs. Yet, despite the seeming importance of the psychotherapist privilege, one recent empirical study—the most thorough study available on evidentiary privileges—raises questions about the instrumental justification, and therefore about the costs of reducing the privilege.

This study,[98] conducted in Texas by a lawyer and a psychiatrist, followed the enactment in 1979 of the state's first privilege law covering psychotherapists.[99] Before 1979, Texas had had no such privilege.[100] The study took advantage of this complete change in the law to address several questions: Would more people enter psychotherapy after enactment of the privilege? Would patients act differently in therapy after enactment of the privilege? Had therapists been compelled to disclose their patient's confidences before enactment, and, if so, with what effect on the therapeutic relationship? To what extent do patients even express concern about confidentiality?

The study used four questionnaires: one was distributed to therapists, one to psychotherapy patients, one to judges, and one to a large random group of adult students in a state university who could represent the general population of potential psychotherapy patients in the state.[101] In addition, the study examined medical insurance data before and after 1979 to determine whether the percentage of the state's population seeking psychotherapy changed after enactment of the privilege.[102]

The Texas study offers some striking, if tentative, conclusions. First, and most important, the presence or absence of a privilege statute seemed to have no immediate or direct effect on the number of people who sought psychotherapy[103] or on patients' willingness to be fully candid with their therapists once they were in therapy.[104] The medical insurance study revealed no significant increase in billings for psychotherapy after the privilege went into effect.[105] Moreover, the surveys of actual patients and potential

---

[97] *See generally* R. SLOVENKO, PSYCHOTHERAPY, CONFIDENTIALITY AND PRIVILEGED COMMUNICATIONS 37–52 (1966).

[98] Shuman & Weiner, *The Privilege Study: An Empirical Examination of the Psychotherapist-Patient Privilege,* 60 N.C.L. REV. 893 (1982).

[99] Act of May 17, 1979, ch. 239, 1979 TEX. GEN. LAWS 512 (codified at TEX. REV. CIV. STAT. ANN. art. 5561h (Vernon Supp. 1984).

[100] Shuman & Weiner, *supra* note 98 at 895.

[101] *Id.* at 896.

[102] *Id.*

[103] *Id.* at 924–25.

[104] *Id.*

[105] *Id.* at 918–19.

patients revealed that the vast majority had never been aware whether their state had a psychotherapist privilege[106] nor had they ever adverted to the question of psychotherapist confidentiality in legal terms.[107] Indeed, the survey of psychotherapists themselves revealed that more than half had been and continued to be ignorant of the status of confidentiality under Texas law.[108] Finally, to the extent that psychotherapy patients revealed any concern about confidentiality, they found assurance of confidentiality in their perception of the personal ethics of therapists, rather than in any legal rule.[109]

The Texas study also yields interesting facts about how confidentiality concerns arise in psychotherapy. Most clients do not seem to require express assurances of confidentiality from their therapists, even in nonlegal terms.[110] Few clients ever raise the issue of confidentiality expressly with their therapists.[111] Moreover, express assurances of confidentiality do not seem to enhance a client's willingness to disclose intimate information freely and fully. Clients with whom the therapist never discusses confidentiality, and who therefore receive no express assurances, are generally no less candid with their therapists than those who do receive express assurances.[112]

The Texas study indicates that patients do not directly rely on privilege laws in deciding whether to seek psychotherapy or to be candid with their therapists. The study therefore suggests that the costs of removing or restricting the privilege law may be much smaller than the proponents of the instrumental justification for privileges argue. But the presence or absence of a privilege law may still have an important *indirect* effect on whether people seek or make full use of psychotherapy. As the Texas study revealed, patients do want confidentiality, but they normally seek assurance of confidentiality in the general ethical conduct of psychotherapists, rather than in any law. Therefore, if as a result of a change in the law, therapists did disclose some confidential information, and if many actual or potential patients learned of these disclosures, people might indeed be deterred from confiding in psychotherapists. Moreover, the Texas study focused on a change in the law that *increased* the legal protection for confidentiality. Thus the study

---

[106] *Id.* at 925–26.

[107] *Id.* at 920.

[108] *Id.* at 920, 925–26.

[109] *Id.* at 920.

[110] *Id.* at 920, 926.

[111] *See id.* at 920 (only 28 percent of patients in study had asked their therapists about confidentiality).

[112] *See id.* at 925–26. Of course, this might not be the case for people who know they have acted improperly, e.g., a sexual abuser. In such situations the potential patient may demand confidentiality. An instance of this is reported in *People v. Stritzinger*, 34 Cal. 3d 505, 668 P.2d 738, 194 Cal. Rptr. 431 (1983). Moreover, the Texas study did indicate that patients would be less candid if their therapists expressly told them that they had no guarantee of confidentiality. Shuman & Weiner, *supra* note 98, at 926.

does not tell us what effect *reducing* legal protection for confidentiality might have on actual or potential patients.

The social cost of removing or restricting the psychotherapy privilege in child neglect or abuse cases may therefore be great, even if people generally do not directly rely on privilege laws. But assessing the costs and benefits of reducing the privilege is a complex matter. A change in the law may have very different effects on different people, depending on a number of factors. The main factor, of course, is whether a person ever learns about the change in the law, or learns that psychotherapists have been disclosing confidential information and thus has reason to change his or her perception of the norms of professional behavior. But the effect of a change in the law may also depend on whether a person has ever abused or neglected her child or thinks that he or she might someday be erroneously charged with abuse or neglect.

To assess the possible effects of restricting the privilege law, and thus to weigh the costs and benefits of changing the law, we suggest that actual and potential patients will fall into a few roughly distinguishable groups. The theoretical classification we offer below draws sharper lines than could really exist in the world, but this rough scheme is useful as a device for addressing these very speculative questions.

First assume a state that has had a psychotherapist privilege but enacts a new law removing the privilege when the therapist has confidential information relevant to a charge of child abuse or neglect against a patient. Second, assume that the legislature must write its new law in general terms and that no practical statute could address the distinctions among people that we examine below. The people in the jurisdiction will fall into the following groups and subgroups.

Group A: Actual patients whose therapists are compelled to disclose patients' confidences to a child protection agency or juvenile court.

Subgroups: A1: Patients ultimately determined by the court to have abused or neglected their children, in cases in which the confidential information proved important to the state's case.

A2: Patients ultimately determined by the court to have abused or neglected their children, in cases in which the confidential information proved unnecessary to the state's case.

A3: Patients ultimately exonerated of abuse or neglect charges, in spite of confidential information from their therapists.

A4: Patients ultimately exonerated of abuse or neglect charges because of exculpatory confidential information from the therapist.

Group B: Actual or potential patients who have never been charged with child abuse or neglect and who have never had their confidences disclosed by a therapist, but who are deterred from seeking or continuing psychotherapy because they learn of the change in the privilege statute or learn of the therapists' disclosure described in Group A.

Subgroups: B1: People who have abused or neglected their children or may mistreat them in the future.

B2: People who have never abused or neglected their children and will never mistreat them but who fear they may someday be erroneously charged with abuse or neglect.

B3: People who merely learn that some therapists disclose their patients' confidences but pay no attention to the particular reason for these disclosures and who are deterred from seeking psychotherapy because they fear that they also may suffer a breach of confidentiality, perhaps for reasons having nothing to do with child abuse or neglect.

Group C: People who are unaffected by the removal of the privilege because they never learn of the change in the statutes or hear of any disclosures.

We can now briefly suggest the likely benefits and costs of removing the privilege under this scheme.

The key benefit is obvious. The change in the law will protect the children of the parents in subgroup A1. Less obviously, the change in the law might benefit the parents in subgroup A4. We cannot tell whether subgroup A4 actually benefits from a change in the law unless we know how many of these parents would have waived the privilege even under the old privilege law, and thus would have ensured disclosure of the exculpatory information anyway.

The costs of removing the privilege are subtler because they vary among the groups.

Removing the privilege is costly in subgroups A1 and A2 because these parents may be deterred from further psychotherapy that might benefit themselves and their children.[113] But these costs are somewhat mitigated

---

[113] The traditional instrumental view of privileges assumes that what deters the client from seeking help is the fear of the mental distress or embarrassment he might suffer if his confidences become public. The client, of course, might also fear that the confidences will be used against him in litigation to deny him some legal right. Technically this second fear of the client may deserve no legal weight. If the client has abused or neglected his child, he has no legitimate interest in avoiding loss of his parental rights. To the extent that the parent reasonably fears unwarranted state intervention, that is a problem the legislature must address under the substantive child abuse and neglect laws, not under privilege and nondisclosure laws. Communications privileges, unlike the self-incrimination privilege, have never traditionally been concerned with the right of the person to avoid adverse *use* of confidential information.

From the child's perspective it is unlikely that coerced disclosure will be harmful. There may be cases, however, when a parent has abused or neglected a child, is in therapy on his or her own, and has not revealed anything coming within mandatory laws, and the therapist has information *needed* to prove abuse or neglect, but in which there is a greater chance of changing the patient's behavior by keeping the state out of the picture, since once confidentiality is breached, the parent will not cooperate with any therapist. This scenario assumes that private therapists are likely to be more successful than court-ordered therapists, even when they do not

once these parents actually come under court control, since the court can require them to undergo psychotherapy if they want to enjoy continued custody of their children. We recognize that court-ordered psychotherapy may be less effective than voluntary psychotherapy, but it surely has some benefit.[114]

Removing the privilege is very costly in subgroup A3, since it unnecessarily deters these parents from future psychotherapy.

Removing the privilege is very costly to both parents and children in subgroup B1, since the removal of the privilege deters these parents from obtaining psychotherapy that may help them to avoid mistreating their children. And unless and until these patients come before the juvenile court, there can be no counterbalancing benefit from court-ordered psychotherapy.

Removing the privilege is costly in subgroup B2, since these parents, who fear they might fall into subgroup A3 above, will be needlessly deterred from seeking therapy. Obviously, it will also prove costly in subgroup B3.[115]

---

know that the parent has abused or neglected the child and may not be treating them with that in mind. We doubt that the chance of success in such cases is great enough to justify leaving the children unprotected, since under the above assumptions no intervention would occur without the therapist's information.

There may also be cases in which a professional breaches his or her client's confidentiality, and the agency or court ultimately finds abuse or neglect, but the confidential information turns out to have been unnecessary to support the finding. Obviously in such cases confidentiality was breached needlessly. Unfortunately, it will generally be impossible to tell in advance in which cases the agency will need the information. A legislative rule therefore must assume the agency's need.

[114] We have discussed previously the special situation of parents who receive court-ordered therapy. *See supra* note 43. They are the group most likely to limit their participation in the therapy for fear that the therapist will reveal unfavorable information, making it difficult for them to regain custody. This is especially likely if the therapist has previously testified against them. Their failure to cooperate can harm children in two ways. First, to the extent it is beneficial to return children whenever possible, some children will not be reunited because the therapist believes that the parents have not fully rehabilitated themselves. Second, if the parents withhold information which leads the therapist to recommend return in situations where the additional information would have resulted in the opposite recommendation, and the child is returned and reinjured, the child obviously is harmed.

We believe that both these results are very unlikely. Most court-ordered therapy continues for many months. Over this time parents will not be continuously "on guard." Moreover, most skilled therapists should be able to make adequate assessments even if the parent is somewhat guarded. Also, it seems likely that the parents will be motivated to cooperate, since if they do not cooperate they may never regain custody or have court supervision terminated. In any case, as we discussed in note 43 *supra*, this information is so important to the decision on whether to return the child that it cannot be excluded by a confidentiality rule.

[115] One other potential cost of restricting confidentiality merits attention. If the information provided by professionals leads to poorer rather than better decisions by the child protection agencies or courts, then we should exclude such information regardless of whether breaching confidentiality has any other costs.

Information from professionals might lead to poorer decisions if it causes either "false

Of course, a scientific cost-benefit analysis is impossible in resolving these issues since we cannot sensibly quantify any of the factors or tell how many parents would really fall in each subgroup. It seems likely that the vast majority of the population is likely to fall into Group C, so that for most people the benefits of removing the privilege will bring no costs. Nevertheless, our classification suggests that any change in the law of privilege requires a very speculative trade-off between serious advantages and serious disadvantages. The social benefit of protecting the children of the parents in subgroup A1 is very compelling. But the costs in the other subgroups examined above may also prove serious. Unable to quantify the factors in this close and speculative question, the legislature must decide whether to err on the side of protecting children from harm or on the side of preventing harmful and unnecessary breaches of confidentiality. As we discuss later, we think the state interest in protecting children is the weightier interest.

The Noninstrumental Argument for Confidentiality

The argument in favor of confidentiality rules need not rest on the instrumental view alone. Indeed, Wigmore's instrumental concern has attracted some academic criticism, precisely because he ascribes no *independent* legal significance to privacy.[116] He assumes that people value their privacy and that professional relationships we perceive as socially valuable require that we ensure this privacy. But his theory apparently would not grant a privilege to a relationship that would continue even if the professional were forced to disclose his or her client's confidences. Many commentators have argued that privacy, as an end and not as a means to instrumental social goals, is itself a ground of privilege: Privilege laws should protect people from embarrassing or harmful public disclosure of intimate

---

positive" or "false negative" decisions. For example, in a case in which the evidence of abuse is not clear—as when the child's injury might have been accidental but the parents' explanation is poor and the child has suffered earlier injuries—testimony from the parent's therapist that the parent had said "sometimes I feel like killing my child" would likely lead a court to find the parent a child-abuser. On the other hand, testimony by the therapist that the parent seemed in control of herself might lead to dismissal.

The key question is whether such circumstantial testimony is likely to be given too much weight and lead to wrong decisions. In the area of civil commitment many commentators have written about the tendency of mental health professionals to over-predict violence. Since a person seeing a psychotherapist is likely to be experiencing some emotional problems, a therapist may overestimate the likelihood that the client would abuse or neglect his or her children.

We know of no evidence, however, that courts place too much weight on the testimony of professionals or that these professionals either systematically overestimate or underestimate abuse or neglect. At present it does not seem likely to us that the information provided by these professionals is going to lead to worse rather than better decisions.

[116] *See, e.g.,* Krattenmaker, *Testimonial Privileges in Federal Courts: An Alternative to the Proposed Federal Rules of Evidence,* 62 GEO. L.J. 61.85 (1973); Louisell, *supra* note 49, at 110–11 (1956).

information, regardless of whether that disclosure in any systematic way deters them from forming or maintaining professional relationships.[117]

The privacy protected by privilege and confidentiality laws is essentially no different from the common law right of privacy protected by tort law[118]— the sanctuary of personality and of intimate thoughts and feelings that the individual wishes to keep free of public disclosure or outside intrusion.[119] Although the courts have shown little inclination to accord any constitutional weight to the traditional evidentiary privileges, many who advocate protecting the privacy of professional relationships draw an analogy to the rather different privacy in marital and sexual relationships,[120] which have received constitutional protection.[121] In fact, the privacy concerns inherent in such professional relationships as the psychotherapist-patient relationship are in some ways even stronger than those accorded constitutional weight, since in the professional relationship the client discloses thoughts and feelings he or she might well be unwilling or afraid to disclose to his or her most intimate friends and family members. The privacy of the professional relationship is thus essentially the privacy of the individual mind, which Brandeis and Warren called the "inviolate personality."[122]

Some American advocates of privilege laws, mirroring the European view of privilege, have stressed the normative aspect of the privilege laws. The literature describing and encouraging the development of the psychotherapist privilege, for example, has often spoken in intensely moral terms. The confidentiality of communications "represents a civilized standard of behavior."[123] A professional's disclosure of a client's confidences is "indecent."[124] "a betrayal,"[125] and an act of "treachery."[126] Presumably, the client would suffer no less moral offense if the professional were forced by the state, against his or her ethics, to disclose them. Behind these norma-

---

[117] *See, e.g.*, R. LEMPERT & S. SALTZBURG, A. MODERN APPROACH TO EVIDENCE 614–15 (1977); Black, *The Marital and Physician Privileges—A Reprint of a Letter to a Congressman*, 1975 DUKE L.J. 45, 48–49; Krattenmaker, *supra* note 116 at 85–94; Louisell, *supra* note 49, at 101, 110–11, 123.

[118] For a discussion of the common law of privacy, see generally W. PROSSER, HANDBOOK OF THE LAW OF TORTS § 117 (4th ed. 1971).

[119] *See* Brandeis & Warren, *The Right to Privacy*, 4 HARV. L. REV. 193, 205–07 (1890).

[120] *See, e.g.*, Black, *supra* note 117. This view was also adopted by the court in *People v. Stritzinger*, 34 Cal. 3d 505, 668 P.2d 738, 194 Cal. Rptr. 431 (1983), at least in a situation where the client asked if the information would be held confidential.

[121] *See Roe v. Wade*, 410 U.S. 113, 152 (1973); *Griswold v. Connecticut*, 381 U.S. 479, 484–85 (1965).

[122] Brandeis & Warren, *supra* note 119 at 205.

[123] R. SLOVENKO, *supra* note 97 at 167.

[124] *Id.*

[125] *Id.*

[126] Louisell, *supra* note 49, at 112.

tive arguments is the notion that invasion of privacy inflicts serious, even catastrophic, mental pain and distress on the client.[127]

The noninstrumental privacy interest may be even stronger for the non-disclosure laws than for the privilege laws. The basis of the nondisclosure laws is in large part that even if the fear of disclosure would not deter the client from obtaining the professional service, the disclosure is unfair in itself.[128] Although the professional in private psychotherapy probably fully shares the client's interest as against the state, the professional or the agency governed by the nondisclosure laws may not be the trusting, faithful friend of the client's privacy.

The nondisclosure laws assume that unless restrained by law, state social and medical agencies, without the client's consent, will compile great amounts of information about the client, much of it not relevant to the particular service the client is receiving, and will disclose that information, or indiscriminately permit its disclosure.[129] Moreover, the prejudicial indignity social service clients often suffer is not the only harm they might fear from disclosure: The professional or agency might intentionally disclose the information to other agencies or institutions that might deny benefits to or take adverse action against the client. Thus the nondisclosure laws need not rest wholly on the rationale that the individual will avoid seeking the agency's service or treatment to avoid these harmful disclosures. Rather, they assume that the individual will seek or receive the service anyway but that it is unfair that he or she suffer the harms of disclosure helplessly.

CHOOSING BETWEEN DISCLOSURE AND CONFIDENTIALITY

Deciding whether to change the current law raises two inquiries. First, we must decide how much disclosure we want, and thus must balance the benefits obtained by recognizing the client's interest in confidentiality with the costs of losing the confidential information. Second, we must address practical and procedural questions in determining how a legislature's substantive preference among or balance of these interests should take shape in a specific statute. The second inquiry has several parts. If less information should be confidential, who should have the power to obtain information

---

[127] Brandeis & Warren, *supra* note 119 at 196.

[128] *See, e.g.,* PRIVACY PROTECTION STUDY COMM'N, PERSONAL PRIVACY IN AN INFORMA-TION SOCIETY, 20–21 (1977) (arguing for statutory creation of a "legally enforceable expectation of confidentiality" to "redress the imbalances" between the individual client and the record-keeping organization.

[129] *Cf. id.* at 21 (advocating procedural rule to allow individual client "to participate in decision of the organization to disclose records kept about him").

from professionals? At what stage of the investigation or proceedings and under what standard of need for the information should the issues be raised? How much discretion should the legislature delegate to the courts, professionals, or child protection agencies in deciding whether confidential information will be disclosed? What procedural rights should the client or professional have in resisting the state's demands for information? We shall address these questions in turn.

The interest with which the instrumental and privacy claims for confidentiality must compete in the area of child neglect and abuse laws is obviously the helpless child's interest in protection from serious and possibly catastrophic harm. More specifically, the confidentiality claims must compete with the possibility that removing the bar of privilege and nondisclosure laws in child abuse and neglect cases may save more children from serious harm than are saved under the current confidentiality laws. To resolve this balance, we must keep in mind that there is nothing novel about deciding that some important social interest justifies an incursion on confidentiality. Established law, most obviously in the numerous exceptions to the privilege and nondisclosure laws we have examined,[130] already recognizes that certain social interests outweigh confidentiality, and empirical studies suggest that professionals themselves recognize that client confidentiality should not be absolute.[131] It is hard to conceive a stronger social interest than protecting children from injury or serious neglect. Thus, though the instrumental argument for confidentiality identifies serious social costs that disclosure entails, we think the instrumental argument must yield to any significant increase in child protection that might result from a narrowing of the confidentiality laws.

Although, as we have noted, it is not subject to measurement or empirical verification, the privacy basis for privilege and confidentiality laws is a strong one. Nevertheless, the child's interest in the greatest possible protection from harm seems even stronger. The parent's privacy interest is in his or her individual mind and conscience and therefore seems powerful in competition with broad or abstract social interests. But the protection of children is not really such a general social interest; rather it is the powerful *individual* interest of the individual child and seems much more compelling than the adult's privacy interest. First, if the child faces physical harm, we are more certain of his or her need for protection than we are for an adult who asserts his or her fear of emotional harm from disclosure. Emotional harm is simply more inchoate than physical harm. Second, even if the dan-

---

[130] *E.g., see supra* notes 61–68, 80–87 and accompanying text.

[131] For a summary of empirical evidence that professionals feel an ethical responsibility to breach their clients' confidentiality in certain circumstances, *see* NOLL & ROSEN, *Privacy, Confidentiality, and Informed Consent in Psychotherapy*, in B. BLOOM & S. ASHER, eds., PSYCHIATRIC PATIENT RIGHTS AND PATIENT ADVOCACY, 175–179 (1982).

ger to the child is only emotional harm, it threatens the child's *development* in a way that it cannot threaten an adult's.

Moreover, even if the parent's privacy interest cannot be empirically measured, we *can* compare the degree of intrusion on privacy that would result from broader disclosure of information about abuse and neglect with other types of intrusion on privacy. A law infringing the confidentiality of communications to enable state agencies or courts to investigate child abuse and neglect does not subject the confidences to indiscriminate, embarrassing public disclosure. The agency and court can keep the confidential information *relatively* safely within the bounds of *non*public administrative and judicial process. In contrast, both legislatures and courts have found that a variety of interests—even the social interest in publication of newsworthy information—may outweigh a person's need for privacy, even when the breach will be far more public.[132]

Finally, the state interest in protecting the child, when it conflicts with asserted rights of the parents, must be viewed in the context of the vast autonomy the state normally grants the parents in caring for the child. The law embodies a powerful presumption that the parents know what is best for the child. Indeed, as we have noted earlier, our proposal *assumes* a narrowly drawn law of abuse and neglect, permitting state intervention only in extreme cases. We know, however, that *some* parents do not properly care for their children, and indeed inflict very serious harm on them. The state therefore can and must retain *some* opportunity to rebut this presumption of parental autonomy and to set at least a low minimum level of parental care that the parents must meet if they are to enjoy this presumption. Moreover, those children who do suffer from serious parental harm usually have no way to ask others to help, and the harm they suffer, before it becomes catastrophic, often remains invisible to the outside world. Therefore, the state must have power to get the information necessary to protect children.

A LEGISLATIVE PROPOSAL

We have concluded that the law governing private communications between professionals and clients should generally favor disclosure of any information that might be useful in investigating or proving a charge of child abuse or neglect. But a substantive decision to prefer disclosure still leaves difficult questions about how the law should carry out this preference. In trying to construct a new law we have focused on the major flaws of the current law. Beyond the failure of the current law to give paramount weight to the state's and child's interest in preventing abuse and neglect, we have

---

[132] *E.g., Virgil v. Time, Inc.,* 527 F.2d 1122 (9th Cir. 1975), *cert. denied,* 425 U.S. 998 (1976).

seen two major defects in the current legal regime. First, the law is uncoordinated: It is not one law, but a patchwork of several laws, which are often overlapping and inconsistent. Second, the law speaks too vaguely, often abdicating to courts and professionals the difficult balancing of the interest in disclosure against the interest in privacy. The result has been to invite uneven and unpredictable treatment of confidentiality and to allow courts and professionals to subvert whatever substantive choices the legislature has expressed.

Therefore, beyond reflecting a preference for protection of children over protection of the client's privacy, the law in this area should be consciously crafted to deal with the specific problems of child abuse and neglect information and must have two essential features: coordination and precision. A coordinated law is one that takes a comprehensive approach to all the situations, in and out of court, in which the need for disclosure may arise, and that expressly preempts any other nondisclosure and privilege laws that might appear to apply. A precise law is one that avoids as much as possible delegating to courts or professionals the decision whether the need for disclosure outweighs the need for privacy in particular cases. Only a statute that speaks with relatively rulelike precision can ensure the consistency and predictability needed in this difficult matter.

The Proposal

We propose the following rules to govern information relevant to proceedings concerning abused or neglected children, *when that information falls outside the coverage of the mandatory reporting laws*. No confidential information disclosed under these rules may be used in any *criminal* proceeding against a parent.

(1) With regard to disclosure of information to a child protection agency out of court:

Whenever a staff member of the state or county child protection agency seeks from a professional any information that the staff member, in good faith, believes might aid in determining whether a parent has abused or neglected, or might abuse or neglect his or her child, the professional *must* yield that information. The agency, of course, cannot simply ask the professional for everything he or she knows about the client. But when the agency defines the perceived threat to the child, the professional must provide any information he or she knows that might help the agency determine the appropriate action, *regardless of any nondisclosure or privilege law*. If the professional refuses, the agency may petition a court to order the professional to cooperate. The court should be required to order disclosures unless it appears that the agency is acting in bad faith.

(2) With regard to disclosure of information in a court, in any court proceeding in which the state seeks an adjudication that a child has been

abused or neglected, or a disposition of the placement of an abused or neglected child, or termination of parental rights:

Whenever any party seeks to introduce evidence regarding the parent or child, the court *must* admit that evidence, according to the jurisdiction's normal rules of relevancy and materiality, *regardless of any nondisclosure or privilege laws.*

Duty to Warn and the Prediction of Dangerousness

William J. Winslade

10

After *Tarasoff:* Therapist Liability and Patient Confidentiality

When the *Tarasoff*[1] decision was handed down, there was fear within much of the psychotherapeutic community that it was a critical, if not fatal, blow to patient–therapist confidentiality. Occasional voices suggested that the court had simply articulated what was, in fact, good psychotherapeutic practice, but most felt that the decision would hinder the therapeutic process and encourage a new set of liability malpractice suits.

If the passage of 10 years does not provide us with a genuine historical view, it at least allows us to see if the *Tarasoff* doctrine has taken root and if *Tarasoff*-type cases occur frequently. A review of the legal literature shows that few cases citing the *Tarasoff* rule have been decided; in general, the effects of the decision have been extremely limited and, indeed, have tended to strengthen psychotherapists' immunity. This suggests that the legal roots are shallow indeed. The effect on therapeutic practice is less clear. But there are grounds for believing that the minority who thought the rule to be merely a legal formulation of sound professional practice was correct.

---

[1] *Tarasoff v. Regents of the University of California*, 17 C. 3d 425, 551 P 2d 334 (Cal 1976). Because this opinion has been so widely cited, other footnotes to the Tarasoff opinion are omitted in subsequent discussion of the opinion. For complete references, see article cited in note 3.

PSYCHOTHERAPY AND THE LAW
ISBN 0-8089-1780-3

THE *TARASOFF* CASE

More than 15 years have passed since Prosenjit Poddar killed Tatiana Tarasoff. That Poddar killed her was never disputed: As Tarasoff ran into her front yard, collapsed, and died, Poddar called the police to report the killing. His original criminal trial resulted in a conviction of second-degree murder. On appeal, the California Supreme Court reversed the conviction because the jury was improperly instructed on the diminished capacity defense. By the time the original conviction was reversed, Poddar had spent 5 years in prison. He was not retried, but neither were the charges dropped. Instead, as a result of an informal agreement between Poddar's attorney and the attorney general of California, Poddar was released from jail with the understanding that he would immediately return to India. Thus Poddar was never ultimately convicted of the crime; he was found neither not guilty by reason of insanity nor guilty but suffering from diminished capacity; he was never excused, exonerated, or pardoned; he was never officially deported. The criminal case of *People v. Prosenjit Poddar*[2] remains in legal limbo.

The civil lawsuit for wrongful death brought by Tatiana Tarasoff's parents against the regents of the University of California, the psychotherapists, and the police also ended inconclusively. The procedural history of the *Tarasoff* litigation has been reviewed extensively elsewhere[3] and need not be reiterated here. But it should be noted that, contrary to popular misconceptions, the now familiar *Tarasoff* rule (see below) was never applied to the *Tarasoff* case. The California Supreme Court decision established only the defendants' *potential* liability by recognizing that, when a therapist failed to take reasonable steps to protect a third party from potential danger at the hands of a patient, there was a cause of action; i.e., a sufficient basis for a law suit. The case never went to trial on the facts. Justice Stanley Mosk remarked that "whether plaintiff can ultimately prevail is problematic."[1] As Poddar was never convicted of a crime, so also the therapists were never held legally liable for violating the *Tarasoff* duty. An out-of-court settlement was reached, and the complaints against the therapists were dismissed with prejudice (that is, the possibility of any further legal action in the civil case was precluded). It is interesting to note that the settlement amount was not officially disclosed, another ambiguous outcome of the Tarasoff-Poddar story.

Given the anomalous outcome of the *Tarasoff* case, it is not surprising that considerable misunderstanding still exists about the precise legal ruling made by the California Supreme Court. The plaintiffs (Tarasoff's parents)

---

[2] *People v. Prosenjit Poddar*, 16 C. 3d 750, 518 P 2d 342 (1974).
[3] Winslade W. J. "Psychotherapeutic Discretion and Judicial Decision: A Case of Enigmatic Justice." In *The Law-Medicine Relationship: A Philosophical Exploration*, S. F. Spicker, J. M. Healey, H. T. Engelhardt, eds. (Boston: Reidel, 1981), pp. 139–157.

asserted in their original complaint that both the psychotherapists and the police should be held liable (1) for failing to *confine* Poddar under California's law permitting the involuntary commitment, evaluation, and treatment of persons dangerous to others and (2) for failing to *warn* Tarasoff or her parents that Poddar posed a danger to her.

The court made it quite clear that California law grants statutory immunity from liability to the publicly employed psychotherapists and police for failing to confine Poddar. The court also ruled that the police were not liable for failing to warn Tarasoff or her parents of her peril, because the police had no special relationship to the patient. The court held, however, that the psychotherapists had no immunity for failing to warn the victim or her parents. Instead, the court formulated a new common law rule, asserting that, in certain circumstances, psychotherapists have a duty to a third party arising out of the psychotherapist's special relationship to a patient. The rule was expressed as follows:

> When a therapist determines, or pursuant to the standards of his profession should determine, that his patient presents a serious danger of violence to another, he incurs an obligation to use reasonable care to protect the intended victim against such danger.[1]

Discharge of the duty may require the therapists "to warn the intended victim or others likely to apprise the victim of the danger, to notify the police, or to take whatever other steps are reasonably necessary under the circumstances."

When Justice Mosk suggested that it would be difficult for the plaintiff to prevail, he was presumably referring to the fact that the therapist *had* asked the police to confine Poddar, and that the police had interviewed him and chosen not to commit him. Additionally, there was evidence that Tarasoff's brother knew about Poddar's fantasies and knew that Poddar possessed a gun; and there was at least the suggestion that Tarasoff herself knew she was at some kind of risk from Poddar. Furthermore, at the time Poddar killed Tarasoff he had avoided therapy for more than 2 months. Given the phrasing of the rule, the question that the court or jury might well have been asked to decide in trial was whether the therapist's actions constituted "reasonable care to protect" the victim.

One of the continuing controversies about the *Tarasoff* rule is whether it has a sound basis in common law tort doctrine. The court said that the duty to third parties arose from the special relationship between the psychotherapist and the patient. The court's reliance on the special relationship doctrine has been criticized because it provides a rather shaky foundation for a novel legal rule.[4] Moreover, the allegedly analogous cases to which the court turns

---

[4] Stone, A. A. "The *Tarasoff* Decisions: Suing Psychotherapists to Safeguard Society." *Harvard Law Review* 90:358–378, 1976.

do not provide much additional support. Extending psychotherapists' duties to protect third parties when treating voluntary outpatients like Poddar logically goes far beyond traditional custody and control cases involving inpatients. Thus it is possible that other courts will reject the legal reasoning of the *Tarasoff* decision.[5]

LEGAL DIRECTIONS: OTHER CASES

Ten years after the *Tarasoff* ruling, in only one case have therapists been held liable for damages resulting from a failure to warn or to take other steps. In *Jablonski v. United States*[6], Veterans' Administration psychiatrists were found to have fallen short of their Tarasoff duties, among others. In this case, Tarasoff liability was based upon the failure of the psychiatrists to foresee the risk to the victim and to warn, explicitly and sufficiently, the victim of her peril. But it should be pointed out that, in this case, the psychiatrists were not merely negligent but reckless[7] in their disregard of detail in (1) taking and assessing the medical history, (2) making a diagnosis and assessing risks of harm, and (3) fulfilling their *Tarasoff* duties. One might conclude that the psychiatrists' conduct in this case was a substantial departure from what most would consider to be good clinical practice.[8]

In *Lipari v. Sears, Roebuck & Co.,*[9] a Nebraska federal court adopted the broad reading of the *Tarasoff* rule that a psychotherapist has a duty to take reasonable steps to protect third persons foreseeably endangered by a known, dangerous patient. On that basis, they held that the alleged failure of Veterans' Administration psychiatrists to hold an outpatient who refused continued care could constitute a cause of action. In *Lipari,* there is no indication that the patient threatened to shoot into a nightclub crowd, nor is it alleged that his victims were known to the therapists. *Lipari* then does not deal with the confidentiality issue evoked by the *Tarasoff* case, namely the failure to protect a known, endangered third party. The federal court noted that no Nebraska state court had specifically accepted or rejected the *Tarasoff* principle. *Lipari,* like *Tarasoff,* was settled out of court before a trial on the facts. Thus it is possible that Nebraska courts may yet reject *Tarasoff.*

---

[5] Courts in at least two states, Maryland and Delaware, have indicated some hesitation about the acceptance of a *Tarasoff* duty: *Shaw v. Glickman,* 415 A 2d 625 (Md Ct Spec App 1980); *Delaware v. Tarbutton,* 407 A 2d 538 (Del Super Ct 1979).

[6] *Jablonski v. United States,* 712 F. 2d 391 (9th Cir. 1983).

[7] Winslade, W. J. "Recklessness." *Analysis* (March 1970), pp. 135–140.

[8] For a review of the numerous cases in which the courts have *not* imposed *Tarasoff* liability, see Mills, M. J. "The So-called Duty to Warn: The Psychotherapeutic Duty to Protect Third Parties from Patients' Violent Acts," *Behavioral Sciences and the Law* (in press). Mills reviews *Tarasoff,* related cases, and judicial policy issues and makes some useful practical suggestions to clinicians.

[9] *Lipari v. Sears, Roebuck & Co,* 497 F Supp 185 (D Neb 1980).

Only one state court has adopted the *Tarasoff* rule, and it expanded the rationale for legal duty to warn. In *McIntosh v. Milano* (a case procedurally and factually similar to *Tarasoff*), a New Jersey Superior Court held that a plaintiff does have a cause of action against a therapist, stating that:

> this court holds that a psychiatrist or therapist may have a duty to take whatever steps are reasonably necessary to protect an intended or potential victim of his patient when he determines, or should determine, in the appropriate factual setting and in accordance with the standards of his profession established at trial, that the patient is or may present a probability of danger to that person. The relationship giving rise to that duty may be found either in that existing between the therapist and the patient, as was alluded to in *Tarasoff*, or in the more broadly based obligation a practitioner may have to protect the welfare of the community, which is analogous to the obligation a physician has to warn third persons of infectious or contagious diseases.[10]

When this case did go to trial, however, the jury found that the psychiatrist was not liable for his patient's homicidal but unforeseeable conduct.

The *Tarasoff* and *McIntosh* rules are legally controversial, primarily because they create a tension between duties to third parties and duties to protect patients' confidential communications. The *McIntosh* court believes that the value of protecting confidentiality is overridden in situations in which a patient presents a danger to others and perhaps to himself or herself. In *Bellah v. Greenson*,[11] on the other hand, the California Supreme Court specifically stated that confidentiality is the overriding concern in cases of danger to self or damage to property. The *Tarasoff* opinion recognizes that confidentiality statutes, such as Section 5328 of the California Welfare and Institutions Code, require nondisclosure of such information. It could be argued that the *Tarasoff* rule applies in California only to situations not governed by statutory confidentiality rules. For example, at the UCLA Neuropsychiatric Institute, an institution specifically named by the legislature to be governed by the Welfare and Institutions Code, the *Tarasoff* rule may not apply because Section 5328 would govern instead.

One might speculate, however, about the California Supreme Court's decision if faced with a conflict between the *Tarasoff* rule and the Section 5328 confidentiality requirements: Would it restrict the *Tarasoff* rule or create a judicial exception to the statute? In its 1980 decision in *Mavroudis v. Superior Court*,[12] a California court of appeal recognized that Section 5328 does not permit disclosure of confidential records. It did admit, however, an exception to the psychotherapist–patient privilege in the presence of conditions evoking the *Tarasoff* duty—under Evidence Code Section 1024. That

---

[10] *McIntosh v. Milano*, 403 A 2d 500 (N J Super Ct 1979).

[11] *Bellah v. Greenson*, 146 Cal Rptr. 535 (Ct App 1978).

[12] *Mavroudis v. Superior Court for the County of San Mateo*, 162 Cal Rptr. 724 (Ct App 1980).

section states there is no privilege "if the psychotherapist has reasonable cause to believe that the patient is in such mental or emotional condition as to be dangerous to himself or to the person or property of another, and that disclosure of the communication is necessary to prevent the threatened danger."[13] On that basis, the *Mavroudis* court ruled that psychiatric records could be obtained by parties to a suit, in pretrial discovery, if the judge examined the records in chambers and found that the conditions described in Evidence Code Section 1024 were present and that there was a readily identifiable victim before the time of the incident.

The Mavroudis court's willingness to allow access to confidential records in a *Tarasoff*-type lawsuit implies that a party will be allowed to bring an action against an institution covered by Section 5328 for violation of the *Tarasoff* duty and thus that institutions governed under Section 5328 are *not* protected by those statutory provisions. By contrast, without specifically accepting or rejecting *Tarasoff,* a Maryland tribunal suggested that *Tarasoff* warnings would be a violation of Maryland's statutory protection of patient confidentiality.[14]

Mavroudis signals further erosion of the psychotherapist–patient confidentiality doctrine in two respects: (1) Confidentiality is probably not protected by other statutes in a *Tarasoff* context; and (2) confidentiality and privacy are further diminished by the judge's *in camera* examination of the therapist's records and the possible release of those records to litigants. If psychiatric records are to be obtained, access needs to be restricted to only those portions of the records directly related to the issues to be addressed in court. These matters go beyond the original concern of breaching confidentiality to warn a victim. Confidentiality may now be breached to further a lawsuit alleging liability of a therapist as opposed to the conduct or potential conduct of the patient involved. Just how much statutory protection of psychotherapist–patient confidentiality still exists in the *Tarasoff* context remains unclear, because the *Mavroudis* opinion addresses this question only insofar as it allows litigants pretrial access to privileged information.

This is a particularly clear case of conflict between statutory law and judicial interpretation, and until it is clarified by either legislative action or judicial decision, therapists must walk a narrow path. They must take care to make their best professional judgments without the security of knowing that their actions are within legal limits and while knowing that their conduct is likely to be subject to retrospective review, including that which is documented or inferred from medical records.

The *McIntosh* opinion described above suggests that confidentiality can be overridden not only in situations where there is danger to others but also in those where there is danger to self. In *Bellah v. Greenson,* however, a

---

[13] *California Evidence Code* § 1024. St. Paul, Minn., West Publishing, 1966.
[14] *Shaw v. Glickman,* 415 A 2d 625 (Md Ct Spec App 1980)

California appellate court declined to apply the *Tarasoff* rule to a suicide case. The court held that confidentiality is the overriding concern when the threatened danger is to self or damage to property. But the court does suggest that therapists may have special duties beyond the bounds of confidentiality in some suicide-related cases, such as suicidal inpatients.

Another class of cases, more distantly related to *Tarasoff*, includes cases dealing with the release of dangerous patients or prisoners from state institutions. Although these cases deal with different kinds of situations than did *Tarasoff, McIntosh, Bellah, Lipari,* or *Mavroudis,* there is an underlying similarity in that all bear upon the nature of the therapist's legal responsibility to the community in protecting innocent individuals from dangerous patients. The *Lipari* court found that an institution and its therapist employees have at least a duty to detain a dangerous outpatient to protect the community. As in *Lipari,* a major issue in these cases is whether government employees are immune from liability regardless of the releasing agency's legal duty.

More far-reaching than the immediate legislation it triggered, the *Berwid* case in New York's Pilgrim Hospital has generated significant questions about the responsibility of therapists for potentially dangerous patients.[15] Adam Berwid, who was hospitalized because of attempts to kill his wife, was given an 8-hour pass. He did not return to the hospital at the agreed-upon time, calling instead to inform the hospital that he had missed a train and would take the next one. Instead, he went to his wife's home and killed her. Berwid was found incompetent to stand trial. On the basis of three psychiatrists' evaluations in the spring of 1980, he was certified as competent to stand trial by a psychiatrist at Mid-Hudson Psychiatric Center, where he was a patient. But Berwid subsequently stabbed his court-appointed attorney with a ballpoint pen, and after months of psychiatric examinations and competency hearings, the court found him incompetent to stand trial once more. When the Mid-Hudson psychiatrists again announced that Berwid was competent, in early 1981, he attacked a member of the hospital staff. A decision to not seek another competency ruling in court was made at that time. Eventually, Berwid was found competent to stand trial, was convicted of murder, and sentenced to prison.

The psychiatrist who approved Berwid's pass was suspended from the hospital, but a grand jury later failed to indict him for criminal negligence. Charges of misconduct were instituted to terminate his employment, then were withdrawn. Over the psychiatrist's objection that he had given up his arbitration claim in reliance on the withdrawal of charges, a New York court

---

[15] Sources of information on the *Berwid* matter include various reports appearing in the *New York Times,* beginning December 9, 1979, and personal communication with Stephen Rachlin, M.D. See also "Professional Liability in the Mental Health Context: Ten Recent Cases," *Mental Disabilities Law Reporter* 4:241–243, 1980.

ruled that the charges could be reinstated. Reassigned to duties not involving patient care, the psychiatrist continued employment until his retirement a few months later. Charges were never renewed.

As a result of the *Berwid* situation, however, the New York legislature prepared legislation requiring automatic notification of all potential victims when any criminally committed patient is given any kind of pass or leave. Currently, such notification is required only in cases of absences. If a civil case is eventually filed in the *Berwid* matter (which is possible since there are surviving children), it is likely to proceed on questions not only about the need to warn but about the timing of such warnings. If so, *Berwid* could make the entire matter of warnings even stickier.

The legislative response to *Berwid* may be political overreaction. But it must be kept in mind that public reaction to such cases is usually quick and intense and seldom involves any understanding of the clinical complexities of cases involving potentially dangerous patients—especially the difficulties therapists have in accurately predicting dangerousness. Although these cases look clear in hindsight, journalistic accounts seldom focus on the size of the population that would have to be restrained (a clear violation of civil rights) in order conclusively to restrain any given individual. This is inherently a statistical problem, one of excessive numbers of false positives, and one that the public has not been well educated to understand.

In several other recent cases involving release on parole, therapist liability was precluded by government immunity for discretionary acts. These cases open the question of whether there is immunity for ministerial, as opposed to discretionary, functions. It will be helpful to look at the cases that address this distinction before considering whether or not the distinction is a useful one in this context.

In *Martinez v. California,*[16] the plaintiff charged that, among others, the state was responsible for a young woman's death because it paroled a sex offender whom the judge had recommended should receive no parole, and had thereby deprived her of her life without due process. The U.S. Supreme Court ruled that the state was not liable because Section 845.8 of the California Government Code states that neither public entity nor public employee is liable for injuries resulting from decisions to parole or release prisoners. Further, it stated that due process did not apply because the state did not cause the woman's death: Her death was the result of a long chain of events, and the decision to parole was only one of many such events.

Martinez is only indirectly related to the *Tarasoff* ruling because it does not involve warning third parties, i.e., there was no way of knowing what specific person might be at risk. It does seem relevant, however, to general questions of therapists' liability for former patients' actions. The decision suggests that public employees cannot be held liable for such harmful actions

---

[16] *Martinez v. California,* 444 US 277 (1980).

as long as they perform their work in accordance with professional standards and in line with some rational state policy. In *Martinez,* the court held that rehabilitation and parole is a rational policy and that the actions of the parole board in paroling prisoners is consistent with that policy. Further, it asserted that the state is free to choose its policies and, having done so, may protect its employees from liability in order to carry out the policy. If the state were not able to provide immunity from liability, it would be impossible to carry out the policy effectively.

The *Martinez* rationale was applied to a later case alleging a county's failure to warn a juvenile's mother, her neighbors, or the police when the county released a juvenile offender known to commit sexual assaults on young children. Within 24 hours of his release to the custody of his mother, the juvenile murdered a neighbor's young son. The California Supreme Court, in *Thompson v. County of Alameda,*[17] dismissed the suit because the decision to release the offender was a discretionary decision that promoted the public policy of rehabilitation through probation and parole, and therefore the county was immune from liability. It also found that there was no direct or continuing relationship between the county and the victim paralleling the special relationship between the therapist and patient in *Tarasoff,* and that the victim was not readily identifiable. The court stated that "public entities and employees have no affirmative duty to warn of the release of an inmate with a violent history who has made *nonspecific threats of harm directed at nonspecific victims.*"[17] It is noteworthy, however, that two justices dissented, saying that *Tarasoff* is not limited to a duty to warn nor to identifiable victims but rather creates a duty of care to all persons foreseeably endangered by a person of known dangerousness.

Both these cases speak to the validity of the state's purposes insofar as they are "rational policies." A parallel, however, might be drawn between *parole* as a rational policy with respect to successful criminal rehabilitation and *confidentiality* as a rational policy with respect to successful psychotherapy (itself a kind of rehabilitation). If the parallel is accurate, then it follows that immunity should also be granted to those who honor confidentiality in the pursuit of successful therapy, even if success is not any more guaranteed than it is in criminal rehabilitation.

A third recent case is that of *Buford v. California.*[18] In April 1978, a Ms. Buford was assaulted and raped by a Mr. Daniels. Daniels had been released from Atascadero State Hospital in January 1976, on "indefinite leave." In June 1977, the hospital changed his status to "unauthorized" leave. Buford argued that the state, as well as its employees, were responsible for failing properly to diagnose, treat, and monitor Daniels. The court held that the state did have a special relationship to Daniels because he was still a mental

---

[17] *Thompson v. County of Alameda,* 167 Cal Rptr. 70, 614 P 2d 728 (Cal 1980).

[18] *Buford v. California,* 164 Cal Rptr. 264 (Ct App 1980).

hospital patient. Even though the hospital had placed him on unauthorized leave, he was not an escaped patient given the nature of his original departure. The state's special relationship was manifested in the several employees at the hospital who were responsible for Daniels' rehabilitation. The court further found that the problem lay not in the *discretionary* decision made by the state and its employees to grant a leave of absence (for which they were not liable under California Government Code, Section 856), but rather with those *ministerial* actions that followed the decision to grant leave. The state was not held liable even for these actions under California Government Code, Section 854.8, but the appellate court left, as questions for the triers of fact, whether or not the therapeutic/rehabilitative personnel at Atascadero had properly performed their "ministerial" duties.

Allowing government immunity for discretionary functions but not for ministerial duties creates anomalous liability criteria in *Tarasoff*-type situations. Generally, a discretionary function is characterized as one involving the balancing of policy considerations; a ministerial act, as one performed according to orders, without the exercise of judgment as to the propriety of the action. For example, development of government regulations is a discretionary function; implementation of them is a ministerial action. Statutory provisions protect many government entities from liability for discretionary functions (although they allow liability for negligence in performing ministerial duties) in part to protect the policy-making powers that are entrusted to government.

Thus the decision to release a prisoner or mental patient has been characterized as discretionary because it involves a decision as to whether the public policy favoring rehabilitation, by release into the community, outweighs that of continued detention. On the other hand, the *Lipari* court stated that when a government psychotherapist judges that an outpatient does not require detention, it is *not* a discretionary function because it does not involve policy balancing. Similarly, the *Tarasoff* court held that a failure to protect a potential victim would be a failure to carry out a *ministerial* duty. By allowing liability for ministerial duties, the court distinguishes between treatment decisions, commitment decisions, and decisions to release a patient (which are discretionary, and for which therapeutic personnel usually have immunity from liability) versus those actions involving followup and oversight after a patient is released into the community.

The underlying concepts in *Buford* and *Martinez,* and those in *Thompson* and *Lipari,* seem to go in different directions. It is not clear, for example, in what way ministerial actions and decisions having to do with monitoring (in *Buford*) and with detaining (in *Lipari*) are not aspects of rational, state-approved policies, when treatment and release or parole decisions are. Ministerial actions in *Buford* seem to be comparable to the therapist's position in *Tarasoff*-type cases, insofar as each is liable for actions, or failures to act, to prevent harm. It is not clear from the discussions whether the court is concerned with actual distinctions between ministerial and discretionary functions or whether it is trying to determine differing standards that would constitute negligence in the two forms.

In *Martinez, Thompson,* and *Buford,* no specific person was known to be at risk. The liability of psychotherapists would seem to depend upon whether or not they made their decisions in agreement with professional standards and in response to some rational state policy. This would apply equally to decisions about release, parole, and followup or monitoring.

These immunity cases are interesting because they discourage litigation in *Tarasoff*-type situations. Plaintiffs' attorneys are less likely to sue when practitioners are directly liable for injuries to third parties than when there are more attractive targets, such as institutional or government defendants, with their so-called "deep pockets." Individual therapists are, to be sure, still potential targets for litigation as well as liability. To date, however, only once have psychiatrists been held liable for damages for violating the *Tarasoff* rule. And, here, the deep pockets of the Veterans' Administration were the target of the litigation. Thus the dire predictions that came from the psychotherapeutic community about the disastrous legal consequences of *Tarasoff* have not been realized.

IMPACT ON CLINICAL PRACTICE

Controversy and uncertainty about the *Tarasoff* case are not limited to its legal significance; they extend also to its general and specific impacts upon therapy. *Tarasoff* is reported to have had a significant impact on the practice of psychotherapy in California. Furthermore, the *Tarasoff* rule has begun to stimulate controversy about appropriate clinical treatment for certain types of patients who present a serious danger of violence to others. The debate about clinical responses, combined with the ambiguity of the legal requirements, make it especially difficult for therapists to determine clinically appropriate and legally responsible professional conduct. Nevertheless, clinicians who are treating dangerous patients can neither wait until theoretical controversies are resolved nor, as in litigation, obtain a continuance.

Tarasoff generated many anxieties and misunderstandings, especially when the first opinion of the California Supreme Court was published in 1974. Not only did it coincide with the peak of the so-called malpractice crisis (at least as reflected in malpractice insurance rates) in California, but also it reflected the growing national concern about professional accountability and government regulation of professional practice. Furthermore, it evoked concern among psychotherapists about the specter of increased litigation—even where liability might not be found.

In 1976, when the revised *Tarasoff* opinion was issued, it was clear that the case might have an impact not only on psychotherapists, their patients, and potential victims, but also on the attitudes of (1) the general public and potential patients; (2) policymakers, such as legislators and judges; and (3) attorneys, especially those who litigate personal injury cases. Although the post-*Tarasoff* situation in California called for careful impact research, only one empirical study of the effects of *Tarasoff* has been published, namely a note in the *Stanford Law Review* that reports the results of a questionnaire survey of psychologists and psychiatrists in California. This study gathered information about (1) "the effects psychotherapists perceive *Tarasoff* has had on their clinical practices; (2) the extent of psychotherapists' knowledge of the case; (3) therapists' general attitude toward confidentiality; and (4) general data on the therapists themselves and their practices."[19] After analyzing their data, the authors concluded that psychotherapists had often given warnings to third parties before *Tarasoff*. The imposition of a *legal duty* to protect third parties, however, created substantial concern, even among such therapists, because they were uncertain about what would constitute compliance. Further, there was an indication that therapists were focusing more attention on their patients' potential for violence and the requisite breach of confidentiality, and that such attention was not necessarily conducive to good therapeutic practice.

Although it is beyond the scope of this chapter to examine critically the methodology or content of the Stanford study, there are questions about the sampling (random selection of psychologists plus all members of the California Psychiatric Association), the somewhat leading questions on the questionnaire, and the unreliability of a self-reporting survey as a basis for an assessment of impact (as opposed to attitudes).

David Wexler has offered additional criticism of this study, especially the interpretation of the data and the theoretical assumptions on which it was based.[20] Nevertheless, the study did identify important issues that warrant further empirical research, namely the impact of *Tarasoff* on clinical practice in California—including changes in disclosures to patients about confidentiality, commitment practices, treatment techniques with *Tarasoff*-type patients, and methods used by therapists to comply with the *Tarasoff* rule. But a questionnaire alone cannot provide the data that are needed; a more systematic and rigorous empirical study is necessary.

Such research has recently been undertaken at Northeastern University in Boston.[21] Investigators there are collecting data to investigate the impact

[19] Wise, T. "Where the Public Peril Begins: A Survey of Psychotherapists to Determine the Effects of *Tarasoff*." *Stanford Law Review* 31:164–190, 1978.

[20] Wexler, D. B. "Patients, Therapists, and Third Parties: The Victimological Virtues of *Tarasoff*." *International Journal of Law and Psychiatry* 2:1–18, 1979.

[21] Bowers, W. J., Givelber, D. J. "*Tarasoff*: Legal Impact on Mental Health Practice." NIMH grant 5 R01 MH 32439-02 (research in progress). Some preliminary findings have been published by Givelber, et al., in "*Tarasoff*, Myth and Reality: An Empirical Study of Private Law in Action," *Wisconsin Law Review* 2:443–498, 1984.

of *Tarasoff* on mental health practices. They are surveying psychiatrists, psychologists, and social workers in private practice with the planned addition of mental health workers who staff institutions in the eight largest metropolitan areas of the country. This survey proposes to identify existing practices among the several groups of mental health care providers with respect to confidentiality, interventions that may compromise it, and where and by whom potentially dangerous patients are seen, as well as levels of confidence in and experience with predicting short-term violence. Studies such as this one are needed to provide factual information from which the actual impact of *Tarasoff* on clinical practice can be measured.

Even without adequate empirical evidence about the impact of *Tarasoff*, however, clinicians confronted with *Tarasoff*-type situations must act. Alan Stone[22] wrote a serious and thoughtful article about the clinical problems raised by *Tarasoff*. Stone contends that the *Tarasoff*-duty—specifically the duty of a psychotherapist to protect identifiable persons threatened with violence by a dangerous patient of the psychotherapist—will undermine "the therapeutic alliance and destroy the patient's expectation of confidentiality, thereby thwarting effective treatment and ultimately reducing public safety." He believes that the type of voluntary outpatient who is potentially dangerous to identifiable others is typically disturbed because of passion, paranoia, or morbid jealousy and argues that the therapist's primary social responsibility in dealing with such patients should be limited to notifying the police, who are better equipped to protect public safety. He claims that "emergency civil commitment generally remains the safest and least destructive way to deal with a crisis of violence in a mentally ill person." As Wexler[23] points out in his criticism of Stone, however, involuntary civil commitment may not be the most appropriate clinical response to the type of patient most likely to pose *Tarasoff* problems. Such patients are not the typically severely mental ill persons who need and can benefit significantly from hospitalization. *Tarasoff* patients often are disturbed because of serious difficulties in specific interpersonal relationships.

Civil commitment, especially if imposed against a patient's will, may imperil the therapeutic alliance more than would disclosure of sensitive information. Furthermore, involuntary civil commitment is, at best, only a temporary measure to avert a crisis, not a sufficient measure for dealing with the usually long-standing interpersonal conflicts that may erupt into violence. Civil commitment may interrupt and briefly postpone violence, but it may not defuse it. Finally, it is not clear that all patients share the grave concern about confidentiality that psychotherapists have. Here also we need some reliable empirical evidence, not merely unproven assumptions and professional prejudices.

In contrast to Stone, Wexler argued that it is necessary to revise funda-

---

[22] *Supra* note 4.
[23] *Supra* note 20.

mental assumptions about clinical practices in treating potentially dangerous patients. Wexler summarized his position as follows:

> . . . my purpose is to assert that the enmity of Stone and others toward *Tarasoff* is bottomed largely on their adherence to an "individual pathology" model of violent behavior which, the literature strongly suggests, is theoretically and therapeutically unwarranted. More important, what *is* apparently warranted, according to those who have seriously studied the type of interpersonal violence that is therapeutically preventable, is an approach that focuses on troubled *relationships*. Ideally, such an approach should involve both the patient and the potential victim, and should therefore often take the form of "couple" or "family" therapy. Finally, it is my thesis that, if taken seriously and followed widely, the *Tarasoff* decision, despite its many obvious drawbacks, has the clear-cut potential of prompting and prodding practicing therapists to terminate their continued clinging to an outmoded "individual pathology" model of violence, and to accept the paradigm of "interactional" or "couple" violence already endorsed by the professional literature.[24]

Wexler carefully analyzed the victimological variables—the nature of the patient, the identity of the potential victim, and the nature and role of the potential victim. He explained the therapeutic implications of victimological theory and specifically applied them to *Tarasoff*-type cases in order to illustrate how an interactionist (rather than individual pathology) model for therapeutic intervention might more successfully avert *Tarasoff* tragedies.

Stone and Wexler present very different views about appropriate clinical responses to dangerous patients. In fairness to Stone, it should be noted that his comments about clinical practice are incidental to his primary critique of the legal logic and practical implications of the *Tarasoff* litigation. Wexler is primarily concerned with implications of *Tarasoff* for clinical practice. Nevertheless, Stone's article is troubling because of his confidence in, or at least reliance on, the efficacy of civil commitment as the best available treatment alternative. Wexler's argument, on the other hand, reads like a brief for interactionist theory. It is not clear that the individual pathology and interactionist models can be so sharply separated in theory, much less in practice.

When there are so many areas of uncertainty and ambiguity, what is the clinician to do? The lack of legal repercussions from *Tarasoff* signals that psychotherapists need not sacrifice professional judgment in this sensitive area. In fact, the profession would do well to maintain a skeptical attitude about any theoretical framework purporting to solve complex, unique, and atomistically irreducible episodes that call for sensitive, thoughtful, and responsible clinical judgments. In many cases, detailed—*very* detailed—case discussions and consultations can help to guide clinical treatment and socially responsible decisions in *Tarasoff* situations, though by no means can they guarantee success. The complexity of factual situations, the inevitable

---

[24] Id. at 4.

uncertainties of human conduct, the difficulties of orchestrating patients, potential victims, families, police, and mental health institutions are likely to defy any neat categorization or fixed plan of action. Treatment decisions must be made pragmatically, subject to revision and redirection in the face of changing circumstances.

It is, perhaps, for these reasons that the California Supreme Court, having promulgated an ambiguous and potentially far-reaching *Tarasoff* rule, also qualified it in important ways:

> We recognize the difficulty that a therapist encounters in attempting to forecast whether a patient presents a serious danger of violence. Obviously we do not require that the therapists, in making that determination, render a perfect performance; the therapist need only exercise "that reasonable degree of skill, knowledge and care ordinarily possessed and exercised by members of that professional speciality under similar circumstances [citations omitted]". Within the broad range of reasonable practice and treatment in which professional opinion and judgment may differ, the therapist is free to exercise his or her own best judgment without liability; proof, aided by hindsight, that he or she judged wrongly is insufficient to establish negligence.
>
> We emphasize that our conclusion does not raise the specter of therapists . . . indiscriminately being held liable for damages despite their exercise of sound professional judgment.

This language may not be very reassuring to therapists faced with the uncertainties of clinical decision making, but at least it acknowledges the difficulties of trying to control human conduct through psychotherapeutic intervention. The essential legal requirement is that the psychotherapist must exercise judgment in accordance with the standards of the profession. Only one case in California applying the *Tarasoff* rule has resulted in a finding of liability. The other recent cases related to *Tarasoff* tend to restrict rather than expand liability, or to reaffirm the scope of immunity statutes. This suggests that the *Tarasoff* case calls attention to a genuine professional dilemma but has not opened, and is not likely to open, malpractice liability floodgates.

Tarasoff-type cases cannot very effectively be prevented or controlled by either legal regulation or psychotherapeutic intervention. Legal regulation recognizing this is likely to be, like the *Tarasoff* rule, tentative and uncertain. We must view, with similar caution, the theoretical clinical approaches to a class of cases that are perplexing precisely because they are so intractable to generalization. Given this uncertainty, therapists would be wise to make decisions about each such case on an individual basis, rather than by trying to find a formula to apply to every instance. This requires the therapist to act with some uncertainty as to his or her legal position but not as to his or her professional responsibility. It is probable that a reflective, well thought out judgment based on professional responsibility will always be the best defense.

C. J. Meyers

11

The Legal Perils of Psychotherapeutic Practice: The Farther Reaches of the Duty to Warn

Psychologists and psychiatrists belong to professional associations that hold that it is virtually impossible to predict violence accurately.[1] If a member of either discipline offers himself or herself to the public as a prognosticator of violent behavior, he or she risks censure by peers for unethical overreaching.[2] Courts of law, however, are not beholden to the official positions taken by professional guilds. They may, and they do, respect or ignore these positions to suit their purposes.[3]

---

[1] See American Psychiatric Association *amicus* brief, submitted to the U.S. Supreme Court in the case of *Estelle v. Smith,* 45 U.S. 454 (1981): "The unreliability of psychiatric prediction of future dangerousness is by now an established fact within the profession . . . The large body of research in this area indicates that, even under the best conditions, psychiatric predictions of long-term future dangerousness are wrong in at least two out of every three cases." See generally A. Monahan, *The Clinical Prediction of Violent Behavior* (DHHS Publication No. [ADM] 81-921), 1981.

[2] See, for example, the comments of the American Psychiatric Association on psychiatrist James Grigson, nicknamed "Dr. Death" and "the killer shrink" in the media because of his uniform predictions in Texas death penalty cases that convicted murderers would be prone to future violence: *Amicus* brief, submitted to the U.S. Supreme Court in the case of *Barefoot v. Estelle,* 103 S. Ct. 3383 (1983), reported in S. Cunningham, "High Court Distorts Results of Research on Dangerousness," *APA Monitor, 14,* 9, 1983.

[3] See, for example, *Barefoot v. Estelle* and *Estelle v. Smith, supra,* where, in both instances, the U.S. Supreme Court found the *amicus* briefs of the psychiatric association unpersuasive. See also *In re William Wilson,* M.H. No 1124-82, D.C. Super. Ct. (April 14, 1983), examined later in this chapter, in which a lower court cites the *amicus* brief from *Estelle v. Smith* and then goes further than the psychiatric association would wish, in holding that psychiatrists are not competent to testify on the issue of dangerousness in ordinary civil commitment hearings.

PSYCHOTHERAPY AND THE LAW
ISBN 0-8089-1780-3

When potential violence is an issue in civil commitment cases, the courts have shown themselves disposed to respect the view that mental health professionals have no special expertise in predicting a patient's imminent dangerousness to self or others. Psychiatrists and psychologists are expected to testify at commitment hearings, but unless they can point to hard evidence of a patient's violent behavior in the immediate past, their expert witness testimony on the issue of imminent dangerousness will be given short shrift.[4]

Unfortunately for the mental health profession, its incompetence to predict violence has been established by legal precedent only in the context of civil commitment hearings. These precedents have created no shield of imperceptiveness to duck behind in malpractice cases. If a party who has been injured by a mental patient is looking around for someone to sue, he or she may find that the most inviting target is the person who was unlucky enough to be the patient's psychotherapist. If the injured party then alleges, first, that the psychotherapist failed to foresee the patient's violent behavior and, second, that the psychotherapist negligently failed to act to prevent its occurrence, a jury might agree.

This chapter addresses the willingness of courts of law to hold psychotherapists accountable for the damage done by their patients. Most especially, it examines the implications of the recently decided *Hedlund*[5] and *Jablonski*[6] cases, and, of their progenitor, *Tarasoff*,[7] and it recommends courses of action for coping with the problems these cases create.

---

[4] The following judicial response is unusual only in that it is part of the record that provided the basis of a landmark "Right to Treatment" decision, *Rouse v. Cameron*, 373 F.2d 451 (D.C. Cir. 1966). It comes from the transcript of the civil commitment hearing held a year earlier, as reprinted in J. Katz, et al., *Psychoanalysis, Psychiatry and Law* (New York: Free Press, 1967), p. 604:

"THE COURT: I know as much about the dictionary, I presume, as the average person. I say to you that the words 'anti-social acts' is so general that it does not help anybody. You have got to tell us concretely what specific things he says and does that differentiate him from a normal person."

"THE WITNESS: Yes, Your Honor."

"THE COURT: . . . I am not going to keep anybody deprived of his liberty on adjectives and generalities, it has got to be verbs and nouns, something that a person does or says that differentiates him from normal people and makes him dangerous. . . ."

"THE COURT: Liberty is too precious to leave it merely with the opinions of psychiatrists. . . ."

"THE COURT: I have a very high regard for the science of medicine, of which psychiatry is a branch, but matters like these are, in the ultimate analysis, for the Court to determine."

[5] *Hedlund v. Superior Court of Orange County*, 34 Cal. 3d 695 (1983).

[6] *Jablonski v. United States*, 712 F. 2d 391 (1983).

[7] *Tarasoff v. Regents of the University of California*, 17 Cal. 3d 425 (1976).

THE RELEVANT CASES

When the California Supreme Court delivered its controversial duty to warn opinion in the landmark *Tarasoff* case,[8] it seemed to be constructing a dangerous trap for all psychotherapists. But the threat implicit in the court's decision, much like the threats most psychotherapists hear their patients make from time to time, dissipated even as it was expressed. Although an important new law would seem to have been created, few litigants were eager or eligible to take advantage of the opportunities it offered. When they tried, they were usually disappointed.

The legal actions that followed on the heels of *Tarasoff* were anticlimactic. First, in *Bellah v. Greenson,*[9] a California appellate court reassured therapists that they were not bound by a duty to warn others when a patient was suicidal. Then, in *Thompson v. Alameda County,*[10] the California Supreme Court reassured therapists further by holding that there was no duty to warn when threats had been directed at an amorphous group.

But recently, two decisions, one from the Federal Court of Appeals and the other from the California Supreme Court, have given *Tarasoff* new teeth.

In *Jablonski v. United States,*[11] the Federal Court of Appeals for the Ninth Circuit upheld a trial court in imposing the duty to warn upon a psychotherapist who had not been told of his patient's murderous intent. The trial court found that the psychotherapist should have discerned his patient's intentions from the ''psychological profile'' implicit in the patient's psychiatric record. The trial court also found that the victim, although warned by several people and aware herself of the danger, had not been ''adequately'' warned.

In *Hedlund v. Superior Court of Orange County,*[12] the California Supreme Court clarified the nature of the duty to warn by stating that it was ''inextricably interwoven'' with the function of diagnosing danger.[13] A failure to diagnose or warn was thus designated an act of professional negligence, i.e., malpractice. The court also extended the duty to warn to include warnings to family members foreseeably located within the ''zone of danger.''[14]

---

[8] *Id.*

[9] *Bellah v. Greenson,* 81 Cal. App. 3d 911 (1978).

[10] *Thompson v. Alameda County,* 27 Cal. 3d 741 (1980).

[11] *Supra* note 6.

[12] *Supra* note 5.

[13] 34 Cal. 3d 695 (1983) at 706.

[14] The *Jablonski* case is precedent only in the federal courts of California. To exploit the ruling, a plaintiff must find an excuse to file suit in the federal court. The offender in *Jablonski* was being treated by a clinic of the Veterans' Administration when he wronged his victim.

JABLONSKI: SUMMARY OF FACTS

On Sunday, July 16, 1978, Phillip Jablonski murdered Melinda Kimball. Their infant daughter, Meghan, then sued the Loma Linda Veterans' Administration Hospital and several named psychiatrists for mishandling her father's case.

Jablonski was first brought to the attention of the hospital by the police. On Friday, July 7, 1978, Isobel Pahls complained to police that Jablonski had threatened her with a sharp object and tried to rape her. Pahls had also been the object of obscene phone calls and other unspecified malicious acts which the police concluded had been committed by Jablonski. Jablonski was the lover of Melinda Kimball, Pahls's daughter. Pahls did not file formal charges against her daughter's lover but instead discussed with the police a plan to pressure him into receiving psychiatric help. Shortly thereafter, Jablonski "volunteered" to undergo psychiatric examination at the V.A. hospital.

The police immediately phoned the hospital and advised the chief of psychiatric services of Jablonski's prior criminal record. (The contents of this record are unspecified in the appellate opinion; presumably, the record contained Jablonski's conviction 10 years earlier for raping the woman who was then his wife.) The police also conveyed Jablonski's recent history and offered their opinion that he be hospitalized. The chief of services stated that he would convey this information to the treating psychiatrist in the outpatient clinic, but he failed to do so. On the witness stand, the treating psychiatrist testified that had he received this information he might have hospitalized Jablonski involuntarily. Why he so testified is not clear, since he appears to have received from Jablonski and Kimball themselves during the first diagnostic session, all the information that he could have received from his chief.

On Monday, July 10, Jablonski, accompanied by Kimball, showed up at the V.A. clinic for his first psychiatric session. At this time the treating psychiatrist learned that 3 days earlier Jablonski had threatened to rape Pahls and that a decade earlier he had served a 5-year prison term for raping his ex-wife. The treating psychiatrist also learned that Jablonski had undergone psychiatric treatment previously, but the patient refused to tell him where that treatment had taken place. The psychiatrist diagnosed Jablonski as a potentially dangerous antisocial personality, but concluded that the situation was not an emergency and that there was no basis for hospitalizing

---

Presumably, any psychotherapist paid with federal funds (by CHAMPUS, for instance or through a community mental health program that shared federal revenue) could find himself or herself maneuvered into a federal court.

Hedlund is binding only in the state courts of California. But, as California has often proved itself a legal bellwether for the rest of the nation, this case, like the original duty to warn case, *Tarasoff,* is not something that mental health professionals in the rest of the country can blithely ignore.

the patient against his will. Jablonski was offered hospitalization on a voluntary basis, but he refused. Faced with someone he considered an evasive psychopath, the doctor demonstrated his pessimism about psychiatry's ability to help a recalcitrant outpatient and scheduled Jablonski's next appointment for 2 weeks hence.

Following the diagnostic interview, Kimball privately confided her fears about her lover to the psychiatrist. The doctor recommended that she leave Jablonski, at least while he was being evaluated, but when Kimball protested on the grounds of love, the doctor warned no further.

No attempt was made to locate Jablonski's psychiatric records. As it happened, some of the records were within the V.A. system's own file and would have been accessible without the patient's consent. The bulk of the records, however, were 10 years old and buried in another system's file. These old records were replete with ominous descriptions and conclusions and contained statements such as, "The possibility of future violent behavior was [sic] a distinct probability."[15] They included the diagnosis "schizophrenic reaction, undifferentiated type, chronic, moderate; manifested by homicidal behavior toward his wife." The V.A. psychiatrist had no legal access to these records, and because of his patient's lack of candor, he was unaware that they existed.

On Tuesday or Wednesday, July 11 or 12, according to the appellate court record, Pahls telephoned the V.A. psychiatrist and complained about the 2-week hiatus. She wanted Jablonski seen immediately, or she would again call the police. The psychiatrist agreed to see the patient again on Friday, July 14. The record also says that the psychiatrist "persuaded" Pahls not to call the police, but it is left ambiguous whether this persuasion consisted merely of an accomodation to Pahls' wishes or whether it comprised something more.

Her lover's psychiatrist was not the only one urging Kimball to leave Jablonski. On Wednesday, July 12, on the advice of her priest, Kimball took her daughter (Meghan) and moved into Pahls' apartment. She continued to see her lover, however, and on Friday she drove him to a session in which he was examined in tandem by his psychiatrist and his psychiatrist's supervisor. Jablonski was still evasive about his past, but he admitted that violent reactions had been a problem throughout his life; as a result, his diagnosis was modified to "antisocial personality with explosive features." Although the supervising psychiatrist concluded that the patient was dangerous to some degree and that the case was an "emergency," both psychiatrists agreed that Jablonski was not homicidal or suicidal and, given the V.A.'s policy for the treatment of nonpsychotic patients, that he could not be involuntarily hospitalized. Jablonski continued to decline the offer of voluntary hospitalization.

---

[15] 712 F. 2d 391 (1983) at 393.

While Jablonski was being interviewed, Kimball fretted outside the office. Yet another doctor, the chief of the psychiatric outpatient clinic, noticed her distress and tried to reassure her. Kimball expressed fear for her physical safety. The doctor commiserated but pointed out that if Jablonski did not meet the criteria for involuntary hospitalization, Kimball could consider staying away from him.

Jablonski was scheduled for psychological testing, given a prescription for Valium, and told to return to the clinic on the following workday, Monday, July 17. This treatment plan did not survive the weekend. On Sunday, Kimball returned to the apartment on an errand, encountered Jablonski, and was murdered.

The trial judge found the V.A. psychiatrists liable on several grounds: (1) failure to record and transmit the information from the police; (2) failure to obtain past medical records; and (3) failure to warn adequately. Each failure was considered a cause of Kimball's death and a separate act of malpractice. The appeals court affirmed this decision.

COMPARISON WITH *TARASOFF*

The facts of *Tarasoff,* the landmark case from which *Jablonski* descends, included the unusual circumstance of a therapist accurately and publicly concluding that his patient was severely mentally ill and homicidal (diagnosis: paranoid schizophrenia) after his patient confided his intention to kill a woman who had spurned him. The attempt to impose involuntary hospitalization on the patient was then subverted by the bungling of the police and the uncooperativeness of the therapist's clinic chief.

The facts of *Jablonski* are more commonplace and, hence, the case has even wider ramifications. *Jablonski* contains no premeditating killer verbally sharing his intentions with his therapist, no therapist deciding that the patient is lethal and ill enough to warrant involuntary hospitalization, and no aborted attempt to confine. The therapists officially concluded that their patient was not severely mentally ill and not homicidal (diagnosis: character disorder). They thought that he was probably dangerous because of his history of sexual assaults, but given the admissions policy of the V.A. hospital and the therapists' interpretation of the law of involuntary detention, they finally concluded that their patient was not suitable for involuntary hospitalization.

In *Jablonski,* the killer threatened no one in the presence of his therapists. The psychiatrists knew that the patient had recently menaced his lover's mother and that 10 years earlier he had been sentenced to prison for raping his ex-wife. But in the case record there is no mention that the patient ever threatened or assaulted his lover, the woman who was to become his victim. The court did not assume, therefore, as had the court in *Tarasoff,* that the identity of the victim had been specified; but it concluded that the identity of the victim was foreseeable because of the client's history of directing his violence toward women with whom he was close. The court termed this historical pattern of behavior a "psychological profile." Because the victim's identity was foreseeable, the psychiatrists were considered liable for not warning the woman about what was in store for her.

Jablonski, therefore, goes beyond *Tarasoff* in a very important way. No longer is it sufficient to warn intended victims of explicit threats of violence confided by a severely mentally ill patient. Therapists must now warn intended victims of threats of violence that may be *implied* by their patients' "psychological profiles." The therapist is responsible for discerning both the identity of the targeted victim and the magnitude of the threat. That is the case even, as in *Jablonski,* when the patient does not appear to be severely mentally ill, is "vague and noncommunicative,"[16] and is willing to share neither his prior psychiatric or criminal history nor his plans for the future.

The *Tarasoff* case never came to trial but was finally settled out of court: The California Supreme Court merely ruled that such a case was triable. But in *Jablonski,* a case that was tried on a *Tarasoff* theory, the trial judge found for the injured plaintiff and against the therapist defendants. The defendants appealed, and the court of appeals, working from the written record, concluded that the trial judge had not done anything that was, in the terms of the Federal Rules of Civil Procedure, "clearly erroneous."[17] He may have been wrong, but the record did not indicate that he was *clearly* wrong; and insofar as the defendants did not prove that the trial judge was clearly wrong, the appeals court was obliged not to second-guess him. The trial court's judgment stands, therefore, and becomes law in the federal courts in the state of California.

IMPLICATIONS OF *JABLONSKI*

Jablonski is a disconcerting case to read, and not merely because the holding will be hard to live with. The case is one of malpractice, tried on several theories and won on all of them. The V.A. was held liable for dropping a number of balls, and the adequate-warning ball was only one of several. The chief psychiatrist failed to relay to the treating psychiatrist information he had received from the police; records of past medical treatment at the V.A. and elsewhere were not retrieved. And although it could be

---

[16] *Id.* at 393.

[17] The phrase "clearly erroneous" comes from the *Federal Rules of Civil Procedure,* a set of rules passed by Congress to govern the operations of the federal district trial and appellate courts: "Findings of fact shall not be set aside [on review by the appellate courts] unless clearly erroneous, and due regard shall be given to the opportunity of the trial court to judge the credibility of witnesses" (*Federal Rules of Civil Procedure,* p. 52 [a]).

argued that neither incident of information slippage had any effect on the therapists' decisions or on the patient's subsequent behavior, the slippage had occurred—and it had been preventable. The psychiatrists had been clearly negligent in not retrieving the V.A.'s own records and in not passing along police information. Even so, it would appear that they had been merely mistaken in not guessing accurately that their patient was an imminent murderer.

There is a further disturbing element in the case. A close reading reveals that the psychiatrist *did* warn the victim, not that she would be killed— because he had not come to so pessimistic a conclusion—but that it would be wise for her to move out of the apartment she shared with the patient and to keep her distance from him during the initial phase of evaluation and treatment. For good measure, the victim was given the same warning the second time that she accompanied her lover to the clinic, this time by a colleague of the treating psychiatrist. Good advice is often easy to give and hard to take. Kimball thanked the doctors but protested that she loved her man. Eventually, however, on the urgings of her attorney, her priest, and a psychological crisis hotline, she did move out. But then, guided by the type of motive one might find in a textbook on victimology, she found an excuse to go back to the old apartment. Her path crossed Jablonski's, and she was murdered.

There is a final irony in the case. Implied but not stated explicitly in the opinion is the proposition that had the V.A. psychiatrists done their homework and assembled all the relevant information from available police and hospital records, they would have concluded that their patient was homicidal. They then would have either hospitalized him or issued more robust warnings to the eventual victim. That proposition appears to be false. The V.A. file that the killer's therapist neglected to retrieve was a sparse account of an earlier outpatient visit and did not hint at violence. The information from the police that was not relayed to the treating psychiatrist by his colleague was no different from information given to him by other collaterals. The account of psychiatric treatment a decade earlier was voluminous and ominous, but the V.A. psychiatrists were blocked from access to this information by ignorance of its existence. Had they been aware of these earlier records, they still would have had to overcome the obstacle of laws protecting the confidentiality of non-V.A. psychiatric records. The patient was disposed to cover up his history rather than reveal it, and he was not willing to sign a release.[18]

---

[18] *Id.* at 393: "Jablonski informed Kopiloff that he had undergone psychiatric treatment previously, but refused to state where he had received the treatment. Kopiloff concluded that the patient was . . . unwilling to share his prior psychiatric history."

In a personal communication with the author, Dr. Kopiloff confirms the implication that the patient refused to sign a release-of-information form.

So the victim was clearly warned, but was she *adequately* warned? The trial court said no, and the appeals court said that the evidence did not demonstrate that the trial court was "clearly erroneous." The multiple warnings from various sources, and the implication that the victim knew that she was assuming risks for the sake of love, were considered irrelevancies for legal, if not practical, purposes. The court wanted someone to pay, and as it pointed out, "There are no meaningful alternative remedies available to the plaintiff."[19]

There were meaningful alternatives available to the court. It could have upheld the malpractice award on the grounds of negligent failure to retrieve records and relay information, but not on the grounds of negligent failure to warn. Some diminishment of the award to the plaintiff might have been necessary, but California's psychotherapists would be operating under a more reasonable law.

HEDLUND: THE FACTS AND THE HOLDING

The facts of *Hedlund* are not as readily available as those of *Jablonski* and *Tarasoff*. The *Hedlund* case is still in litigation, and the principals are maintaining a discrete public silence. The following, then, is the plaintiff's version of the facts of the case, which the California Supreme Court, as it was obliged to do at this stage of litigation, assumed to be true.[20]

LaNita and Stephen Wilson, coincidentally sharing the same last name but related only by romantic entanglement, sought counseling from Bonnie Hedlund, a psychological assistant working under the professional supervision of a licensed psychologist, Peter Ebersole. Some time thereafter, on April 9, 1979, Stephen assaulted LaNita with a shotgun. LaNita, who was cornered in her car with her 4-year-old son, Darryl, threw her body over the boy, successfully shielding him from physical injury but sustaining wounds that eventually led to the amputation of her leg. Stephen ran from the scene, turned the gun on himself, and committed suicide.

On November 12, 1980, more than a year and a half after the carnage and more than 6 months after the statute of limitations had expired for filing suits alleging simple negligence, LaNita and Darryl sued Hedlund and Ebersole, claiming that the two therapists had been *professionally* negligent and that therefore the usual 3-year statute of limitations for medical malpractice

---

[19] *Id.* at 397.

[20] The *Hedlund* court was asked to decide only whether the complaint as formulated legally warranted a trial. When asked to judge in such a preliminary matter "it normally is improper for a court to look beyond the pleading itself to determine whether or not a challenge should be upheld. It is not the obligation of the court to determine whether the allegations are true, but only whether, if true, they state a sufficient claim or defense." J. Friedenthal and A. Miller, *Sum and Substance of Civil Procedure,* 2d ed. (CES, 1979) at 121.

suits should apply. The would-be killer had told the therapists that he intended to do serious bodily harm to LaNita, the suit alleged, and they should have known, "in the exercise of the professional skill, knowledge, and care possessed by members of their speciality,"[21] that Stephen presented a serious danger of violence to LaNita. Therefore, the pleading continued, the therapists had failed in their professional duty to warn LaNita of the danger. Darryl, in his turn, alleged that the therapists' duty extended to him for the following reason: It was foreseeable that, if the threat was carried out, a little boy was likely to be in the vicinity of his mother and might be injured. Darryl was not claiming that he should have been warned but only that the therapists, because they did not warn his mother, should have their liability extended to him. Darryl, though physically unscathed, made the plausible claim that he had suffered emotional distress during the assault and its aftermath.

The court gave LaNita and Darryl all that they asked for, and more than was needed to bring the suit to trial. In *Hedlund* (as in *Tarasoff*), the soon-to-be-violent patient allegedly told his therapist that he intended to inflict serious bodily injury upon his victim. As Justice Mosk pointed out in his dissent in *Hedlund* (as he had similarly done in *Tarasoff*), because it can be argued that the defendants had "actual knowledge" of their patient's intent to do harm, there was no need for the majority of the court to "muse . . . about the result that would follow if defendants merely *should have known* of the threatened violence."[22] But muse they did: The majority chose to go beyond the facts of the case presented to them and dwell instead on what the clinicians knew or should have known.[23] In *Hedlund* they stated explicitly that a "negligent failure to diagnose dangerousness in a Tarasoff action is as much a basis for liability as a negligent failure to warn."[24] Thus the court made explicit what alarmists thought they saw in *Tarasoff* from the beginning.

Until now, when referring to *Tarasoff* as a modern malpractice case, one had to be careful to specify that the classification was only figurative. Technically, the plaintiffs in *Tarasoff* had not alleged professional malpractice. The "duty of due care" imposed by the court was an extension of the common-law duty to protect from harm those toward whom a party had a "special relationship." *Tarasoff* broke new ground by declaring the relationship between a psychotherapist and the readily identifiable potential victim of his or her patient to be something special enough to warrant a duty. But

---

[21] 34 Cal 3d 695 (1983) at 700.

[22] *Id.* at 710.

[23] *Id.* at 707, 708: "In its text, the opinion employs such terms as failure to 'predict' behavior, and flatly declares that a negligent act occurs 'when the therapist has or should have diagnosed dangerousness,' as if that subjective characteristic would be revealed through a stethoscope or by an X-ray." J. Mosk, *Dissenting Opinion.*

[24] *Id.* at 703.

Hedlund went further, declaring the warning aspect of the psychotherapist's duty to be part and parcel of the diagnostic aspect. Misdiagnosis is a type of malpractice, and failure to warn, assumed to be based upon misdiagnosis, becomes malpractice too. A person who alleges that he or she was injured because of a psychotherapist's failure to give a warning therefore is entitled to have 3 years (the statute of limitations governing malpractice), rather than 1 year (the statute of limitations governing simple negligence), in which to file a lawsuit against the offending therapist.

The facts of *Hedlund*, including as they did a talkative patient making explicit threats of violence toward the eventual victim, resembled the facts of *Tarasoff*. The facts of *Jablonski* seem to stand apart: There, the patient was close-mouthed, imposing on his therapists a task of inference; the patient's threats of violence toward the eventual victim were implied by his history of assaulting women and from his "psychological profile." But the holding of *Hedlund*, with its inextricably interwoven duty to diagnose danger and duty to warn, lines up a jump ahead of the holding of *Tarasoff* and stands shoulder to shoulder with the holding of *Jablonski*. Both recent decisions can be interpreted as demanding of psychotherapists that they apply the standards of their profession to recognize explicit, and implicit, stigmata of dangerousness in their patients and that they intervene to protect readily identifiable and notifiable victims. Alan Stone's lament about *Tarasoff* rings louder than ever: "One can only wonder what it means to apply standards to skills that do not exist."[25] The *Hedlund* and *Jablonski* courts are willing to allow this rhetorical query to become a question for the jury.

The *Hedlund* court also ruled that LaNita's 4-year-old son, Darryl, had a separate cause of action against the psychotherapists and could sue them in his own right, because it had been foreseeable that he would be emotionally traumatized by the (predictable) attack on his mother. This section of the holding weds two lines of cases, those descending from *Tarasoff* and those descending from another landmark California Supreme Court decision, *Dillon v. Legg*.[26] In *Dillon*, a mother alleged that she was present when a defendant, driving negligently, ran over and killed her young child, and as a result, she suffered emotional trauma and physical injury.[27] The court responded by formulating three questions, the answers to which were to be used as guidelines in determining whether emotional trauma was foreseeable and whether plaintiffs could recover for the breaching of a duty of due care

---

[25] A. Stone, "The *Tarasoff* Decisions: Suing Psychotherapists to Safeguard Society," *Harvard Law Review*, 90, 358–378, 1976, at 371.

[26] *Dillon v. Legg*, 68 Cal. 2d 728 (1968).

[27] In 1968, it was necessary to allege co-requisite physical injury in order to recover for emotional trauma. A subsequent California Supreme Court decision, *Molien v. Kaiser Foundation Hospitals*, 27 Cal. 3d 916 (1980) changed the rule. It allowed suits in which only emotional and psychological trauma were alleged, opening the way for cases like Darryl's.

owed to them. The questions were (1) was the plaintiff nearby at the time of the accident; (2) did the plaintiff experience the effects of the accident first-hand; (3) were the plaintiff and victim closely related?

The *Dillon* court concluded that because the answer to all three questions was "yes," the mother's emotional trauma had been foreseeable; the driver had breached the duty he owed to her and could be sued. "Surely," said the court, "the negligent driver who causes the death of a young child may reasonably expect that the mother will not be far distant and will, upon witnessing the accident, suffer emotional trauma."[28]

LaNita Wilson's son, Darryl, was, of course, on the scene when his mother was injured, seeming to satisfy all three of the *Dillon* criteria. We may ignore the fact, as the court did, that the mother was not the victim of a negligent driver but of an intentional assailant and that the alleged negligence of the psychotherapists—their failures to diagnose dangerousness and to warn—occurred a great distance from Darryl, far, to use the language of *Dillon,* from his "sensory and contemporaneous observance."[29] Plugging the *Hedlund* facts into the *Dillon* formula, the court *could* have said, "Surely, negligent psychotherapists who fail to diagnose their patients' dangerousness and fail to warn their patients' intended victims may reasonably expect that if the victim is the mother of a young child, the child will not be far distant from the scene of victimization and will, upon witnessing the scene, suffer emotional trauma." What the court did say was, "The possibility of injury to Darryl if Stephen carried out his threat to harm LaNita was no less foreseeable than the harm to the mother in *Dillon v. Legg.* We conclude, therefore, that in alleging his age and relationship to LaNita, and defendant's negligent failure to diagnose and/or warn LaNita of the danger posed by Stephen, Darryl has stated a cause of action."[30]

Coping with the Duty to Warn

Jablonski and *Hedlund* broaden the frontiers of liability and increase the likelihood of suit. But they have the practical effect of reducing conflicts imposed by *Tarasoff,* thereby easing decision-making for the honest and perceptive psychotherapist who is earnestly trying to reconcile the interests of his or her patient and the public. Despite their wrongheadedness (or perhaps because of it), both decisions make it easier for psychotherapists to know what to do when they are confronted by patients whom they think are dangerous.

The court's official holding in *Tarasoff* was not self-evident. Although popularly known as the "duty to warn" case, the duty eventually imposed

---

[28] *Id.* at 741.
[29] *Id.* at 740.
[30] *Id.* at 707.

was broader: "To take whatever . . . steps are reasonably necessary under the circumstances . . . to protect the intended victim against . . . danger."[31] Warning the intended victim is only one means toward this end, but one that the court implied would have been appropriate behavior in that particular case. The court went on to inject more ambiguity and conflict by reminding psychotherapists of their countervailing duty *not* to warn: "We realize that the open and confidential character of the psychotherapeutic dialogue encourages patients to express threats of violence, few of which are ever executed. *Certainly, a therapist should not be encouraged to reveal such threats:* such disclosures could seriously disrupt the patient's relationship with his therapist and with the persons threatened. *To the contrary,* the therapist's obligations to his patient require that he *not* disclose a confidence *unless such disclosure is necessary to avert danger to others,* and even then that he do so discretely, and in a fashion that would preserve the privacy of his patient to the fullest extent compatible with the prevention of the threatened danger."[32] *Tarasoff* can therefore be said to impose a duty *not* to warn except in unusual circumstances, and then the warning should not be a shout but rather a discrete whisper in the ear of the targeted victim.

The court's reasoning was consistent with this interpretation in the subsequently decided *Thompson v. Alameda County.*[33] There, a teenage boy, an inveterate molester of small children, had confessed to the officer who had last arrested him his intention to kill his next victim. Despite the presence of this threat in the probation record, the molester was released from juvenile hall on a pass. He promptly molested and murdered one of his neighbor's children. The bereaved parents of the victim sued the county probation department for not warning them of the danger posed to their son. They claimed that had they known that the neighborhood menace was again at large, they would have taken precautions to protect their little boy. The court did not contest the parents' scenario but held that the probation department had no duty to warn about those who had made "non-specific threats of harm directed at non-specific victims."[34]

In this case, there was no readily identifiable victim to inform discretely, but rather a large amorphous public group—neighbors—to whom it would have been impracticable to broadcast warnings wholesale.

If the *language* of *Tarasoff* was full of double messages, taking away with one clause what it gave with the other, the *lesson* of *Tarasoff* was relatively straightforward: "Behave the way this therapist behaved and you will be punished." The therapist had been clinically perceptive and socially responsible in his handling of the case. He had sought second opinions from

---

[31] 17 Cal. 3d 425 (1976) at 431.
[32] *Id.* at 441; emphasis added.
[33] 27 Cal. 3d 741 (1980).
[34] *Id.* at 754.

more experienced colleagues and supervisors before taking prudent action. He had scrupulously documented all his moves. But, to use the language of behavior modification, the court did not positively reinforce this behavior. Instead, they shocked the therapist and his colleagues by saying that he could be held liable for the injuries inflicted by his patient.

"Behave the way this psychotherapist behaved and you will be punished." To escape punishment, you have to do something *more* than the defendants did in *Tarasoff;* for instance, you could warn, suggested the court.[35] To escape punishment, you could also do something *less* than the defendants did in *Tarasoff,* although the court did not address itself to this troublesome issue.[36] For example, a psychotherapist could avoid this category of problem entirely by refusing to treat patients with a high potential for violence. Because they commit violent crimes more than a hundred times more frequently than middle-aged white housewives, young, black, single males could invariably be rejected as patients by established therapists and referred to a hungrier colleague or to a public clinic. Once a patient had been taken on, however, the situation would call for more subtle evasion. If appearing to discern dangerousness in a patient places psychotherapists in jeopardy, they could play it safe by appearing to see no evil. If they were naturally imperceptive, they could be honest, of course (blessed are the obtuse for they are immune), but if they were cursed with insight, they could pretend. They could either make the ominous appear innocuous by not recording it or, if their consciences permitted sins of commission, they could record falsely. Of course, such therapists would not give themselves away by warning anyone.[37]

No one is saying that *Tarasoff* ensures evasion and dishonesty. It merely rewards them and discourages their opposites. *Jablonski* and *Hedlund,* if they stand as law, will be much more even-handed. Every psy-

---

[35] It is a little-known fact that the killer in the *Tarasoff* case claimed during his trial for murder that he had warned the victim himself. So too the victim in *Jablonski* had been warned, if not by the killer, by two doctors, her clergyman, her lawyer, and a psychological hotline. And, if my unofficial sources are correct, the adult victim in *Hedlund,* although she alleges the opposite in her pleading, had also been warned. A sample of three cases is a poor basis for generalization, but it is sufficient to stimulate one's sense of irony.

[36] The dissenters, however, did note the chilling effect that the decision could have on the relationship between therapist and patient. (*Id.* at 460.)

[37] An empirical study published two years after *Tarasoff* became law indicated that a significant number of the psychotherapist respondents admitted to modifying their recordkeeping in order to reduce their vulnerability to suit. And almost one-fifth reported "feeling tempted to avoid probing into sensitive areas of therapy, including matters of dangerousness." (Note: "Where the Public Peril Begins: A Survey of Psychotherapists to Determine the Effects of *Tarasoff,*" *Stanford Law Review, 31,* 165–190, 1978, at 182). Candor about deviousness is uncommon, so the study probably underestimated the defensive maneuvering triggered by *Tarasoff.*

chotherapist unfortunate enough to have a patient who does damage will now be vulnerable. Those who warn and those who do not both warn inadequately if the warnings are not strong enough to prevent damage. Ignorance is no excuse when it is a professional's obligation to be knowledgeable. And knowledge is no protection for the therapist unless it also protects the victim. Practically, warnings ignored by an eventual victim might well be deemed inadequate when viewed with the wisdom of hindsight.

Because *Jablonski* and *Hedlund* eliminate the advantages of appearing ignorant, the path lies open for displaying foresight again. Two general courses of action immediately suggest themselves, as follows.

ONE POSSIBLE COURSE OF ACTION

Therapists can become society's whistle-blowers, although once the word gets out, they will have little to blow about. When they do blow, they will have to blow loudly and record their performance because if someone gets hurt anyway, they will want to counter allegations that they did not warn *adequately*. To form an effective shield against third-party liability, therapists may have to adopt a strategy similar to that implied by the language of California's new child abuse reporting law, by which it is mandatory for therapists to report any "reasonable suspicion" that child abuse has occurred.[38] It would now become advisable for a therapist to warn discretely any identifiable victims who could be informed of any "reasonable suspicion" that a patient had targeted them for violence. Cassandras, prophets of doom, purveyors of bad news, informers, squealers, and finks play a useful role in society, but they are not rewarded with esteem or popularity. And they may get sued anyway, if the warnings of the future turn out to be the ineffectual protection they were to victims of the past.

Ethically, therapists should advertise their new status and issue a Miranda-type warning to new patients that the therapist is an agent of society first, the patient second, and that any conflict will be resolved in favor of the former. But, practically speaking, such warnings would become superfluous. The word would get out, and violent patients would soon learn to keep their own counsel.

Of course, if therapists try to play it safe and warn defensively whenever danger is in the air, they will, human limitations being what they are, ring a lot of false alarms. And without statutory protection of the sort that the California Legislature included in its child-abuse reporting law,[39] overeager whistle-blowers risk being sued by their patients for breaching confi-

---

[38] California Penal Code, § 11166.
[39] California Penal Code, § 1172.

dences and for defamation. Conceivably, they also risk being sued for negligently inflicting emotional distress upon the person whom they warn.[40]

ANOTHER POSSIBLE COURSE

Therapists can continue to be society's safety valve, encouraging patients to think the unthinkable out loud and not let secrets ferment to something stronger. Therapists can keep their mouths shut when they believe that their patient is just letting off steam, no matter how violent his or her imagery, but if they become persuaded that the patient represents a danger to either a specified victim or to the public at large, they could then do something more effective than shouting that the intended victim had better watch out.

Calling the police, for example, despite the unfortunate events that come to mind from the facts of *Tarasoff,* is likely to be a more effective preventive stratagem than warning the victim. Had the psychotherapist of Tarasoff's killer been able to follow through on his original plan to press for the involuntary hospitalization of his patient, the name of his patient's victim might never have been linked to the phrase "duty to warn." Warning, it seems, should be the last resort of those powerless to intervene in any other way. It should never be a hair-trigger response to the first whiff of danger. It will always be a poor substitute for the power to restrict a threatening mental patient's freedom to act.

SUMMARY

What, then, should a psychotherapist do when treating a potentially violent patient, if doing what is sensible, reasonable, ethical, and moral may or may not prove to be an adequate defense in court? There is no pragmatic advantage, even in the short run, to practicing a craven analogue of defensive medicine, i.e., unless the therapist can avoid dangerous patients altogether, the strategy is unlikely to work. Whatever therapists do, a small and unlucky minority will find a hand reaching for their pocketbooks when a patient or former patient does damage.

---

[40] In California, psychotherapists in community mental health clinics, who practice under the auspices of the Lanterman-Petris-Short Act (LPS), would appear to be especially vulnerable. They risk suits for treble damages if they "willingly and knowingly" release confidential information to unauthorized parties, including potential victims, unless those in jeopardy are "federal and state constitutional officers and their families" (*California Welfare and Institutions Code,* § 5330).

The best course of action, in this less than best of all possible worlds, would seem to be to follow the dictates of your conscience and your principles, support your colleagues if misfortune catches them short, lobby for sensible corrective legislation, and wait until the voices of reason outlast the voices of panic. Such professional behavior will not confer immunity from liability, but it will foster the pride of the therapist, the prestige of his or her profession, the health of the patient, and the safety of the public. Meanwhile, though behaving admirably, be sure to pay your insurance premiums on time.

TARASOFF, JABLONSKI, AND *HEDLUND* AS HARD CASES

Law is one of the few games in which the decisions of umpires and referees generate more commentary than the actions of the players. When Holmes wrote his dictum that hard cases make bad law,[41] he was not referring to the trial courts, where a hard case for one side can mean an easy win for the other, but to the appellate courts; there, a justice's strongly held preconvictions about the larger issues of politics, policy, and morals can combine to overpower wisdom and logic.

The cases that have been examined in this chapter make bad law. They are administrative directives that have made a bad situation worse. They aim for the prudential "better safe than sorry," but they achieve the perverse "tell the truth, or pay the consequences." The courts may rationalize that therapists will protect society from danger as they try to protect themselves from liability. But responsibility has been delegated where there is little power—little power to discern imminent homicidal behavior and, hence, little power to intervene until after damage has been done.

The courts in *Tarasoff, Jablonski,* and *Hedlund* did not find a reliable agent for protecting society and preventing damage. Instead, they chose someone who can be blamed for the damage after the fact, a "fall guy" who can be made to foot part of the bill. Psychotherapists have reachable assets, something most murderers do not, and, most especially, psychotherapists are covered by insurance.

Perhaps the most important effects of expansive duty to warn decisions are those contrary to the courts' stated intention of protecting potential victims. The decisions tend to encourage patients with violent inclinations to avoid seeking help and to avoid confiding in a psychotherapist, and they encourage psychotherapists to make prudence the better part of valor by

---

[41] "Great cases like hard cases make bad law." *Northern Securities Co. v. United States,* 193 U.S. 197, 400.

avoiding this type of case.[42] Mutual avoidance of this sort increases rather than lessens public peril, even if psychotherapy is no more effective as an antidote to violent inclination than the tactic of counting to ten before acting. To the extent that avoidance is not always possible, the duty to warn decisions encourage unnecessarily breached confidences, abortive attempts at treatment, defensive record-keeping and, if their promise of increased liability is ever realized, higher insurance rates.

What "felt necessities of the time" made *Tarasoff, Jablonski,* and *Hedlund* hard cases? What "prevalent moral and political theories" pressed judges to burden psychotherapists with responsibility for the destructive actions of patients? What "intuitions of public policy, avowed or unconscious" or "prejudices which judges share with their fellow men" led the courts to ignore evidence that would seem to make the inability to predict dangerousness a fact beyond controversy?[43]

The following factors are worth considering:

(1) *Feelings of sympathy for the victims:* Although frequently mentioned by clinicians when they try to make sense of these decisions, the emotional pressure to compensate victims or their heirs for their terrible losses is less important than common sense would seem to indicate. Courts come to accept that there are some wrongs for which there is no legal remedy. The losses to the parties were indeed terrible in these duty to warn cases, but one must recall that disaster and catastrophe are commonplace events in the world of legal complaint. In context, the appeal to emotion is not extraordinary. The sentimental desire to right a wrong, therefore, could not *in itself* have generated sufficient momentum to create new law.

(2) *Feelings of punitiveness toward individual defendants:* Clinicians sometimes express the view that the courts in these decisions might have been punishing the defendants for some especially outrageous or odious conduct, unmentioned in the official version of the case but nevertheless determinative of the case's outcome. Some "thing" is postulated, hidden in the swamp of underlying facts, which may have exerted an invisible pull on the justices and on justice.

Sometimes this kind of view grows from general conviction about the nature of the moral universe: if someone is getting punished, there must be a

---

[42] Several of the respondent therapists in the Stanford study volunteered the information that *Tarasoff* had caused them to discontinue treating potentially dangerous patients. Because the investigator had not thought to include this question in her questionnaire, she did not have a measure of the frequency with which psychotherapists would admit to this defensive and presumably detrimental practice. *Supra* note 37, at 188.

[43] The quotes are from Holmes again, the sentence following his most famous aphorism, "The life of the law has not been logic: it has been experience; the felt necessities of the time, the prevalent moral and political theories, intuitions of public policy, avowed or unconscious, even the prejudices which judges share with their fellow-men, have had a good deal more to do than the syllogism in determining the rules by which men should be governed." (Reprinted in *The Life of the Law,* John Honnold, Ed. [New York: Free Press, 1963], p. 3.)

good reason; since no good reason is apparent, it must be hidden. But usually the view grows from specific knowledge about the facts of a particular case: In *Tarasoff*, for instance, the killer's psychotherapist seems to have behaved with exemplary rectitude, but the psychotherapist's clinic chief does appear to have behaved outrageously: He subverted his subordinate's treatment plan by refusing to allow him to continue his efforts to have the patient hospitalized; he contacted the campus police and arranged to destroy the request for assistance that had been written by the psychotherapist; he ordered the psychotherapist to falsify clinic records by expunging all reference to the divulgence of confidential information and to the threats that prompted its divulgence.[44] "As in the Watergate case, the attempts to conceal may have greater consequences than the original error," commented a justice of a lower appellate court who heard the case.[45] Someone clearly deserved to be punished, and punishment there was, although the official reason for the punishment (the holding "failure to warn or otherwise intervene,") may have been less the real reason than was the outrageous behavior—countermanding a valid treatment plan and falsifying official records.

According to this view, the court would be likened to federal prosecutors trying Al Capone for failure to pay his income tax. But to the best of my knowledge, such things are just not done at the appellate court level, at least not in so crass a manner. The justices are not supposed to have access to facts other than those that are included in the transcript of the trial, those that are placed before them by the parties to the appeal or by friends of the court, and those that are common knowledge and of which they can take "judicial notice."[46] If they have special knowledge of the facts of a case above and beyond what is presented to them, they should withdraw from the deliberations. Appellate court judges are higher level jurists who have a tradition to uphold: They are supposed to focus on the larger issues of the law and not be swayed by extraneous facts, no matter how egregious those facts may appear to be. Even the justice quoted earlier, who invoked Watergate and who was extremely sympathetic to the cause of the surviving Tarasoffs, went on to write, "Although the defendant's attempts to destroy the records cannot be condoned, plaintiff's claims . . . bear no relation to [the clinic chief's] alleged attempts to conceal the nature of that prescribed treatment or his motives in so doing."[47]

---

[44] See "Brief for Respondent Moore" at 168, *Tarasoff v. Regents of Univ. of Cal.*, 529 P.2d 553, 118 Cal. Rptr. 129 (1974).

[45] See *Tarasoff v. Regents of Univ. of Cal.*, 33 Cal. App. 3d 275 (1973), reprinted in A. Brooks, *Law, Psychiatry and the Mental Health System* (Boston: Little, Brown, 1974) at 1115.

[46] "*Facts Judicially Noticed*. On a challenge to the pleading the court will consider unpleaded matters so universally known that they cannot be refuted, including scientific principles, historical events, and matters of local public record." (J. Friedenthal and A. Miller, *Sum and Substance of Civil Procedure*, 2d ed. [CES, 1979], at 121.)

[47] *Id.* at 1115.

The worst swamp of facts that I know of in a duty to warn type of case, facts crying out for some way to remedy a wrong, are those underlying *Thompson,*[48] the case of the child molester given a pass from juvenile hall despite his stated intention to kill his next victim. The parents of the molester's eventual prey sued the probation department for releasing the potential killer without warning his neighbors. The molester had been given a pass on the advice of his psychotherapist, chief of a clinic set up to advise the probation department about psychologically disturbed probationers. But, as later came to light, the pathology of the patient was mirrored in the pathology of the psychotherapist: His patient, the molester, was one of the psychotherapist's homosexual lovers. This psychotherapist had recommended a pass, the better to effect a romantic tryst with his juvenile patient.[49] The psychotherapist had been blinded by love (or lust) to his patient's destructive potential, but his egregious behavior, for which he eventually lost his license to practice,[50] and his appallingly bad judgment had no effect on the court's holding in the case. *Thompson* was decided by the same court that had decided *Tarasoff,* but it was decided the other way around: it distinguished a nonspecific death threat to nonspecific neighborhood children from the specific threat to shoot the specific Tarasoff, and it held, therefore, that there was no duty to warn.[51] The court was not officially aware of the corrupt relationship between the child molester/killer and the child molester/ psychotherapist when it first considered the case, but when it *was* made aware of these extraordinary facts and was asked by the plaintiff to reconsider its holding, it refused to do so. The factual atrocities did not alter the legal principles.

(3) *Feelings of hostility toward psychotherapists:* Although some therapists have become convinced that the courts are trying to persecute them as a profession, and with that conviction have become angry, whimsical, or fatalistic depending upon how they tend to respond to unwonted abuse, some others, prone to feelings of unworthiness and guilt, see their current predicament as a natural extension of undeserved success—not success in predicting, but success in self-advertisement. As one commentator on an earlier draft of this chapter wrote, "The mental health professions have sold themselves so well to the public that the public expects a great deal from the mental health professions . . . especially . . . that the mental health professions will be responsible for either curing or preventing individuals with aberrant behavior from inflicting harm on other people."[52] Having made their bed, so to speak, psychotherapists are now being forced to lie in it.

---

[48] *Thompson v. Alameda County,* 27 Cal 3d 741 (1980).

[49] See W. Carlsen, "A Weird Sexual Twist in Suit on Boy's Slaying," *San Francisco Chronicle,* August 31, 1980, p. 3.

[50] Case D-212, Board of Medical Quality Assurance, Psychology Examining Committee, February 1, 1980.

[51] *Supra* note 49, at 754.

[52] Anonymous comment from reviewer.

There is undoubtedly truth in the foregoing commentary. It should be noted, however, that the duty to warn decisions coincide with a period of diminishing prestige and credibility for psychotherapists. In the 1950s and pre-Vietnam 1960s, when psychotherapists' stock was at its highest and even more was expected of the profession, no court imposed "responsibility for curing or preventing"[53]—or for warning. Courts are conservative institutions and may be a generation behind the times, but if the courts have "bought" the mental health "package" and are inordinately respectful of psychotherapists' abilities, they have a peculiar way of showing it. In the civil arena, they honor those abilities only retroactively and in the breach: that is, a psychotherapist who demonstrates an absence of ability by failing to divine his or her patient's violent future acts is considered blameworthy for being negligent, but a psychotherapist who claims to discern potentially violent inclinations in a patient and tries to impose restrictions on the patient's freedom to actualize those inclinations may find that the court views his or her claim with suspicion.

A striking example of a court's acknowledgment of this dual attitude lies in a recent District of Columbia Superior Court decision. Stating that "the ability to predict future dangerousness is not one generally accepted by the psychiatric profession"[54] and citing Monahan, Shah, Diamond, and Ennis and Litwak,[55] the court held that expert testimony predicting future dangerous behavior is *inadmissible* in a civil commitment hearing "because the state of scientific knowledge does not permit the assertion of a reasonable psychiatric opinion on the issue of whether a person is likely to injure himself or others."[56]

The court then went on to face the challenge of *Tarasoff*. Based as it was upon an assumption that psychotherapists can predict dangerousness reliably, *Tarasoff* would seem to be inconsistent with a decision to exclude such predictions from commitment hearings. Ingeniously, the court found in *Tarasoff* that a patient's interest in confidentiality (the interest that would be violated if the psychotherapist exercised a duty to warn) does not reach the same constitutional proportions as the interest in freedom raised by civil commitment hearings—the interest that would be violated if a psychothera-

---

[53] See, for example, R. Slovenko, *Psychiatry and Law* (Boston: Little, Brown, 1973) at 407: "As a general principle of law, a physician is not a guarantor of a cure; he does not warrant a good result; he is not an insurer against mishaps or unusual consequences; and he is not liable for honest mistakes of judgment. . . . In effect, the law says that a patient assumes the risk when he submits himself to medical or psychiatric care."

[54] *In re William Wilson*, M.H. 1124-82, D.C. Super. Ct., April 14, 1983.

[55] A. Monahan, *The Clinical Prediction of Violent Behavior*, DHHS Publication No. (ADM) 81-921, 1981; S. Shah, "Legal and Mental Health System Interactions," *International Journal of Law and Psychiatry*, 4, 219, 1981; B. Diamond, "The Psychiatric Prediction of Dangerousness," *University of Pennsylvania Law Review*, 123, 439, 1974; B. Ennis and T. Litwack, "Psychiatry and the Presumption of Expertise: Flipping Coins in the Courtroom," *California Law Review*, 62, 693, 1974.

[56] *Id.*

pist testified in a commitment hearing.[57] In other words, the confidence a psychotherapist can have in a prediction of violence may be high enough to trigger a duty to warn, but it may not be high enough to warrant the admissibility of the prediction as evidence in court. Apparently the court is comfortable in imposing an obligation on a psychotherapist to share his or her confidential revelations and conclusions with anybody "reasonably situated" to protect an intended victim (such as the police or the victim himself), while prohibiting the psychotherapist from sharing comparable information with the committing court. In the District of Columbia, presumably, psychotherapists may conspire to have their patients arrested, but they may not use a court to railroad their patients to a mental hospital. The courts, it would seem, have not bought the mental health package, but have devised one of their own.

(4) *Feelings that the civil rights of mental patients should be protected:* All of the more expansive duty to warn decisions have been made by courts that are liberal on the issue of a mental patient's right to refuse treatment. It is now more difficult than at any time in living memory to confine an unequivocally mentally ill person to a mental hospital against that person's will. This difficulty was exemplified by the facts of the *Tarasoff* case itself, which demonstrated, among other things, the powerlessness of the therapist in question to hospitalize his dangerously mentally ill patient. Sanctioning the decline of quarantine as a means of social control, but dissatisfied with a void, the duty to warn courts have turned to historical precedent for an alternative model of dealing with carriers of a dangerous"disease." The leper colony-like mental hospitals of the past have been abandoned in favor of local outpatient treatment programs, augmented by timely recourse to a warning bell. The courts, however, have hung the bell around the doctor's neck rather than the patient's, since lunatics, unlike lepers, cannot be expected to sound their own alarms.

As Stone has pointed out,[58] the tragedy of Tatiana Tarasoff is part of the price society pays for the protection of the mental patient's right to be different and to be unfettered by involuntary hospitalization. Neither society nor the court, rhetoric notwithstanding, is willing to pay this price—certainly not in an era of ascendant crime rates and feelings of public vulnerability akin to panic. Hence the desperate search for alternatives, including the proposal to use symbolic "patches" like the duty to warn, when it is clear that we lack reliable technology to spot potential leaks.

(5) *Feelings that those who profit should indemnify:* In the field of product liability law, there is a trend toward making the manufacturer the insurer of a defective product, whatever the defect and whether or not the manufacturer knew (or could have known) about the presence of the defect.

---

[57] *Id.*
[58] *Supra* note 25, at 378.

As a matter of public policy, courts have decided that no one is better situated to idemnify a lucklessly injured consumer than the manufacturer of the defective product that caused the injury. Moral fault on the part of the manufacturer is not necessarily implied, as it always is when there are allegations of negligence; all that need be proven is a substantial link between using the defective product in a foreseeable manner and suffering the injury. The courts are saying that losses should be borne not merely by the victim, but also by the manufacturer who, even if without fault, nevertheless has profited from the transaction that resulted in injury. The loss must also be borne by the victim's uninjured fellow consumers, who have to share the cost of compensating the unlucky few by paying higher prices for the product. Thus shared, the losses become more tolerable for all. Textbooks on the law of torts, the law of injuries and remedies, label this development the "theory of strict liability."

Duty to warn is a relatively new phrase in the law of psychiatric malpractice, but it has venerable status in the law of product liability.[59] It is an established principle of law that manufacturers are liable, under a theory of negligence, if they knew (or should have known) of concealed dangers lurking in their products but failed to warn users of those hidden risks.[60] When strict liability supplanted negligence as the dominant theory under which most product liability cases were tried, duty to warn survived as an excuse for legal complaint, but it took a less common-sensical form. For instance, the New Jersey Supreme Court (a court that vies with California as a pacesetter in product liability law) recently ruled that Johns Manville Corporation can be held liable for marketing asbestos in 1930 and failing to warn, *at that time*, against dangers that arguably were then scientifically unknown.[61] From there it does not take a great imaginative leap to believe that therapists are liable for allowing their patients to roam free and for failing to warn against dangers which may be knowable only in retrospect.

That is a leap that the courts, in the expansive duty to warn cases, are approaching tentatively but that lawyers, with more to gain from expanding the frontiers of liability, are taking on the run. In *Moscowitz v. M.I.T.*,[62] a recent *Tarasoff*-type case, a Manhattan jury awarded $10.3 million to a woman whose former boyfriend doused her with sulfuric acid. The Massachusetts Institute of Technology was held liable, on the grounds that the school's psychiatric facility failed to help the man and failed to warn the victim about the man's threats toward her. The victorious lawyer, capsulizing his argument in a statement to the press, said, "Why shouldn't [therapists] have to warn? They're putting a lunatic into the stream of commerce.

[59] See, for example, *Rosenbusch v. Ambrosia Milk Corp.*, 181 App. Div. 97, 168 N.Y.S. 505 (1917).
[60] See W. Prosser, *Law of Torts*, 4th ed. (St. Paul: West, 1971), at 646, 647.
[61] *Beshada v. Johns Manville Products Corp.*, 90 N.J. 191 (1982).
[62] *Moscowitz v. M.I.T.*, 14/86/79.

Everyone should be responsible for their product. [The patient] is their product.''[63]

Although a New York jury presumably bought this argument, no appellate court has been willing to go so far. The federal district court in Colorado, for instance, where John Hinckley's psychiatrist found himself sued by his patient's nonpresidential victims, considered the possibility of adopting a strict liability standard for psychotherapists, but rejected it. Citing ''cogent policy reasons for limiting the scope of the therapist's liability,'' the court held that making therapists ''ultimately responsible for the actions of their patients'' would be like imposing a ''strict liability standard of care [in which] therapists would be potentially liable for all harm inflicted by persons presently or formerly under psychiatric treatment. Human behavior is simply too unpredictable, and the field of psychotherapy presently too inexact, to so greatly expand the scope of therapists' liability.''[64] Such an imposition, writes a commentator, ''would effectively preclude therapists from treating any patient who might turn out to be violent, unless they and their insurance companies were willing to accept the risk, which is unlikely.''[65]

Courts that have not addressed the issue of strict liability directly are, however, imposing a near equivalent under a different name. When the *Jablonski* court holds that a psychotherapist must not merely warn but must warn ''adequately,'' the impression is compelling that, practically speaking, an adequate warning is one that succeeds in averting injury and an inadequate warning is one that fails. No injured party ever received adequate warning, or so it is likely to appear to a jury armed with the wisdom of hindsight.[66]

When the *Hedlund* court holds that a psychotherapist's duty to diagnose danger is inextricably interwoven with his or her duty to act to avert it, the impression is equally compelling that, practically speaking, any injury caused by a patient to a ''predictable'' victim—lover or spouse, to take the most plausible instance—will be deemed a danger that should have been diagnosed, warned about, and averted. Or so it is likely to appear to that same jury armed with the same wisdom.

POSTSCRIPT

Five factors contributing to the development of the duty to warn were examined in the preceding section: (1) sympathy for particularly unfortunate victims; (2) punitiveness toward particularly errant defendants; (3) hostility

---

[63] D. Berreby, ''Forcing the Therapists to Pay,'' *National Law Journal, 5,* 19 (Jan. 1983).

[64] *Brady v. Hopper* (83-JM-451, D. Colo.), September 14, 1983.

[65] *Mental Disability Law Reporter, 7,* 6 (1983) at 449.

[66] See, for example, Fischhoff, ''Hindsight ≠ Foresight: The Effect of Outcome Knowledge on Judgment under Uncertainty,'' *Journal of Experimental Psychology: Human Perception and Performance, 1,* 228 (1975).

toward an oversold profession; (4) compensation for expansion of the rights of mental patients in an era of ascendant crime; and, (5) the influence of mainstream product liability law on the eddy of psychotherapeutic malpractice cases.

Factors 4 and 5 weight more heavily to my way of thinking, than do factors 1 and 2 (factor 3 hovers somewhere in the middle), but I think no factor has been without effect. Taking a leaf from the notebooks of psychotherapists who have developed a grammar and a vocabulary for understanding and explaining weakness and failure, we might say that all the factors are significant, although weighted differently, and that the courts' behavior during the legal development of the duty to warn was, if not inevitable, *overdetermined*.

Explaining the past is a respectable occupation. It takes only a little ingenuity to make what has already happened seem inevitable or overdetermined. But predicting what is yet to come is a suspect pursuit, best left to gamblers, oracles, and boards of parole. Will psychotherapists' legal duties toward their patients continue to expand? Will the courts adopt a strict liability standard outright and impose it upon psychotherapists? Will the cost of psychotherapy have to include the price of remedies for patients' *subsequent* wrongdoings? Will the profession survive the surcharge?

Or will improvements in the laws of civil commitment lead to alternatives more attractive than the sounding of alarms? Will a receding crime rate diminish the concern with early warning and encourage the courts to establish policies likely to ease rather than increase public anxiety? Will psychotherapists lobby successfully in the legislature to pass statutes to protect their profession? Will a psychotherapist's duty to warn become an odd footnote in the history of the law of torts?

Although my hopes are implied in this chapter, I have no tools to make reliable predictions and no inclination to hazard a guess. Fortunately, in the present instance, I at least have no duty to speak when discretion urges me to be silent.

PART V I

Professional Liability

Ronald Jay Cohen

12

The Professional Liability of Behavioral Scientists: An Overview*

A record amount of malpractice litigation against physicians during the last decade has sensitized practitioners in all health-related professions to the need for an adequate understanding of the legal framework in which they function. Practitioners in the field of behavioral science, including psychologists, psychiatrists, social workers, psychiatric nurses, occupational therapists, and others have taken cognizance of a foreboding constellation of societal factors that may make them more vulnerable than ever before to the receipt of a summons and complaint alleging malpractice (Cohen, 1979; Cohen & Mariano, 1982; Stone, 1977; Green & Cox, 1978; Bernstein, 1978.) Thorough knowledge of a professional specialty is a necessary but no longer sufficient condition for the successful practice of that specialty; a knowledge of the law is essential.

NEGLIGENCE, MALPRACTICE, AND PROFESSIONAL LIABILITY

Stated generally, all adults have a legal duty to conduct themselves in a fashion that at least measures up to the way that any ordinary and reasonable person would behave under the same or similar circumstances. If a person's unintentional behavior falls short of this "ordinary and reasonable person" standard, the behavior is described as "negligent." Negligence is formally

* Reprinted, by permission of John Wiley & Sons, Inc. The Professional Liability of Behavioral Scientists: An Overview. Cohen, R.J. *Behavioral Sciences and the Law, 1* (1), pp. 9–22. Copyright © (1983, John Wiley & Sons, Inc.)

defined as "conduct which falls below the standard established by law for the protection of others against unreasonable risk of harm."[1,2] In litigation, the burden of proof is on the plaintiff; the plaintiff must prove by the preponderance of evidence that the defendant was indeed negligent.[3] The elements of proof required to prove the tort of negligence are (1) duty on the part of the defendant, (2) breach of that duty, (3) causation, and (4) damages.

Members of professions, like the citizenry in general, are also legally bound to behave in ways consistent with the proverbial "ordinary and reasonable person." Persons acting in their professional capacity, however, are additionally held to a higher standard, that of any ordinary and reasonable person in their profession acting under the same or similar circumstances. If the professional's behavior unintentionally falls below this higher standard, the term "malpractice" applies; malpractice refers to negligence in the execution of professional duties. If the professional is a lawyer, one speaks of legal malpractice; a physician, medical malpractice; a psychologist, psychological malpractice; and so forth. The elements required to prove malpractice are the same as those described above for negligence. The place of malpractice within the general schema of the law is illustrated in Figure 12-1.

An understanding of what malpractice is, is best complemented by a knowledge of what it is not. It is not malpractice if the professional fails to bring an extraordinary amount of skill, knowledge, or expertise to bear on the problem; the professional, as stated by Chief Justice Tindal in the 1832 case of *Lanphier v. Phipus,* is not charged by law to be brilliant: "Every person who enters into a learned profession undertakes to bring to it the exercise of a reasonable degree of care and skill; he does not undertake, if he is an attorney, that at all events you shall gain your case, nor does a surgeon undertake that he will perform a cure, nor does he undertake to use the highest possible skill." Jurow and Mariano (1972) have emphasized that professionals are not guarantors of good results:

> Professionals, including psychologists, physicians, attorneys, engineers, accountants and others, do not guarantee to accomplish a particular result or cure. But once he undertakes treatment of a patient, the psychologist, in the same way as the physician and surgeon, is obligated to conduct his examination and treatment in a skillful, competent, and professional manner. The psychologist holds himself out as possessing the skill and knowledge commonly possessed by members in good standing of the psychology profession, and is consequently liable for harm or injury for failure to meet current professional standards. (pp. 224–225)

---

[1] Restatement 2d, Torts § 282 (1965).

[2] Our presentation of the concept of negligence and of related terminology is necessarily brief and simplified. The interested reader is referred to Prosser (1962) for a detailed and thorough discussion of these legal concepts.

[3] This is true except for the relatively rare instance wherein a case is decided on the basis of a doctrine that the negligent act need not be proven; it is sufficient to demonstrate that, but for the negligent act, the plaintiff could not have been injured.

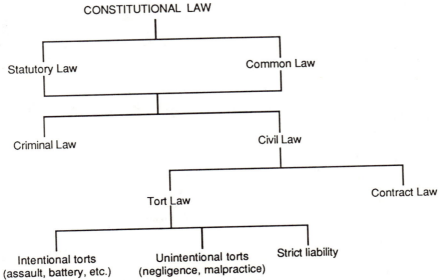

Figure 12-1. The Place of Malpractice within the Law
From *Legal Guidebook in Mental Health* by Ronald Jay Cohen and William E. Mariano, ©*1982* by The Free Press. *Reprinted by permission.*

Technically, it is not malpractice if the act or omission in question was intentional on the part of the professional. As we have noted, malpractice is to the professional what negligence is to the lay person, and both imply that the negative effect or outcome was unintentional. Still, the wide range of actions or omissions that professionals could potentially be held liable for is referred to as "malpractice" in common parlance. An illustrative listing of some intentional as well as unintentional torts appears in Table 12-1.

A psychiatrist, for example, who is instrumental in committing an involuntary patient to a mental institution and who then administers medication to the patient against the patient's will might be sued for "malpractice" on grounds such as assault, battery, false imprisonment, and malicious prosecution. For protection against such claims, insurance companies offer *professional liability* insurance—colloquially but inaccurately referred to as *malpractice* insurance—the former term being all-inclusive with respect to intentional and unintentional acts and omissions.

The Duty of the Professional

Reviewing the elements of proof for malpractice, it can be seen that it is the plaintiff's burden to prove that the defendant owed a duty of due care. This element is usually but not always a straightforward matter of establish-

Table 12-1
Some intentional and unintentional torts

Intentional	Unintentional (Negligence)
Torts to Person	Negligence based on duty of due care
Battery	Breach of duty of due care
Assault	(malpractice) including special
False imprisonment	affirmative duties to prevent harm
Torts to Property	Duty to prevent suicide
Trespass to land	Duty to prevent assault to third
Trespass to chattels	parties
Conversion of chattels	Other
Other	Negligent misrepresentation
Intentional or fraudulent	Negligent causing of emotional
misrepresentation (deceit)	distress
Intentional causing of emotional	Negligent invasion of privacy
distress	
Intentional invasion of privacy	
Malicious prosecution	
Abuse of the process of law	

From *Malpractice: A Guide for Mental Health Professionals* by Ronald Jay Cohen, ©*1979 by The Free Press. Reprinted by permission.*

ing that a professional–client or doctor–patient relationship arose. In *O'Neill v. Montefiore Hospital,*[4] for example, a question before the court was whether or not a doctor–patient relationship arose as the result of a telephone conversation. The now deceased Mr. O'Neill had presented himself with his wife (the plaintiff) at the Montefiore Hospital emergency room complaining of chest pain and asking to see a Hospital Insurance Plan (HIP) doctor. He was told by the nurse that the hospital had no connection with HIP but that she would try to get him a HIP doctor. The nurse telephoned an HIP doctor and Mr. O'Neill was overheard to say during the course of the conversation, "Well, I could be dead by 8 o'clock." What happened next appears in the court record:

> When the deceased concluded the telephone conversation, he informed the nurse that Dr. Craig had told him to go home and come back when HIP was open. Mrs. O'Neill, however, asked the nurse to have a doctor examine her husband since it was an emergency. Disregarding the request, the nurse told her that their family doctor would see Mr. O'Neill at 8 o'clock, to which he again replied, "I could be dead by 8 o'clock."

When examination or treatment at the hospital was refused, the plaintiff and the deceased left and returned home on foot, pausing occasionally to

---

[4] *O'Neill v. Montefiore Hospital,* 11 App. Div. 2d 132, 203 N.Y.S.2d 436 (1960).

permit him to catch his breath. After they arrived at their apartment, and as the plaintiff was helping her husband to disrobe, he fell to the floor and died before any medical attention could be obtained.

The appellate court in *O'Neill* held that "the jury could have concluded that Dr. Craig undertook to diagnose the ailments of the deceased and could have decided whether he abandoned the patient, inadequately or improperly advised him, or, conversely, made a proper diagnosis fully appropriate under the circumstances, or offered an examination which was rejected." The court therefore reversed the lower court's dismissal of Mrs. O'Neill's complaint and ordered a new trial. Although *O'Neill* is presented here primarily for illustrative purposes, the possibility of a comparable situation arising with respect to the duty of a mental health professional is everpresent. What, for example, is the duty of the clinician contacted by telephone by a suicidal or homicidal person wishing to undertake therapy but uncertain about what he or she will do in the next hour or so?

Another question of duty arose in *Rainer v. Grossman*[5] wherein it was alleged that the opinion of a medical school professor expressed at a professional conference made the professor liable for malpractice. The *Rainer* court did not find this to be the case:

> As a teacher of doctors, defendant used as a teaching vehicle cases presented to him by his pupils. It is conceded that his opinion became part of the total information upon which one of those pupils, Dr. Rainer, drew in giving advice to his patient.
>
> Presumably every professor or instructor in a professional school hopes, expects or foresees that his students will absorb and apply in their own careers at least some of the information he imparts. Does he thereby assume a duty of care and potential liability to those persons who may ultimately become the clients or patients of those students? We think not.

Another exceptional situation with respect to the professional's duty involves the duty not to the client but to some third party. Physicians as well as other health professionals are required by law to report to the appropriate authorities the diagnosis of certain contagious disease, cases of child abuse, and related diagnoses deemed to be in the interest of public health and safety. Additionally, physicians have a duty to warn a patient or responsible family members of the dangers to the family of a contagious disease (*Hofmann v. Blackmon*[6]). An extension of this duty to warn endangered third parties to the field of behavioral science appears in the decision by the Supreme Court of California in *Tarasoff v. Regents of the University of California*.[7] Tatiana Tarasoff died at the hands of Prosenjit Poddar.[8] Poddar

---

[5] *Rainer v. Grossman*, 31 Cal.App.3d 539, 107 Cal.Rptr. 469 (1973).

[6] *Hofmann v. Blackmon*, 241 So.2d 752 (Fla. App. 1970).

[7] *Tarasoff v. Regents of the University of California*, 131 Cal.Rptr. 14, 551 P.2d 334 (1976).

[8] *People v. Poddar*, 10 Cal.3d 750, 111 Cal.Rptr. 910, 518 P.2d 342 (1974)

had been in therapy with a psychologist employed at the University of California, Berkeley, Counseling Center, and had indicated to his therapist his intention to murder an unnamed but readily identifiable person (Tarasoff). As a result of the civil suit brought by the parents of the deceased, the Supreme Court of California ruled that psychotherapists have a duty to warn endangered third parties of their peril; in the oft-cited words of the court, "The protective privilege ends where the public peril begins."

Professionals who supervise the psychotherapeutic or psychodiagnostic work of others may themselves be "endangered third parties" with respect to legal jeopardy if substandard supervision leads to a negative result. According to the legal doctrine of *respondeat superior* ("let the master respond"), "masters" (employers, supervisors, corporate entities) can incur vicarious liability for the acts of their "servants." Cohen and Mariano (1982) elaborate:

> Psychologists, psychiatrists, and other mental health professionals who supervise the work of training psychotherapists must be responsive[9] to the needs of the supervisee and of the patient if they are to avoid liability under the doctrine of *respondeat superior*. In too many training institutions today, psychotherapy supervision is set up on a *pro forma* once-a-week or once-a-month basis. It would seem to the present authors that this standard, upon which the profession has expressed approval by its silence, is too low. If some harm or injury befalls the patient of the student psychotherapist because the supervisor improperly failed to take into account the specific and unique needs of the patient and the supervisee, then it would seem that the doctrine of *respondeat superior* would be applicable. (p. 315)

In addition to exposure to legal jeopardy for improper supervision, mental health professionals must exercise due care in their referrals to fellow practitioners lest they be liable for the malpractice of another; the referral is an act of professional judgment and as such is capable of incurring liability.[10] Professionals who serve on peer review committees are exposed to the possibility of a malpractice lawsuit when a claim is made that they failed to exercise their responsibilities with due care.[11] In his survey of malpractice claims against psychologists, Wright (1981) noted that an "area of substantial exposure to claims of malpractice is service in the governance of psychological organizations and structures, particularly as an ethics committee member, a member of a licensing board, and so on" (p. 1492).

---

[9] See, for example, "Responsive Supervision of the Psychiatric Resident and Clinical Psychology Intern" (Cohen and DeBetz, 1977).

[10] *Cestone v. Harkavy*, 243 App. Div. 732, 277 N.Y.S.2d 438 (1935).

[11] *Corleto v. Shore Memorial Hospital*, 138 N.J.Super. 302, 350 A.2d 534 (1975).

Breach of Duty

The yardstick used by the court to determine if a legal duty was in fact breached is referred to as the *standard of care*. The court will under most circumstances look to the standards of the profession and examine how the ordinary and prudent practitioner of the profession would have acted under the same or similar circumstances in order to define the applicable standards. Exceptions to this general rule are when the applicable standard is defined by statute and when the court deems the profession's standard to be too low (as in *Tarasoff*[12] and in *Helling v. Carey*[13]). "Ordinarily, a doctor's failure to possess or exercise the requisite learning or skill can be established only by the testimony of experts" (*Lawless v. Calaway*[14]). An exception to this rule is the instance in which the court invokes the doctrine of *res ipsa loquitur* ("the act speaks for itself"), which holds that the mere fact that injury occurred under a particular set of circumstances bespeaks negligence. This doctrine was invoked in *Rodriguez v. State,*[15] a case involving injury to a 5-year-old profoundly retarded resident of a state mental hospital. Another instance that obviates the need for expert testimony is when, in the opinion of the court, a jury is qualified to determine if malpractice occurred. This *doctrine of common knowledge* was invoked by the court in *Steinke v. Bell,*[16] a case in which a dentist extracted the wrong tooth: "We think laymen, looking at this case in the light of their common knowledge and experience, can say that a dentist engaged to remove a lower left second molar is not acting with the care and skill normal to the average member of the profession if, in so doing, he extracts or causes to come out an upper right lateral incisor." In *res ipsa loquitur* cases, the plaintiff is required to prove injury only and not a particular standard of care or a specific act or omission. In cases in which the doctrine of common knowledge is invoked, the plaintiff has already proved damage and an act or omission by the defendant, and the effect of the invocation of the doctrine is to let the jury decide what the applicable standard is.

Defining the applicable standard of care in the mental health profession tends not to be as straightforward a task as it is with respect to other professions. Stated succinctly, the problem is that if you ask two psychotherapists—even two psychotherapists who subscribe to the same school of psy-

---

[12] Both the American Psychological Association and the American Psychiatric Association filed an *amicus curiae* brief in *Tarasoff* (citation is in footnote 7 above) arguing that the duty to warn was not required by professional standards and in fact would be counter to the psychotherapeutic process.

[13] *Helling v. Carey*, 83 Wash.2d 514, 519 P.2d 981 (1974)

[14] *Lawless v. Calaway*, 147 P.2d 604

[15] *Rodriguez v. State*, 355 N.Y.S.2d 912

[16] *Steinke v. Bell*, 107 A.2d 825 (1954)

chotherapy—about their opinion on a particular course of treatment, you are likely to get two (or more) different opinions. In treating phobias, for example, one behavior therapist might have a predilection for systematic desensitization while another might believe that implosion is the treatment of choice. Needless to say, the variance of opinion increases exponentially if expert psychotherapists from other schools of therapy are consulted. The law prefers no one form of treatment over another, and it will usually measure a practitioner's professional behavior by the standards of his or her own school of treatment,[17] provided that that form of treatment is supported by at least a "respectable minority" of the members of the profession. Harris (1973) has noted that such minorities are legion in the field of psychotherapy and that the courts have in some cases "shifted the burden to the doctor to justify the use of unorthodox methods" (p. 419).

Persons who hold themselves out to the public as specialists in some professional area will be held to a higher standard of care—that of the specialist—than the presumably less trained nonspecialist. This is so even if the professional in question has falsely represented herself or himself as a specialist.[18] Nonprofessional psychotherapists cannot, technically speaking, be sued for malpractice as that cause of action is reserved for licensed members of a recognized profession:

> Those persons who are either licensed or members of professions sanctioned by the state, must follow the standards of care of their professions or they may be subject to either liability for negligence, or loss of license, or criminal penalties. Those people who practice outside the law are either quacks or nonprofessionals not yet under the state's statutory umbrella. Since no standards are established for their reputed professions, someone injured by their "care" will have to rely on tort theories other than malpractice. (Harris, 1973, pp. 408–409)

Although the quack[19] cannot technically be sued for malpractice, he or she will be held to the same standard of care that the properly credentialled professional being (mis)represented would be held to.[20] Sometimes the court, on the basis of the situation before it, will elect not to hold the defendant to the standard of a mental health professional even though the defendant's work closely resembled or was in many respects indistinguish-

---

[17] *Nelson v. Dahl,* 174 Minn. 574, 219 N.W.941 (1928)

[18] In *Simpson v. Davis* (219 Kan. 584, 549 P.2d 950), for example, a dentist who performed endodontic work was held to the standard of an endodontist.

[19] According to Black (1968, p. 1403) a quack is a "pretender to medical skill which he does not possess; one who practices as a physician or surgeon without adequate preparation or due qualification." We might substitute "psychotherapeutic" for "medical" and "licensed mental health professional" for "physician or surgeon" in this definition, but we are still left with a disturbing question: To what standard should the burgeoning number of formally unlicensed psychotherapists be held?

[20] *Whipple v. Grandchamp,* 261 Mass. 40, 158 N.E. 270, 57 A.L.R. 974.

able from the work of a psychiatrist, psychologist, social worker, or other licensed mental health professional.[21]

Causation and Damages

Causation in the legal sense is a relatively complicated concept that encompasses such factors as the foreseeability of the outcome and the effects of intervening variables. Damage is defined as "loss, injury, or deterioration, caused by the negligence, design, or accident of one person to another, in respect of the latter's person or property" (Black, 1968, p. 466). In its plural form, damages additionally refers to monetary compensation for a loss. *Compensatory* damages are awarded by a court to compensate a successful plaintiff for her or his loss. *Punitive* damages are awarded by a court to the plaintiff to punish a defendant for the recklessness, wantonness, or heinousness of his or her actions or omissions. As Rothblatt and Leroy (1973) note, proving the elements of causation and damage in a malpractice proceeding involving a mental health professional is no easy task:

> Besides proving that the psychiatrist has breached the requisite standard of care in some specific detail, the plaintiff must also demonstrate causation and damage. Because the natural pathological development and prognosis of mental disease is not well known, it is frequently difficult to state to a reasonable degree of medical certainty whether the application or omission of a particular procedure at a specified time caused mental injury to the patient. Thus it is often difficult for the plaintiff to prove the element of causation. The task is simplified, however, if the alleged negligence in some manner caused or encouraged the patient to sustain or inflict tangible physical injuries upon himself or others. Indeed, this characteristic is typical of almost every successful suit. In this situation, proof of the injuries in addition to proof that ordinary and prudent therapeutic techniques would have prevented the damage may sustain the burden of proof.
>
> The plaintiff who complains of exclusively mental injuries may also have a difficult time proving the element of damages. Not only are his allegations intangible and difficult to demonstrate to the judge and jury, but they also tend to be somewhat speculative because of the state of knowledge about mental illness. Even where improper procedures have been used to institutionalize a person in need of mental care, the courts may absolve physicians from liability by finding that the patient was not injured by receiving the treatment he needed. (p. 264).

The courts have increasingly become more liberal with respect to their recognition of—and compensation for—emotional distress as an injury. Illustrative of the types of actions that have succeeded in this area are the

---

[21] See, for example, the discussion of *Bogust v. Iverson* (10 Wisc.2d. 129, 102 N.W.2d 228) and *Previn v. Tenacre, Inc.* (70 F.2d 389) in Cohen and Mariano (1982).

following: in *Chavez v. Southern Pacific Transportation*[22] the claim of "severe traumatic neurosis" was made after a Hispanic railroad worker injured his back, an injury that healed after 9 months but left him depressed. It was alleged that the depression was intensified as a result of his Mexican-American "machismo" tradition. Chavez was awarded $1,300,000, and the verdict was not appealed. In *Vanoni v. Western Airlines*[23] it was held that "shock to the nerves and nervous system" constituted physical harm. The shock in this case was fright as a consequence of the negligent operation of an airliner. In *Cauverian v. DeMetz*[24] it was alleged that the negligent infliction of emotional distress caused the victim to become mentally unbalanced. In *Samms v. Eccles*[25] damages were awarded to the plaintiff as a consequence of the emotional distress she suffered when the defendant exposed himself and propositioned her.

WHAT CAN YOU BE SUED FOR?

As a mental health professional, regardless of whether you are primarily involved in psychotherapy, psychological assessment, consulting, research, or some related professional endeavor, you are exposed to the potential of professional liability. A cause of action is the basis of a lawsuit, and the causes of action that have been cited in suits against behavioral scientists have been quite varied. In general, any intentional or unintentional action or failure to act that impinges on the patient's rights is actionable.[26] Thus, for example, you may be sued on grounds such as assault, battery, wrongful death, false imprisonment, sexual or marital harm, abuse of psychotherapeutic process, breach of confidentiality, breach of contract, breach of right to informed consent, false imprisonment, defamation . . . the list goes on. Detailed descriptions of these and related causes of actions appear in Cohen (1979) in Cohen and Mariano (1982), and elsewhere.

---

[22] *Chavez v. Southern Pacific Transportation*, Los Angeles Superior Court No. C-134638, October 2, 1979.

[23] *Vanoni v. Western Airlines*, 247 Cal.App.2d 793.

[24] *Cauverian v. DeMetz* 188 N.Y.S.2d 627.

[25] *Samms v. Eccles*, 11 Utah 2d 289, 358 P.2d 344.

[26] This is not to imply that professionals will be held liable for honest errors in professional judgment that result in negative outcome. The courts have long recognized that behavioral science is not an exact science (e.g., *St. George v. State*, 283 App.Div.245, 127 N.Y.S.2d 147) and that prediction of violence and other behavior cannot be made with precision (e.g., *Taig v. State*, 19 App.Div.2d 182, 241 N.Y.S.2d 495). The court in *Taig* held "if a liability were imposed on the physician or the State each time the prediction of future course of mental disease was wrong, few releases would ever be made and the hope of recovery and rehabilitation of a vast number of patients would be impeded and frustrated. This is one of the medical and public risks which must be taken on balance, even though it may sometimes result in injury to the patient or others."

Psychiatrists, as physicians, will, of course, be more prone than their colleagues in the field of mental health to be sued for allegedly improper conduct with respect to the prescription and administration of medication, the administration of electroshock therapy, or hospitalization. Wright (1981, p. 1487) has observed that for psychologists, "the greatest [malpractice] risks are incurred in those areas of psychological practice designated as *evaluation*." Indeed, the import of a psychological evaluation can have momentous consequences for the person being evaluated. The evaluation may result in the denial of employment, denial of promotion or transfer, denial of child custody, denial of probation, or the diagnosis of, or failure to diagnose, suicidal or homicidal potential.[27] In contrast to the situation in psychotherapy, in which the professional and the client have ample time to establish a good working relationship, the assessment situation is more often than not brief, to the point, and almost adversarial in nature from the perspective of the (frequently unwilling) examinee.

AVOIDING LEGAL JEOPARDY

If one day you are served with a summons and complaint alleging professional misconduct or substandard service, expect to read a laundry list of horrible things about yourself since lawyers will frequently cite every possible cause of action they can scare up, hoping to prevail on at least one. Do not panic and do not call the patient to reconciliate, berate, or apologize and beg for mercy—do not call the patient. Notify your malpractice insurance broker or carrier immediately,[28] and discuss the case only with your attorney, and no one else except under the advice of your attorney. If your attorney has been appointed by your malpractice insurance carrier, question him or her as to prior experience in this area and satisfy yourself that this is the right person to defend your personal savings and professional reputation. If your codefendant in the suit is your employer (e.g., a private hospital, the state, etc.), I strongly advise you retain your own counsel and politely reject your employer's offer of joint legal representation by one attorney; the rationale here is that you will be better off if you have someone in the courtroom representing your interests exclusively. Never assume that your family attorney or lawyer friend is capable of representing you in the action by virtue of his or her admission to the bar; retain a specialist in the area. One psychologist for whom I acted as a consultant made the grave error of

---

[27] Consult the chapter entitled "Legal/Ethical Issues in Assessment" in *Psychological Testing and Assessment* (Cohen, Montague, Nathanson, & Swerdlik, in press) for a detailed discussion of this area.

[28] Notwithstanding the fact that many clinicians have argued against the "tyranny of the shoulds," you *should* carry malpractice insurance.

allowing a lifelong attorney friend to represent him. Suffice to say that the results of that error in judgment were disastrous for the psychologist's personal health and economic well-being.

Most malpractice actions are settled out of court at the claim stage; it is simply more economical to do it that way than to go the potentially long and expensive litigation route. Out-of-court settlements do not impute blame but instead merely indicate that the suit is being dropped for some unspecified reason in return for an agreed-upon dollar amount. If your insurance carrier wants to settle but you insist on "going the distance," be prepared to do so at your own cost and expense. If, for whatever reason, the case does go to trial, thorough preparation is essential. Organize all of your notes and reports so that you can crisply recite what was done on what date, your interpretations if any, your plans if any, and so forth. Thoroughly review the professional literature pertinent to the issue and have your attorney brief you on how best to comport yourself in pretrial discovery proceedings and in court.[29] In court, communicate effectively and avoid what I have elsewhere referred to as "WWT" errors:

> Many mental health professionals, to their detriment, make what might be termed "What's-wrong-with-that?" (WWT) errors in their court testimony. When a supposedly revealing statement about a patient's pathology compels the majority of the jury to ask themselves, "What's wrong with that?" a WWT error has been made. For example, suppose "Mr. Citizen," the patient, is forcibly taken from his home by the police, handcuffed, and packed into a police car in full view of his friends and neighbors. And suppose "Dr. Smith," a psychiatrist, testifies that the patient was verbally abusive and hostile to the therapist on admission. Jury members are likely to ask themselves. "What's wrong with that? Who wouldn't be verbally abusive and hostile under such conditions?" This is especially true if Mr. Citizen appears to be composed and "normal" in the courtroom. Smith may compound his WWT error by going on to say something like, "Further, Mr. Citizen denied that he was mentally ill." Again, jury members—who are more likely to identify with a patient than a psychiatrist—are likely to ask themselves, "What's wrong with that? I would deny it under the same circumstances." To weaken his testimony still further, Smith might testify that the patient's denial of mental illness demonstrated lack of insight, which was evidence of mental illness. Although all of Smith's statements might make sense to experienced mental health professionals, they will probably not make much sense to the lay people of the jury. WWT errors can be avoided with some forethought, factual documentation, and practice in presenting professional opinion to lay audiences. (Cohen, 1979, pp. 280–281)

If you are dissatisfied with the final disposition of the matter, you can, on the advice of your attorney, appeal. Regardless of the disposition of the case, one option you may want to discuss with your attorney is that of

---

[29] Fifteen guidelines with respect to handling pretrial depositions as well as other suggestions regarding courtroom behavior appear in Cohen (1979, pp. 276–281).

instituting a countersuit. The countersuit will be most effective when the initial suit was instituted on patently frivolous grounds, and the plaintiff's lawyer might be held liable for abuse of process of law, malicious prosecution, or barratry. The countersuit is least effective—even something that will get you into a lot more trouble—when it is employed in reflex action fashion as a retaliatory measure.

Claims Prevention Strategies

An oral surgeon who was sued for malpractice after a patient swallowed one of his tools reflected, "No man sued for malpractice ever wins completely . . . You can't know what it's like to go through such an ordeal—until you do it. One day you're a respected, confident professional man. The next day your ability is being debated in court, with all your friends and patients looking on—and wondering" (Balliet, 1974, p. 73). Indeed, given the amount of apprehension, loss of time, and loss of income most malpractice actions entail, it is meaningless to talk about winning or losing and more constructive to speak of how losses can best be cut. What follows are some claims prevention strategies designed to keep the process server away.

Perhaps the primary triggering factor in most malpractice litigation against private practitioners—regardless of the causes of action listed in the complaint—is a fee dispute; to allow a client to run up a large bill is to invite litigation when you try to collect. Personally, I have tried to make it a policy for therapy patients to pay on a per session basis. Such a policy is not only a good claims prevention strategy but it also cuts down on book-keeping time and time spent preparing and mailing out bills and notices. I make it a policy to collect fees for psychological assessment and for certain types of consulting in advance, if possible. Exactly how the individual practitioner handles fee collection will depend on the nature of the practice, personality factors of the practitioner, and related factors. The point here is that *some* policy that prevents the running up of large bills is a necessity.

If your work is primarily in the area of psychological evaluation, be conversant with the validity of the tests and methods you use and take care to employ the appropriate test or measure for the particular situation and the particular examinee. You should also have a well-defined and systematic method of interpreting test findings and be able to support your conclusions in court. If the results of the testing are to be transmitted to any third party, the examinee should be aware of this prior to the testing and should, if necessary, give his or her informed consent for such transmittal of the results. Test records, protocols, reports and related documents must be stored in a manner that makes them reasonably secure from persons not privileged to read this confidential material.

Like the psychological assessor, the psychotherapist must also take reasonable precautions to safeguard from unauthorized eyes privileged information such as therapy notes, records, and reports. Assure your individual patients of confidentiality, and get assurances from your therapy group members regarding the confidentiality of the communications there. If you do marital or family therapy[30] or consulting to business,[31] you should be familiar with the legal issues of privacy and confidentiality as they apply in those settings. If you use an automated test-scoring service in your clinical practice, you had best have a sound understanding of the test and its scoring and interpretation lest you look rather foolish in court. If you treat persons who may at some point become dangerous to themselves or others, it is important for you to have a contingency plan to put into action if the need arises. You are not obligated to accept into treatment all prospective patients who show up at your door. Once you do accept a patient, however, you are legally obliged not to abandon her or him; continue to treat until the patient leaves for whatever reason or you mutually agree that therapy should be undertaken by another therapist or terminated. All policies with respect to matters such as missed sessions due to sickness, vacation, and so forth should be clearly set forth at the onset and informed consent to treatment, to the extent that such consent is feasible,[32] should be obtained. If you employ methods involving touching or physically cathartic behavior in your treatment, you are probably much more likely to be sued for injury arising out of therapy *per se* than the therapist who relies exclusively on verbal behavior.

In concluding this brief, noncomprehensive list of claims avoidance strategies, it should be pointed out that in supervising the professional work of others it is best to structure the number of hours given to the unique needs of the supervisee and the client as opposed to some *pro forma* schedule. Remember that if you are in a partnership you can potentially be held liable for the tortious behavior of your partner. Premises liability can be avoided by keeping your work space neat and in reasonably good repair. Know the limits of your competence, and do not practice beyond those limits. If your ability to work effectively should at some point be compromised, take some time off to obtain personal help; this is the most cost-effective way of handling such a situation in the long run. In general, keep in mind that you owe your patients, clients, research subjects, corporate consultees—anyone whom you deal with professionally—a duty to act skillfully and carefully. Finally, keep abreast of the law as it affects professional practice in the behavioral sciences through regular perusal of pertinent literature. As we noted at the outset, sound professional practice is a necessary but insuffi-

---

[30] A review of some of these issues appears in Margolin (1982).

[31] An analysis of some of the issues here is provided by Carey (1981).

[32] For a real-life illustration of the problems in obtaining informed consent prior to beginning therapy, consult Cohen (1977). The article is a rejoinder to the many comments generated by an earlier case study (Cohen & Smith, 1976) in which a Christian Scientist relinquished her obsessive symptoms only after she stopped believing in Christian Science. Further discussion of the issues raised by this study appear in Cohen (1979, pp. 76–83) and in McLemore (1982).

cient condition for avoiding allegations of malpractice; a knowledge of the law is essential.

REFERENCES

Balliet, G. (1974). Thirteen ways to protect yourself against malpractice suits. *Resident and Staff Physician, 20 (4)*, 70–73; 75.

Bernstein, B. E. (1978). Malpractice: An ogre on the horizon. *Social Work, 23*, 106–112.

Black, H. C. (1968). *Black's law dictionary* (rev., 4th ed.). St. Paul: West Publishing.

Carey, J. P. (1981). Business ethics, employee privacy and the management of insurance information. *Review of Business, 3*, 21–24.

Cohen, R. J. (1977). Socially reinforced obsessing: A reply. *Journal of Consulting and Clinical Psychology, 45*, 1166–1171.

Cohen, R. J. (1979). *Malpractice: A guide for mental health professionals*. New York; Free Press.

Cohen, R. J., & DeBetz, B. (1977). Responsive supervision of the psychiatric resident and clinical psychology intern. *American Journal of Psychoanalysis, 37*, 51–64.

Cohen, R. J., & Mariano, W. E. (1982). *Legal guidebook in mental health*. New York: Free Press.

Cohen, R. J., & Smith, F. J. (1976). Socially reinforced obsessing: Etiology of a disorder in a Christian Scientist. *Journal of Consulting and Clinical Psychology, 44*, 142–144.

Cohen, R. J., Montague, P., Nathanson, L. S., & Swerdlik, M. E. (in press). *Psychological Testing and Assessment*. New York: St. Martin's Press.

Danzon, P. M. (1983). An economic analysis of the medical malpractice system. *Behavioral Sciences and the Law, 1(1)*: 39–44.

Green, R. K., & Cox, G. (1978). Social work and malpractice: A converging course. *Social Work, 23*, 100–105.

Harris, M. (1973). Tort liability of the psychotherapist. *University of San Francisco Law Review, 8*, 405–436.

Horan, D. J., & Milligan, R. J. (1983). Recent developments in psychiatric malpractice. *Behavioral Sciences and the Law, 1(1)*: 23–38.

Jurow, G. L., & Mariano, W. E. (1972). Law and private practice. in G. D. Goldman & G. Stricker (Eds.), *Practical problems of a private psychotherapy practice*. Springfield, Ill.: Charles C. Thomas.

Margolin, G. (1982). Ethical and legal considerations in marital and family therapy. *American Psychologist, 37*, 788–801.

McLemore, C. W. (1982). *The scandal of psychotherapy: A guide to resolving the tensions between faith and counseling*. Wheaton, Ill.: Tyndale.

Prosser, W. L. (1971). *Law of torts* (4th ed.). St. Paul, Minn.: West Publishing.

Rothblatt, H. B., & Leroy, D. H. (1973). Avoiding psychiatric malpractice. *California Western Law Review, 9*, 260–272.

Slovenko, R. (1983). The hazards of writing or disclosing information in psychiatry. *Behavioral Sciences and the Law, 1 (1)*: 109–127.

Stone, A. A. (1977). Recent mental health litigation: A critical perspective. *American Journal of Psychiatry, 134*, 273–279.

Wettstein, R. M. (1983). Tardive dyskinesia and malpractice. *Behavioral Sciences and the Law, 1(1)*: 85–107.

Wright, R. H. (1981). Psychologists and professional liability (malpractice) insurance: A retrospective view. *American Psychologist, 36*, 1485–1493.

William E. Mariano and Derek Wolman

13

Boundaries Between the Law and Behavioral Therapies

"Professional liability" is an umbrella term encompassing all activities conducted by psychotherapists in their professional capacity for which they can be held civilly liable. Professional liability then is not a special area of law, but rather a convenient term that describes the legal problems of professionals in the conduct of their special relationships with their patients.

Unlike a situation involving two strangers however—as for instance two people who are involved in a car accident—where only social duty (the duty of ordinary care) gives rise to liability, a therapist–patient relationship is held to a higher standard. The applicable standard is the degree of care that would reasonably be expected from other therapists practicing in the field.

Possibly the most vexing problem for the psychotherapist in this area is the clash of philosophies between clinical practice and the law. The therapist looks to his or her patient's mental processes to determine the proper treatment for that patient. The law, on the other hand, looks to the facts of a situation and applies them to the various rights and duties of patients and therapists, as it has defined them, to determine whether or not any violation of these rights and duties has occurred. Obviously, there is a clash of these two philosophies when the therapist's best judgment for appropriate treatment infringes upon the legal rights of a patient or violates a legal duty owed to the patient by the therapist. Conversely, when the mandates of the law dictate or limit the form of treatment the therapist provides his or her patient, the law interferes with the therapeutic process.

PSYCHOTHERAPY AND THE LAW
ISBN 0-8089-1780-3

Under the circumstances discussed above, therapy may constitute tortious conduct on the part of a therapist. This can be illustrated by the following examples:

1. A therapist may determine that a certain degree of physical contact will be therapeutic to his or her patient; however, any nonconsensual touching, or imminent threat of such touching, may constitute a battery or an assault.
2. A therapist may decide that his or her patient is in need of a certain kind of treatment, but, without the patient's informed consent to that treatment, the therapist may breach his or her professional duty of care to the patient by administering it.
3. A therapist may determine that a patient would be best served by informing a spouse, parent, or other relative of certain aspects of the patient's condition, but to do so without the patient's consent may constitute a breach of confidentiality. The therapist must therefore be aware of his or her legal duties to the patient when acting in a professional capacity and of the legal limitations on the therapy to be provided.

ASSAULT AND BATTERY

Legally, an assault is said to have occurred when one person, without his or her consent, is placed in apprehension of a harmful or offensive touching by another person. A battery is said to have occurred when the nonconsensual harmful or offensive touching has taken place. "Harmful" touching is usually defined as that which causes pain, injury, and the like. "Offensive" touching is usually defined as that which would be offensive to a reasonable person's sense of dignity. With the advent of psychiatric medication, other physical forms of treatment, and individual and group therapy methods that may call for therapist–patient and patient–patient touching, the potential for liability on the grounds of assault and/or battery has risen dramatically.

Hammer v. Rosen (7 N.Y. 2d 376, 198 N.Y.S. 2d 65 [1960]) exemplifies the view that any physical contact construed as assaultive between therapist and patient is unacceptable. Left open are questions such as (1) whether or not contact necessary to calm the patient is proper or (2) whether or not there is liability when the touching is consensual. Finally, what are the implications of the court decision in *Hammer* for the development of novel modes of therapy?

In *Hammer* the court found, "[concerning the defendant's argument] that there was no expert testimony to support the plaintiff's charge of malpractice, the simple answer is that the very nature of the acts complained of bespeaks improper treatment and malpractice and that, if the defendant chooses to justify those acts as proper treatment, he is under the necessity of offering evidence to that effect. In point of fact, the defendant can hardly urge that the plaintiff must call an expert to demonstrate the impropriety of the assaultive acts charged against him in view of the acknowledgement, contained in his brief in this court, that any mode of treatment which involves assaults upon the patient is 'fantastic.' "

Given the *Hammer* ruling that practitioners generally have no right to "assault" their patients, the question arises whether or not the administration of a drug for the benefit of the patient, and in the course of developing a new method of treatment—but without the patient's consent—amounts to an actionable assault. *Stowens v. Wolodzko* (396 Mich. 119, 191 N.W. 2d 355 [1971]) reflects the current judicial opinion on this issue. The *Stowens* court held that the patient retains the right to control the treatment at all times. Thus the administration of a drug without consent, regardless of the beneficial or suspected beneficial results, is deemed an assault and a trespass upon the body of the patient.

In *Stowens,* the plaintiff's husband had applied to the probate court to have her committed to a state hospital. The two defendants certified that the plaintiff should be committed, and the probate court so ordered. The plaintiff was taken to a hospital, where she remained for 11 hours, and she was then released when the emergency order was rescinded. The court, quoting the Michigan Court of Appeals (19 Mich. App. 126, 172 N.W. 2d, p. 503), summarized its opinion by saying the "sanctity of one's body is such that a possible absence of pain and suffering in its unwarranted and non-consensual touching does not eliminate the need for protection from, or compensation for, such touching in the absence of a court order or an emergency. Any submission by plaintiff, no matter how benign, was not voluntary. It was not necessary that she violently resist at every juncture as a prerequisite to recovery for assault and battery if her lack of consent was clearly manifested."

LACK OF INFORMED CONSENT

Definition of Informed Consent

"Informed consent" is a court-made doctrine with a definition and rationale that are succinctly stated in the following excerpt from the opinion in *Sard v. Hardy* (291 Md. 432, 379 A. 2d 1014 [1977]:

> The doctrine of informed consent, which we shall apply here, follows logically from the universally recognized rule that a physician, treating a mentally competent adult under nonemergency circumstances, cannot properly undertake

to perform surgery or administer other therapy without the prior consent of his patient . . . . In order for the patient's consent to be effective, it must have been an "informed" consent, one that is given after the patient has received a fair and reasonable explanation of the contemplated treatment or procedure . . . .

The fountainhead of the doctrine of informed consent is the patient's right to exercise control over his own body, at least when undergoing elective surgery, by deciding for himself whether or not to submit to the particular therapy. . . . Other courts have bottomed the physician's duty to disclose on the fiducial quality of the physician–patient relationship. . . . Whatever its source, the doctrine of informed consent takes full account of the probability that unlike the physician, the patient is untrained in medical science, and therefore depends on the trust and skill of his physician for the information on which he makes his decision . . . .

Simply stated, the doctrine of informed consent imposes on a physician, before he subjects his patient to medical treatment, the duty to explain the procedure to the patient and to warn him of any material risks or dangers inherent in or collateral to the therapy, so as to enable the patient to make an intelligent and informed choice about whether or not to undergo such treatment . . .

This duty to disclose is said to require a physician to reveal to his patient the nature of the ailment, the nature of the proposed treatment, the probability of success of the contemplated therapy and its alternatives, and the risk of unfortunate consequences associated with such treatment . . . The law does not allow a physician to substitute his judgment for that of the patient in the matter of consent to treatment.

The opinion in *Sard* discusses the following three elements of the cause of action arising from a practitioner's failure to obtain informed consent prior to treatment:

1. The scope of the practitioner's duty to warn and whether the duty is to be measured by a professional standard of care or a general reasonableness standard;
2. Whether or not expert medical testimony is required to prove the standard of care; and
3. The appropriate test for proving a causal connection between the failure to disclose and any injury or damage that might result.

The notion that therapists and other health service providers have a legal duty to make a full and frank disclosure of all facts pertinent to the illness or condition and the treatment was clearly enunciated in the case of *Nathanson v. Kline*, 350 P. 2d 1293 and 354 P. 2d 670 (1960). In *Nathanson*, the defendant, a radiologist, failed to inform a breast cancer patient of the risks of cobalt radiation treatment. The radiologist knew he was "taking a chance" with the treatment that he proposed to administer and that such treatment involved a "calculated risk." The patient conceded that she con-

sented to treatment, thus eliminating any claim for assault and battery, but she contended that "the nature and consequences of the risks of the treatment were not properly explained to her."

After reviewing the law, the court found that "where a physician or surgeon has affirmatively misrepresented the nature of the operation or has failed to point out the probable consequences of the course of treatment, he may be subjected to a claim of unauthorized treatment." This is not to say that a doctor is obliged to tell the details of all possible consequences. The court continued: "It might be argued . . . that to make a complete disclosure of all facts, diagnoses, and alternatives or possibilities which may occur to the doctor could so alarm the patient that it would, in fact, constitute bad medical practice."

There is, therefore, a balance to be struck in deciding how much treatment-related information to disclose to a patient. That balance, however, is clearly in favor of disclosure. As the *Nathanson* court held, if disclosure "would seriously jeopardize the recovery of an unstable, temperamental or severely depressed patient," a privilege to withhold a specific diagnosis probably exists on therapeutic grounds. In the ordinary case no such warrant for suppressing facts exists, however, and a substantial disclosure should be made to the patient prior to treatment.

BREACH OF CONFIDENTIALITY

The right of privacy, as embodied in the Fifth Amendment of the Constitution and elsewhere, is a long-cherished right in our society. Under the provisions of the Fifth Amendment, one cannot be compelled to testify against one's own self-interest. States, as a matter of public policy (not constitutional right), have enacted statutes that have extended this right of the person to refuse to disclose certain information. The privilege has been extended to other people with whom the person shares a special relationship, e.g., attorney, physician, psychologist, priest, husband or wife, and so on.

In addition to the statute law and rules of privilege, there is also a practice or custom, derived from professional standards of practice and codes of ethics, of a duty not to disclose information (i.e., the rule of confidentiality) obtained in the course of psychotherapeutic treatment.

Patients of clinicians have a right to expect that the confidentiality of the patient–therapist relationship and the communications therein will be assured. In general, therapists have been granted by law the same right to privileged communication as that enjoyed by physicians and lawyers. It is important to note the distinction between the rules of confidentiality and the concept of privileged communication. As stated succinctly by Jagin, Wittman, and Noll (1979), "Whereas confidentiality concerns matters of communication outside the courtroom, privilege protects clients from disclosure in judicial proceedings'' (p. 459).

Breach of confidentiality can serve as the basis of a malpractice action. The practitioner who fails to exercise reasonable care in maintaining the confidentiality of patients' communications may be subject to disciplinary action by his or her professional association and/or by the government body charged with the regulation and control of the profession. Some patients have also brought suit against clinicians under a theory of breach of contract. The claim here is that the practitioner breached an implied contract to maintain confidentiality.

There is a duty on the part of the therapist not to disclose information obtained in the course of the therapist–patient relationship. This duty not to disclose is an affirmative duty imposed upon the practitioner, and its breach constitutes an invasion of the patient's right to privacy. Every jurisdiction also has laws stating that certain communications made by patients to practitioners cannot be required to be disclosed by a court.

Horne v. Patton (291 Ala. 701, 227 So. 2d 824, 1973) states the general view of the patient's right to privacy and the therapist's duty to maintain confidentiality. This case involved disclosure by the clinician-defendant of certain information to the patient-plaintiff's employer; this information, acquired during the course of the therapeutic relationship contravened the instructions of the plaintiff. In determining whether or not the unauthorized disclosure of a patient's treatment record constitutes an invasion of that patient's right of privacy, the court looked to *Hammonds v. Aetna Casualty & Surety Co.* (243 F. Supp. 793, N.D. Ohio, 1965), involving disclosure of medical information concerning the patient to the patient's insurer, wherein that court stated:

> When a patient seeks out a doctor and retains him, he must admit him to the most private part of the material domain of man. Nothing material is more important or more intimate to man than the health of his mind and body. Since the layman is unfamiliar with the road to recovery, he cannot sift the circumstances of his life and habits to determine what is information pertinent to his health. As a consequence he must disclose all information in his consultations with his doctor—even that which is embarrassing, disgraceful, or incriminating. To promote full disclosure, the medical profession extends the promise of secrecy referred to above. The candor which this promise elicits is necessary to the effective pursuit of health; there can be no reticence, no reservation, no reluctance when patients discuss their problems with their doctors. But the disclosure is certainly intended to be private. If a doctor should reveal any of these confidences, he surely effects an invasion of the privacy of his patient. We are of the opinion that the preservation of the patient's privacy is no mere ethical duty upon the part of the doctor; there is a legal duty as well. The unauthorized revelation of medical secrets, or *any* confidential communication given in the course of treatment, is tortious conduct which may be the basis for an action in damages.

The court continued:

> Unauthorized disclosure of intimate details of a patient's health may amount to unwarranted publicization of one's private affairs with which the public has no legitimate concern such as to cause outrage, mental suffering, shame or humiliation to a person of ordinary sensibilities. Nor can it be said that an employer is necessarily a person who has a legitimate interest in knowing each and every detail of an employee's health. Certainly, there are many ailments about which a patient might consult his private physician which have no bearing or effect on one's employment. If the defendant doctor in the instant case had a legitimate reason for making this disclosure under the particular facts of this case, then this is a matter of defense.

The court then turned to the issue of breach of contract in the defendant's disclosure. Again the *Horne* court relied on *Hammonds* and quoted the following from that case:

> Any time a doctor undertakes the treatment of a patient, and the consensual relationship of physician and patient is established, two jural obligations (of significance here) are simultaneously assumed by the doctor. Doctor and patient enter into a simple contract, the patient hoping that he will be cured and the doctor optimistically assuming that he will be compensated. As an implied condition of that contract, this Court is of the opinion that the doctor warrants that any confidential information gained through the relationship will not be released without the patient's permission. Almost every member of the public is aware of the promise of discretion contained in the Hippocratic Oath, and every patient has a right to rely upon this warranty of silence. The promise of secrecy is as much an express warranty as the advertisement of a commercial entrepreneur. Consequently, when a doctor breaches his duty of secrecy, he is in violation of part of his obligations under the contract.

A therapist should be aware that the right of confidentiality is the right of the patient and not the right of the therapist. Once the patient waives this right, the therapist is free to use his or her discretion in disclosing information about the patient. Waiver by the patient also removes any privilege that the therapist may possess to refuse to reveal information when ordered to do so by a court of law.

In re Lifschutz (85 Ca. Rptr. 829, 2 Cal 3d 415, 467 P. 2d 557, 1970) illustrates the rule that the patient, not the therapist, enjoys the right of confidentiality. Dr. Joseph E. Lifschutz, a California psychiatrist, was judged in contempt of court and jailed for refusing to obey a court order instructing him to answer questions and produce records relating to communications with a former client. Lifschutz sought a writ of *habeas corpus* claiming that the order was invalid for a variety of reasons, including the infringement of his personal constitutional right of privacy, his right to practice his profession effectively, and the constitutional privacy rights of his patient. The court did not agree and found as follows:

In separating the interest of the psychotherapist from that of the patient for the purposes of analyzing this contention, we conclude that the compelled disclosure of relevant information obtained in a confidential communication does not violate any Constitutional privacy rights of the psychotherapist.

The court recalled the United States Supreme Court discussion in *Griswold v. Connecticut* (381 U.S. 479, 85 S.Ct. 1965), in which the high court explicitly explained that the constitutional right to privacy belonged to the *patients* and not to the physicians. In *Lifschutz,* the court added:

It is the depth of intimacy of the patients' revelations that give rise to the concern over compelled disclosure; the psychotherapist, though undoubtedly deeply involved in the communicative treatment, does not exert a significant privacy interest separate from his patient.

Regarding Lifschutz's other claims, namely the violation of his right to practice his profession and the privacy rights of his patient, the court noted that when the patient (as in this case) has put his or her medical or psychological record in controversy by making a claim of mental and emotional distress, the making of such a claim acts as a waiver of the patient's privilege to exclude any information that may be necessary to prove his or her allegations.

Because the information relevant to the proof of such a claim is in the control of the patient and not the party from whom recovery is sought, the burden is on the patient, at least initially, to show that certain confidential communication, are not directly related to the issue of injury. On this point, the more general the claim pleaded, the more difficult it will be to determine what information is relevant; thus more information may be subject to production. In determining, however, whether or not certain communications sufficiently relate to the mental condition at issue, the court is still obliged to safeguard as much information as possible—in accord with the basic privacy interests in the privilege. On this point, the Lifschutz court concluded: "In general the statutory psychotherapist–patient privilege [is to] be liberally construed in favor of the patient."

DUTY TO WARN

As noted in *In re Lifschutz,* the status of psychotherapist–patient communications is not absolutely privileged nor completely exposed to public light. The privilege lies instead in a "grey area" somewhere between. One aspect of where the privilege lies was revealed in *Tarasoff v. Regents of the University of California,* 131 Cal. Rptr. 14, 551 P. 2d 334, 1976). In that case, the duties of the therapist to his patient and to society at large were examined in a context in which a therapist's duty to both incurrd a direct conflict.

In *Tarasoff,* Lawrence Moore, a psychologist at a California university's mental health clinic, was sued when his patient, Prosenjit Poddar, killed a woman named Tatiana Tarasoff. Prior to Tarasoff's death, Moore believed that Poddar posed a danger to her by virtue of certain statements Poddar made to him. Moore notified the campus police that Poddar was dangerous and should be hospitalized. The police, however, after talking to Poddar, determined that he was rational and failed to detain him. Subsequently, Moore's superior at the clinic directed that no further action be taken to detain or hospitalize Poddar. The superior also requested that the police return Moore's letter concerning Poddar and ordered all records of the matter destroyed. Two months later the murder occurred.

The parents of the victim sued the therapists at the clinic. The Supreme Court of California, in overturning a trial court's dismissal of the case, found that when a therapist determines, according to the applicable standards of his or her profession, that his patient "presents a serious danger of violence to another" he has a duty "to use reasonable care to protect the intended victim against such danger." A therapist is obliged to take whatever steps are reasonably necessary under the circumstances. Warning a potential victim is only one of the possible steps a therapist may choose to take, and may or may not be appropriate or adequate in a particular case.

By its decision, the California Supreme Court applied the general principle that "whenever one person is by circumstances placed in such a position with regard to another . . . that if he did not use ordinary care and skill in his own conduct . . . he would cause danger of injury to the person or property of the other, a duty arises to use ordinary care and skill to avoid such danger." Nonetheless, in recognizing the duty that therapists have to third parties when their patients pose a danger to others, the court outlined a number of considerations to be balanced *against* that duty. Chief among these are the foreseeability of potential harm to a particular victim, the degree of certainty that this victim has indeed suffered injury, the closeness of the connection between the patient's conduct and the injury suffered (causation), and the burden on the therapist (as well as the consequences to the community) of imposing a duty to exercise care with resulting liability for breach.

Foreseeability is the most important element in establishing the existence of a duty. In ordinary circumstances, only the person whose conduct causes the injury "owes the duty of care to those who are foreseeably endangered by his conduct." But for a duty to arise on the part of a therapist to take active steps to avoid foreseeable injury, he or she must stand in some special relationship with the person whose conduct needs to be controlled. In *Tarasoff,* the court found that the therapist–patient relationship was "special" in this sense, giving rise to a duty to take affirmative action to prevent a foreseeable risk caused by the conduct of the patient.

Establishment of this duty creates an obligation on the part of the therapist to use "that reasonable degree of skill, knowledge, and care ordinarily possessed and exercised by members of [the profession] under similar circumstances." The therapist need not be correct in his or her evaluation, only able to use his or her best judgment—within the broad range of reasonable practice and treatment—to avoid liability.

In *Tarasoff,* circumstances were such that the therapist's duty was to take reasonable care to protect the potential victim from a high risk of serious harm. Other situations that a therapist may encounter could give rise to varying degrees of likelihood and/or seriousness of harm to persons outside the therapist–patient relationship. The clinician must determine the response that will appropriately safeguard against the foreseeable danger and, at the same time, have the least detrimental effect on his or her patient and the treatment. A therapist must then balance the need for confidentiality in the therapist–patient relationship with his or her duty to the community at large: that is, to protect third parties who are endangered by the potential conduct of the patient. The therapist's obligation under *Tarasoff* rests upon the outcome of this balancing act.

To help determine when a clinician has complied with the obligation to take reasonable steps to safeguard others from the injurious conduct of his or her patients, the paramount criteria are these:

(1) *Contribution to Risk.* When a therapist has contributed to the risk presented by a patient, the therapist's responsibility to safeguard is increased. He or she will be held to a higher standard and thus be required to exercise greater accuracy in judging the patient's dangerousness.

(2) *Type of Harm Anticipated.* The more dangerous the harm anticipated, the more likely some preventive action should be taken.

(3) *Probability of Harm.* The higher the probability that the patient will take some action causing harm, the more imperative that preventive action be taken. Aids to predicting the likelihood of harm include past conduct, specificity of threats made, duration of the threatening behavior, and evidence of specific plans for carrying out the threatened conduct.

(4) *Patient's Consent.* If the patient consents to warning or otherwise safeguarding the potential victim, this suggests that the appropriate response would be to act in accordance with the patient's consent; even so, it would still need to be determined whether so acting would be enough to satisfy the therapist's obligation. In a legal context, reliance on the patient's consent could incur the danger of being construed as involuntary and thus ineffective, leaving the therapist open to a claim of breach of confidentiality.

(5) *Value of Warning the Patient.* On this point the therapist must ask: Will the potential victim benefit from warning? Will the victim heed the

warning? Is the threat narrow enough that an identifiable victim can be warned? If the threat is to a large group or to the general public, a warning may be ineffectual.

(6) *Impact upon the Psychotherapeutic Process*. In determining what course of action to take, if any, the therapist must consider which alternatives will be least detrimental to his or her patients' well-being.

These criteria are by no means an exhaustive list of consideration regarding when to risk breaching confidentiality in order to meet the countervailing duty to warn. As the law in this area develops more fully other considerations will no doubt come into play, and these and other criteria will be more clearly defined.

CONCLUSION

The boundaries between law and behavioral therapy are constantly changing due to new developments in both these fields. To insure the safe practice of psychotherapy, the therapist must constantly balance these interests. Whether or not the right balance is struck is always a matter of hindsight, however, the therapist can reasonably safeguard his practice by using his knowledge of the duties and obligations that the law requires of him to weigh the propriety of his conduct toward his patients.

* C. Hofling, Law and Ethics in the Practice of Psychiatry, 1981, New York, Brunner/ Mazel, Publishers pp. 119–134.

INDEX